KANT AND FINE ART

KANT

AND

FINE ART

*An Essay on Kant and
the Philosophy of
Fine Art and Culture*

SALIM KEMAL

CLARENDON PRESS · OXFORD
1986

Oxford University Press, Walton Street, Oxford OX2 6DP
Oxford New York Toronto
Delhi Bombay Calcutta Madras Karachi
Kuala Lumpur Singapore Hong Kong Tokyo
Nairobi Dar es Salaam Cape Town
Melbourne Auckland
and associated companies in
Beirut Berlin Ibadan Nicosia

Oxford is a trade mark of Oxford University Press

Published in the United States
by Oxford University Press, New York

British Library Cataloguing in Publication Data
Kemal, Salim
Kant and fine art : an essay on Kant and
the philosophy of fine art and culture.
1. Kant, Immanuel—Contributions in
aesthetics   2. Aesthetics
I. Title
111'.85'0924   B2799.A4
ISBN 0–19–824927–6

Library of Congress Cataloging in Publication Data
Kemal, Salim.
Kant and fine art.
Bibliography: p.
Includes index.
1. Kant, Immanuel, 1724–1804—Contributions in
aesthetics.   2. Aesthetics, Modern—18th century.
3. Culture—Philosophy—History—18th century.
I. Title.
B2799.A4K45 1986   701   86–8696
ISBN 0–19–824927–6

Set by Wyvern Typesetting Limited, Bristol
Printed in Great Britain
at the Alden Press, Oxford

Acknowledgements

MANY people have helped me at different stages of this book. I am happy to record my thanks to them.

Dr Michael Tanner, Corpus Christi, Cambridge, helped and encouraged my work; Dr Gerd Buchdahl, Department of the History and Philosophy of Science, University of Cambridge, and Professor R. W. Hepburn, University of Edinburgh, commented on an earlier version of some of the material in this book, and they have supported my work since then.

The President and Council of Wolfson College gave me encouragement and aid, first during my initial tenure as Fellow and also more recently, on my return to Cambridge, when the familiar academic environment of Wolfson College has helped me in completing this book.

An anonymous Adviser at Oxford University Press who read my typescript made many helpful suggestions. By following them, this book has been improved considerably. I have to thank Teddy Garick also: he proof-read an earlier draft, which is now almost entirely redundant, in spite of his being innocent of knowledge of Kant.

I have been lucky also with editors. Angela Blackburn has been helpful. Parts of this book have appeared in different versions in parts of papers published in the *British Journal of Aesthetics* and *Kant Studien*, and I am grateful to the Editors for permission to use the material here. Dr Manfred Kleinschnieder has been especially generous in helping me far beyond the call of an Editor's duties.

Dr Alan Bishop, Dr John Rhodes, Miss Penny Lea, and John Cathie have contributed more than they know to my welfare at Wolfson College. Professor Bob Ridell preferred his help unstintingly when I needed it. I am grateful also to Dr Jonathan Powers and, at the University of Western Ontario, to Professor Martha Williams and Professor Harold Johnson, for their many kindnesses.

People at AUB made me welcome in the good days of 1981. Dick Scott helped, as did Majid Fakhry; Ilyas Bu-Saleh and Suzy Katchadurian gave heart and hope. Professor David Makinson supported my work then and later; Waddah Nasr enabled me to obtain a grant which Elie Salem, erstwhile Dean of Arts and Sciences, generously made available for my work. To Ken Ferguson and Nabil Matar I owe a deep and special thanks, as I do to the Birberi family, who gave me shelter and succour at a time when they themselves faced the gravest dangers.

Above all, my deepest gratitude is owed to Jane Baston, and it is appropriate that this book should be for her and for my parents.

Wolfson College, Cambridge   SALIM KEMAL
1986

Contents

Abbreviations

The following abbreviations have been used:

I

Anthropology	*Anthropology from a Pragmatic Point of View*
'Conjectural Beginnings'	'Conjectural Beginnings of Human History'
Doctrine	*The Doctrine of Virtue, Part II of the Metaphysics of Morals*
'End'	'End of All Things'
'Enlightenment'	'What is Enlightenment?'
First Introduction	*First Introduction to the Critique of Judgement*
Foundations	*Foundations of the Metaphysics of Morals*
'Human Race'	'An Old Question Raised Again: Is the Human Race Constantly Progressing?'
Justice	*The Metaphysical Elements of Justice, Part I of the Metaphysics of Morals*
KrdpV	*Critique of Practical Reason*
KrdrV	*Critique of Pure Reason*
KrdU	*Critique of Judgement*
'Old Saw'	'On the Old Saw: That May be Right in Theory But it Won't Work in Practice'
'Orientation'	'What is Orientation in Thinking?'
Prolegomena	*Prolegomena to any Future Metaphysics that will be able to Present Itself as a Science*
Religion	*Religion within the Limits of Reason Alone*
'Strife'	'Strife Between the Faculties'
'Universal History'	'Idea for a Universal History From a Cosmopolitan Point of View'

II

AEM	*Letters on the Aesthetic Education of Man*
SR	*The Science of Rights*
VS	*The Vocation of a Scholar*

III

BJA	*British Journal of Aesthetics*

JAAC	*Journal of Aesthetics and Art Criticism*
KS	*Kant Studien*
PAS	*Proceedings of the Aristotelean Society*
RM	*Review of Metaphysics*

IV

GR	General Remark
R	Remark

In the Notes, references to *KrdrV* are given to the First (A) and Second (B) editions only. References to *KrdU* are given only by the Section, followed by the pagination of the Meredith translation and then the Academy Edition pagination. References to the *Critique of Teleological Judgement* are identified by inserting 'II' before the pagination. References to other texts are given with the abbreviation, followed by the pagination of the translation used and the Academy Edition.

I

Introduction

THIS book examines Kant's justification of aesthetic necessity. As we shall show, this requires us to understand the role of fine art in Kant's argument for 'an intimate and obscure' unity between theory and practice.[1] In turn, this leads us to examine the relation of Kant's aesthetic theory to his writing on epistemology and ethics, and to the lesser works on culture, history, religion, and anthropology.

As the account of aesthetic necessity to be proposed gives a central place to art and artistic beauty, we may begin by considering whether it is not precluded by other aspects of Kant's thought. There are a number of distinctions underlying Kant's theory which at the very outset, given the conclusions he draws from the preceding *Critiques*, cast doubt on his justification and argument. For example, he differentiates our theoretical understanding of a causally determined nature from the practical exercise of reason and freedom; and his distinction seems so thorough that it is difficult to conceive how they might be unified. Similarly, Kant carefully distinguishes cognitive and moral from aesthetic judgements; between understanding, imagination, and reason; natural from artistic beauty; questions about the possibility of aesthetic judgements from ones concerning their necessity; between a symbolic relation to morality and one that supports morality; reason from nature; and so on. All these elements must be interrelated consistently if his theory is to make good its claim to be coherent.

It has been argued against Kant that his theory, on its own grounds, cannot prevent aesthetic necessity from being determined by a moral interest without also denying that the moral imperative can interact with aesthetic practice;[2] that the distinction of aesthetic from cognitive judgement renders the former entirely subjective and idiosyncratic;[3] and that aesthetic judgements possess a necessity like that of cognitive judgements.[4] Other critics have supposed that Kant unsuccessfully sought an epistemological account of intersubjective validity *and* necessity;[5] or that Kant proposes that aesthetic judgements are necess-

ary for the reason of their symbolic relation to and analogy with the
moral good[6] but that his arguments are unsatisfactory.[7] Yet others have
argued that Kant distinguishes between form and content but is unable
to interrelate them; or that form must be associated with natural beauty
alone while expression is allegedly conterminous with fine art.[8]
Sometimes it is also proposed that natural beauty has precedence over
artistic beauty;[9] and that this raises questions about their respective
claims to necessity.

Epistemology and Kant's Critique of Judgement

A perspective common to a number of the competing positions mentioned in the last paragraph is that of epistemology. They stress that
although there are differences between the three *Critiques*, the *Critique
of Judgement*, like its precursors, is concerned principally with the
transcendental possibility of judgements. Accordingly, they attend to
questions about the nature and structure of aesthetic judgements,[10] to
the mental operations that constitute them,[11] their differences from
moral or cognitive claims,[12] and the conditions that must be satisfied for
a defence of particular aesthetic claims to be meaningful or legitimate.[13]
As these questions are given an epistemological slant, their answers seek
to extend to aesthetic judgements the modes of thought Kant applied to
claims for objective experience and knowledge. They assess the justification of the peculiar universality or intersubjective validity of our
aesthetic judgements by pointing to the presence of similar 'subjective
conditions' and mental operations in different subjects, and then explain
Kant's account of aesthetic necessity as if it were comparable to that of
cognitive judgements.[14] Thus, if aesthetic judgements have to do with
pleasure, then, in order to understand whether and how they can claim
necessity, we may compare them with cognitive claims that, say, a stone
is hard.[15]

   Although this epistemic approach has yielded many significant
insights, it leaves out of account a very important part of Kant's thinking:
artistic and cultural activity. For to understand our aesthetic lives, we
must deal with our activity in judging and constructing the objects we
find beautiful. It is unsatisfactory to understand aesthetic judgement
only in terms of mental operations, without examining its role as an
activity in our lives. And we must also consider the nature, distinction,
and interrelation of natural beauty and fine art—the objects of beauty.
More especially, we must understand the construction and presentation
of the latter. For our ability to make a distinction between the two sorts

of objects itself invites comparisons of their value and character, and it raises questions about the possibility of human activity, the realization of our intentions in a world apparently governed by causal determinations, and our relation to other subjects through such a realization.

Although many of the crucial ideas involved here have their origin in the First *Critique*, an epistemological slant is unable to do justice to the features of Kant's theory we mentioned in the last paragraph. If the *Critique of Judgement* were concerned only with the legitimacy of a priori synthetic judgements, of their necessary conditions, structure, and operation, then fine art as an object of judgement would become of secondary importance. Even if it were acknowledged that the issues Kant raises permit a dual perspective—of judgement and the objects judged—it would be argued that the first perspective determines that natural objects are our best examples.[16] Their existence may be explained simply by pointing to material natural causes, and any consideration of the human action necessary to producing a work replete with artistic qualities seems irrelevant. For if they differed in any significant way from natural objects, a consideration of works of fine art would introduce issues—of their nature, existence, and production, or of ascriptions of value—that were quite separate from and irrelevant to an interest in the nature of aesthetic judgements on any object, be it natural or an artefact.

Further, this epistemological slant seems to lead to an unsatisfactory understanding of some of the concepts Kant uses in the Third *Critique*. The symbolic relation of beauty to moral good, for example, comes to be seen as a means of justifying aesthetic necessity.[17] Not only can Kant's proposal that beauty involves moral issues now be shown to fail because of inadequacies in his account of symbolic relations, but it may be proposed that a justification of aesthetic necessity must be sought in the epistemology of aesthetic judgements.[18] However, the account of symbolic relations which Kant presents in Section 59, in which he compares the universality, interrelation of faculties, immediacy, and disinterestedness of aesthetic and moral claims, can be seen either as one based on the forms of judgement or as one emphasizing the act of judging. And for the formal similarity between judgements to constitute a symbolic relation, we must first examine the context in which they are made in order to show why these rather than other resemblances are significant. But this requires us to consider aesthetic response, appreciation, and activity as part of the conception of reason and rational action which Kant develops in all his critical writings. And that leads us to extend our concern beyond epistemology and the formal character of judgements: we must consider the activities of constructing works of art and judging beauty in order to understand how they contribute to our rational and moral lives. The symbolic relation between beauty and morality then appears not as an attempt to justify the necessity of aesthetic judgements on the basis of a similarity of form, but as a heuristic device Kant uses to indicate that an argument for aesthetic necessity must depend for its success on the rationality of aesthetic activity.

Similarly, the *sensus communis* may be understood as a feature of the operation of our minds. In making reflective judgements, it may be proposed, we use the *sensus communis* as a principle of reflection for our estimation of the order of representations. However, the *sensus communis* as a 'public sense' and an 'ideal norm' may be seen also in terms of relations between individuals. Not only is it something we rely on in order to justify the deduction of taste, it also serves as a principle for constructing a unity between subjects capable of reason and feeling; and so it may be understood to be a practical principle guiding our actions. Indeed, this leads us to see beauty as the basis for a unity between 'theory' and 'practice'.

If the *sensus communis* can be seen as a practical norm, then questions of aesthetic necessity clearly take us beyond epistemology. For the transcendental possibility of judgements at best only provides a warrant for making aesthetic judgements, and neither implies any conclusions about our particular judgements nor, hence, justifies the necessity attaching to these instances. And although it makes sense to say that the possibility of taste, based on the use of commonly possessed cognitive faculties, is an epistemological matter, nevertheless, given that Kant's account of aesthetic necessity seems to involve the *sensus communis* as a practical norm, we may expect that the matter will be unsatisfactorily dealt with as an epistemological issue. Thus, aesthetic judgements may have an epistemic necessity in one sense because they are transcendentally possible, but, in another sense, the demand which we make of other subjects—the necessity of particular aesthetic judgements—is 'of a special kind'[19] which 'comes to be *exacted* from everyone as a sort of *duty*'.[20]

Although we have made an issue of the merely epistemological account of aesthetic judgements, we must be careful not to make too much of it. Our contention is not that epistemological issues are absent from the Third *Critique*, nor that the latter text shares no similarity with the first. Many of the crucial ideas, such as subjectivity and objective judgement, empirical and transcendental deduction, and their commensurate necessities, have their origin in the First *Critique*. However, there are substantial differences in the conclusions Kant arrives at concerning cognitive and aesthetic judgements in relation to these ideas—differences which lead us to expect, for example, that the two sorts of judgement will be capable of very different sorts of necessity. And if we tend to think of aesthetic judgements in terms of cognitive ones, and try to gain the second sort of certainty about both, we will be diverted from giving proper credence to Kant's arguments for the practical value of beauty and fine art.

Transcendental and Empirical Necessity

The distinction proposed above, between the possibility of aesthetic judgements and the necessity ascribed to our particular claims about the beauty of specific objects, is natural to Kant's critical idealism. As with the *Critique of Pure Reason* and the *Critique of Practical Reason*, in the Third *Critique* a concern with transcendental possibility can be differentiated from an interest in articulating the distinctive order and necessity we ascribe to experience. The distinction is usually unheeded even in the case of the earlier *Critiques* and is worth recounting because it reveals an important feature of Kant's aesthetic theory.

In the *Critique of Pure Reason* Kant answers Hume's scepticism by justifying the transcendental necessity of using certain categorical concepts: to have experience is to obtain a unity or organization of representations that cannot be described except by using concepts of an objective world. Causality is one of these categorical concepts and its application gives subjects' perceptions a unity that makes it possible for us to conceive of them as perceptions of objects existing independently of subjects in space and time.

Kant goes on to deny that the empirical knowledge of objects can be derived from a transcendental use of 'cause'. Categorical concepts only constitute our experience of objects. Transcendental arguments legitimate the application of causality to our experience, and ensure that our search for causal relations is not a pointless task, but they cannot tell us which specific causes will be found in experience.[21] Thus, the argument of the Analogies only shows that nature in general is grounded in causality. To discover actual instances of causality we must resort to contingent actual experience.[22]

Evidently, for Kant, a satisfactory account of experience must satisfy two considerations. First, we must use concepts of an objective world in order to have experience at all. Second, we are interested ultimately in providing a coherent body of empirical knowledge within which an event may be placed and so explained. Kant writes that 'systematic unity is what first raises ordinary knowledge to the rank of science—that is, makes a system out of a mere aggregate of knowledge'.[23] Accordingly, while categorical laws provide the conceptual framework necessary for experience to be possible, this minimal coherence cannot legislate comprehensively over all the diverse relations between objects and events that occur in nature.[24] Therefore, science sets out to discover the systematic character of nature in detail by investigating the experience made possible by categorical principles.

Kant considers the distinction between categorical and systematic necessity further, in the Transcendental Dialectic of the *Critique of Pure Reason*, in terms of the analogy, distinction, and interrelation between the cognitive faculties of understanding and reason. His interest in gaining a totality[25] becomes a concern with whether our knowledge of nature, based on the categories of understanding, can be organized as a systematic unity in which 'the totality of things, in their interconnection as constituting the universe', can be understood by us.

The activity of conceptualizing how events in nature are to be ordered and organized is said to be the task of reason. Reason 'will determine, according to principles, how understanding is to be employed in dealing with experience in its totality'.[26] Clearly, the unity provided by reason is '*not* the unity of a *possible experience* but is essentially different from such a unity, *which is that of the understanding*'.[27] For Kant, reason has 'as its sole object the understanding and its effective application. Just as the understanding unifies the manifold in the object by means of concepts, so reason unifies the manifold of objects by means of the idea.'[28] And, in Section V of the *Critique of Judgement*, Kant suggests that a priori transcendental laws have limitations that lead us to seek a necessity drawn from empirical lawlikeness. Although all causal relations in nature presuppose a transcendental deduction, nevertheless, because different sorts of objects have distinctive natures, they also have diverse determining causes and depend on different natural laws, each of which 'brings necessity with it, although we do not at all have an insight into this necessity'.[29]

Here, the analogy between understanding and reason allows an analogous use of 'cause'. While our understanding necessarily uses concepts in order to constitute its objects, the discovery of causal connections in empirical nature is used to satisfy our desire for a systematic unity of empirical cognitions.[30] In the latter, reason is concerned with nature 'as a *system of causal interconnections*'.[31] And Kant proposes[32] that in the discovery of empirical lawlikeness causality is the basis of a rule, 'the principle of causality', which we use to develop a systematic unity between different parts of our experience and to give lawlikeness to an apparently uniform and regular sequence of empirical events.[33] Causality was used in a similar way to constitute events and objects out of a uniform train of representations.

But while there are analogies between reason and understanding, there are also differences. Although Kant draws a parallel between the activity of reason—ordering and unifying our knowledge of empirical events into a systematic whole—and the activity of understanding—conceptualizing our experience—it should be clear that the principles used by reason to gain unity—its ideas—are not derived from nature and do not allow us to gain experience of some 'rational objects' in any way parallel to the exercise of understanding and our constitution of the objects of experience. Ideas have only 'the reality of a schema [of sensibility] . . . . They should be regarded only as analoga of real things, not as in themselves real things'.[34]

In the *Critique of Pure Reason*, Kant goes on to provide a deduction of that systematic unity as a law of reason, arguing that unless we presupposed that a unity and valid objective order were obtainable we would 'have no reason at all, and without reason, no coherent employment of the understanding, and in the absence of this, no sufficient criterion of empirical truth'.[35] But this claim to objective validity is not a claim to anything like objective existence.[36] It cannot be constitutive of experience, and at most may claim validity as a necessary supposition in our organization and regulation of a unified system of our knowledge of nature.

The analogies and distinctions between understanding and reason are instructive. For something similar is present in the *Critique of Judgement*, where we may make the same distinction between the transcendental possibility of aesthetic judgements and their necessity. But there are also differences between the two texts.

To treat the similarities first: the transcendental deduction of aesthetic judgements justifies our expectation that rational agreement with other subjects over a feeling is possible. But at most this shows that there are a priori principles underlying our aesthetic experience. For the universality or subjective general validity defended in Kant's deduction only suffices to legitimate discourse about fine art and natural beauty—a discourse in which our defence and explanation of preferences is accepted as a rational procedure. Yet our response to and appreciation of objects is something that occurs in experience. Just as the discovery of general laws of nature is an empirical matter, one based on the experience legitimated by a transcendental deduction of categories, similarly discovering which objects generate a generalizable response depends on our actual responses and on an assessment of the intersubjectivity of pleasure, where the possibility of the latter is justified by a transcendental deduction.

Consequently, we may say that the transcendental deduction has a limited scope, and comprehends only a part of our aesthetic experience. It warrants only the rationality of our attempts to justify and explain our appreciation of objects generally. But whether a particular justification is successful, so that a subjective response may be generalized over other subjects, can only be assessed by seeing whether others in fact share our pleasure. For to justify an aesthetic judgement is to enable another subject to gain the same response. And only when we have a way of dealing with the actual occurrences of this experience can we make sense of warranting a demand that they should agree with our judgements or that they have a duty to do so. However, because a deduction of taste covers only the general possibility of a claim to intersubjectivity or universal validity, it is unable to deal with the necessity of particular judgements in the sense of explaining why others should attempt to gain that pleasure. And a lot more needs to be said about successful aesthetic judgements, of the claims we may make of others in the case of particular judgements, and of the reasons why others should participate in the same activity.

Just as Kant acknowledged the need for an additional justification of the necessity of cognitive judgements under empirical laws—one separate from the necessity deployed through the transcendental deduction of categories—we must now recognize that, in addition to the force aesthetic judgements claim on the basis of their transcendental deduction we need a justification of the demands which particular aesthetic judgements make upon us. And Kant seeks to justify this necessity of aesthetic judgements by arguing that the pursuit of beauty through understanding, criticizing, and evaluating fine art is an important activity.

This leads us to introduce the issue of differences between cognitive and aesthetic necessity. For, as we said, Kant holds that aesthetic necessity 'is of a special kind',[37] and its justification must show 'how the feeling in the judgement of taste comes to be exacted from everyone *as a duty*'.[38] Although aesthetic response occurs in our actual experience, clearly its necessity is not like that of cognition. It is peculiar in being neither obviously cognitive nor simply moral: because it is based on a feeling of pleasure, we cannot predicate beauty of objects as if disagreements between subjects could be resolved merely by considering the state of objects.[39] Further, we may know a priori that others are able to appreciate the beauty of an object, but they need not feel compelled to do so.[40] And moral compulsion is unable to evoke our pleasurable aesthetic judgements.[41]

Moreover, if aesthetic judgements are necessary, they must possess a distinctive force. Instead of seeing them as either cognitive or moral, Kant argues that in aesthetic judgements 'the theoretical faculty gets bound into unity with the practical in an intimate and obscure manner'.[42] And the context of Kant's claim, his earlier contention that practical reason has primacy, together with evidence gleaned from the range of his writings on ethical subjects, all suggest that he proposes a practical necessity for our aesthetic judgements. While it is the burden of this book to defend this proposal, we can say here that theoretical necessity is an unsatisfactory modality for beauty. Because aesthetic judgements are based on a subjective feeling, and as beauty denotes our experience rather than objects,[43] our aesthetic experience is best understood as a relation between subjects. It is capable of a practical necessity which we will not understand unless we go beyond considering only epistemological issues.

From Epistemology to Nature and Art

It may seem less than obvious that we must extend our concern beyond epistemology in order to understand Kant's theory. After all, few commentators have done so, and Kant himself not only admits that he seeks a deduction of 'taste, i.e. of judgement upon the beauty of *things of nature*', but he also holds that 'this will satisfactorily dispose of the problem for the entire faculty of judgements'.[44] Not only is the deduction concerned to argue merely that individuals may accept the possibility of rational agreement with others over a judgement based on their *'own* feeling of pleasure in an object',[45] but even the practice of describing *objects* as beautiful, we are reminded,[46] is really illicit because strictly beauty is an experience of *mind* in judgement rather than a quality of objects. Thus, even where the object of beauty is considered, natural objects are given priority by virtue of our interest in epistemology.

An emphasis on nature is justified further by arguing that its beauty is the experience of a 'beautiful thing' whereas fine art is merely the 'beautiful *representation* of a thing'.[47] Thus, because the object is natural, its beauty seems to have a value that cannot be ascribed to the beauty of a mere representation. Natural beauty is capable of an 'immediate interest' which is 'akin to the moral' but which fine art either cannot possess or gains only because of its similarity to natural beauty. As an analogy between beauty and morality forms the basis of Kant's claim for aesthetic necessity, the immediate interest that natural beauty possesses will make an understanding of natural objects central to justifications of aesthetic necessity. Further, Kant asserts that fine art is beautiful in so far as 'it has the appearance of nature',[48] and it may be noted that his references to fine art are confined to one part of the *Critique*.

Another reason adduced to relegate fine art to a secondary position turns on one interpretation of Kant. By this account, aesthetic judgements are disinterested because they are not determined by concepts.[49] By contrast, if objects are recognized as human artefacts, they must be identified as the product of an intention under some description.[50] Consequently, judgements upon works of fine art must be determined by the application of concepts, and thus must be deprived of their disinterestedness. Fine art, it is said, is 'impure' for being 'described as beautiful under the condition of a definite concept',[51] and judgements of taste upon it are 'dependent'.[52] By contrast, natural objects are 'free' beauties and 'no concept is here presupposed of any end'.[53] Hence judgements of taste upon them are 'pure'.[54] The inference seems to be that natural objects permit a purity of response that fine art is incapable of making available, and so the former must be elevated above the latter wherever that response is valued.

Natural beauty may be thought to deserve precedence also for a 'representational priority' because objective nature provides a standard for representation in fine art. Kant touches on this in his discussion of the role of mechanism in fine art, and suggests that aesthetic representation must borrow some elements from our experience of objects in nature,[55] even though an artist may transform that experience in accordance with the rules of representation practised, say, by a particular school of painting. And even if the artist refuses to let his representation be completely restricted by the causal relations determining the object, it must still be seen as the 'effectuation of an end'. Apparently nature must be represented in particular ways to allow various expressive intentions to be realized. And the artist must relate his expressive work to representations of the empirical world if it is to avoid becoming implausible or obtuse, bodiless, and evanescent.[56]

However, if objects of nature are given this representational priority, it is one conditioned by our artistic expressive intentions. For example, where the artist's intentions are at odds with or, hindered by, the object represented, either he must manipulate his representation to realize his expression or, where the latter cannot be effected without making it a poor representation, another vehicle must be found for his expressive intention.[57] Thus, the representational and expressive features may be said so to interpenetrate each other that no clear answer can be given to questions of which, in any particular work, has priority over the other. It is possible to represent a man in a painting without giving every detail about him that may be needed in our actual experience. We need only give the details necessary to aesthetic and expressive intentions. Conversely, our aesthetic intentions may be changed by the mode of representation used. And the proposal that nature has precedence for its representational priority can be rejected because representation is conditioned by expression.

Nor can we infer that Kant provides a deduction of *natural* beauty without mentioning *artistic* beauty because fine art is somehow secondary or that its possibility derives from the former. When Kant confines his search for a deduction to 'judgements upon the beauty of things of nature',[58] he makes no mention of a separate deduction of aesthetic judgements on works of art because he seeks only to justify the possibility of judgements generally. Rather than imply that natural objects have aesthetic priority, if Kant can show that judgements on objects of nature are possible he will have shown that they are possible on works of art. For judgements retain their character in spite of differences in the objects judged, and natural objects are unable to claim any sort of 'deductive' precedence over fine art.[59] The possibility of judgements of taste concerns the 'subjective factor which we presuppose in all men'. It examines rational and feeling *man* and *his* capacity for making judgements, and is unconcerned with the priority of one object over another. As Kant makes clear, there 'are two kinds of objects *which in the judgement of mere taste could scarcely contend with one another for superiority*.'[60] If fine art has precedence over natural beauty, or vice versa, its priority is not a result of the fact that the deduction is addressed to one sort of object rather than the other. And that Kant's deduction is of judgements upon one sort of object fails to imply that they are valued more highly than works of art.

Morality and Beautiful Objects

We may also reject claims for the precedence of natural beauty which are based on a particular conception of the relation between disinterest and morality.[61] In arguing for this precedence, Kant is thought to hold that the beauty of nature inspires a feeling 'akin to the moral'. Given that the permanence and necessity of beauty are gained through association with morality, the separate relation of beautiful natural objects to morality may contend for precedence over artistic beauty's symbolic relation to morality. For Kant beautiful natural objects are valued for sustaining our moral behaviour and aspirations. This may be explained as follows.

The Newtonian conception of a causally determined order of nature which was legitimated by Kant in the *First Critique* seems to be entirely antithetical to the demand for freedom and the exercise of moral reason examined in the *Second Critique*. Where all objects are thought to be causally determined, there seems little possibility of seeing some events or objects as the result of free action on the part of an agent. In the *Third Critique*, by developing teleological thinking in its application to nature, Kant may be said to show that the natural order can be conceived of as other than simply determined according to causal connections. It is conceived of as determined to certain ends. With the occurrence of natural beauty, nature exhibits a finality directed to an accord with the harmonious relation of freely exercised faculties. Nature shows that it can have an end which is not antithetical to human ends and so is not indifferent to moral ends. When we appreciate natural beauty, therefore, we make a pleasurable judgement of taste and, in addition, feel pleasure in being able to make this judgement on objects.[62] The occurrence of natural beauty supports us in thinking that nature has some regard for us and our exercise of a free rationality. And this is of great help in our efforts to persevere with moral behaviour, suggesting, as it does, that a nature which, by the Newtonian conception, seems uninterested in freedom and human responsibility, not only has some regard for reason but, in instances of natural beauty, seems able to cooperate with or satisfy the demands of rationality.

It is a great stimulus to moral effort and a strong support to the human spirit if man can believe that the moral life is something more than a mortal enterprise in which he can join with his fellow men against a background of a blind and indifferent universe until he and the human race are blotted out forever. Man cannot be indifferent to the possibility that his puny efforts toward moral perfection may, in spite of appearances, be in accord with the purpose of the universe . . . .[63]

The feeling that natural beauty inspires on this account is a feeling 'akin to the moral'.

But this relation to morality is not one of analogy or symbolism. That is, by 'akin to the moral' Kant means that it supports moral feeling and behaviour, not that it is analogous to, or symbolic of, morality. It gives the beauty of nature an importance because nature appears to be art, as if it had freedom and a rational will at its base.[64] Moreover, it appears that nature is sympathetic to, or at least co-operates with, the effort to attain human ends. But the importance of natural beauty is not moral—it affords us hope but cannot provide a moral justification for our exercise of will. Rather, the importance of natural beauty lies in exhibiting the possibility that we can act in the hope of achieving a moral end in a world not entirely indifferent to our moral aspirations. Thus, the relation it bears to morality is one of supporting moral feelings and aspirations, not one of analogy.

Kant does not clarify which sort of connection to morality is deemed fundamental to the universality and necessity of beauty. That is, he does not clearly say that the permanent value and exemplary necessity of beauty must be understood through the support given to morality by our experience of natural beauty—which might exclude artistic beauty or make it imitative of nature—or in terms of an analogy and symbolic relation of beauty to morality—which could leave natural beauty in a secondary role.[65]

In Section 52 of the *Critique of Judgement*, for example, Kant faults fine art because its pleasures are superficial and temporary so long as it is not related to morality in some way. Where we are concerned to enculture the mind, the suggestion is, the important connection to morality is one which disposes the mind to moral ideas.[66] Fine art may be able to do this by its reflectiveness and its concern with the possible developments and limits of human rationality. But fine art can be amoral too, neither connected to moral ideas nor concerned to dispose the mind to attend to them. By contrast, natural beauty cannot but be related to moral aspirations because its beauty has an immediate interest which sustains the moral hopes of men. Thus, comparing the two, while fine art *can* be related to moral ideas, it need not be; and we cannot, therefore, unequivocally value fine art without first discovering whether or how the relation to morality is entertained. By contrast, with natural beauty we know the relation to morality to be concomitant with the experience of beauty. What is important to both, here, is that beauty must dispose the mind to moral ideas and thus support our moral aspirations.

On the other hand, in Section 59, Kant relates beauty to morality as the symbol of the latter.

Now, I say the beautiful is the symbol of the morally good, and only in this light . . . does it give us pleasure with an attendant claim to the agreement of everyone else, whereupon the mind becomes conscious of a certain ennoblement and elevation above mere sensibility to pleasure from impressions of sense and also appraises the worth of others on the score of a like maxim of their judgement.[67]

And the suggestion here is that beauty is universal and claims exemplary necessity in a way similar to morality. It does not derive its necessity from reassuring mankind about the viability of its moral hopes.

Further, with regard to the precedence claimed for natural beauty, in at least one instance in Section 42 Kant refers to the matter of nature's design as if the latter were a factor 'in addition' to the main argument for interest in natural beauty.[68] As this occurs at the end of a paragraph whose substance seems to rely on an *analogy* between aesthetic and moral *judgements* to explain our immediate interest in natural beauty, it must give us more reason to pause before dismissing fine art on the grounds that it cannot possess an immediate interest. The case for an immediate interest is made here in terms of an *analogy between judgements*, and nature's design seems to be only an additional factor on which to base its possession of an interest.[69] Given that a symbolic relation is based on an analogy between two elements, and given that we may yet be able to rely on a symbolic relation to morality to justify our interest in fine art, all is not lost for fine art's claim to priority.

Fine Art over Natural Beauty

Indeed, we can use the symbolic relation of beauty to morality to argue that the contention between artistic and natural beauty, which is based on their respective relations to morality, must be resolved in favour of fine art. First, natural beauty bears a relation to morality which, so to speak, is merely an external one. Beautiful natural objects are given precedence for supporting our moral endeavours, not for any aesthetic merit. Second, the elements which underlie the analogy with moral good are constitutive of both natural and artistic beauty, but fine art is better able to bear that symbolic relation to morality.[70] Our experience of beauty is constituted through reflective judgement on an object, and there is an analogy between moral good and that reflection: in both we seek to maintain a similar balance between the demands of reason and the inclinations of nature. Further, we can contrast this with an immediate interest in natural beauty, where our experience is given importance for its support of moral aspirations, not for its similarity to morality. Nor does our understanding of the reflective judgement which constitutes natural beauty tell us anything about its role in supporting morality. It is only after an object has been judged beautiful that an immediate interest is associated with it: the moral interest associated with natural beauty is engaged only after an object has been judged beautiful on the basis of a reflection that bears analogies with moral good. Consequently, if we were to compare the analogy between beauty and moral good with the support beauty gives our moral endeavours, the analogy must be deemed more fundamental as it has to do with the very constitution of the beautiful rather than with an interest that will be associated with one sort of object once it has been judged beautiful.[71]

At one place, we saw, Kant appears to contend that beauty's support of morality must be constitutive of fine art; and if this contention were successful, it would show natural beauty to have precedence over fine art. Kant claims that if the fine arts lack all relation to moral ideas, they become insipid, because they cannot claim to have any independent value, and they leave our disposition in a perverse state,[72] bereft of expansion or strengthening. That is, an amoral fine art can neither claim exemplary necessity nor be judged beautiful. It 'can only serve as a diversion'.

Our need to bring fine art into combination with moral ideas may then be compared with the situation of natural beauty. And Kant writes that for 'disposing the mind to moral ideas', natural beauty is 'in general the most beneficial' because it possesses an immediate interest. This claim implies a contrast between the support natural beauty gives to moral effort and the possible absence of such support from fine art, and the suggestion is that the relation to moral ideas that fine art must bear is similar to that already borne by natural beauty. It would not be enough, it seems, for fine art merely to express moral ideas. If fine art is to claim to be more than just a 'diversion', its relation to moral ideas must be constitutive of beauty. That is, *to be judged beautiful* fine art must be brought into combination with morality in a way comparable to the support natural beauty gives to morality. And this implies that it is the support it gives to morality that is fundamental *and* constitutive of our experience of beauty, not the analogy between beauty and morality.

Such an argument is, at best, an aberration on the part of Kant. It tries to impose on fine art conditions that stem from the character of natural beauty. The suggestion is that in order to be judged beautiful fine art must support morality in just the way that natural beauty does. But this illegitimately extends to fine art demands which natural beauty must satisfy. Natural objects are not brought into relation with morality in order to be judged beautiful. It is only once their beauty is acknowledged that an immediate interest is associated with them. Yet because Kant proposes that natural beauty's relation to morality must serve as a standard for fine art, the implication seems to be that a role supporting morality is also constitutive of the beauty of art. If it did not support morality, it seems, our pleasure in appreciating a work of fine art would be merely diversionary. So, *in order to be beautiful*, fine art must support our moral endeavours; and the case differs from natural beauty, in which an immediate interest comes to be associated with our experience of beauty. But to impose this requirement on fine art is to imply that a moral interest must determine our judgement of beauty. And if this were Kant's intention he would contradict his own demand for disinterested-ness—the requirement that moral interests should not determine a judgement of taste or our experience of beauty.

Further, we can show that Kant did not think that the more fundamental relation of beauty to morality was to give support to our moral aspirations. After all, in the *Critique of Judgement* Kant wants to show that reason and nature are conterminous by discovering a balance between them. He focuses on man and holds that selfconscious 'social communication' and 'social spirit' are proper to or 'befit' mankind. This exercise of reason can be contrasted with 'the lower life of animals' without implying that we must suppress our animal character and natural being. Kant writes that a balance between reason and nature that is gained through the use of reason as social spirit cannot 'dispense with' nature; and even if 'nature will ever recede into the background', it cannot be allowed to disappear. Thus, consonantly with these emphases on a balance between reason and nature, it is more appropriate and fruitful to stress that beauty bears analogies with moral good, combining nature and reason, sensibility and freedom, natural inclination and law, in similar ways.

Kant accepts that in the course of social development the forms of social spirit that grow out of a basis in nature can become more clearly social in character and less natural. The self-formation of a social character through communication and the developing 'social spirit befitting mankind' consists, in part, in natural determinations being replaced by social determinations in culture, politics, and morality. Elsewhere,[73] Kant identifies human nature as the repository of our creative energies, thus linking human reason to the natural world. Accordingly, if the natural and animal part of our being is suppressed, then, we will be left, 'eventually, with no permanent example retained from the past'. Consequently 'a future age will be in no position to form a concept of a happy union of the highest culture with the force and truth of a free nature sensible of its proper worth'.[74] To circumvent such a forgetting and to prevent our natural creative potential from eroding under pressure from social organization, we look to the relation of nature to reason contained in the highest moral good. The latter identifies for us the proper balance between the two elements. So far as aesthetic activity participates in the development of our 'social spirit' it takes morality as a model and seeks that balance or 'mean between *higher culture* and the modest worth of *nature* [which] forms for taste also, as a sense common to all mankind, [a] true standard'.[75] Thus, as fine art is characterized in terms of *humaniora*[76] and 'the faculty of being able to *communicate* universally one's inmost self', it concerns 'the befitting social spirit of mankind, in contradistinction to the narrow life of the lower animals'.[77] The significance of morality here is just that it does not forget its relation to sensibility and nature; and the dual determination of an ultimately insuperable natural basis and the continuing transformation of this by man implies that the development of man's social character is a vitally important matter because it is in men and their objects, in their nature and relationships, that those determinations are most clearly worked out.

In the experience of beauty, taste is the proper relation of genius to reason, of purposive nature to rational faculties, of human nature to the social spirit of mankind. And although taste links reason to nature in the case of both natural beauty and fine art, in the latter it is human nature, of which genius is a function,[78] that is important. It bears reference to construction and creativity, to expressive freedom and universality. By contrast, natural beauty is a balance between reason and a nature to which purposiveness and construction are ascribed by judgement on the basis of an analogy with art. It provides a mean in which nature only shows itself to be co-operative with reason and conducive to human ends, and although natural objects are valued for their part in this balance, such value really results only from the way we look to nature.[79]

It is by reference to this background that we may use morality as a model of the relation between reason and nature in order to understand the relation of fine art to natural beauty. The Highest Good mediates the relation of reason to nature. Happiness, which Kant understands as the satisfaction of natural impulses, is conditioned by the requirement that we treat each other as ends.[80] Nature is essential but subordinate to the demands of reason, for although it can never be extirpated, moral behaviour demands that natural impulses be conditioned by the superior stipulations of moral law. Nature must be seen in the context of reason, and the satisfaction of natural impulses is dependent on the requirements of rational behaviour.[81] Accordingly, if beauty is symbolic of morality, nature's subordination to reason may be expected to form some part of that symbolic relation. As nature will be conditioned by the freedom presupposed in fine art, our experience of natural beauty will be circumscribed by that of fine art. In the proper relation of reason to nature the former serves as an unconditioned and unqualified value. If that is taken to be something about artistic and natural beauty, the Highest Good's mediation between reason and nature leads us to accept that, first, natural and artistic beauty are not identical and, second, are two sorts of objects that remain irreducible to each other even while they are both objects of taste and part of the experience of beauty.

Further, natural beauty exhibits nature's purposiveness, showing that nature is conterminous with reason, and invites an immediate interest through its support of our moral aspirations. In a sense, natural beauty procures a balance between reason and nature from the latter side, showing how far nature can enter into a relation with reason. In this sense, artistic beauty participates from the side of reason, exhibiting reason's part in the subordination of nature. Fine art is known to depend on genius which, in turn, is based on a human nature that, further, is discontinuous with ordinary nature in several ways. Men are subject to nature but also capable of rationality. This involves a particular relation between the two; while some part of our behaviour may be understood in terms of susceptibility to natural inclinations, human nature must also be seen in the context of moral necessity. The satisfaction of natural inclinations is a good conditioned by the needs of moral behaviour: and ultimately reason's relation to nature in artistic beauty is one within the realm of practical reason.

However, this cannot exclude man's natural being because man's social spirit arises out of his natural being in the course of developing social practice. Such growth is part of a process that begins with creative projects, for which there must be scope in nature. Although mechanistic nature does not contain an analogy for creativity, one can be discovered through a teleological conception of nature by which a nature formerly thought to be causally determined can be understood in terms of purposes and projects. If there is no analogy in Newtonian deterministic nature for a constructive and 'technic' sense of purpose, one is ascribed by analogy with the social practice exhibited in art and fine art. And without denying the causal determinations that constitute our experience of nature, through natural beauty we see how far nature can enter into accord with reason. It faces us with the limitations that preclude this balance and with the potential there is in nature for developing their harmony.

Clearly, both artistic and natural beauty are to be valued. The former cannot ignore its basis in nature through genius and our sensible experience, while the latter must try to attain standards set by a fine art cognizant of its basis in nature. But, as should be clear now, art's relation to nature goes further. Not only are they in accord through natural and artistic beauty, but the former is conditioned by our understanding and experience of the latter. Interest in natural beauty is based on nature showing itself to have a regard for man's rational ends. Nature is valued for its part in our attaining moral ends, but this evaluation is possible only because nature is like art. As Kant affirms, *'the sole basis'* of our immediate interest is that 'the beauty in question is nature's *handiwork'*.[82]

Further, fine art may have its basis in nature, but in addition it is a participant in man's cultural development. In keeping with the demands of the highest good, the beautiful brings about a constant but moderate discipline of our inclinations, and by a continuous cultural labour and growth it promotes the resolve to do one's duty. While a more detailed account of fine art's participation in culture will be given later, for the present it is important to note that in our cultural and aesthetic experience fine art circumscribes our approach to nature and its beauty.[83] We judge nature by criteria that belong to art and its presupposition of free actions. Natural beauty at best merely augments our 'disposition to good', especially by bringing to our attention the natural characteristics that 'are the aesthetic receptiveness of the mind to the concept of duty'.[84] And again, it is fine art, with its ontological commitment to the existence of freedom, that shows us which aspects of nature should be the objects of our concern.

Thus, just as the highest good contains a *heterogeneous* unity between moral and natural goods,[85] similarly Kant intends to unify nature with art without mixing them together. By relating them so that one is the ground for what worth we ascribe to the other, both are valued, but one unconditionally and unqualifiedly and the other so far as it is consistent with and conditioned by our pursuit of the first. That is, our response to nature is determined by the demands of reason and our exercise of creativity: artistic beauty is seen as the unconditioned and unqualified development of a free autonomous will that accepts only those limitations essential to communication and understanding, while natural beauty's entry into the field of communication, first, is conditioned by its ability to satisfy criteria native to art, and second, qualified by its lack of commitment to the existence of freedom.[86]

We have seen that to the question whether nature or art must be given precedence, one answer is that neither is superior because each possesses a distinctive value. Beautiful natural objects are valued for their support of our moral endeavours while works of fine art are better able to bear a symbolic relation to morality.[87] However, this answer is inadequate. The precedence claimed for natural beauty is not based on an aesthetic value: it is superior only for supporting morality, not for the features which constitute its beauty. Natural objects are ascribed aesthetic qualities by analogy with fine art—nature is not based on free purposive action nor capable of any expressiveness or universality except where it is 'regarded as such' because of similarities it bears to our experience of fine art. In terms of its ability to satisfy judgements of taste, then, fine art may claim precedence. But Kant proposes also that the necessity of beauty must be understood by reference to its symbolic relation to moral good; and that relation turns on requirements which are more properly fulfilled by fine art than by natural beauty. Moreover, the analogy between beauty and morality suggests how we may inter-relate the different aspects of fine art to natural beauty and also gain another reason for giving fine art precedence. Moral good is related to nature as the unconditioned and unqualified member that sets the standard for nature. If beauty is analogous to moral good, then we may expect this relation between a rational will and nature to be exemplified in both and may suppose that fine art is related to natural beauty as the unconditioned and unqualified member of a heterogeneous unity. Indeed, it is clear that the capacity for sustaining a symbolic relation, which is possessed by fine art, lends itself to just such a relation, so that we can give precedence to artistic beauty while remaining conscious of the basis of art in nature.

The main problem with such an account is that it remains incomplete. At best the precedence of fine art is based on its symbolic relation to moral good, but no argument has yet been given to justify their relation. And, when we look at the analogies listed by Kant in Section 59, it appears that of the four put forward, only the first three serve to describe their common characteristics. The fourth seems to do more. It suggests that Kant is using the symbolic relation to make an argument from analogy that justifies the exemplary necessity of beauty—that he is not merely pointing to similarities in their immediacy, disinterestedness, and universality. So we must consider whether beauty's symbolic relation to morality constitutes aesthetic necessity. And, in the present context, the question may be raised in terms of fine art's precedence.

Priority and Kant's Argument for Aesthetic Necessity

Fine art's priority over natural beauty was shown to depend on a symbolic relation between beauty and moral good. But Kant also says that beauty's claim to 'the agreement of everyone else' can only be justified 'in the light of' that relation, and he has been understood to assert that beauty gains necessity because of and through symbolizing moral good.[88] Kant himself is seen to support this reading through his hints that our experience of beauty must be comprehended in terms of a 'supersensible ground for unity between moral and theoretical under-standing'[89] and his assertions that beauty effects a transition from sense to moral feeling.[90] To penetrate further into fine art's precedence over natural beauty, then, we must assess whether it cannot be justified by arguing that a symbolic relation to moral good gives artistic beauty a necessity that natural beauty claims only by analogy.

Both Crawford and Elliott refer to the symbolic relation in order to justify aesthetic necessity; but it is not clear that the analogy lends itself to this argument. For an argument based on a symbolic relation to succeed, it is necessary to exhibit the presence of some relevant similarities between beauty and moral good that permit us to ascribe the further similarity of their necessity. It must be understood, naturally, that several differences will remain, for beauty only has a subjective exemplary necessity while morality claims objective lawfulness, and so on. Unfortunately, it is not clear that Kant is arguing in this manner. Beauty's analogy with morality appears to be viewed by Kant as the *basis* of their symbolic relation; and if beauty successfully symbolizes moral good because of analogies between them, then aesthetic judgements must possess necessity before we can entertain the idea of an analogy between the two elements. If a comparison between the two rests on their respective claims to necessity, among other things, then it cannot without circularity be argued that their symbolic relation justifies aesthetic necessity.

Once we assume that their analogy rests on a common possession of necessity, we will be unable to accept a justification of aesthetic necessity like Crawford's which supposes, first, that beauty symbolizes the basis of morality and, second, holds that whatever symbolizes the basis of morality demands our attention.[91] Where we seek an account of necessity, to hold to the last point is to beg the question because there cannot be a symbolic relation unless certain analogies with morality are already present. In this case, beauty must already have a basis like that of morality and therefore be analogous in a relevant way. It will then be rendered necessary in a manner similar to that of morality, thus allowing it to symbolize the latter. By contrast, we may hold that for Kant beauty symbolizes morality because both are valid in similar ways in spite of other differences that result from beauty's basis in a subjective experience and morality's claim to possession of an objective principle.[92]

A similar criticism may be levelled against Elliott when he argues that its analogy with morality makes beauty of special interest.[93] His claim may very well be true, but it does not explain or justify the claim to necessity that beauty must make in order to be analogous to, and symbolic of moral good.

Cohen's account of the relation of beauty to morality differs from those proposed by Crawford and Elliot, though like them it ignores important differences in the relation of morality to natural and artistic beauty. In any case, Cohen's argument depends on a formal analogy between aesthetic and moral judgements; he claims that this gives us reason to look on the former with favour. However, if this favour is morally important, it needs to be shown at least why the analogy between morality and beauty is important. And that must depend on some account of aesthetic necessity—which Cohen does not provide.[94]

There are several reasons for holding that their common possession of necessity is a basis for the analogy between beauty and morality. It is possible to provide a justification of aesthetic necessity that does not depend on a symbolic relation to morality, and such a justification is likely to provide a more fruitful conception of aesthetic practice. At the same time, there is good reason to distrust a justification of aesthetic necessity which is based on the symbolic relation of beauty to moral good. It is wrong to argue that beauty is analogous to the moral good *and* that moral good is necessary in some ways and that *therefore* the beautiful is necessary because it is like the moral good. First, the relation of analogy is wildly imprecise. Unless it is clear which similarities are significant, *any* assumption of necessity will remain arbitrary. And where criteria for assessing significance are present, there we have an account of necessity that is more basic than one based on analogy. In the case of moral good and beauty, the analogy rests on similar 'rules of reflection' and 'causality'—suggesting that their common supposition of freedom and, hence, of necessity, is the basis of their symbolic relation, not its result. Second, to derive necessity in the way set out above is to make morality constitutive of beauty by saying that an object is beautiful and so possesses necessity only if it is like the moral good. To argue successfully for this would cause beauty to lose its disinterestedness, and an object would be thought beautiful only if it satisfied certain moral requirements and for the reason that it satisfied them. Third, it is not clear how such an argument could be made. It is far from obvious how a similarity between beauty and moral good allows necessity to be extended to the former. If it is only a symbolic relation, then the necessity attaching to moral good, which is allegedly extended to the beautiful because of their similarity, could be said to be merely a 'symbolic' necessity in some way commensurate with the symbolic nature of their relation. Yet it is difficult to see what sense can be given to such a 'symbolic' necessity or to the extension of necessity from moral good to beauty on the basis of some analogy between them.

Although the priority of artistic over natural beauty cannot be defended by deriving aesthetic necessity from beauty's symbolic relation to moral good, this does not render the latter vacuous or show Kant's statement about it to be misleading. While it is unable to justify aesthetic necessity, beauty's symbolic relation to morality has an important role to play. For Kant may be understood to use the analogy with moral good to characterize beauty in a way that indicates which factors are relevant to justifying aesthetic necessity. As we saw, Section 59 of the *Critique of Judgement* focuses in the main on particular symbolic relations. It examines monarchy's association with a handmill for example, thereby considering a relation that is specific in its content when compared to that between beauty and moral good generally. Examining particular relations may be of help in understanding the more general one, but in the latter case we cannot suppose Kant merely to be setting out technical rules for choosing individual representations and generating a symbolic content. If he were, then, because of the substantive moral content involved, we would expect a more detailed account of the criteria we must use in judging their analogy and a clearer delineation of how a subject is to grasp a symbolic relation in the many particular judgements of taste he makes. Instead, it may be proposed, Kant's concern is with the role of beauty in the system of reason and morality—with the relation between freedom and nature. The symbolic relation to moral good brings to light the practical connotations of our experience of beauty: it emphasizes Kant's fundamental interest in the place and promise of humanity. Rather than interpret Kant's construction of a symbolic relation as an attempt to derive aesthetic necessity, we should see it as a heuristic device proposing that although our experience of beauty is unlike both cognitive and moral activity, nevertheless in many respects it may still be characterized through certain analogies with the second.

Kant's presentation in Section 59 explains their analogy in terms that range beyond both the four formulae mentioned earlier and the relation explained by reference to a handmill and the monarchial state.[95] His presentation contains a stronger substantive content than either the formal or particular terms can adequately grasp. It talks of 'appraising the worth of others' and so of judging their adequacy. Kant says also that taste gives 'the law to itself',[96] suggesting that where genius creates objects capable of sustaining judgements of taste, and so ensures that a creative and free imagination is in accord with the lawfulness of understanding, it is similar to our moral life where in our choices (*Willkur*) we attempt to realize the moral law (*Wille*) rather than follow sensual desires. Similarly, Kant writes of the '*intelligible*' to which taste 'extends its view', proposing that our experience of beauty involves treating individuals as subjects who are ends in themselves and capable of appreciating the exercise of imaginative freedom. In this context Kant also mentions the 'Subject finding a reference to something connected with the ground of freedom', and this can be explained as a reference to our capacity for reason. The interconnections proposed here are the domain of culture; and Kant goes on to emphasize that a reference to the intelligible 'brings even our higher *cognitive* faculties into common accord', suggesting that his interest lies in showing, through our experience and understanding of beauty, that there is no contradiction between theory—which involves the use of cognitive faculties; intersubjectivity—the common accord of faculties; and a reference to the intelligible—that is, to our character as free and reasoning but natural beings. Leaving further clarification until later, all this can be taken to show that our capacity for sensual experience is far from being always opposed to the exercise of practical reason. It is possible for there to be an accord between nature and practical reason that allows intersubjectivity—in the sense of treating other subjects as ends in themselves, even where their sensuous nature is involved—instead of supposing that subjectivity implies subjugation to private, sensuous inclinations.

The importance of such an accord should be obvious. As Kant makes clear in his Preface and Introduction, his intention is to see how theory and practice are conterminuous by discovering what room there is in the experience of nature for our 'intelligible' character. The analogies presented above together go to make beauty, an experience in the phenomenal world, similar to morality and, so, symbolic of it. Kant is proposing that beauty be understood in terms of a freedom involving a concern for others and their worth 'from a practical point of view', based on an accord between reason and nature. But whatever these analogies suggest, they do not constitute an argument for necessity. Although it seems at times as though Kant is relying on the symbolic relation to explain aesthetic necessity, his real argument is found elsewhere. It ranges over the aesthetic and teleological parts of the third *Critique*, depends on the priority of fine art, and requires us to consider especially those other of his writings in which he puts forward a theory of culture.

While fine art's priority over natural beauty has been exhibited sufficiently, an argument proposing that aesthetic necessity must be justified through fine art's relation to morality still has a long way to go. Even while we deprecate claims made for natural beauty, we must explain and understand the production of fine art. To give precedence to fine art is to stress aesthetic activity, which Kant explains by reference to genius's creative activity. Not only is it doubtful that such freedom is possible in a causally determined nature, but we need some account of what genius might be. Further, we must give some explanation of how the understanding, criticism, and evaluation of beauty gain necessity, and that account must depend on genius and fine art in some way or raise further doubts about fine art's claim to precedence. Moreover, we must consider whether the account of necessity that seems to be presented in the Deduction is successful and whether that makes redundant other explanations of necessity.[97] The best place to begin this justification of aesthetic necessity is in a consideration of the nature and existence of fine art, whose possibility and production, in turn, must be explained by

understanding genius. We shall embark on that in Chapter II. Before
that, we must deal with another issue.

Critique *and Theory*

In considering the question of aesthetic necessity we have argued that a
merely epistemological interest will be inadequate. This may be said to
follow also from the character of Kant's critical enterprise. The first two
Critiques examined different areas of the relation between reason and
nature. In the *Critique of Pure Reason* Kant argues to the necessary
conditions of our knowledge of nature, while, in the *Critique of Practical
Reason*, Kant continues an argument begun in the *Foundations of the
Metaphysics of Morals*. The last text examines the supreme principle of
morality and its variations; and the second *Critique* is concerned to argue
that it is possible for imperfectly rational creatures like us to act
according to that principle. And its Analytic, accordingly, ends with a
section on the conditions which must be satisfied for the concepts of
good and evil—the concepts of objects of practical reason—to be
applicable.

An issue left unargued in these writings concerns the extent to which
our knowledge and experience of nature are conterminous with both the
nature of imperatives, as outlined in the *Critique of Practical Reason*, and
the duties proposed in the *Doctrine of Virtue: The Metaphysics of Morals*.
We need to question not only whether and the extent to which moral
concepts are capable of application, but also the extent to which our
experience of nature prepares us to accept moral principles. When Kant
concludes in the First *Critique* that our experience is bound to causality,
this lends itself to the inference that moral actions are precluded
because the freedom to act is excluded by the force of natural causal
necessity. That is, our understanding of theory militates against its
relation to practice. As we have already seen, however, the issue of
natural necessity is more complicated than this suggests, for the
conclusion that causal necessities structure nature is unsatisfactorily
defended unless it is accompanied by an adequate account of the
systematic order given to our empirical knowledge of nature.

Kant explores this issue in the Dialectic of the *Critique of Pure Reason*
and in the Introduction to the *Critique of Judgement*. He develops an
argument that an a priori principle of finality or purposiveness is
presupposed in our constructing a systematic order for our knowledge
of nature. And, on the basis of this principle, he affirms later that
although we must rely 'on mere mechanical laws' to explain events in

nature, the latter are not 'solely possible to this way, that is, to the exclusion of every other kind of causality'.[98] Ultimately, the character of our experience of nature permits us to conceive of some objects in the empirical world as the result of human actions. Again, the details of this argument will be considered later;[99] but it is clear, in the context of this exploration of theory's relation to practice, that an understanding of the ascription of values will be quite inadequate if it fails to consider the problems associated with explaining human activity in producing valuable objects, including ones valued for their beauty. Conversely, a study of practical reason must include consideration of the value of the aesthetic objects produced by human activity.

This concern with the interrelation of experience to value and action is not simply a matter of following Kant's interest in architectonic structure. Rather, it is essential to understanding our own activity through Kant's critical method. For transcendental arguments examine experience, as it were, from inside, and set out the conditions which legitimate the claims we make of it. And this makes the issue of totality or, at least, unity, more important. For unless we can exhibit an interrelation between the separate parts of whatever is made possible on the basis of a priori principles, their very fragmentation must force us to admit an inadequacy in our method. We would 'know' the separate parts yielded by transcendental deductions but be incapable of understanding how activity in one partial system can penetrate into another while, at the same time, being unable to reject the supposition that they bore some interrelation through ourselves as knowing and acting subjects.

That said, it is another matter to argue that considerations of totality or unity apply to our experience of beauty and to aesthetic activity. Indeed Kant himself may seem to deny it when he argues that his *Critique of Aesthetic Judgement* can contain no doctrinal part or any critical 'metaphysics' whose legitimacy is ensured through transcendental arguments. Instead, 'with judgement critique takes the place of theory',[100] because judgement does not constitute any objects. It only serves to give intersubjective validity to our experience of the representation of objects constituted on the basis of the necessary conditions examined in the first and second *Critiques*.

In the Introduction Kant elaborates on this purely critical role. Not only is a 'critique of the judging subject and its faculties of knowledge the propaedeutic of all philosophy',[101] but aesthetic judgements are the ideal vehicle for this critique since they 'alone contain a principle introduced by judgement completely a priori as the basis of its reflection upon nature'.[102] Evidently, a critique of aesthetic judgement examines the subject's use of rational capacities by considering what sort of logical status we give to a part of our experience. And no substantive conclusions about the nature of the subject or about objects seem to follow from this alone because critique is directed only towards the 'subjective factor' in man.

However, even if judgement contains no doctrine, there can be a theory of fine art. For, as Kant goes on to say, 'the whole ground will be covered by the Metaphysics of Nature and of Morals'.[103] Judgements are upon objects or their representations in the empirical world, whose existence must be accounted for either by reference to natural causes alone or by combining reflective judgements with an ontological commitment to the existence of freedom. Critique may 'take the place of theory'; but even while judgement must be subject to critical scrutiny, it is exercised on objects and their representations, and we must understand their nature and existence in relation to our pleasurable judgement. Hence, in an important sense, judgements on works of fine art gain their metaphysics from 'the whole ground of philosophy and its division into theoretical and practical parts'.[104] And this book is concerned to raise some issues in that philosophy of fine art, in which theory is united with practice through judgement.

The Argument

Ultimately, the best defence of the issues touched on in this Introduction is provided by presenting the details of Kant's theory, to show that aesthetic necessity is justified through the relation of fine art to morality. Here, by developing a coherent and defensible account of Kant's thought we also argue against other commentators. Some of the differing emphases and interpretations found in commentaries are a consequence of the way Kant presents the argument. Thus, the attempt made by various authors to justify aesthetic necessity through a symbolic relation to morality is based on what Kant seems to propose in the *Critique of Judgement*. By contrast, the attempt to justify aesthetic necessity on epistemological grounds alone can be blamed on an incorrect assessment of the larger task of the *Critique of Judgement* to link theory with practice—even if Kant is guilty of explaining the possibility and the necessity of taste in different places and of using differing terms. And by developing certain aspects of Kant's theory we propose to show its coherence over aspects which are usually neglected.

For example, we will give considerable importance to the relation of fine art to culture and morality. Very few recent commentators have considered how the quasi-objective necessity which Kant ascribes to beauty may be explained through this relation. They either prefer to limit attention to the *Critique of Judgement* and the *Critique of Pure Reason*[105] or seek a relation of beauty to morality which bypasses the role of beauty and fine art in culture.[106] By explaining the relation between the *Critique of Aesthetic Judgement* and Kant's 'lesser' writings on history, anthropology, and religion, and his work on moral theory and on teleology, we can show his distance from other thinkers and correct those commentators who have ignored this part of his theory.

These points refer to Part I on 'Fine Art and Culture'. Once we acknowledge the crucial role of fine art in our understanding of beauty, the production of fine art and its role in culture and nature become important issues. In Part I, beginning with 'The Production of Fine Art', we present this aspect of Kant's theory. First, we examine his account of the creation of works of fine art. Because of his conceptions of beauty and of art, it is not clear that Kant can maintain that there is such a thing as fine art.

Next, in 'Fine Art and Culture', we show what Kant makes of the concept of culture and how it contributes to our conception of fine art. Very little work has been done on this part of Kant's theory: because interest usually centres on epistemological questions, the relation of aesthetic judgements and beauty to politics, culture, morality, history, and anthropology is usually ignored. As a result, fine art's ability to unite theory and practice, the experience of nature and the exercise of reason, is inadequately understood when, really, it is crucial to Kant's justification of aesthetic necessity and to the issues of warranting a subject's demand that others should agree with his or her aesthetic judgements and their duty to do so. Aesthetic and cultural activity are a corner-stone of this examination of intersubjectivity. And Kant's efforts to include subjectivity within the compass of rational human activities enhances the comprehensiveness of his complex understanding of human will. Consequently, their exclusion will impoverish his conception of our actions.

Accordingly we look briefly at the notion of culture held by English aestheticians—such as Hutcheson, Hume, and Shaftesbury—or, by historicists—such as Herder—or transcendentalists like Schiller, and then present Kant's understanding of culture. This involves us in contrasting culture with politics and morality, in distinguishing skill from disciplinary and progressive culture, and in explaining the social and historical features of culture. Further, Kant's account can be shown also to differ from developments proposed by Fichte and Schiller.

Only then do we return to fine art, to show how it contributes to progressive culture and, it may be suggested, serves morality and cultural duty. Indeed, it may be the latter that goes to justify aesthetic necessity. As we said, for our argument it is important to follow the details of Kant's conception of fine art and culture. It allows us to avoid the pitfalls which some commentators have not been able to avoid, and we can show that Kant's theory is far from being so abstract and pure that it makes no specifiable claims in relation to works of fine art. For although Kant's argument often works at a very abstract level, we can see also the sort of activity it is intended to justify.

In any case, by placing fine art in this context we raise another issue: that of its possibility. If fine art can be produced, it must be possible for artists to intervene in the operation of determinate natural causes in some way in order to attain their goals. In 'Fine Art and Natural Necessity' Kant's writings on teleology are used to suggest how such intervention might be possible. We consider whether moral and cultural progress are compatible with a scientific understanding of nature, and examine whether science is compatible with the presuppositions of autonomy and subjectivity involved in culture. It is argued that scientific generalizations are unable to explain or be substituted for the universality claimed by culture.

This argument further locates the claim that a justification of aesthetic necessity is based on fine art's participation in a culture that pursues the highest good. For by arguing that the proposed intervention is possible, not only do we reject claims that Kant's deduction of experience disallows all conceptions of objects as works produced by a rational will, but by showing what room there is in nature for our intelligible character and for the relation of theory to practice, we also show how the Third *Critique* goes to provide the support Kant's justification needs.

It is next, in Part II, in 'The Necessities of Taste, Fine Art and the *Summum Bonum*', that we turn to questions of necessity. Kant proposes that aesthetic judgements have subjective or objective necessity depending on their presupposition of a *sensus communis*. First, the issue of the transcendental possibility of taste is distinguished from that of its necessity; second, it is shown how the *sensus communis* serves as an ideal norm for aesthetic judgements and their claim to necessity. However, the nature of aesthetic judgements, as shown in the deduction, precludes us from using the *sensus communis*, as an epistemological ideal norm, to 'demand' agreement from other subjects. It is proposed that the *sensus communis* be seen as a practical demand, and this is defended by showing that as a 'public sense' it is similar in form to the practical demands Kant justifies in politics, law, and morality.

And in 'Culture and Morality: Aesthetic Necessity', we examine the justification of aesthetic necessity. We propose that it depends on the contribution that fine art makes to our moral lives: Kant wants to provide a unity between theory and practice, or nature and reason, and between individuals in a community. Accordingly, aesthetic judgements are made by autonomous individual subjects on the basis of a feeling that Kant takes to be universalizable over other equally autonomous subjects. Fine art, thus, occasions a judgement which, despite using cognitive faculties, succeeds in taking account of subjects as rational and feeling ends in themselves. And Kant's justification proceeds by arguing that a duty of culture in general, derived from the supreme principle of morality, warrants a subject's demand for a dutiful assent from others to a subjective but universalizable judgement. We then develop the positive argument further and raise a number of questions about Kant's claim to unite individual with community, theory with practice, reason with nature, or consciousness with interpretation. If beauty is unable to gain necessity through participation in a culture that claims to satisfy moral reason, then the unity of Kant's critical enterprise itself would be shattered.

In this way, this book examines Kant's theory of beauty. And although it restructures issues from the *Critique of Judgement*, it avoids introducing premises alien to Kant. Instead, in the main, it relates the text to other of Kant's writings and so emphasizes concepts and arguments whose significance is sometimes lost in detailed study of only some of his works.

Two other points may be made here about this book. As we intend to show that Kant actually has a theory of artistic beauty in the *Critique of Judgement*—rather than an interest only in establishing a connection between the two earlier *Critiques*—we use examples of fine art to illustrate a number of points. And rather than use examples which would have been familiar to Kant, and in the hope of avoiding the two prejudices that first, Kant would not have recognized modern art as art and, second, that his theory is too abstract to be applicable there or anywhere else, the examples presented are drawn from modern art.

Further, although a fairly close reading of texts is necessary at most points in order to show that Kant does hold the views we attribute to him, nevertheless, because extensive quotation will overburden and could swamp the argument of this book, most quotations have been placed in notes at the end of the book. Indeed, all the notes are intended as end-notes—which may develop points made in the main body of the book but whose absence from there should not hamper the reader.

PART I
FINE ART AND CULTURE

II

The Production of Fine Art

IN Chapter I we examined the moral connotations borne by beautiful objects. Although we could not say unequivocally that either sort of object had priority over its rival, it was clear that the ascription of immediate interest was not sufficient to justify giving priority to natural beauty. And, at best, interest was only 'externally' associated with natural beauty. Further, although natural beauty may be capable of bearing a moral interest because it satisfies our need to discover a congruence between reason and nature, it seems that Kant thinks this is a merely peripheral issue—something 'in addition' to the major justification of interest in beauty.

By contrast, when we consider a symbolic relation to moral good, not only is fine art better able to bear this relation, but it does so on the basis of elements constitutive of and 'internal' to beauty. And as the existence of its symbolic relation to morality could arguably enable fine art to support our moral endeavours, it could claim an immediate interest also. Fine art, then, is the primary object of beauty.

Another reason for giving importance to fine art is pointed out by Burch. He argues, rightly, that Kant turns to fine art at Sections 43–8 because he recognizes the importance of art for an exploration of what we might call our aesthetic activity and its intentionality. Burch concludes that 'since to experience a thing's beauty is to perceive it as free, spontaneous, and a creative product of purposiveness, to experience a thing's beauty is to perceive it as a work of art'.[1]

If these reasons justify the importance given to fine art, showing that it is the active principle in any comparison with natural beauty, they also raise other issues. For to comprehend this aesthetic activity we must understand the nature and possibility of fine art and must consider whether other features of Kant's system allow for this role. For example, although we have relied in part on a symbolic relation to explain the claims made for fine art, Kant's account of symbols remains irredeemably obscure; and when we try to gain clarity by attending to the underlying analogies, it is to find that their nature and possibility have not been justified. Thus, the supposition that there is a rational will underlying both the production of fine art and our moral lives needs to be justified by explaining how a free rational will can be said to determine objects in nature. Similarly, we need to justify singling out *these* analogies between beauty and morality from all the other ones available: a task which Kant presents us with at the end of Section 59 by pointing to the substantive content underlying his four formulae.

The need to consider these issues is compounded further in the case of the production of fine art by an apparent contradiction in Kant's claim. To illustrate: we may be tempted to suppose that a work of fine art is a beautiful object[2] intentionally produced by rational human activity.[3] But this proposal seems to make two incompatible claims. For while intentional activity is that following rules determined by some end, where these rules result from the determinate employment of the understanding and its concepts to grasp that end,[4] the aesthetic character of fine art[5] is such as 'does not permit the judgement on the beauty of its products being derived from any rule that has a *concept* for its determining ground, and that depends, consequently, on a concept of the way in which the product is possible.'[6] That is, it appears that an aesthetic judgement on a work cannot be determined by a concept, not even the concept guiding the production of the work. Consequently, the object cannot be considered both beautiful *and* a work of art. If we recognized it as a work of art, we would apply a concept to identify the end and so make an aesthetic judgement impossible. Conversely, when we judge it beautiful, its nature as art seems irrelevant, and it cannot be seen as fine *art*.

We may attempt to reconcile the two claims by distinguishing our judgement on the work from the rules determining its production; but this will not patch up the contradiction. For Kant asserts that 'a product of fine art must be recognized to be art and not nature'.[7] Thus, judging that an object is a work of fine art must involve knowing that it is the result of human making.[8] And that, in turn, requires us to see it as intentional 'under a definite concept'[9]—the description which determines rules for its production. Consequently, again we cannot judge that a work is fine art because the latter requires us to see the object as both beautiful *and* a work of art.

We may be able to reconcile the two claims if we emphasize the notion of 'genius'. Fine art can 'presuppose an intention', we may say,[10] so long as it can depend on genius 'for its possibility',[11] because of the nature of genius and its part in the production of fine art. But this claim must be qualified to be understood. For Kant's association of genius with fine art, rather than being simply one of an intention with the product of actions, has at least three senses: genius denotes the process of production of art generally, including fine art; it also covers creativity in works; and, lastly, denotes a feature of the rational will to which we refer in explaining the possibility of an artist's actions in the empirical world. Given the claim that genius makes fine art possible, these different senses must be examined if we are to understand the nature and production of fine art. And it is this task that will engage us in the present chapter.

Thus, another reason for examining the production of fine art is to show that Kant can speak coherently of objects as both beautiful *and* art. For if he cannot then there is no point to the whole enterprise of arguing for fine art's role in justifications of aesthetic necessity. But, as we suggested, Kant does have an explanation of fine art. And, moreover, other benefits accrue to understanding this explanation.

The two following chapters result from corresponding pressures. Given that we understand the production of fine art, we must also explain its role in our lives. Therefore the next chapter examines the relation of fine art to culture. This is especially important as it is a feature of Kant's theory which is often either ignored or insufficiently stressed. But we are motivated to consider the role of fine art in culture not merely in order to counter others' disregard. Rather, a positive argument for the necessity of judgements of beauty will be seen to depend on fine art's contribution to culture.

The chapter following, on 'Fine Art and Natural Necessity', shows that the account of Kant's theory of fine art which we have presented is compatible with the rest of his system. It must seem that this is not the case because works of fine art exist in the phenomenal world of nature— one which is given over to natural causality. Therefore, we must justify the claim that they are part of our cultural self-development in spite of their location; for if they are merely part of a general causal determination, they would not suit our attempts to develop ourselves.

This requires us to make explicit another sense of genius. If talk of human intentions and of our production of objects is to be meaningful, some objects in the phenomenal, causally determined world must be conceived of as the result of our actions. Here, if art generally depends on our actions,[12] then because it is genius that 'gives the rule to art',[13] genius can be construed as a feature of the rational will, underlying actions, which 'makes possible' the beauty of art—a claim which requires us to consider how the vocabulary of transcendental necessity enters the case. Indeed, this is important to understanding the role of fine art in Kant's attempt to unify theory with practice and reason with nature. Although aesthetic necessity cannot be justified through a symbolic relation to moral good, by arguing that artistic activity and the appreciation of fine art are morally valuable we may warrant a subject's demand that others should agree with his aesthetic judgements. Their value is explained by reference to fine art's participation in a culture guided by moral reason and, in turn, fine art's participation in culture is explained by showing that its production depends on genius as a rational will producing works of fine art—works whose appreciation and understanding develop a community between finitely rational beings.

Notwithstanding the schematic nature of the last paragraphs, it should be clear from what has been said above that it is difficult to overestimate the importance of 'genius' to Kant's conception of fine art.

Genius and the Production of Fine Art

When Kant uses genius to denote a human capacity for producing an object, he is using it merely as an analytic concept.[14] We do not necessarily express approval when we describe an object as a work of genius; and, as such, genius is neutral between inventing, producing works of art and fine art and, it will become clear later, constructing theories in science.[15] However, elsewhere Kant adds that we reserve the terms genius for people possessed of 'an exemplary originality of talent'.[16] In doing so, he seems to be trying to capture a sense of creativity by qualifying some genius as 'vast' or as having a particular intensity,[17] and the qualifications apparently lead to ascriptions of value or approval. But whether such ascription is successful will depend on whether the positive account of genius and art, which we have yet to give, is open to these qualifications.

Before turning to the issue of value we must deal with something else. A process of production is implicated in that we would have no business describing an object as art if we were to deny the presence or possibility of any process of production. But this does not imply that we would be unable to understand or appreciate a particular work unless we understood the particular process of its production. For while there is a conceptual relation between art and the process of production, there is also a causal relation between a particular process and its product. Thus, any work of art must have been the result of a process, and some particular process must be the cause or sufficient condition of the existence of each particular product. But our response to the work need not be determined by the particular process of its production. So, for example, we judge the success of a work of mechanical art[18]—say a working model of an intricate process—by considering the adequacy of its movements to our cognition of that intricate process. And it is not necessary to know how its movements are caused in order to appreciate their similarity to those of which it is a model.[19] That is, knowledge of the process by which the object is produced need not add to our response.

In the case of 'aesthetic fine art'—fine art—a slightly different situation obtains. The end there[20] is to satisfy a judgement of taste; and, as we have seen, the distinction between process and product goes too far for it precludes the possibility of describing the object as fine *art*. This is because we cannot describe an object as art unless we know it to be constructed, and we cannot know that unless we see it as intentional 'under a definite concept', even though we may not know how that intention was realized. Yet, our judgement on the beauty of the work cannot be determined by the rule or concept by which the object is constructed.[21] So, either we describe it merely as a beautiful object, or, it seems, we must use the concept or rule determining its production and so fail to judge its beauty. In the first case, however, the process becomes separate from and totally arbitrary to the experience of beauty; in the second, we seem unable to judge that it is a work of art that is beautiful. Both alternatives are unsatisfactory because they preclude an understanding of fine art, its production, or its nature.

There is, naturally, a third possibility, which would be feasible even if the dilemma posed were ill founded. In the case of fine art we have a process of production which is not determined by a concept in that the rule becomes clear only when the product is gained. That is, whatever rule there is must be gained from the product once that is formed.[22] And we may present a positive account of genius in the production of art by following what Kant says of fine art.

In Section 46 of the *Critique of Judgement* Kant presents four characteristics which go to make up a positive account of genius. Their point is not a psychological one. Rather than being concerned with the psychological processes by which we produce, apprehend, and respond to objects, Kant wants to show that the production and appreciation of fine art can legitimately be said to be intersubjective. He is investigating the special conditions genius must satisfy in order to produce intentionally something that satisfies the epistemological character of judgements of taste—that is, singular judgements which are incapable of proof in some sense, but yield a 'feeling of life' which is insufficiently determinate to count as experience yet claims validity over all subjects through its foundations in the rational faculties.

The four characteristics of genius are that (1) [it] is a *talent* for producing that for which no definite rule can be given . . . ; consequently *originality* must be its primary property; (2) that its products must at the same time be models, that is, be exemplary; (3) it gives the rule to [its product] as *nature* . . . ; (4) nature prescribes the rule through genius not to science but to art, and this also only as far as it is to be fine art'.[23]

The first property of genius shows that it is an ability to generate works without following determinate given rules—it is the ability to *originate* works of art. First, as art, works are the result of a process of production; second, because they are works of *fine* art, genius in their production is neither guided by 'a determinate concept of the end' nor, consequently, can possess a definite rule for production but, third, must be an ability to produce without the guidance of *given* rules. Thus, on the one hand, so far as genius is a talent for producing fine art, the nature of the object requires that genius must be a capacity for production without determinate goal-derived rules. However, on the other hand, because we are concerned with art and so with a process of production, some rule must be present,[24] for otherwise it will be an arbitrary set of actions or motions. As the only given rules for a product—the ones derived from the definite concept of a goal—cannot be found in fine art but as, nevertheless, there must be rules, which must come from somewhere, and as genius is defined as that 'which gives the rule to art', Kant moves on to say that genius must be the capacity to create, or to originate independently the rules that are present. In other words, given that the general concept of art implicates production, our ability to produce or create fine art must operate in a particular way. Although there *is* production in fine art, there is no definite goal or rule, and any ability that is to count as one of producing fine art must be able to satisfy the requirement of production—that rules must be present—yet must do so in the absence of guidance from determinate rules and goals. Consequently, it must be capable of originality in this literal sense of originating the rules present in fine art.[25]

However, the ability to originate rules does not necessarily constitute originality. In claiming that originality is a *consequence* of the ability to generate rules, Kant is trying to give origination the sense we give to creativity.[26] But the latter bears a connotation of novelty which is not clearly associated with the ability to originate rules. Indeed, such association is precluded because we cannot use something true of the process of production to describe the product. While these are causally related, they differ conceptually, and we may determine the originality of a product without raising issues concerning the manner of its production. This may be seen by examining what counts as 'production in the absence of rules' in fine art.

We may describe a process as one in which we do not follow rules because we only make piecemeal decisions as we proceed. The initial decision to paint rather than sculpt, for example, can be exemplified in our concern with pigments; and the choice of blue rather than burnt sienna and of chrome yellow in preference to aquamarine may be decisions we make as we develop a painting. And, in these cases, we deny the determining presence of rules because the result of earlier piecemeal decisions is not apparent before the end and no previously given end determines the choices we make. Before the work is completed we are unable to know the consequences of the earlier decisions for the whole work, and we may be able to discover the rule that is present only through the completed work. That is, it is only when the painting is finished that we discover, through the painting, what rule is present.

Further, this absence of a rule does not prevent us from knowing that a work is complete. There can still be an end, for that is the moment at which we cannot make any more choices without destroying or going against some past choice. If a painter uses cold colours, has successively introduced blue, grey, green, and zinc-white on a blue base, and used them in a configuration that accepts the addition of chrome yellow, he may be unable to progress further by using other hues of yellow or by adding red, because their introduction would destroy the balances that have been procured. Where chrome yellow in combination with the cold colours will make the painting seem brittle, the further addition of a dramatic scarlet would overwhelm that brittleness. Thus, it is only when chrome yellow is added that the painting becomes brittle, so that only then does it become clearly what the painter is after; and it is also the point at which, regardless of whether the work is good or bad, the painter's choices come to an end.

Although this may be a plausible account of how we proceed to make choices in the absence of a rule, nothing about originality has been secured. For the rule we later discover to be involved in our independent choices need not be original just because the painter, as it were, recreated or re-invented it in constructing the work. The choices made may do no more than follow steps already taken by another artist. Accordingly, while the absence of rules refers to our procedure, questions of originality refer not to the process of production or its relation to the finished product but to the relation of similarity or dissimilarity which a finished product bears to other products. And to deny the distinctions just made is to conflate an account of genius given in terms of our sense of originality with one given in terms of the conditions for bringing about works. For the explanation of how a work is produced differs from what it means to describe an object, or the action in producing it, or the producer, as original.

We must, then, treat the absence of rules and the presence of originality as two separate claims, and can proceed by stressing, with Kant, that originality as a feature of creativity is the first requirement of genius. Obviously, genius is now being used to mean 'creativity' and to describe the product, rather than as the ability to originate or give the rule to art, which is about the process of production. Although Kant uses 'genius' with both meanings, we shall refer to the latter as genius and the former as creativity. And we can claim that genius is a condition for creativity because the ability to originate rules is exercised in generating original objects. That is, if the product is original, new rules will be generated in the process of production rather than already given ones being followed.

Kant's second characteristic of genius, that its 'products must at the same time be models, i.e., exemplary', also describes the process of production, though its principle aim is to tell us of the product. It is a consequence of origination, where each work is produced without following rules in the relevant sense, that works are models or examples. In relation to the production of objects, they serve to demonstrate the feasibility of a process and its product, and stand as models showing what can be done. The point of saying that they are models is that each work cannot function except as a model for other processes of production because of the nature of a process of originating rules. For works neither follow established rules in the manipulation of material to ends nor are mere skill. The rules present in the formed objects are ones originated by genius. Consequently, for genius, at best other works are models for 'following', and they neither influence nor are influenced by imitation: they do not provide rules for constructing another object.

If works are models and can enter into the process of production of other works only as models for following, then where they are chosen as models there they are exemplary. However, their exemplarity is not constituted by their service as models. While they can only be models, not every model is exemplary. Not every work will be chosen as 'a standard or rule for estimating'[27] other works, though every work can be a model. And just as origination may be a condition for originality, similarly, their nature as models may be a condition for their exemplarity. Further, just as the originality of a work is not guaranteed by its origination, its ability to serve as a standard will not be assessed merely by reference to its nature as a model. That is, creativity differs from genius. Moreover, we saw that the nature of works as models was a result of their origination, and it may be that originality will have consequences for our assessment of its exemplarity. In any case, by characterizing genius as the origination of models, we are explaining what it means to say that 'fine art is only possible as a product of genius'.[28] These characteristics show us how we must think of fine art. But genius does not also ensure the presence of creativity in works. And before we go on to consider other features of genius, it is appropriate to examine the way in which originality and exemplarity are assessed.

Usually, originality is ascribed to the producer in that the ability to produce original works is something he or she possesses.[29] But this ascription would be decided by focusing on the product. Not every work produced by the author need be original, and in order to ascribe creativity to the person, we must first be able to distinguish and value those works which are original. That is, we must be able to describe *works* as original and must have some reason for relating the product to its producer.

A mode of assessing originality which Kant finds acceptable is that of comparative analysis. Writing of the autonomy of taste, he avers that taste 'stands most in need of examples of what has in the course of culture maintained itself in the longest esteem', where these examples are for 'following', not 'imitation', and may be used to estimate the influence an author exerts on others.[30] Accordingly, in rectifying and extending judgements of taste, we must 'investigate the faculties of cognition and their function in these judgements'. It requires 'illustration, by the analysis of examples',[31] of the response they generate in subjects. And this explanation of how objects are to be understood and appreciated can be extended to questions of originality because the latter would be recognized in the same way. By the analysis of examples we would reveal 'a new rule that could not have been inferred from any preceding principles or examples'.[32]

As an example of such a procedure, which indicates broadly how a more careful analysis of works will reveal their originality, we may compare the works of Cézanne and Matisse with the mural character of Renaissance painting. A theme common to all three is the representation of three-dimensional objects on two-dimensional surfaces by using the resources available in oils and brushes. But the later works are distinguished by their sensitivity to the play of light and colour in establishing the solidity of shapes. By contrasting them with the older interest in uniting different shapes and figures into a perspectival unity, we establish their originality, showing how the nature of painting itself was changed by the development of various techniques to think through, or present in paintings, an aesthetically satisfactory relation of fine art to reality. For Cézanne's oddly-shaped objects present in two dimensions something that is really an experience of three-dimensional objects: by extending the edges of the represented object, he hopes to recover the experience we have when we walk around a vase; and, by balancing blues against reds, he seeks to provide unity within a work. Matisse, similarly, sets aside the natural spectrum in order to use other colours in various hues and, in works such as *La Fenêtre ouverte* (1905), combines an unnatural spectrum with a careful manipulation of brush strokes to recover the experience of the play of light. In all these cases a careful analysis will tell us more about the works, explaining our interest in them in ways which reveal their originality.[33]

Of course, originality is not simply a matter of novelty, and when Kant seeks to distinguish original and hence creative products from '*original* nonsense' he says that the former must be 'exemplary'. We must, then, look to the latter to explain creativity. For Kant, exemplariness covers, first, the intelligibility of a work, and second, its value. The former develops the distinction between process and product in that it is necessary to make a distinction from 'original nonsense', since were creativity defined by reference only to the process, then the nature of the product and our comprehension of it would be irrelevant. The work could be said to be creative and original just because of the way it was produced.[34] By contrast, for Kant, to assess creativity we must understand and assess the work and, therefore, it must at least be capable of being understood.

Clearly, the work of art, the product, is being given importance in assessments of creativity. Further, to be original rather than merely novel, the work must have some value; and Kant seems to propose that this value is based on the explanatory power of a work. Accordingly, a comparative analysis must not only include considerations of dissimilarity and understandability but also assess the explanatory value of works. And if this is an unfamiliar way of appraising works of fine art, its viability can be shown by presenting some examples. Thus, *Majas on the Balcony* involves a self-consciousness of its status as a representation. Through the posture of Jenny Class the painting is seen to bear a particular relation to the audience—because her gaze cannot but remind us that she appears within a painting, amid a design made up of extended diagonals and rectangles. Similarly, *The Vase* is constructed by Cézanne to appear as it would in our experience of a real vase: its presentation and our understanding depend on recognizing that its audience is looking at a painting of a real vase. Matisse also constructs *La fenêtre ouverte* in the knowledge that it is a representation that uses an unnatural spectrum to illustrate something about the way light operates. And the explanatory power of these paintings consists in the way their rule deals with and exemplifies a concern with and resolution of problems that artists must overcome in using their material. In this case, the problem is that of representation, and their explanatory power resides in their indication and resolution of the problems faced in gaining aesthetically satisfactory representations. They provide valuable models of what it is possible to achieve, which may lead others to discover and solve other problems, and will serve as standards with which we can compare other attempts.[35]

Although a more detailed account is called for, it is in terms of explanatory value, I suggest, that we must understand Kant's claims that exemplary works, first, 'though not themselves derived from imitation . . . must serve that purpose for others, i.e. as a standard or rule for estimating',[36] and, second, that a genius puts 'freedom from the constraint of rules so into force in his art, that for art itself a new rule is won—which is what shows a talent to be exemplary'.[37]

We have said that creativity requires originality and exemplariness, which are discovered through a comparative analysis of the novelty, comprehensibility, and explanatory value of works of art. The third characteristic of genius which Kant puts forward is that it gives the rule to its products 'as nature'. This serves to justify the importance of the work or product, a claim Kant develops in part in Section 47 by arguing that genius 'furnishes a rule' which cannot be formulated as a prescription and must 'be gathered from the performance, i.e., from the product'.[38] It is related to the requirement of exemplariness in that works of fine art, for example, must serve as models *as fine art*. That is, the rule is articulated only in the work itself, and must be gained from the product understood as fine art. Moreover, by justifying the importance we give to works, it explains why creativity is assessed by looking at the product rather than the process or the producer.

We may begin with the absence of prescriptive rules. Kant's claim is addressed to the formation of rules in what is specific to a particular work,[39] and he wants to show that we will fail to formulate prescriptive rules even though we can recognize order in a work. One condition for such a formulation is that, as prescriptive rules tell us what must be done, we must identify the end which is sought before, or at least separately from, the effort to gain that end. Only if this is possible can there be prescriptive rules for attaining the required goal. However, in order to refer to the goal—in this case, to indicate the order present or expressed in the work—it is necessary to point to the work itself. For the work *is* what the producer intends to create: *it* is the explanation, exhibition, and exposition of whatever originality she or he possesses. Hence we cannot satisfactorily formulate prescriptive rules for constructing art because to have such rules the producer must be able to issue instructions telling someone what is to be done. But the instructions he would have to issue would be the work itself—that is what must be done. That is, the work is what the instructions would consist in, for only in constructing the work need the producer discover the rule being used. Consequently, the rule can be gathered only 'from its performance'—the object.[40]

The work itself, then, is important because that is where the new rule is embodied. Kant develops this claim about the absence of prescriptive rules in fine art when he explains the development of artistic traditions. The latter do not occur because we abstract and apply prescriptive rules but because one artist influences another in a particular way. Kant maintains that the product of genius 'is an example, not for imitation but to be followed by another genius—one whom it arouses to a sense of his own originality in putting forward freedom from the constraint of rules so into force in this art that for art itself a new rule is won'.[41] Leaving aside psychological explanations of the process by which one creative mind evokes similar originality in another, the material point is that both artists' creative work will be assessed by applying the same criteria: ones yielding rules discovered in the works themselves and providing a continuity between them.[42]

Accordingly, creativity is exhibited in a work; uncreative labour consists in slavishly imitating another work of fine art or in following prescribed rules. The explanation given makes it easier to understand why Kant says that 'genius' gives the rule to its products 'as nature'. First, nature is to be contrasted with grace. What a man does 'through his own efforts' and, so, for which he can be held responsible, 'in contrast to what he can do with supernatural assistance, can be called *nature*, as distinct from grace'.[43] To refer to nature in this context, then, is to say that the work is a product of human action rather than divine intervention. Second, Kant talks of nature in order to refer to that which, as it were, guarantees the validity of creative work. Accordingly, when he looks to subjects as the source of rules, for example in fine art, Kant relates works to 'the nature of the individual': the artist, 'by virtue of the harmony of his faculties',[44] guides his own and the audience's reaction, thereby judging a work by standards gained from his nature— that is, by using the rational faculties and sensitivity to experience that he possesses by nature. Moreover, this reference to the nature of the subject serves an epistemological interest: a work can be exemplary because the deduction of aesthetic judgements is taken to show that a relation of faculties gained by one subject can be gained by others. So that the rule present is given by human nature, and occasions a subjective response, but the latter is far from being private, dependent on personal or idiosyncratic preferences, or a feeling that owes its uniformity to causal regularities.

In summary, then, we began by making a distinction between the process of production and the product. Though we would not call an object art and also deny it could be the result of a process of production, we do not need to explain its particular process in order to appreciate or understand the particular product. The above distinction helps us to understand the concept of genius. The ability to originate rules describes the process of production while originality is ascribed to the product. Similarly, works of art, because they are originated, relate to each other as models. This describes the process of production; but exemplarity is ascribed to the product. As originality and exemplarity are distinct from origination and the nature of works as models, we cannot assess the former couple simply by the latter. Rather, originality is assessed through a comparative analysis of the novelty of works, for it is a relation between products, not one between product and process. By referring to novelty, Kant is trying to capture the sense we generally give to creativity. But novelty by itself is an insufficient guarantee of the presence of creativity because there can be 'original nonsense'. Accordingly, Kant proposes that creative works are exemplary, and explains the latter by reference to explanatory value. Thus, creativity requires originality and exemplariness which are discovered through an analysis of the novelty, comprehensibility, and explanatory value of works. Further, the emphasis on works, on the product, can be justified by the third characteristic Kant attributes to genius: its similarity with nature. Kant develops this point by saying that the rules furnished by genius must be 'gathered from the performance, i.e., from the product'. The work itself is important because the 'new rule' is embodied in the object: the work *is* what the rules or instruction would consist in, and its adequacy is assessed by our nature so far as we are, by nature, rational and animal. In any case, the product itself is important, and the process of its production need not be known, or is known only from the product. This suggests, moreover, that creativity is initially ascribed to works, and only by extension are the ability to produce such objects and 'the mind with this ability'[45]—the person—said to be creative or have genius. We will return to this last point later. For the moment, we may say first, that genius denotes the process of production where we originate rules which serve as models, and, second, that creativity requires the embodiment of originality and exemplariness in works. The latter are assessed by comparative analysis of the novelty, comprehensibility, and explanatory value of works.

These characteristics of genius allow us to resolve the sort of dilemma we posed at the beginning of this chapter. The difficulty was that if we were to identify the object as a work of art at all, we would have to use the concept of the object which determined its production; and this would seem to preclude making an aesthetic 'concept free' judgement of taste on the object. Consequently, either the judgement would have to ignore the fact that the object was a work of art, or, if the latter were recognized, it would fail to be a judgement of taste. In either case, we would not judge a work to be fine art because the latter requires both that the object is a work of art *and* that it satisfies a judgement of taste *as* a work of art. However, as Kant uses 'genius' to show that we may plausibly talk of producing an object even though we do not have a concept of the end in determining production, then we may recognize that it is a work of art without thereby being precluded from making an aesthetic judgement which is free of concepts in the relevant way. The process of production is not determined by a concept of an end although a rule is present and

can be derived from the object. And as the end is discovered only when
the object is judged, its rule only becomes clear just when it is said to be a
beautiful product of human action—when it is said to be a work of fine
art.

Further, by arguing that works serve as models, Kant develops his
claims for the production of art in the following way. He shows that the
absence of a concept determining the production of art need not lead us
to deny the influence one product may have upon the production of
another. Thus origination is neither merely arbitrary nor simply
determined, and we can provide some account of the production of
works generally, even placing particular works within that general
account, without precluding the possibility of valuing some works as fine
art—as beautiful and artistic.

Similarly, by explaining that genius furnishes rules which must be
gathered from the product, Kant makes clear that our interest must turn
on the object and its nature. We understand that it is art by examining
the object itself, so that not only is the rule derived from the object, but
also it is the object that is judged beautiful. Accordingly, beauty turns on
the nature of the object—the features which make it a work of art.
Consequently, not only are its artistic properties and its beauty both
involved in judging the work to be fine art, but we cannot judge it
beautiful unless we recognize that it is a work of art.

Such a conclusion resolves the dilemma posed above. Where we
began with the difficulty that we seemed unable to judge an object
beautiful and to identify it as a work of art, we see now, first, that we can
identify the object as a product of genius without having to suppose that
its production is determined by the concept of an end, and indeed,
second, that we cannot understand the work of genius except through
the object—its performance—which is judged beautiful. The two,
beauty and its mode of production, go together.

Although this may show that we can describe objects as works of fine art,
Kant's conception of genius raises other issues. For instance, although
we have claimed repeatedly that creativity and genius characterize art,
fine art, and science, when Kant puts forward the fourth feature of
genius he seems to deny this by writing that nature 'prescribes the rule
through genius [first] not to science but to art, and this [second] only so
far as it is to be fine art'.[46] To show that genius and creativity are
generally applicable, we must examine this last characteristic and then
see whether the first three must be restricted to fine art.

Creativity, Genius, and Science

Kant argues for the restriction of genius to fine art by saying that
what is accomplished in science is something that *could* have been learned.
Hence it all lies in the natural path of investigation and reflection according to
rules, and so is not specifically distinguishable from what may be acquired as the
result of industry backed up by imitation. So all that *Newton* has set forth in his
immortal work on the Principles of Natural Philosophy may well be learned,
however great a mind it took to find it all out, but we cannot learn to write in a
true poetic vein, no matter how complete all the precepts of the poetic art may
be, or however excellent its models. The reason is that all the steps that Newton
had to take from the first element of geometry to his greatest and most profound
discoveries were such as he could make intuitively evident and plain to follow,
not only for himself but for everyone else. On the other hand no Homer or
Wieland can show how his ideas, so rich at once in fancy and in thought, enter
and assemble themselves in his brain, for the good reason that he does not
himself know, and so cannot teach others. In matters of science, therefore, the
greatest inventor differs only in degree from the most laborious imitator and
apprentice, whereas he differs specifically from one endowed by nature for fine
art.[47]

The claim seems to be that science excludes all 'proper' originality
because it only seeks to discover what is in the world whereas the artist
constructs and develops objects to express ideas. Whether the most
important practitioner of science is able to grasp the interrelation
between a vast range of empirical objects and events or whether its most
humble agent conducts a study of some minor event, science proceeds
in both extremes by following objective rules. The nature of the subject
is irrelevant, it seems, and the object is of paramount importance.[48]

In thinking this of science, however, Kant seems to have forgotten his
earlier discrimination of a constitutive use of understanding from the
regulative use of reason. As we saw, he argued that in science it is the
regulative use of reason that gives order to cognition and experience.
The argument of the Analogies shows only that nature *in general* is
grounded in causality. While this legitimates the application of causality
to experience, it cannot tell us which causes will be found in actual
experience.[49]

Consequently, a satisfactory account of experience must satisfy two
considerations: first, we must use concepts of an objective world in
order to have experience at all; and, second, we must provide a coherent
body of empirical knowledge within which an event may be placed and
explained.[50] That is, the conceptual framework provided by the categories could not legislate comprehensively over all the diverse relations

between natural objects and events. The task of science is to order our knowledge of the latter and so to discover the systematic character of nature in detail through the empirical investigation legitimated by categorical principles. And the activity of conceptualizing how our knowledge of events in nature is ordered and organized becomes the task of reason. That is, in science it is the regulative use of reason that gives order to cognitive experience.

There is, therefore, a qualitative difference between reason and understanding. The important contrast with the constitutive role of understanding is that regulative ideas could in principle have been used to give a different organization to our knowledge of nature. And as an organization of our knowledge of nature is the production of a theory about the relation of events, the qualitative distinction mentioned above implies that competing theories about natural events and their order are not assessed solely by reference to nature. Rather, our understanding of natural events is guided by ideas and theories, which are assessed by their own criteria—of generality, continuity, coherence, and simplicity, among others, Kant suggests—and constructed by scientists in order to investigate nature. Consequently, we cannot expect that a minor intelligence would only take a longer time to test and develop every part of a theory proposed and tested with greater ingenuity or more efficiency by a major intelligence. For a 'shallowpate' or minor intelligence may not only be unable to formulate such a theory but, as we 'question nature' on the basis of certain principles, and as the theory itself will establish the 'natural pattern of investigation and reflection according to rules', he will be unable to begin to examine nature except on the basis of that theory.[51]

Naturally, a scientist must propose his theory in a way that allows it to be understood; and 'even Newton' will have to explain all the steps he takes, from first principles to the conclusions that are his greatest discoveries. But the justification and explanation of his theory is not an account of how it occurred to him. Just as Wieland and Homer may be unable to explain how an idea occurred to them, so Newton's psychology might be opaque to himself and to us. Nevertheless, all three of them, whether their work is aesthetic or scientific, must make their work communicable; and Newton is not less original just because he uses scientific terms, nor because he can explain his discoveries. Indeed, if Homer and Wieland were unable to articulate their aesthetic discoveries in a comprehensible fashion, not least in a work of fine art, we should be very reluctant to laud their genius.

That is, the justifications given by Newton, Homer, and Wieland will differ because their presentation is constrained by the nature of their discoveries. Science and art—scientific theories and works of fine art—are dissimilar because each bears a distinctive relation to the rational and feeling subject; but this does not turn on the presence or absence of creativity. The distinction between them goes to establish that a subject may participate in different activities, but it does not imply that he is creative in one but not in the other.[52] By arguing as he does, Kant wrongly conflates creativity with the production of a particular sort of object.

All this leaves us with the onus of explaining just what the contrast between art and science resides in; and that will be considered later. For the present, Kant's fourth characteristic may be left aside—or understood as saying that the aesthetic character of its object will place certain constraints on creativity, while its scientific character may pose other requirements.

It is clear also that the three characteristics of genius apply to science as they do to art. For example, a call for originality can be satisfied by science as well as by fine art. It may even be argued that originality in science and fine art will be discovered in the same way: by a comparative analysis. Similarly, that genius 'gives the rule to its product as *nature*' means only, first, that creativity in science denotes human action; and second, that it is a rational and intelligible exercise whose conduct is legitimated by the transcendental deductions and our possession of rational faculties. There *are* also questions of the distinctive ways in which the faculties are employed in cognition and of their relation to the deductions; but these are a matter of differences in our conceptions of the objects produced. They do not imply a qualitative distinction in creativity.

Although an element of the third claim—that prescriptive rules are absent—when combined with the requirement of exemplarity—that works stand as models for fine art—seems to exclude science—because the latter is more than a model and does seem to involve prescriptive rules telling us how we should organize our knowledge of the mechanisms governing natural events—the exclusion is only apparent. For one thing, our ignorance of psychology does not lead us to deny the presence of rules in a scientific theory. Further, as with fine art, the construction of a scientific theory does not require us to possess a set of rules which are formulated independently of the theory. There are, of course, rules in the sense that not every proposition will count as part of a theory—just as there are rules involved in constructing a painting or sculpture. And one difference between scientific and artistic work may be that the former must be presented in ways that allow us to falsify propositions, at least by generating contradictions within a theory, while particular works of fine art must be appreciable by rational and feeling subjects rather than being dependent on the falsifiability of propositions. However, these are not rules which determine whether we describe a product as imitative or creative. Just as, in the case of fine art, we were able to say that the *work* is the exhibition, explanation, and exposition of the artist's originality, so too we may say that a theory embodies a scientist's originality. And in each case we would understand and judge the work in its own terms: science by its ability to explain the behaviour of objects; works of art by their satisfaction of aesthetic judgements. In both cases, the author does not issue instructions about what is to be done because the theory or work itself is what is to be done. Only in constructing the theory need the scientist discover what theory he is constructing. And while, naturally, there will be particular requirements that the scientific theory must satisfy, which may differ from those demanded of the artist, this is only a matter of differences in our conception of the objects being produced. And they do not turn on the presence or absence of creativity.[53]

The scientific theory, thus, may be exemplary, embodying some part of what is creative work in science, just as a work of art was said to be exemplary as a model. Prescriptive rules are absent here, just as they are absent in creating art or fine art, and we may ascribe the work to 'nature', may describe it as original, can compare the explanatory power of theories, and so on. We may not, however, be prepared to say that scientific theories are intransitive, and are unlikely to accept that they are inherently indeterminate or equivocal. To explain this further, we must look to differences in our approaches to the objects produced in science and fine art.

Kant on the Nature of Fine Art

By referring to the faculties of mind that constitute genius, Kant shows that we are dealing with a rational procedure. Accordingly, we may expect that our response to and construction of fine art can be accommodated within the deduction. This, in turn, indicates that we are concerned with epistemological issues; and by making them explicit we can show how the requirements of fine art differ from those native to science.

Fine art can be characterized as depending on an indeterminate relation of faculties and a commensurately particular reference to a subject's capacity for reason *and* feeling. And Kant's claims can be formulated in the following way: in the case of fine art we are concerned with factors that are, first, capable of being presented, second, to subjects as rational and feeling beings who, third, by means of metaphors, images, idioms, and other imaginative products, fourth, communicate a 'subjective state of mind'. Our concern is with a universally valid response which itself serves to promote or inhibit communication.

Kant's certainty that fine art must be capable of presentation rests in part on the importance he gives to the product. The objects of fine art are capable of a general conformity to the laws of the human understanding. Accordingly, fine art must 'actualize a possible object' in that it must be experienced in the phenomenal world and so must satisfy the transcendental conditions necessary for experience to be possible.[54] That is, creativity and meaning are exhibited and embodied *in* the work we experience. There is not some entirely separate meaning or intention 'beyond' the work that we decipher by using the work as a means.

Explanations of the last three parts of Kant's claim are interdependent, and we may begin with the imaginative products involved. This clarifies the nature of our 'aesthetic understanding' of the object[55] by attending to Kant's explanation of the process of constructing and appreciating fine art—to assertions about the nature and function of rational faculties.

Kant's claim is that by contrast with cognition, in which imagination provides the representations that we order by applying concepts of an objective world, in the production of fine art the imagination actively 'remodels experience'. It allows us to 'feel our freedom from the law of association (which attaches to the empirical employment of the imagination) so that the material supplied to us by nature in accordance with this law can be worked up into something that surpasses nature'.[56]

There are a number of points being made here. First, Kant is contrasting our ordinary experience with whatever it is that we gain in fine art. The difference is marked initially by reference to 'the law of association' that governs experience: the causal regularities which govern objects in experience no longer determine the associations we make. And the suggestion seems to be that in so far as experience is necessarily causal and in so far as concepts can only be of an objective world, our response to fine art is neither sufficiently determinate to count as experience nor conceptual. Nevertheless, second, Kant proposes that this indeterminate and non-conceptual response bears some relation to experience. We respond to fine art 'through the medium of a concept',[57] and in this response it is experience that we 'remodel'. The material we reorganize is that provided by 'nature in accordance with' law. Third, in this response 'we feel our freedom' where we have 'worked up' that material 'into something that surpasses nature'. It appears that the artist changes our experience by reorganizing it, putting forward configurations that do not follow natural determinations or are not governed by the causal regularities found in nature. And he does this in order to gain a different perspective. This perspective is best described as aesthetic, its lack of conceptual clarity or univocal and determinate meanings being contrasted with the use of concepts following rules established in the experience of objects and the organization of our knowledge into a system of science.[58]

This perspective is no less rational for being free of empirical associations. And it becomes the task of reason to consider how this aesthetic content—metaphors, images, and other imaginative products—is to be organized. In it language and thought contain ambiguities which cannot be resolved simply by comparing them with rational or moral ideas. Instead, because of their indeterminancy, they need a distinctive organization. Having explained the absence of lawful associations by which this thought is produced, and seeing that the flow of imagination is 'formless', Kant seems to consider the whole process reminiscent of and complementary to the quality of 'striving for something beyond experience' that is found in ideas of reason. The two perspectives may differ in the associations their objects possess, but both contain a sense of reaching beyond experience.[59] From this, Kant moves on to say that in our response to fine art *aesthetic* ideas convey ideas of reason by 'interpreting them to the sense'. That is, by definition no experience can be adequate to an idea in that no object or metaphor can be seen to exemplify every meaning of an idea that is, itself, used to organize the experience of objects or the relation of images and metaphors generally. But so far as the organization is owed to the use of an idea, then the structure and content given can exemplify something of the idea. And so Kant proposes *aesthetic* ideas as the themes that unite our thoughts on works—just as rational ideas serve to order our knowledge of nature. In order to appreciate and understand fine art, we use reason as a guiding force to discover the similarities, patterns, and themes present in our thoughts as metaphors, images, and other imaginative products. Here, reason qualifies the indeterminate notion of similarity in order to focus attention on a set of possible meanings. Thus, for example, Malraux's phrase that man is 'a little pile of dirty secrets' must be understood, in *Days of Hope*, in relation to constructing a community of individuals during a time of political upheaval. It is not so much a reflection on laundry lists as a way of leading us to see men as private possessors of concealed desires and unconscious habits.[60] And it constitutes the expressiveness of a work of fine art.

We see that expression is conceptually indeterminate.[61] Kant explains it is something in which 'language . . . binds up the spirit (soul) also':[62] we add to experience a subjective resonance and value it lacks in 'empirical employment'.[63] This subjectivity is a very important feature, for it establishes expression as a matter of interpretation and appreciation, and distinguishes it from experience dependent on explanation by reference to causal determinations. For to see expression in fine art as a case of interpretation, not only do we take it to possess a conceptually indeterminate order, but we suppose a subject to be the source of that order. That is, works are expressive because of their relation to subjects, and this may be explained as follows.

Although expression is subjective and free of empirical associations, it remains rational and intentional. Properly, rules result from the determinate employment of the understanding and its concepts. And as purposive intentional activity is that toward an end and following rules determined by that end, Kant's claim that works of fine art are devoid of ends may seem to imply they must be irrational and cannot be intentional. However, it is only by contrast with such determination that Kant denies the presence of ends in fine art: the end is not determined by the *cognitive* use of concepts.[64] And the absence of such a *concept* does not imply that expression lacks an end because we can discover a different source for aesthetic order and unity. Thus, Kant looks to the subject as the source of order, and attributes the production of a work to 'the nature of the individual' where order is obtained 'by virtue of the harmony of faculties'. In creating a work, the artist comes to know that it is completed when he has run out of choices, and the viability of choices is judged by standards gained from his nature—his possession of rational faculties and a sensitivity to experience. Thus works are assessed by their appropriateness to a state of mind—the pleasurable judgement of a harmonious relation of faculties—rather than judged by their success or failure in following rules determined by a particular determinate end.

The presence of conceptual indeterminacy, of more thought than can be contained in a concept, of associations that do not follow the laws relevant to the empirical employment of concepts, of feelings, the reference to a subject and to his intentions in creating and appreciating a work, together with a commensurate assessment by reference to an indeterminate or general relation of harmonious faculties, all go to characterize expression and our engagement with fine art.[65] They are crucial to any construction *and* appreciation of fine art, being vital equally to the artist constructing works and the audience responding to them.[66] And Kant exhibits his consciousness of their mutual involvement by making taste—a 'critical faculty'—part of the execution of a work.[67] Taste complements the productive faculty of genius, 'qualifying it at once for permanent and universal approval'.[68] For not only must genius be made communicable in a work, but for thoughts to be communicated the audience must participate, as it were, in reconstructing the work, its ideas, and their associations, and must gain the pleasurable judgement they portend. Whether a particular work is fine art is determined by what it is possible to understand—and that is not decided by the artist alone. Thus, the work is dealt with in a particular way. The complex of thoughts that makes up the judgement does not contain univocal meanings of the sort that conceptual knowledge gains through organization into a system of science. Disagreements between subjects cannot be resolved by reference to a system of scientific knowledge to assess the truth or falsity of claims. Instead, because of the autonomy of aesthetic judgements, their resistance to others' judgements, differences can only be settled by persuasion: we deploy examples and comparisons in order to enable another to make his own judgement. Here, subjects must be treated as rational and feeling ends in themselves, and works and our appreciation of them must be capable of being part of a dialogue between subjects.[69]

In all these ways, then, fine art differs from science, and creativity will be exhibited by producing objects possessing these different natures.

It is clear that the process of production guarantees nothing of the value of the object. Yet some writers have held that it did.[70] Similarly, some have maintained that genius gives us access to some realm 'beyond' present reality.[71] Although Kant does not hold the latter position, it has been thought that he did, and we will further our understanding of Kant's conception of genius and creativity by contrasting his position with that held by other writers. Further, there is another feature of genius which we have mentioned but not examined. If works of art are produced by us, it must be possible for the producer to intervene in some way in the causal natural order. On occasion Kant says that genius makes fine art possible, and the transcendental connotations involved here must be understood to see whether they are compatible with Kant's argument that all our experience is necessarily causally determined. The issue requires another chapter, but will be introduced in this one. In any case, we will next contrast Kant's account of genius with one which is sometimes confused with it.

Kant on Genius

Some of Kant's contemporaries criticized their world from the perspective of an ideal unity between man and nature that allegedly was enjoyed by the ancient Greeks. That 'naïvely' immediate unity with nature has been lost, Schiller claims, except in the case of genius, and ordinary mortals are forced to suffer the torment of a bifurcation between free rational action and an implacable nature. Such estrangement leads to ignorance. Consequently, true education has been lost and a 'paper culture' substituted that encourages 'pedants, sextons, the half-educated, apothecaries, to come forward'.[72] Few people are aware of this split, it seems, so Herder and Hamann propose to expose to the 'philistines their own nakedness, to unclothe and transfigure them' so that they realize the superficiality of their Francophile 'good taste' and are led to seek an alternative to their 'undistinguished and uniform culture'.[73] They seek to contrast our present reality with another realm of unity and human fulfillment.

Art gives access to this transcendental realm, providing the truly educated with a satisfaction that their bisected lives could not encounter in this world. And it is genius which explores and interprets that other realm of truth through art. Having access to deep powers, the genius possesses an innate and divinely ordained creative potential whose inexorable pressures he must succumb to, without caring for mortal needs or the niceties of etiquette. A possession of skill will not serve the end of unity and fulfilment because it is merely a facility with present reality. Only genius has the aptitude and possesses that extra dimension which allows the artist to penetrate into and perceive the perfect order through art. He is able to call on deep irrational forces and, some reckon,[74] must suffer martyrdom in order to interpret the esoteric order of truth and make it accessible to the ordinary mortals living in this deficient world. Naturally, given the chasm he has to span, his creations can seem like incoherent babbling to those lacking his gifts, and he may be condemned to isolation from his fellow men.[75]

The genius then, for these writers, provides a bridge between nature and man's capacity for rational freedom by interpreting the realm of freedom and fulfilment to others. It implies the existence of a special individual whose possession of a gift empowers him to penetrate to a transcendental and true reality, lying beyond the ordinary world, through artistic activity and expression. Indeed, the activity of genius in producing works goes to justify the value we give, so that a work is valuable because it is created by a genius.[76] Further, his talent separates the genius from ordinary men; and though not all the writers mentioned do so, most restrict application of the concept to the creator of art. Similarly, most of them allow art alone any access to the world beyond present reality.

Against such claims, Kant warns that it is necessary to exercise care. Elsewhere he states that

a type of ordinary man, called the *man of genius* (he should rather be called the ape of genius), has forced himself under the sign 'genius'. He speaks the language of a man exceptionally favoured by nature, pronounces laborious study and research mere bungling, and pretends that he has seized at one grasp the spirit of all the sciences, but administers it in small doses that are concentrated and potent. Like the quack and the charlatan, this type is quite prejudicial to progress in scientific and moral cultivation, when he knows how to hide his wretchedness of purpose by handing down his dogmatic pronouncements on religion, politics and morality from the seats of wisdom on high, like one of the initiated or an authority. What can one do against this but laugh and continue patiently on our way with diligence, order, and clarity, taking no notice of these imposters?[77]

By contrast with his contemporaries, Kant distinguishes the process of production from the product and recognizes that each may be understood separately. Where others would forego learning and research in order to dispense a wisdom whose authority derives from their special spiritual capacity, and so is justified by its source, they would also deny the need for a process of production which can be understood. For them the genius is an individual who is special because he possesses this mysterious power to penetrate to a true reality, and there is no sense in talking of a process by which this gift works. Moreover, where Kant seeks a way of understanding the product without relying on explaining the process of its production, for the other writers the value of the product is determined by the nature of the gift whose possession explains its production. For Kant, not only is an assessment of creativity independent of origination, but the former must be understood by reference to the nature of the object. Neither of these qualifications need be accepted by those who value the work for its being produced by a genius.

Further, where other writers hold that genius could only be inspired in being motivated by some divine, mystical pressure, Kant understands genius as human activity. Certainly works by a genius 'inspire' others, but where some think this is as mysterious an event as the creation of a work, Kant explains it by pointing out why works can only serve as models and involve a conceptually indeterminate expressiveness. Our appreciation and production of fine art do not depend on this transcendental, perhaps spiritual, realm whose influence is inspirational. Rather, it is a result of our activity and nature, as opposed to grace, and its appreciation is not restricted to those who possess genius. Instead, works of fine art have significance for all human beings: they are produced by and for human beings,[78] and so may be considered an expression of humanity rather than the product of a mysterious power possessed by the select and with a source in some separate world to which only the special few have access.

Indeed, it is only if the Kantian synthesis between reason and nature breaks down that such transcendental claims gain plausibility. For example, Kant does not and need not accept the speculative metaphysics which is part of the others' attachment to a true and transcendental reality. And like other sceptics he was seen to charge that a genius who is esoteric in principle cannot be distinguished from one who is merely incoherent. Instead, Kant proposes that there is a rational and universalizable response to works. That our appreciation of fine art is not determined by a concept neither renders its communication mysterious nor leaves open the possibility that, when 'nature gives the rule to art through genius', some transcendental Nature brings about a common, if unintended, response. Either such a response is the result of causal factors, making our aesthetic response something irrational—a consequence even those writers find unacceptable—or the generality of our response is guaranteed, as Kant claims, by the very fact of human activity in nature. Works embody intentions. It is if the absence of conceptual clarity in fine art had to be explained by reference to an author's intentions, and if the latter existed separately from the work, that a complete account of expression would require us to ask about the 'real' expression or meaning a work contains and to seek the 'real' creator who somehow introduces meaning into the work as far as an imperfect material allows. This, in turn, would lend itself to answers attributing the work to 'Nature' or to 'Genius' or 'Spirit' outside man.

Another temptation to ascribe the creation of fine art to transcendental sources is based on the absence of an end in fine art. As there is no end, the activity of genius cannot have rules determined by that end. And this too may seem to invite other explanations of how a genius communicates or develops his ideas at all. If we were to accept the sort of faith and religious transcendentalism that writers such as Hamann were prepared to countenance, we could claim that if genius does not use rules that we understand, perhaps it uses rules that we do not completely understand but which we may believe to be insightful because they are divinely inspired. That is, when conjugated with such transcendentalism, its very aesthetic nature seems to preclude the possibility of referring to a rational intention to explain the creation of a work of fine art as an intelligible object. But this would be the case only if there were no end in fine art, and we have seen that Kant can argue that there can be an end in spite of an absence of given rules. Similarly, the temptation to discover some transcendental reality becomes less plausible when we understand that Kant's references to 'Nature' are to our present world and activity, and that the distinction of science from fine art is based on epistemology rather than ontology.[79]

The contrasts suggested above also indicate a problem with Kant's account. We used 'genius' to comprehend the production of fine art. 'Genius' was given at least two senses: first, the ability to originate works and, second, creativity. A third sense of genius, as a feature of the rational will underlying our production of art, has yet to be discussed. Now, one thing unites these three senses: Kant's unargued but vital assumption of individuality. It is clear, for example, that the concept of creativity could be applied to the product of our actions, leading us to compare independently produced objects and to describe them as original or exemplary rather than as merely imitative. But, at the same time, Kant ascribes creativity, as a capacity for producing such new objects, to persons.[80] His manœuvre is similar to the one he makes in moving from good actions to an individual's moral personality and capacity for good acts.[81] Both assume that we explain something about the occurrence of objects and actions by showing that they are unified in a single personality. But such a unity is merely spurious—for it is not a capacity for action that is described as creative but the action and its product. As an object is the basis of consideration, any reference to a 'creative person' will be determined by our understanding of the object. And there is no guarantee that the unity of a work is better explained by referring it to an individual as a unified entity. Thus, there seems to be little reason beyond prejudice for describing a person as creative when not all his actions will be creative, and those of his works that are so described will be assessed by the criteria which attach to works, not personalities.

This does not argue against the fact that we are still concerned with subjectivity rather than with the behaviour of natural objects. Whether we can ascribe it to an individual or not, we must ascribe fine art to some subject who creates the work—although it remains questionable whether any facts about his empirical biography which we find relevant to the explanation of any single work may be sufficiently unified to constitute a personality or always useful to any explanation.

Other questions are raised by the claim that works of fine art are produced by us. While we now know that Kant's talk of fine art is coherent with other claims, we do not as yet know that fine art, as 'production through freedom',[82] is possible in the empirical world. In this context, Kant's assertion that fine art 'requires genius for its possibility'[83] refers us to the rational will. And we may need to be reminded of Kant's contention that philosophy 'is divisible into the theoretical and practical. But the territory upon which its realm is established, and over which it exercises its legislative authority, is still always confined to the complex of the objects of all possible experience, *taken as no more than phenomena*'.[84] Thus, the role attributed to genius raises questions concerning how human intentions are realized in a causally determined world. There, we may suggest, the production of fine art is a special case of the more general relation between rational intentions and causality, and we need to show that fine art is possible.

The Possibility of Fine Art

Kant asserts that 'art has always got a definite intention of producing something'.[85] As art, fine art is the satisfaction of an intention to construct objects in the empirical world. It requires the artists' intervention into the system of phenomenal natural causes to gain an end. And we must explain how objects, in an empirical world determined by a natural causality operating independently of men, can be said to be the result of intentional human intervention. Thus the existence of fine art raises questions that cannot be solved by considering only matters of taste.

Of natural beauty, God is taken to be something like a material condition responsible for the existence of objects in phenomenal nature.[86] Similarly, in the case of a work of art, 'some work of man is always understood'. Yet these ascriptions to man and to God are not made by taste. Taste is only a critical faculty that judges objects according to their appropriateness to a relation of faculties. If it ascribes purposiveness, as it must do, it is not concerned with whether the source of purposiveness is man or God or anything at all. For purposiveness is only a sort of logical condition of making a judgement of taste. But Kant also wants to give an account of the possibility of taste in terms of what might be called material conditions, and so proposes man (and God) as the source of the purposiveness that is a logical condition for taste. However, this ascription to a source is illegitimate in so far as we are concerned with reflective judgements alone because, being merely regulative, they do not make any commitment to the existence of freedom. They presuppose only the purposiveness of nature generally, and that only when it is essential to comprehension. Yet an ontological commitment to freedom is essential if we are to show that fine art is possible as a result of human activity.

The need to make an ontological commitment in order to explain the possibility of rational ends in nature suggests that we must look beyond the *Critique of Aesthetic Judgement* to the second part of the *Third Critique*, on teleology, and to Kant's writings on culture and history. These seek to combine physical with moral teleology, and argue for nature's synthesis with freedom and reason. It is only by looking at those arguments that we can understand Kant's certainty that intentions can be realized in nature and so give substance to his claim that the *Critique of Judgement* bridges the gap between theory and practice.

Kant examines teleological judgements to show that we may conceive of ends in nature; and we discover that some ends may be conceived of as human products. That is, he qualifies conclusions arrived at in the First *Critique*. Formerly he had argued that the order of nature is causally determined and 'cannot admit of a free causality'.[87] Now he allows that we are unable to show that 'every other sort of causality'—freedom—must be excluded.[88] Indeed, if we can justify the use of teleological judgements, we can, first, conceive of some objects as possessing an order which we must ascribe to 'an intelligent cause',[89]

and, second, understand it to depend on 'the causality of conceptions of
. . . rational agents'.[90] This implies that there are objects in the natural
world whose structure and design is compatible with the supposition
that there exists a rational will who is responsible for the order
perceived. Kant sometimes expresses this interrelation between rational
will and objects in the natural world by saying that works of fine art bear
reference to a *rational* nature 'in the Subject itself'[91] or as the claim that
human *rational* 'nature in the individual must give the rule to art'.[92] In
the specific case of fine art this means that an aesthetic judgement—
which depends on a comparison between an object and the relation
faculties[93]—must be related to a reflective teleological judgement—
which permits us to conceive of objects in terms of their finality or as
ends—and combined with a judgement making an ontological commitment to the existence of freedom—which permits us to see the object as
a work, a rational end. It is in justifying the last that genius involves
transcendental conditions for the possibility of fine art, showing that
taste may be combined with a commitment to the existence of freedom.

The introduction of this matter serves to place fine art in a wider
context. While reflective judgements of teleology permit us to identify
and characterize some objects as products of action by rational agents,
this answers only our doubts about nature's tractability. It shows we can
conceive of ends. But other problems are raised by the claim that
freedom exists and that we may synthesize freedom with reflective
judgements in order to explain the rational will's action on an object of
nature. To deal with these problems, we are led to treat more general
questions about the relation between reason and nature. And given that
the exercise of reason brings a range of questions of its own, we must
consider the wider context of the relation of freedom to natural
necessity.

It seems, then, that instead of explaining the relation between reason
and nature, an explanation of the existence of fine art must presume that
such an explanation is available. It raises issues—of how the antinomy
between mechanical and teleological principles can be resolved and the
latter combined with a commitment to the existence of freedom without
contradicting the former, and so on—which must be examined.
However, before we proceed to that, it may be best to see just what must
be shown to be possible. For only when we are clear on that will it be
necessary or feasible to examine the solution on which the existence of
fine art presumes. That is, whatever we learn of fine art from its
participation in culture, if anything, will indicate the criteria its existence

or possibility must satisfy. For example, as man's capacity for reason is linked to his subjugation to nature, we may expect that any rational end he sets himself is bound to effect the relation of nature to reason itself. This can be understood to mean that men are capable of a freedom from nature that is still possible in the phenomenal world, and it is this sort of freedom which must be understood and shown to be possible. Similarly, if we are to accept the demand that subjects pursue fine art through constructing and appreciating particular works, and if we are to show that this is possible, we must understand what this involves in nature and how the relation of reason to nature is expected to change either of these elements.[94]

Of course, culture does not appear by accident in the example given. Our interest is in comprehending the nature of the rational ends that satisfy aesthetic judgements. To understand the interaction between reason and nature involved in the construction and appreciation of fine art, the most useful procedure would be to examine Kant's writings on culture. For Kant maintains not only that aesthetic judgements presuppose culture but also that the two are interconnected in numerous other ways.[95] Indeed, it is through culture that Kant examines the relation of reason to nature that underlies our experience of fine art. For example, he writes that in the latter, judgement 'finds reference in itself to something in the subject itself and outside it, and which is not nature nor yet freedom, but is still connected with the ground of the latter, i.e., the suprasensible'.[96] This passage refers to the particular situation of man as a natural being capable of freedom; and culture is directed precisely at understanding these peculiarities of his position. Culture is defined as the production in man of an aptitude for setting and understanding ends in nature: it involves a freedom from nature, commensurate with setting ends, which yet is possible in the phenomenal world.

Kant also gives judgement generally a wider role: it is a 'mediating concept between the concepts of freedom and nature' whose mandate it is to probe the unity possible between nature and reason in order to clarify our capacity for action. One reason for examining and developing the motion of finality underlying judgement is to explain the order of nature generally in terms of ultimate and final purposes.[97] And Kant's conclusion is that these purposes comprise cultural activity and our promotion of moral reason.[98] Here, then, a concern with genius and its construction of a fine art that satisfies judgements of taste may be linked, at least formally, with culture.

It is likely that Kant expresses this relation when he writes that culture is a true standard for taste.[99] If genius, as human activity toward rational ends in nature, is understood, it may be suggested that it is because fine art participates in culture. Just as the existence of culture is owed to the possibility and necessity of conceiving of objects in nature according to ends and of the order of nature according to a system of ends,[100] similarly, fine art as the product of genius also depends on the use of teleological principles, and an understanding of culture will yield a fuller explanation of the activity of genius in fine art.

Further, fine art and the exercise of taste are part of culture and its creation of a community. First, as an aptitude for setting ends, culture is concerned with man's experience in the phenomenal world. Yet, while culture is not morality, nevertheless noumenal freedom provides culture with a 'guiding thread'.[101] Because it is human activity, it is imperative that culture strive toward moral perfection; but we cannot comprehend its attainment of that goal so long as culture is part of nature and the phenomenal world. However, second, elsewhere Kant defines culture only as the ability to set any end whatsoever, not merely those ends derived from the supreme principle of morality through moral law. In either case culture must be understood in the context of moral activity. And if beauty presupposes culture and bears significant analogies with moral good[102] in spite of being part of the phenomenal world, then we can argue that it is impossible to understand fine art without considering its interaction with culture and morality. Indeed, understanding the relation between fine art and culture promises much more: it holds out hope of explaining and justifying aesthetic necessity.

Kant presents interconnections between beauty and culture in yet other ways. He asserts that taste has a relation to morality which refers to society and culture. Not only is taste a kind of *sensus communis* or public sense,[103] it is also 'morality in one's outward appearance'.[104] The contradictory expression in the last quotation serves to indicate that there are moral matters underlying the social nature of taste. It is public and intersubjective, inviting an appraisal of the subjects making judgements. And taste can be given these characteristics because fine art plays a particular role in the development of culture: for 'the ideal of morality belongs to culture'.[105]

That beauty bears a symbolic relation to morality casts yet more light on fine art's participation in culture and on the justification of aesthetic necessity. Beauty allows us some semblance of moral experience through its analogy with moral good; and participation by an increasing number of people in this semblance of moral experience contributes to cultural progress. Just as moral imperatives, which also guide culture, are obligatory only to a finitely rational being like man, similarly, beauty is appreciable only by creatures who are both animal *and* rational. While moral good gives priority to rational requirements over natural inclinations, beauty depends on a harmony between nature and reason. And just as moral good comprises in part the requirement that we treat persons as ends, similarly the experience of beauty and the construction of fine art must treat subjects as ends. Moral behaviour involves persuasion and a use and appreciation of arguments, just as the appreciation of fine art involves persuasion and a dialogue between subjects. Neither can countenance that one's will or judgement be imposed upon another. Further, morality's reliance on reason is intimately tied to its use of universality as a criterion in moral argument and persuasion. Similarly, the beautiful depends on a judgement that is intersubjective, and its object is capable of being appreciated by other subjects. All these characteristics tell us of the nature of beauty's participation in culture and suggest how its necessity may be justified. The appreciation of beauty and the construction of works of fine art are not a means to the end of cultural progress; they are themselves part of that progress. As we shall see in the next chapter, beauty works to produce an aptitude to determine the will by reason, independently of sensual inclinations, by exploring the harmonious relation possible between reason and nature.

III

Fine Art and Culture

HAVING placed fine art in the context of a general relation of reason to nature, we must enquire further into its character. It was proposed that reflective judgements may be used to classify some phenomenal objects as works constructed by rational human agents. This raises the matter of reason itself. Before showing that reason can be actualized in nature, we must display the different forms that realization takes.

In the last chapter culture was put forward as the natural location for fine art, meaning that an important set of problems pertaining to the construction and appreciation of fine art occurred in common with other cultural products.[1] Now, Kant holds that differences between cultural and other human products depend on the relation between reason and nature involved. More than a mere taxonomy of our exercise of reason as cultural, political, or moral, depending on its relation to nature, these divisions exhibit the distinctive relations individuals enter into with one another and the consequences this has for the way they undertake the demands of practical reason.[2] To explain this further, in this chapter we will examine Kant's concept of culture, clarify its distinction from politics and morality, and argue that fine art participates in a morally valuable cultural development towards a community of individuals.

It is unusual to interrelate fine art, beauty, and culture in the manner proposed. Culture is rarely mentioned in the *Critique of Aesthetic Judgement*, and most commentators have ignored it. Their interest usually centres on epistemological questions about both the possibility of taste and the necessity of beauty.[3] But as our concern is with fine art, we must attend to the existence and creation of works, and must understand the nature of artistic activity. Consequently, we must examine its participation in culture. And as Kant does not set out details of the latter in any single place, we must develop his position and compare it with that of other writers.

Kant's turn to culture and the *activity* of fine art is highlighted by the analogy between beauty and moral good. However, culture itself has sometimes been understood in terms of our responsiveness to varied stimuli. This approach, which raises epistemological issues, implicates an unsurprising relation of beauty to culture. It is found in the work of authors whose influence on himself Kant acknowledged.[4] Were culture related to beauty in their way in the *Critique of Judgement*, it would be synonymous with taste, so that a person who possessed taste or culture would be someone with a *sense* of beauty that is significantly like other senses.[5] Some men, by that account, have a 'sense of beauty', which is *'our power for receiving this idea* of beauty'.[6] As the capacity to appreciate beauty is a sense and is possessed by only some individuals, the ethical benefits accruing to its exercise are gained only individually. Not only is taste personal in this sense, but further, when best it is also innate. While custom and teaching may increase 'our power of receiving or comparing complex ideas, yet it seems rather to weaken than strengthen the ideas of beauty'.[7]

Later English aestheticians preferred to talk of the aesthetic sense, if at all, as an acquired sense. But they still conceived of taste and culture in terms of subjectivity and responsiveness to external stimuli; and the cultivation of taste remained the culture of an individual sensibility. In some cases it was argued that only a few individuals could hope to gain such sensibility. Further, it was often separated from pragmatic social reality. The 'study of the beauties either of poetry, eloquence, music or painting' give some men 'an elegance of sentiment to which the rest of mankind are strangers. The emotions which they excite are soft and tender. They draw off the mind from the hurry of business and interest'.[8]

Kant proposes a more complex account than the one suggested above, for he sees culture as a project in which we are actively engaged. Our experience of beauty leads to cultural progress in a way that is more than the merely personal development of individuals. Sometimes Kant gives beauty a negative role in cultural development, much like the one given by earlier writers.[9] In this vein he restricts beauty to ameliorating the effects of regressive natural tendencies.[10] But other features of culture are examined by Kant in his later works on history, politics, anthropology, and religion, in addition to the work on teleology. What he proposes there yields a description of culture in which fine art, far from being a matter of responsiveness or a factor ameliorating the effects of our natural being, is actively engaged in cultural change and man's self-development out of nature and toward reason. To see this, we must examine what Kant has to say of culture.

Kant on Culture

Kant describes the task of culture as the 'production' in man, a rational and animal creature, of the 'aptitude and skill for all manner of ends for which he may employ nature, both internal and external'.[11] It is more than the ability to appreciate ends for it includes the power man has to set and work for ends of his own choosing.[12] Elsewhere,[13] Kant comes to associate culture with the struggle for moral perfection.[14]

The task of culture progresses through skill and discipline. To have skill is for an individual to possess a technique for controlling and using nature.[15] But it is only the development of means, for Kant, and can give no guidance in establishing the objective validity of the ends to be pursued. Yet the latter is essential 'if an aptitude for ends is to have its full meaning'.[16] And through culture as discipline man develops the aptitude for choosing ends, learning 'to prevail over the rudeness and violence of inclinations' and thereby initiating our control of natural sensuous impulses in order that reason may play its proper role in deciding on ends. Given that men should be moral and that their choice of ends and means ought to be determined ultimately by moral reason, it is possible to extrapolate, with Meredith, that culture tries to develop in man the aptitude of a being who is free.[17] It seeks to bring about the conditions necessary to following the moral law and the exercise of rational freedom.

In proposing culture as a task Kant is not prepared to give up either nature or reason entirely for the sake of the other. He wants to see if 'one might, within civilisation, remain a man of nature'.[18] Cultural development, then, is based on a distinction and relation between discipline and skill and between man's animal and rational character. These two divisions do not coincide, and the relation of these contraries goes to form Kant's account of culture.

Kant holds that men are capable of setting and consciously working towards particular ends.[19] We may explain animal behaviour without supposing that we must attend to their self-understanding; but to explain human behaviour it is necessary to be cognizant of what the actors construe themselves to be doing—that is, our conception of a satisfactory explanation must include consideration of the ends which agents take themselves to be trying to attain, for Kant, because there is always a rational will underlying actions.

We can give more details of this general concern with ends. Kant draws a contrast between reason and nature, and maintains that men may be motivated either by reason or natural inclinations. Accordingly, to explain their behaviour we consider either their reasoning about ends, which motivates them to act in one way, or their sensual ends, such as the satisfaction of particular bodily desires, which will motivate them to action in another way. But, further, Kant reckons that to be motivated by natural desires alone is to be subjugated to nature and inclination. And as only reason can justify the choice of particular ends, to be motivated to an end by desire or inclination alone is to have an end unjustified by reason. Further, not only are reason and nature contrasted, but Kant also affirms that they are sometimes in opposition to each other. Men may be prevented from attaining to reasoned ends because they prefer to be motivated by natural impulses to sensual ends.

Moreover, Kant contends that to be motivated by nature alone, to try to satisfy merely sensual desires, is to seek ends whose satisfaction serves only the individual himself. The contrast between reason and nature, thus, for Kant, becomes a conflict between individuals possessing similar desires but, because of a 'truculent egotism' founded on the search for exclusively individual contentment, rivalling each other for the satisfaction of their own sensual inclinations. Individuals become isolated from each other in the pursuit of exclusive natural inclinations, and treat each other as means to the satisfaction of their own purposes.[20] Here the use of skill in the pursuit of sensual ends may still serve to promote culture, but the development occurs only through the iniquity of war and violence.[21]

Kant sets out the details of such iniquitous progression in the essays on history.[22] His intention is to show how an accidental interrelation between diverse individuals and groups, each devoted to its own concerns, can yet produce a peaceful cosmopolitan society.[23] That is, the existence of a natural 'history' outside human control does not necessarily imply that man's reason is doomed to remain unactualized. Kant holds that reason 'cannot command one to pursue an end that is recognized to be nothing but a fiction of the brain',[24] and these essays show that a history of accidental interrelations between means-based, self-interested, and sensually motivated individual monads—one which might have been thought to preclude the possibility of actualizing reason at all—in fact can lead to a positive development.

However, the best that may be expected from promoting skill in the service of sensual ends is the development of a civic community. This is an association between individuals in the pursuit of their own interests, and men can 'expect to acquire a skill for [the construction of a civic community] only at a late date'.[25] This civic community is contrasted with an ethical one, and their differences must be understood by looking to the situation they endeavour to rectify as well as the different paths that correction takes.[26]

A civic community consists of laws which, if they exist at all, 'are, as a class, laws of coercion'.[27] An *external* compulsion exerted by a powerful *public* authority induces individuals to follow given rules of behaviour. Both the problem and its resolution are based on supposing that although we are not interested in what motivates individuals, we are concerned with the effects of their behaviour. Unity between individuals in a civic community is merely formal and external because it is based on a public standard they can be compelled to accept: if the standard could not be enforced, unity would collapse.[28] Consequently, a civic community has authority only so far as its rule can be enforced. And its members may behave according to the law, even carrying out right actions, but there is no guarantee that these are moral actions, undertaken because they are the law. Such associations, developed through skill, can as well be formed by 'a race of devils',[29] each prepared to accept certain constraints on his own actions in order to pursue freely his personal interests without heed of morality.

Kant contrasts this community with an ethico-civil state where individuals 'are united under non-coercive laws, i.e., *laws of virtue* alone'.[30] Individuals' motives become of central importance, and their actions cannot be coerced for the sake of some external public order. Moreover, because the duties of virtue apply to 'the entire human race',[31] their rational force, and the domain of the ethico-civil condition, is unlimited. Thus, our humanity includes the capacity for reason, which is exercised when men carry out good and right actions for the sake of their moral value. Morally, intentions are important: it is not enough to carry out right actions for the wrong reasons. And if devoid of morality, culture remains mere 'splendid misery'[32] and 'bustling folly':[33] a pleasure without worth and an activity without direction. That is, culture will fail to eliminate its vices[34] so long as it is conceived of only as a civic community or the development of means and if man's capacity for rationally choosing ends is allowed to remain dormant.

Athough this unsatisfactory development is the only one possible 'so long as [culture] proceeds without plan'[35]—where there is merely skill in the service of unreasonable ends—Kant also gives culture a wider role.

While the development of skill through war, violence, and self-interest may eventually give rise to a peaceful cosmopolitan society,[36] it will also have served its purpose when that society is formed. By contrast, it is in conditions of perfect peace that culture finally comes into its own. Only 'in the state of perfect culture would perpetual peace be of benefit to us, and only then would it be possible'.[37]

This distinction marks a qualitative difference rather than a change that follows in time. Kant goes on to talk of culture as discipline, and *this* depends on a relation of reason to nature which differs from that involved in skill. Rather than be content with constructing a civic community, culture as discipline is directed toward the creation of a community in which 'no member shall be a mere means, but should also be an end, and seeing that he contributes to the possibility of the entire body, should have his position and function defined by the idea of the whole'.[38] If a person is to be an end, and his position defined through the interaction and institutions of a social whole, then those institutions must reflect and permit his moral self-legislation. For this, it is necessary to consider men not only as physical beings but also as moral ends.[39]

Kant further develops the nature of unity between men treated as ends in his political philosophy, whose laws are also 'as a class, laws of coercion'.[40] And this interest too must be placed in the context of practical reason and its contrast with nature.

Between Politics and Morality

Underlying Kant's examination of political life is a supposition that had no place in his conception of a civic community. The political unity between individuals that is gained through coercion is in some sense morally wrong, because it denies an individual's autonomy, but is still morally *necessary*. Coercive laws can at least lead to *right* actions, so that where necessary an individual may be forcibly prevented from impairing the possibility of another's *good* action.[41] Accordingly, the political domain too covers only a formal peace in which we strive to establish some consistency in the behaviour of each person, regardless of moral motivations. But coercion is given a moral justification of sorts which the civic community does not claim.

Kant insists that reason can liberate men from 'already existing hindrances which, it may be, do not arise unavoidably out of human nature but are due to a quite remediable cause, the neglect of pure ideas in making laws'.[42] Laws may be absurd in that they are not rational ends:

they merely institutionalize past practices or are based on authority and relations of power and obedience rather than possessing a rational, justified legitimacy.[43] To prove their illegitimacy, however, is not to dissolve the coercion behind such irrational laws and political organizations. Nor can we expect to find compulsion entirely unnecessary. Rather, we must justify and legitimate the coercive rules and system of balances and checks which citizens are expected to follow.[44]

Thus, people are treated as moral ends and ascribed a capacity for rational autonomy. But, in addition, the claim is that the possibility of the latter may be generated by using legal and political systems to restrict the conflict between individuals that results from an opposition between nature and reason. However, in spite of this moral slant, Kant's political theory 'does not require that we know how to attain the moral improvement of men, but only that we should know the mechanism of nature in order to use it on men, organizing the conflict of the hostile intentions present in a people in such a way that they must compel themselves to submit to coercive laws'.[45]

Politics too, then, is based on an interest in attaining a formal, if reasoned, peace between individuals. If so, then the promotion of enlightenment is passed over to practices such as culture and virtue. Cultural and moral practices may motivate us through reason fully as much as political or legal compulsion can motivate us to follow political laws, but their justification does not countenance the existence of coercion. Culture explores the extent to which the interrelation of reason to nature permits a unity between men—a unity we may introduce as follows.

At first the differences between culture and politics seem merely artificial. We saw that since culture as *skill* is merely the development of means, its exercise leads to conflict and compulsion because individuals seek to dominate each other in promoting the satisfaction of their own physical ends. The difference between culture and politics here is that although both involve coercion, skill cannot provide anything like the justification of compulsion to which politics may appeal. While political coercion can be imposed legitimately by an external, public body, culture as skill has no standards by which to claim legitimacy at all, even though it leads to cultural development. But this contrast seems partial and abstract since culture as *discipline* is similar to politics in being coercive. However, if culture as discipline involves any compulsion, it is a self-willed restriction that brings unity between individuals on the basis of subjects' own aptitudes for accepting certain rules to govern their own behaviour. By contrast with culture's emphasis on individual consciousness, political coercion must be restricted to a concern with individuals only so far as they play a public role. That is, coercion is legitimated not by reference to subjects' consciousness but by reference to their positions in a social whole. And in both these ways, politics differs from culture.

Of course, there may be instances in which political rules do not need to be enforced, since agents readily accept, on moral grounds, that they must observe the laws regulating relations between themselves simply because they are legitimate laws. But in these cases of a balance between morality and politics, the interesting comparison will be between culture and morality rather than politics and culture; and that will be considered later. In any case, even where subjects regulate their interrelation by consenting to political rules, perhaps in a way reminiscent of the development of culture as discipline, we must continue to distinguish the two cases because it is *possible* for a public body legitimately to *enforce* a unity between individuals subject to political rules. A similar compulsion cannot be deployed in the case of culture since its unity is attained and a rule created just so far as subjects *choose* to participate in it.

Finally, where the existence of a balance between politics and morality renders implausible or redundant the reminder that coercion is possible, we may still distinguish culture from politics on the basis of Kant's argument that only one political form is capable of exemplifying a state of harmony between morality and politics—a form which has no analogy in culture and instead invites a separation between political and cultural freedom. Kant argues that only a republican form of government will ensure that men are citizens as well as subjects in society with others. In a republic the sole ruler is the public and universal law; it provides the only condition in which each individual can be given his due.[46] And its corollary is the rejection of democracy *as a form of rule* in which all individuals' desires must be given equal significance, regardless of their origin or object, because men can, so to speak, vote for whatever they desire. By this argument, democracy as a form of rule is based on an artificial and formal equality which effectively prevents the public realm from being responsive to differences between individuals. Any and all desires come to be treated as if they had equal validity, and the public realm is determined by the force of the private desires of subjects rather than by the particular needs of different citizens. In effect there is no escape, even in public life, from the demands of arbitrary personal desires.

Kant's solution turns on, first, separating the realm of personal and cultural freedom from that of politics and, second, restricting the latter. The law becomes 'the ultimate end of all *public* right'.[47] And, as with other obligations, Kant defends legal and political rights by reference to duty and morality rather than utility or the search for private satisfactions. But in addition, he claims that as it is suitable for application to all subjects *only so far as they are citizens*, this prevents the law from becoming distorted by private interests. For by restricting its application to our public roles and obligations as citizens, we prevent its intrusion into other spheres of our lives.[48] And because a republican form of government recognizes that citizens are also subjects who pursue their own needs in lives outside the compass of the legal or political spheres, it can sustain a real individuality in democracy as a *form of life*, where subjects choose and promote their own desires, secure in the knowledge that their actions will not be hampered by others nor theirs impair the freedom of others.

Leaving aside questions about the nature of the republican freedom being proposed, we see at least that Kant intends to restrict politics to a unity in the public behaviour of citizens. This leaves the rest of social life to other practices like culture and virtue, and suggests other distinctions between culture and politics. Whereas politics concerns only the public behaviour of citizens, culture involves an aptitude or consciousness, and an inner, personal interrelation between subjects as rational and feeling beings. And although both politics and culture are public, at least in some sense involving communication between individuals, there is an important difference. Culture, most clearly in fine art, seeks to show that subjective feelings are 'public' in that they can claim universal validity over others and, so, can promote a unity between individuals on the basis of their subjectivity.[49] By contrast, the unity gained in politics is public in that it applies to relations between individual citizens seeking to generate commonly accessible conditions in which each individual's moral and personal development will not be hampered by others' wrong or immoral behaviour, and the rules governing relations between citizens are not based on or determined by how they feel towards those rules.

Clearly cultural freedom does not subsist outside society and history, in some realm of quite private individuals: it proceeds through a public but intersubjective and individual engagement in constructing a society suited to human needs. Consequently, Kant's distinction between politics and culture avoids the error of those aestheticians who associate 'private' with 'strictly individual', 'public' with 'social', and then go on to propose that a philosophical distinction between them leads to a difference in the quality of their experiences. The latter would only force culture to become part of a reified individual and private world and, given its distance from public or common standards, an agent of élitism.

In this comparison, culture and morality were supposed to have a similar regard for the consciousness of persons. There are also contrasts between culture and morality to be considered.

Skill is the use of reason as technique or means; where it is subjugated to nature it is directed to ends determined by sensual inclinations. Men are considered as physical ends and nature may be said to lead reason. Now, 'natural inclinations, considered in themselves, are good, not a matter of reproach, and it is futile to want to extirpate them'.[50] Surely 'nature has not endowed men with instincts and capacities in order that they should fight and suppress them'.[51] But Kant's inclusion of nature does not exclude reason, for the two are not always or necessarily opposed.

While culture begins where men set themselves apart from other animals by thinking of themselves as ends, it is not enough to think of men only as physical ends.[52] They must also be considered as beings capable of reasoning about ends. This requires that nature be subjected to reason in that we should pursue only the natural inclinations compatible with treating persons as rational creatures capable of reasoning about ends. That is, motivation determined to rational ends is given priority over motivation determined by natural inclinations to physical ends. And an important part played by culture, here, is the negative one of disciplining natural impulses in order that men may be motivated by reason. So, in comparison with the relation of reason to nature underlying morality, if Kant defines virtue as 'the *power*' to 'master one's inclinations when they rebel against the moral law',[53] then culture in its negative role as discipline develops, to the greatest possible extent, our power for making choices. Further, where virtue is 'the possession of a moral strength of will' to be motivated by reason, there it is culture's task to promote and exercise our ability to determine the will by reason. 'Virtue is the principle of personality functioning as the hypothetical member of a kingdom of ends',[54] and culture seeks to bring the personality to recognize and act on that principle. Further, Kant writes of virtue as the *ideal* of humanity in its moral perfection. It is the ultimate moral character a person may expect to achieve. There, he is 'in possession of himself' and not only able to overcome natural inclinations whenever they threaten to conflict with moral imperatives but also able to acquiesce in moral feeling. Rather than contrast this ideal with culture as discipline, the latter may be differentiated as belonging to the other end of the same scale. Thus, while virtue is an ideal of humanity, culture as discipline is the *emergence* of humanity—of individuals capable of being considered as reasoning, moral ends—out of subjugation to nature.

But it is inadequate to Kant's enterprise to consider only discipline and skill. In addition to these features, culture has a positive role in establishing a relation between nature and reason, and this makes it progressive. Contrasting with skill, progressive culture concerns ends rather than means; and unlike discipline, it does not simply control natural impulses. Beginning with the relation of reason to nature, through cultural practices like fine art,[55] progressive culture develops and exercises our capacity for reason. Starting with our animal and rational character, progressive culture proceeds to increase our capability for using the latter. 'Culture progressively interferes with [nature] by altering the conditions to which it was suited'—by changing the very relation between nature and reason from which it began.[56] Progressive culture brings about more than a rejection of those conflictive natural characteristics that prevent individuals from entering a positive relation with other subjects. It furthers the task of 'making man more than man' by developing 'the dispositions of mankind considered as a *moral* species'.[57] Eventually, the culture we construct 'will be strong and perfect enough to become a second nature. This indeed is the ultimate moral end of the human species'.[58] And we shall consider this again, later.

Kant's concept of culture contrasts with that of German historicism. Herder can serve as an example of the latter. He contends that the application of the concept of culture must be restricted to *particular* patterns of social life. It involves a feeling of belonging to a cultural group and implies that different cultural wholes are incommensurable with each other.[59] He argues for a plurality of cultures and emphasizes specific products—which are meaningful within a particular culture— rather than giving importance to human capabilities generally. Consequently, he holds that culture is collective rather than personal, and that artefacts express their particular cultures rather than promote a normative search for individual moral development.[60] And, unlike Kant, the historicists hold that culture does not make a normative claim to legitimacy. Whereas Kant gives it significance for its promotion of moral perfection, for the historicists culture is simply what is empirically given, and claims attention for its uniqueness.[61]

Kant stresses the development of human capabilities generally instead of proposing a need to gain any particular product. But while culture is a process of gaining mastery over nature and over the barbarism of conflictive individualism, Kant does not intend to exclude nature entirely nor to suppress individuality. Although their natures may lead individuals into conflict with each other, Kant does not attribute to man an aggressive instinct that culture must overcome by repressing individuality. Rather, cultural practice seeks to promote individual development as a basis for moral behaviour.

At the same time, Kant's concept of 'social unsociability'[62] shows that he is cognizant of a tension between individual and group. Members of a civic community are threatened by the possibility that others may treat them only as a means. Hence skill can be contrasted with disciplinary or progressive culture as the subjugation of an individual to a society in which he is seen as a physical end, and a means only, as compared with an individual's liberation to be himself and, in community with others, to be more than an accidental correlation between reason and nature. Its promotion of an aptitude for reason, further, gives culture a normative interest in the search for human perfection. And it is through this normative interest that culture claims legitimacy.

Culture, Society, and History

Whether it is disciplinary or progressive, and by contrast with any increase of skill in the service of nature, to promote culture is not to develop individuals alone. When satisfying his natural inclinations a subject is motivated towards ends which are exclusively individual. But progressive and disciplinary culture deal with '*man as such* (*humanity, really*)'[63] and concern persons generally as morally capable beings.

Only an autonomous individual can carry out actions that are imputable to himself alone and so express and develop his moral personality. But, even so, his actions must bear reference to other persons in a unified moral community. His moral judgements must exhibit consistency, for if they are to be an expression of his moral personality they must form a unity. They cannot be made piecemeal and without integrating them through a considered assessment of past behaviour and the likely pattern of future actions. Similarly, his behaviour must be able to satisfy others' moral demands if it is to satisfy his own, and so must be consistent with the judgements of other moral agents.[64] That is, an agent's moral behaviour is autonomous but continuous with the total moral history of men working to create an ethical community.[65]

Kant holds that reason possesses an interest in striving for totality in this manner. As we saw, Kant's interest in this striving[66] becomes a concern with whether empirical nature can be known as a systematic unity in which 'the totality of things, in their interconnection as constituting the universe' can be comprehended by us.[67] His interest is part of a search for consistency and completeness, to show that our comprehension is public, objective, and unified. The actions and intentions of moral agents are similarly united in the search for an ethical community, and the realization of the latter *in this world* unites the system we construct into a totality under practical imperatives. Further, freedom formally implies spontaneity and, so, some sort of discontinuity between acts; but because an agent is a moral personality possessing a disposition, we may expect continuity and a consistency in his acts. Moreover, Kant holds that we cannot 'pursue an end that is recognized to be a mere fiction of the brain'.[68] Therefore we must have a regard for the consequences that flow from a single act, its conjunction with other of our own acts, and their coherence with those of others. Reason requires us to aim at a systematization of our actions and intentions.[69] And so far as we are beings in nature and among other subjects, moral activity must integrate consideration of our existence in nature with that in society. That is, the ethical community must promote the 'highest as a social good'.[70]

Kant refers to this integration when, first, he states that an individual must show himself capable of legislating for himself as a member of the Kingdom of Ends and, second, then explains the realization of morality in social terms.[71] And as he consistently stresses the concept of community in his many ethical writings, it may be expected also to extend over cultural practices. Basically Kant thinks that the development of reason gives culture an impetus toward a social totality like that of moral thought and action. He asserts that 'man is destined by this reason to live in society with other men',[72] and this destiny includes culture in its provenance: 'culture consists in the social worth of man'.[73] His justification for this conclusion is based on his conception of the object of culture's disciplinary and progressive features. Culture promotes to the greatest possible extent our ability to determine the will to rational ends. To develop our ability to use reason is to increase the rational autonomous part of our character—the part whose exercise also liberates us from natural causation and inclination. Thus, so far as man's reason has priority over his animal being, individuals are autonomous agents; and Kant holds that to promote this ability to set rational ends is to develop humanity. But, further, '*humanity itself* is a dignity',[74] Kant writes, and to develop one's own humanity cannot be to disregard the humanity of others. Any conclusions based on an individual's use of reason must apply to others on the basis of their use of reason.

Indeed, an individual's humanity seems to depend on others'. Kant insists that man has 'an inclination to associate with others', and explains that this is 'because in society he feels himself to be more than man, that is, more than the developed form of his natural capacities'.[75] The features additionally ascribed to him include both the capacity to use reason and the development of the capacity for reason. And it is only in society that man can feel himself 'to be not merely a man, but a man refined after his own kind',[76] because only with other human beings can he be fully human; only with other people can he expect to be considered a person. Although history contains innumerable instances in which men have been maltreated by others and had their humanity transgressed against, nevertheless, only by comparison with other people will an individual's capacity for humanity be fully explored. Dogs, rivers, cabbages, and sharks react to him in very different ways. A comparison and interaction with such objects may permit an individual to discover more about himself, but because of their inherent limitations Kant would find such self-discovery inadequate to the fullest development of humanity. Thus, attributing moral rights to animals may enrich the quality and range of our own moral lives, but because animals cannot initiate actions in a way that permits us to impute approbation or blame to them, they cannot be moral beings like us. Our capacity to determine the will to rational ends is incompletely exercised if it is compared only with inanimate things or irrational beings.

The point being made here concerns the significance we give to propositions about men, but perhaps we should make clear that a reference to social unity does not imply that culture or morality are socially determined, as if society determines what is good or culturally sensitive.[77] The fact that a person's freedom is restricted in one society does not make such repression 'moral in that society'—unless that restriction can be shown to follow from the supreme principle of morality by way of empirical generalizations about that society. And to seek to show that is to accept the demand that particular actions be legitimated by appeal to moral reason rather than to social practices. Similarly, in pointing out that morally and culturally sophisticated individuals are related to each other in a society, Kant is not setting out a necessary condition for their behaviour and implying that only people living in societies can show moral or cultural sensitivity in their actions. Rather, he is pointing to the sort of questions and procedures that are relevant to moral and cultural considerations. To feel oneself more than an animal only in society is to acknowledge that morality and culture are relations between people. Only as a person and in society with others can man expect to progress to living '*under* moral laws'.[78]

Other points about culture's relation to society must be made. Although men strive for the goal of moral perfection, in which our capacity for reason is fully developed, they cannot expect to gain perfection by themselves or 'within their mortal span'. Moral perfection is unattainable for the individual by himself: radical evil is a permanent danger simply because men have an animal, physical character. And the impetus to totality implies that perfection is acquired only by the human race in history. Further, this cannot be the case if the race is considered according to the 'generic notion (*singulorum*)'. The latter circumscribes only their non-rational, natural existence; and, instead, we must think of our race as 'a totality (*Ganza*) of men united socially on earth'.[79] Clearly, cultural progress does not promote the activities of a series of self-regarding individuals who are perpetually in conflict, and Kant holds that in promoting reason culture sustains a universal and social, as opposed to an exclusively individual, good. Nevertheless, it is individual moral autonomy that is being sought as individual perfection. Kant's hope is that his arguments have shown just how the individual and the moral or cultural community are in harmony. We shall see later how fine art seeks to resolve the tension between individual and community.

In any case, culture may endeavour to make possible moral behaviour, but it does not engender morality. While culture can be judged by its success in bringing men to be motivated by reason to moral ends, it does not determine which ends are morally necessary.[80]

Further, a progressive culture will be historical. The finitude of man's reason, its need to develop and understand itself in relation to nature, shows history to be a genuine part of Kant's system.[81] Cultural activity and products are among the agents and objects that constitute our rational history. And cultural activity is itself altered by the changes it effects in the relation of nature to reason.

But culture is not historical for Kant in the way that it is for Hegel. The latter argues that historical development is dialectical in that the progress of *Geist* includes a rational nature and is constituted by the development of both subject and object. By contrast, Kant stresses that progressive culture is only the development of subjects in a community and that the self-realization of reason does not simply incorporate objects in the way in which, for Hegel, all that is real is rational. Indeed Hegel and others were to criticize Kant for just this 'positivism' or 'non-identity' that he allowed the object to retain.[82] Further, Hegel argues that the attainment of the end of history—the self-realization of reason—makes its earlier stages at worst redundant or, at best, causes them to be sublimated into some final whole. So the part played by religion and art in historical progress, for example, is superseded by the coming of philosophy.

Kant holds a position that is more sensitive to differences in the relation of reason to nature and individual to community. While accepting that culture is historical and that it poses different questions and problems at different moments of its development, he contends that distinctions between culture, nature, morality, and politics describe distinctive but permanent features of humanity. Cultural progress does not make itself redundant because reason is not all inclusive and substantial. Instead of arguing that culture becomes unnecessary at just that point where the development of history must be comprehended in terms of the motivating force of reason in pursuit of negativity, Kant uses culture to try to understand the relation of nature to individuals possessing the capacity for rational freedom.

It is because Kant does not put forward a dialectic like Hegel's, yet holds that the cultural development of subjects must be supported by an ordering of nature, that he must argue for some unity between nature and reason. Such a unity is evinced in the relation of physical to moral teleology. The possibility of realizing the *summum bonum* warrants our attributing a teleological order to nature in which man stands as the ultimate end of nature.[83] Further, that a *summum bonum* is progressively realized suggests a moral teleology or order of ends where man, 'under moral laws', but in empirical nature, is the final end to be gained. Kant thinks this requires that moral teleology encompass a physical teleology:[84] nature must be capable of being seen as an objectification of morality—so that moral law governs the individual's social and psychological character—and the empirical existence of ends must be such that they can be recognized as constituents of a moral teleology. By contrast with Hegel, by whose conception rational Nature and developing Spirit manifest an ultimate homogeneity in substance and progress, Kant applies the concept of nature in culture primarily to human beings and includes physical nature only so far as it is under human control.

Cultural development is not a matter of contemplation, but a practice whose projected future confers meaning on its past. Progress is judged by the increase of enlightenment and self-determination—advances in productive and technical power will not count by themselves. But such cultural progress requires some norm if the social nature ascribed to it above is to bear a contrast with a 'society' formed by chance. Kant's intention is to oppose an accidental development of culture as skill with a progress that claims intersubjective validity. It is only if we possess some norm that we can progress beyond both the concatenation of sensually motivated individual interests, grouped in a civic community formed merely through culture as skill, and the public and external but coercive order provided in a political commonwealth. Without a normatively binding intersubjective standard, Kant's claims for the social good which culture promotes will founder inside a merely private sphere, unable to realize the impetus to totality that was said to be involved in morality and culture.

Before we examine the norm and its determination of cultural progress, we must understand how fine art enables us to participate in culture.

Fine Art in Culture

Only a being who is both animal and rational can appreciate beauty. Fine art is an expression of humanity; and only such a creature may change and develop himself through culture. Further, an understanding of our participation in culture through the construction and appreciation of fine art must take account of the analogy between beauty and moral good proposed by Kant.

Beauty is not simply a duplicate of moral good. If it were, we would need to account for the limits and means of such duplication. By one account, we would have to be able to reduce the organizing principles used in fine art to moral ones. But this would push duplication toward replication when, it may be, a comprehensive reproduction of moral good in cultural experience is unnecessary. More importantly, such replication may be said to be unobtainable because of both our animal empirical character and the nature of our experience of beauty. To justify the unlikelihood of replication, we must examine the relation between culture, our experience of fine art, and the highest good, in order to show both what distinguishes each from the other and what unites them. Briefly, what unites morality, politics, and culture is that in each activity we seek to realize the supreme principle. Their distinction consists in each mediating the supreme principle of morality on the basis of its emphasis on a particular conception of the animal and rational character of man. That is, rather than actualizing the imperative in some uniform manner, each possesses a distinctive justification and rational force; and the history of each actualizing of the supreme principle can be combined into a single purely moral story only at the cost of distorting the different facets of our natural and rational character.

For example, to search for a straightforward similarity between fine art and morality serves the former ill because it removes the aesthetic dimension from consideration. Fine art could lose its reality in this comparison if its existence and importance were determined by reference to a moral good that contains all that might be said about rational compulsion and human freedom. Here fine art bears an analogy to moral good as an image to some reality, denying its aesthetic character for the sake of moral requirements in such a way that it would be valued only for its moral qualities.

Kant's enquiries into politics and culture reject such a conception. Political and cultural practices, where fine art is a good example of the latter, will not simply be dissolved into morality but must be understood as separate mediations in the development of a human world. And they have moral value for being what they are rather than for imitating the moral good: the autonomy of fine art must be able to survive its relation to moral good. Nevertheless, a study of fine art cannot be concerned with its sources and character only as an aesthetic object, but must also consider its engagement with and effect on the social world we construct. And Kant begins his explanation of fine art's participation in culture by proposing that aesthetic intention, genius, may be developed as a skill through the taste, possessed by the artist himself, that is required in the execution of works of art. Taste gives form to a work, where form is 'the *means* by which [the product of genius] is universally communicated'.[85] An artist

having practised and corrected his taste by a variety of examples from nature or art, controls his work and, after many and often laborious, attempts to satisfy taste, finds the form which commends itself to him. Hence this form is not, as it were, a matter of inspiration or even a free swing of the mental powers, but rather a slow and painful process of improvement, directed to making the form adequate to his thought without prejudice to the free play of those powers.[86]

As an example of this process we may take Renoir, who came to refine an Impressionist technique of painting and used the relationship between colours and carefully judged tones and textures to give volume and density to represented objects. Rather than use sketched outlines for this task, he preferred to blur outlines altogether, as in the *Rower's Lunch* (1879–80), where glasses and cutlery are represented by their highlights alone while colours making up the human figures merge at their edges with other colours. By contrast, the Classicists would have marked outline forms and not sought to represent objects in so close a relation to their background. Renoir's was a technique or skill developed through experience and exercise in order to represent objects without using the rules of perspective and construction employed by artists, say, in the Renaissance. And to understand the Impressionists' reasons for developing their new techniques or for Cézanne's need to develop his technique, we must understand the history of fine art and its participation in the development of culture, in which an artist uses his taste to make his work 'orderly and polished' and to give guidance, 'directing and controlling [genius] so that it may preserve its character of finality. It introduces a clearness and order into the plentitude of thought'.[87]

But even though it serves to make an artist's work communicable, taste is not determined by an interest in social communication.[88] It merely ensures that genius's creative but uncritical faculty does not cause a work to degenerate into incomprehensible and confused 'original nonsense'. Moreover, this submission of genius to taste is 'freely willed'. It is intended to be a means of making the work understandable and accessible to the artist himself as much as to his audience, for in clarifying a work to himself the artist also clarifies it for others. If taste has an interest, it is in clarity, not social communication. And if fine art is disciplinary, it is so to the extent that clarity and coherence depend on some sort of order and consistency. Taste does not blindly impose order on natural inclination.

Such discipline points to other features of fine art. It was said that fine art participates in culture by promoting unity between individuals. Moreover, the experience of fine art bears analogies with moral good. These analogies may be used to understand the nature of fine art's participation in culture. Just as moral good emphasizes a respect for man's rational character, seeing autonomous acting individuals as ends in themselves, similarly, the clarification and discipline present in fine art show it capable of sustaining and encouraging a relation between subjects as rational autonomous beings. But, further, as fine art also depends on thinking of subjects as beings possessing natural characteristics which are in harmony with their own and others' rational capacities, fine art also participates in constructing the unity between individuals, in reason and feeling, which is the end of culture. This may be explained further.

Just as moral good regards the person as an autonomous rational being who is an end in himself, similarly, judgements of taste and our experience of beauty are bound to see individuals as autonomous, reasoning, and experiencing subjects, and to treat them as ends in themselves.[89] Being disinterested, judgements are determined by their appropriateness to the standard of a harmonious general relation of rational faculties rather than by the application of some determinate concept. This appreciation of beauty may be called a rational end because of the manner in which rational faculties are involved.

The rational ends are ones in which individuals must gain *for themselves* a harmony of rational faculties. As an object is considered beautiful 'solely in respect of that quality in which it adapts itself to our mode of taking it in',[90] every judgement is 'required to be an independent judgement of the individual himself'. Consequently, Kant writes, 'taste lays claim simply to autonomy'. Disapproval or approval by others 'affords no valid proof' of an individual's taste.[91] That is, a judgement cannot be made for the subject by others; and this militates against any attempt at coercion.

Yet autonomous judgements are defensible and taste 'extends its claims to *all* subjects'.[92] Their defence cannot be the presentation of a fact to verify a truth claim, nor like a correct logical argument whose denial is merely self-contradictory. Instead, in spite of the fact that its beauty is free of the cognitive use of determinate concepts, our response to a work must be justified or 'defended by examples and comparison'. Examples and comparisons are put forward to convince a subject, who dislikes Manet's *The Balcony* because he dislikes women with parasols, that he has failed to understand the work. He could subsequently be persuaded of its aesthetic value were his attention turned to the basis of its complex composition of elongated rectangles and crossing diagonals; to its colours, tones, and textures; to its references to Goya's *Majas on the Balcony*; and to its self-consciousness that it is only a representation.[93] Here, to explain and justify a judgement we 'investigate the faculties of cognition and their function', illustrating, 'by the analysis of examples, their mutual subjective finality, the form of which has been shown . . . to constitute the beauty of their object'. Explanation relies on the 'mutual relation' of faculties and, 'consequently, [to reducing] their accordance or discordance, to rules'.[94]

The experience of fine art permits discussion and cultivation of the ability to appreciate works; but the discussion is not a proof that another subject must accept unless he himself feels an accord between the object and a harmonious relation of rational faculties in a judgement of taste. Thus, by their very nature, judgements of taste are bound to be persuasive. At most we may change other subjects to our point of view by putting forward an analogy with moral persuasion in what may be called 'aesthetic argument by comparison and example'. It is successful when another subject is enabled to gain the experience of beauty for himself.[95]

Just as moral persuasion seeks to bring a subject to carry out his duty, similarly, aesthetic persuasion seeks to bring another subject to make a judgement of taste. Both moral and aesthetic persuasion are addressed to other subjects' or persons' capacity for reason and its accord with nature. Persuasion respects the autonomy of an individual and treats his capacity for reason and appreciation as an end. Thus, our experience of fine art is not only public and persuasive but is also intersubjective and promotes our humanity through unity with other subjects. Kant proposes this clearly in his account of the creation of works of art. It involves a submission of genius to taste which prevents fine art from disintegrating into confusion. Submission is freely willed and undertaken as a means of ensuring the coherence and, so, accessibility of a work. Like the acquiescence to moral law (*Wille*) by choice (*Willkur*) that establishes an individual's claim to autonomy and moral personality, the acquiescence of genius to taste makes its product capable of judgement by other subjects.

Thus, Kant can hold that taste treats subjects as subjects and that it develops a respect for others because it furthers our awareness of them as beings capable of understanding, appreciating, and judging a work. Fine art provides an experience whose intersubjectivity is exhibited in its regard for others as rational and feeling subjects. Judgements are not imposed on others; the consent sought from individuals, and the relation of nature to reason that is sustained, promote a community between subjects. And Kant can affirm both that a person is treated as an end in himself and that, therefore, in making a judgement which he considers justifiable, the individual, as it were, declares his autonomy and value.

Consequently, our experience, construction, and appreciation of fine art can develop a community in which we sustain a *real* unity between individuals considered as discrete, rational, and feeling subjects. It is not a formal unity that subsumes them all under one category by reference to some commonly possessed property, but is a unity based on a pleasurable experience in which nature is in harmony with our capacity for reason. Consequently, Kant can contend that fine art promotes culture by developing to the furthest extent a unity between subjects as rational and feeling beings capable of appreciating ends in a way that characterizes us as members of a moral species.

Further, Kant can add to his explanation of the nature of such unity by comparison with the ideal of a *sensus communis*. The latter is contrasted with common human understanding or common sense.[96] Common sense may be seen as the actually existing, unordered, and fragmented collection of habits of thought and behaviour of men, that need not possess a coherence within an individual consciousness, let alone bear reference to an objective social unity. Common sense is subjective in a pejorative sense, being a set of beliefs or 'obscurely represented principles'[97] which may be accepted by individuals but is not necessarily based on any rational, universal criteria.[98] Consequently, common sense can be isolating: as when most subjects behave according to rules which are imposed by force or custom[99] and distance themselves from anyone who acts in an 'unruly' manner—even though the latter may be rational and moral. Common sense can be uncritical, individual, and subjective: an acceptance of experience as arbitrary, a passivity toward events which can be controlled, and a susceptibility to prejudice.[100] It forms a world of conventions where laws and rules, in spite of the regularities of behaviour which their imposition may occasion, do not possess any unity. It results in a social world determined by compulsions that remain irrational and 'other', and it fails to understand that nature is subject to lawful determinations.[101]

By a *sensus communis*, in contrast, we are to understand 'the idea of a *public* sense, i.e., a critical faculty which in its reflective act takes account (a priori) of the mode of representation of everyone else, in order, *as it were*, to weigh its judgement with the collective reason of mankind, and thereby avoid the illusion arising from subjective and personal conditions which could easily be taken for objective, an illusion that would exert a prejudicial influence upon its judgement. This is accomplished by weighing the judgement, not so much with actual, as rather with the *merely possible* judgement of others'.[102]

This concern with 'possible judgements' may be understood as, first, a concern with the possibility of other subjects making the judgements we make. Second, and complementary to the first, it incorporates such claims about our human character as are revealed by the nature of cognitive faculties in judgement. In this regard, Kant argues that the human mind cannot but be aware always of what is possible. Our understanding 'cannot avoid the necessity of drawing a distinction between the possibility and actuality of things'.[103] This distinction is made because 'possibility signifies the position of a thing relative to our conception generally, and to our capacity for thinking, whereas actuality signifies the positing of a thing in its immediate self-existence apart from this conception'.[104] If the 'understanding thinks it—think how it will—then the thing is represented as possible'. God and the perfect will create what they know and will what the moral law expects, but because men possess understanding rather than intuitive knowledge and as they have only an imperfectly rational will, they must deal with what could or should exist. It is part of the situation of men that if a thing 'does not exist, we may yet always give it a place in our thoughts, or if there is something of which we have no conception, we may nevertheless imagine it given'. The concept of 'possibility' gives room for the development of conceptions in imagination and also projects their realization: it refers to man's potential for understanding and acting in a world he did not create. When Kant states that in our construction of the *sensus communis* we must 'weigh' our judgements with 'the *merely possible* judgements of others', he is affirming our humanity in pointing to a development of those capacities which characterize us as men rather than gods or animals. But he is also indicating more than this.

He is also proposing a particular development. Weighing a judgement 'with that of others' introduces considerations of what could be. Artists and their audience reflect upon a work, judging its adequacy to a harmony of rational faculties; and, by doing so, subjects judge not only the work but also themselves. For their assessment of the appropriateness of the object also leads to reflection upon their own adequacy to the work. Through such reflection we participate in culture, where subjects 'progressively interfere' with nature and alter 'the very conditions to which [culture] is suited'.[105] Aesthetic activity changes the very relation between nature and reason on which it depends for its appreciation. Thus it makes 'man more than man' by cultivating individual judgement through a dialogue based on the common possession of a capacity for reason and feeling. As 'a kind of *sensus communis*',[106] taste provides us with a 'mere ideal norm'.[107] Of course, judgements claim only '*exemplary validity*', exhibiting the sort of unity it is possible for individuals to attain. And not only in our engagement with fine art but also in progressive culture generally, our intention is to seek 'that which forms the point of reference for the harmonious accord of all our [that is, of every subject] faculties of cognition—the production of which accord is the ultimate end set by the intelligible basis of our nature'.[108]

Kant develops the cultural role of fine art further in one direction when he argues that different fine arts may be ordered into a hierarchy on the basis of their analogy to our usual modes of communication.[109] Thus, our understanding of the role of fine art in culture will be furthered by considering the proposed hierarchy—if only to see how communication is taken to promote a unity between rational and feeling individuals.

Kant's hierarchy is not unique—nor is it intended as such. He develops this one because he is trying to construct a unity between rational and feeling individuals. The creation and appreciation of works depends on exercising our rational and subjective character. Reason and feeling are held in a delicate balance through the individual's own action of judging, and we make a claim to universality by which all other beings like ourselves are joined in a community because of their capacity for autonomous action, reason, and feeling. What is revealed about individuals is exhibited in their participation in making universally valid judgements, and so the proposed hierarchy will tell us something of the contribution fine art makes and how it succeeds in its task.

Expression and Culture

Kant's hierarchy suggests that we cultivate our humanity as we produce and appreciate fine art. Kant begins by dividing the fine arts by reference to their analogy with different 'modes of expression of which men avail themselves in speech, with a view to communicating themselves to one another as completely as possible, i.e. not merely in respect of their concepts but in respect of their sensations also'.[110] And this tells us of the relation between individuals that fine art can sustain.

Kant takes '*word, gesture and tone* (articulation, gestulation, and modulation)'[111] as his starting-point. Corresponding to these are the arts of speech—rhetoric and poetry—in which thought is expressed in words, formative arts—painting, sculpture, and architecture—in which we give sensuous embodiment to ideas much as we communicate through gestures, and the play of sensation—music, and shows of 'pure' colour—where we use the emotional qualities of sounds and colours, as we do tones of voice, to convey moods, imperatives, and so on. Underlying the divisions is the suggestion that linguistic conventions are basic, and that gestures and tones depend on the first, for this tallies with the deduction in which Kant suggests that the existence of an objective language provides a basis for our understanding and appreciation of objects in aesthetic judgements.

In spite of their differences, each mode of fine art is capable of universality because each involves such an interdependence of expression and form as permits it intersubjective validity. Works are made communicable by giving soul, spirit, or expression, in *forms*[112] presented 'in language or painting or statuary'. The freedom of imagination, whose order is the expression of aesthetic ideas, is grasped by the appreciation of form, where to gain expression is to gain form.[113]

The division of the arts shows that each involves an order which is communicable. Accordingly, Kant's estimate of the comparative worth of fine arts depends on assessing how the imagination in expression serves to cultivate us. For these different fine arts each sustain a relation between the individuals who are engaged in appreciating and communicating works which maintain a balance between feeling and reason. They cultivate us by bringing us to engage in or perform a similar balance so that another subject's experience is gained by us, and his humanity, his reflective estimation of the universalizability of the state of his own capacities, resonates in our experience.

To develop this further, Kant examines the given divisions to see which of the different fine arts is most versatile in communication and will have a greater aesthetic worth—for its unity of expression and form will be more valuable for being better able to explore the balance between feeling and reason, in expression and form, which is universalizable over all subjects.

Clearly, it is no accident that Kant considered the division of fine arts in terms of expression and communication, for he has set a store by their ability to cultivate us in the special way open to beauty and its universalizable pleasure. We feel our humanity by performing an act—making a judgement—which we must do for ourselves, but which carries other and more authority than a mere personal preference. For it is a matter of our humanity that we should be able to act in this way and so too a matter of our recognition of each others' humanity where we make judgements which are universalizable yet autonomous, rational yet dependent on a feeling, personal yet communicable. As Kant holds, there is an aesthetic ground for constructing such a hierarchy because each fine art 'supplies a culture to the mind, expanding our faculties'[114] and enabling us to feel our humanity in a different measure from the others. And ultimately the justification for developing this hierarchy, for ordering our experience along these lines, is that such communication is what encultures the mind; and cultural endeavour, in turn, is morally valuable. In dividing *and* ordering the fine arts as he does, Kant is accepting the validity of a practical justification of our experience of beauty.[115]

In cultivating a unity between individuals in reason and feeling Kant gives first place to poetry. It

invigorates the mind by letting it feel its faculty—free, spontaneous, and independent of determination by nature—of regarding and estimating nature as a phenomenon in the light of aspects which nature of itself does not afford us in experience, either for sense or understanding, and of employing it accordingly on behalf of, as a sort of schema for, the supersensible.[116]

The imagination is liberated from cognitive restrictions and permits us to think of reality from the point of view of the rational *and* feeling subject. And to the expressive unities in which the imagination is given form, the subject responds with an intersubjectively valid pleasure.

The importance of poetry to culture may be understood by contrast with rhetoric and by comparison with the formative arts. For rhetoric uses imagination to delude other subjects, robbing 'their verdict of its freedom'.[117] Although such an art may be used for a morally justified end,[118] its means also abnegate moral purposes.[119] By its irrational and untruthful persuasiveness, by denying the rational autonomy of other subjects, rhetoric denies itself validity. By contrast, poetry is 'straight-forward and above board'. While it claims universal validity and, thus, brings our subjectivity into the public sphere, it is a rational business, which treats subjects as rational and feeling ends in themselves. While rhetoric brings about a change of heart by speech without allowing others to weigh an issue, poetry dissembles only for the sake of entertainment, and does so guilelessly, leaving to individuals their autonomous judgements, their own exercise of reason and feeling in relation to others. Our exercise of thought in understanding the aesthetic ideas expressed, and in appreciating their order, strengthens those powers, giving us a greater dexterity for and deeper appreciation of ourselves and others as united, rational, and feeling ends.

Similarly with the formative arts, of which painting especially 'penetrate[s] much further [than other formative arts] into the region of ideas, and in conformity with them give[s] a greater extension to the field of intuition'.[120] It is better able to satisfy the criterion of culture supplied to the mind, by which there is an 'expansion of the faculties whose confluence, in judgement, is necessary for cognition'.[121]

The descriptions of particular art forms and the resulting claims are obviously questionable, but they serve to show us the end to which Kant directs fine art: cultural development towards a more widely understood and deeply felt unity between rational and feeling individuals treated as autonomous ends in themselves. It is a culture that exists and develops so far as we develop and create it in our individual actions, and is promoted better by different art forms. And although the particular importance Kant claims for each form may be mistaken, we may expect that fine art—its expression and the form or order that constitutes a work by virtue of the relation between individuals that it sustains; the universality of its pleasure; the singularity of judgement; and its autonomy—will be able to tell us something about man. But it does not succeed by providing a set of generalizations which are applicable to all men: the truths about man which we gain from fine art will show themselves in the actions—based on the autonomous unity of reason and feeling, the community of individuals formed, the universalizability that depends on participation—in which men reveal their humanity and participate in progressive culture.

To understand this fully we must examine Kant's justifications for the necessity of progressive culture and the possibility of other subjects making the judgements we make. These issues require separate chapters, and before turning to them we must develop the account of fine art and culture presented above. We have relied on an understanding of participation in culture that in significant features is equally applicable to natural beauty. But we have usually spoken only of fine art, and while consideration of its participation in culture helps clarify issues relating to genius as aesthetic intention and creativity, these do not justify ascribing fine art priority over natural beauty. For an explanation of disciplinary or progressive culture which proposes that they promote our power to choose by exploring the compatibility of nature with reason does not exclude natural beauty from contributing to this exploration. Further, if necessity is to be justified by reference to participation in culture, then because both fine art and natural beauty promote unity between individuals in reason and nature, neither can claim to be more privileged than the other.

Nevertheless, we should stress the central role of fine art. In the absence of fine art and the activity of genius, beauty's analogy with morality would remain partial and the extent of its participation in culture would be the poorer. If beauty were not understood through fine art, it would only be a matter of responsiveness, and while it may as such contribute to disciplinary culture it would be a case of only appreciative judgement. By acknowledging the productive activity of genius in the analogy between artistic beauty and moral good, we can see both as intentional activity subject to rules: genius ruled by taste and choice by moral law. Further, just as our being moral requires us not only to judge the moral value of actions but also to act ourselves, similarly, in the absence of genius' creative activity in producing and appreciating works, beauty would contribute to culture in a very partial and unsatisfactory manner. This is because both genius and choice involve an exercise of freedom. And the better we understand genius, the more clearly we may distinguish the imaginative freedom involved in creating and appreciating fine art from the play of imagination necessary to an appreciation of natural beauty. Whereas the former depends on its object being constituted by an exercise of imaginative freedom, our appreciation of an object of nature does not have such dependence. At best, we ascribe creativity to natural objects by analogy with fine art. Consequently, we may reject the claim of natural beauty to full participation in the progressive cultural task of producing and developing an aptitude for *setting* ends rather than merely responding to aesthetic ends.

Two other objections to this account of fine art and its participation in culture are, first, that it submerges fine art in culture and leads us to lose sight of aesthetic value, and second, that it is not yet clear that cultural behaviour and artistic intention, understood as a grasp and use of meanings, are possible in the phenomenal world.

The first objection is only partially correct at best, and even then only lays an obligation on us to provide further arguments.[122] We have suggested that fine art's participation in culture is a corner-stone of Kant's conception of intersubjectivity. It depends on a harmony between reason and nature such that the development of man's natural being need not lead to conflict between people nor cause us to treat other subjects as means only. The nature and role of genius allows us to see fine art as part of culture, and the distinctive character of fine art resists submersion in culture.

Indeed, at first it seems that fine art is a model for cultural development, and is able to play a unique and exemplary role because of its analogy with morality. It could be claimed that, by contrast with other varieties of cultural activity, beauty not only brings about the highest good but does so by resembling that end, making available to experience a surrogate for the highest good.[123] Where other cultural activity strives for an end it cannot resemble, beauty apparently seeks to realize the highest good by making the sort of demands that the highest good makes. Like the highest good, it is claimed, beauty is constituted by a harmony between reason and nature[124]—unlike culture as skill which is commensurate with a conflict between reason and nature—and requires that subjects be treated as rational ends and be persuaded to an experience they must have for themselves. This may be contrasted with, say, the ethical state of nature,[125] in which evil individuals may be coerced to behave in ways they do not wish. Beauty is effective by duplicating *in experience* the state that is its end. This seems to give it a special status: it tries to be what it wants to become. This claim may also be used to ground the assertion that 'it must be said once and for all that man only plays [through pleasurable aesthetic experience] when he is a man in the full meaning of the word, and he is fully human only when he plays'.[126]

To attribute such a unique and exemplary role to beauty would be mistaken. Leaving aside difficulties in formulating the position outlined above,[127] the fact that beauty plays a distinctive role in culture does not make it exemplary. For beauty participates in culture without being all that culture is about. To argue for the latter on the basis of an analogy between beauty and morality would be to ignore other features of the relation between nature and reason: the conflict between them; the limitations imposed on men by their animal being; the pursuit of moral perfection through a continuing struggle for virtue rather than by means of a universalizable pleasure, and so on. Each of these features is a part of culture because it promotes the ability to set and gain rational ends. And those practices cannot be said to be less capable of doing that just because they do not, like beauty, symbolize morality.

Nor can beauty be given an exemplary status for its resemblance to morality—unless it be argued that by being experienced a symbol takes on the place and power of what it symbolizes, perhaps in the way a cross is revered for its symbolic relation to the Crucifixion.[128] This is not something that Kant would argue for: he recognizes the different ontological commitments made by nature and reason.[129] In any case, this claim would require a further argument to show that the resemblance between elements depends on an unmediated identity. Further, if symbolic relations were taken to work in that way, the fact that they rest on an analogy would mean that *any* cultural activity could symbolize morality in some way, on the basis of *some* resemblance, and could claim the necessity claimed by beauty through *its* symbolic relation and resemblance to moral good.

As beauty cannot be shown to be exemplary on the basis of its distinctive resemblance to morality, and given that various sorts of cultural activity may be distinguished, rather than search for an exemplary model or expect to discover a homogeneity we should see culture as a heterogeneous collection of activities which are unified under an obligation to satisfy cultural duty. By such an account, fine art's participation in culture would require and permit a justification of *aesthetic*, because cultural, necessity.

Further, to see culture as a heterogeneous collection of activities will serve to correct doubts voiced by asking why it is necessary to associate fine art with cultural or moral necessity at all in order to justify aesthetic necessity. Given that aesthetic judgements are possible so far as we are right to suppose a priori that other subjects are able to make them, it is not clear that anything else is required. Neither association with moral good nor the proposed participation in culture seems to add anything to the universality or subjective general validity justified in the deduction of taste[130]—and nothing more is needed. The deduction suffices, it may be said, because it legitimates the understanding and criticism of fine art. And that is all a *Critique* can do. However, because it only shows that aesthetic judgements are possible, the deduction does not do enough. Its argument is that individuals making aesthetic judgements are engaged in a practice in which the justification and explanation of preferences makes sense. But the defence of particular judgements is an empirical matter that is based ultimately on a subjective finality experienced by individuals. While we can defend our claim that ours is an experience of beauty, the success of such a justification, which is an argument for the generalizability of a particular judgement, can only be measured by others also being able to gain that experience. Without some account of the fact that others are able to share that experience, the demand for others' assent, which is objective necessity, is not warranted. Yet a deduction of the possibility of taste does not show why others should attempt to gain that experience—this is something that needs to be justified. And Kant seeks to do this by arguing that the pursuit of beauty through the understanding, criticism, and evaluation of fine art is an important activity. Steps in this argument have been taken by urging that its symbolic relation to morality does not justify the necessity of beauty, that the relation between fine art and morality is complicated by fine art's mediation with culture, and that the pursuit of beauty is one among other sorts of cultural activity. By doing this we prepare grounds for justifying the claim that Kant ascribes 'objective' necessity to beauty by relating its pursuit to morality through cultural duty. Aesthetic activity is important to morality because it promotes culture in our attempts to gain the highest good.

Our claim would be, then, that an obligation to cultural duty and to the effort to gain the highest good gives a heterogeneous unity to various cultural activities. If it did not satisfy cultural duty, then the pursuit of beauty would lack justification, and our appreciation of beauty and our construction of works of fine art would be at best only examples of differing relations between reason and nature. That someone else did not share a judgement would be of no more consequence than if he did. Or, conversely, if the justification of beauty were entirely independent of, though similar to, morality, to lead a good life it would be enough to pursue beauty without regard for any moral consequences. In the first case aesthetic judgements would fail to be much more than the expression of untested individual preferences or the self-satisfied pursuit of personal obsessions. In the second case it would be difficult to accept something as a good life if in it we were expected to appreciate Wagner and Mahler or to understand Benjamin and Kanafani but remain unperturbed by the destruction of a people or their dispersal from their homeland.

We may bring out the limitations of such claims by contrasting Kant's theory with that put forward by Schiller.[131]

Kant, Schiller, and Fichte

An objection to the theory of fine art and culture we ascribed to Kant is that it owes too much to other writers. It may be thought that a similar proposal was made by Schiller. But Schiller's interest in fine art differs from Kant's, and it is necessary to distinguish the latter's work from Schiller's development of it. For Schiller learnt from others as well as from Kant, and if similarities between the two remain, they also show that there is a great deal of room for debate between them. People have presented their differences in various ways,[132] depending on their interests in particular Schillerian texts. Our interest is in understanding the relation of beauty to culture to see what answers Kant and Schiller think beauty gives to questions about man.

Both Schiller and Kant give fine art priority over natural beauty. But the latter maintains that there is a close relation between the two forms of beauty. His concern with artistic beauty leads him to examine how it prefigures our appreciation of natural beauty. And while fine art shows how reason may be developed in conformity with the limits of nature, one of the limitations imposed on fine art is that it must be like nature.[133] By contrast, when Schiller gives priority to art, he also separates it from nature. Fine art now somehow transcends practical reality. It gains an autonomy that leads it away from complementing nature by developing and fulfilling our aims through activity in an area left free by nature (as for Kant) to making possible a contrast between nature and fine art as illusion and reality. For Schiller, 'actuality is overpowered by appearance and Nature by Art'.[134] Apart from the different notions of nature and appearance being used by Kant and Schiller,[135] it is evident that for the latter the autonomy of fine art will enable it to penetrate beyond what is actual to a further reality. And this ability gives fine art its necessity. Only to

idealistic art is given the capacity, *and indeed the task*, of grasping the spirit of the universal and of forcing it into a corporeal form. Even art cannot present reality to the senses, but by its creative power it can reveal it to the imagination, and thereby become truer as an everyday reality and more real than any experience.[136]

Fine art can and should undertake the task of 'expressing'[137] what Schiller takes to be reality.

Fine art has the ability to become a 'truer' or 'more real' experience because of its relation to ordinary experience. Schiller asserts that 'true art' makes men

'truly free . . . by arousing, exercising, and developing a capacity to remove the sensual world, which otherwise oppresses us as a crude raw material and weighs upon us as blind force, into an objective remoteness, transforming it into the free work of our own spirit and enabling us to attain mastery over matter through ideas'.[138]

This is not quite in agreement with Kant. Fine art was shown to be expressive and, so, for Kant, able to give us some semblance of an experience of ideas and, thus, of the noumenal realm and moral ideas. However, as we saw, the expressiveness of fine art is not, for Kant, a ground for justifying aesthetic necessity. And where he may seem to suggest that it is, we can show it to be an aberration on his part that leads to a moral determination of taste and consequently to a loss of disinterestedness.[139] By contrast, Schiller thinks it is the task of fine art to reveal something of reality through imaginative expression, and he proposes that this purpose is the basis of the necessity of beauty.

Further, Kant differs from Schiller in that he does not contend that the harmony between nature and reason exhibited in beauty is determined by a moral end. Whereas Schiller argues that to achieve a balance between reason and nature is to attain a harmonious soul—so that a person may be criticized for belonging too much to nature *or* too much to reason—Kant holds that the attainment of a balance is determined by the demands of reason—so that a moral fanatic may misapply his reason but cannot apply too much reason in being moral. While Schiller appeals to a conception of nature in which reason itself is embraced,[140] Kant argues only that fine art shows how the mind may be developed in harmony with a nature 'directed to our disinterested delight'. And he maintains that the two aspects of nature and reason remain distinct.[141]

Other examples may be given to show that differing accounts of the relation between mind and nature lead Schiller and Kant to give contrasting accounts of fine art. Nor do the two give similar explanations of the relation between individuals. Consequently, they give contrasting accounts of the cultural role of fine art. Many of their contrasts must be accounted for through Fichte's influence on Schiller,[142] and can be seen in the notions of 'Person' and 'Empirical Ego' or in the relation between art and politics proposed by Schiller.

Fichte argued that freedom is finite and depends on the conditions of its realization. He maintained that it is possible and necessary to give a deduction of the social and political regulations underlying any relation between rational beings.[143] While Kant argues that the question of political rights has to do with a prior understanding of individual moral freedom, Fichte holds that the political realm must be given autonomy from and priority over moral being. Further, Fichte reckons that the community can have priority over the individuals who constitute it, so that a State is the political agency of the community and *gives* a particular freedom and individuality.[144]

It is this priority of State over individual, of politics over morality, that underlies Schiller's argument in the opening letters of the *Aesthetic Education of Man* that fine art is a preparation for politics. Through its ability to 'grasp the universal' and to 'master matter', fine art develops in men the individuality legitimated by a State. Fine art presents, and in other ways gives individuals their experience of, a notion of universality which is commensurate with the demands of State and communal life.[145] It becomes a means of educating men by leading them, and it is subject to an external political necessity. Accordingly, it seems that Schiller conceives of fine art as a means to a political end, in a fashion similar to Fichte's, in *The Vocation of a Scholar*, where culture is limited to skill and described as a means to the end of man's harmony with himself.[146] At best, Schiller seeks through pedagogic art to realize the obligation which Fichte expects the State to realize through educational institutions.

By contrast with Schiller and Fichte, Kant accepts that fine art requires skill and as such may play some role in political life. But he looks elsewhere for justifications of aesthetic necessity. Artistic beauty may be a preparation for morality, for Kant, but that does not make beauty a *means* to a moral end. Thus, making a judgement of taste is not a *means* either to developing humanity or to the realization of morality: to make the judgement *is* to promote our humanity. It is this difference that is suggested by saying that fine art participates in progressive culture and is not merely a *means* to educating men to the end of a political community. Kant ascribes necessity to beauty and finds an analogy between beauty and morality on the basis of their autonomy, their purposiveness, and their ability to treat subjects as ends in themselves. He does not subject individuals to the demands of a State which is the political agency of a community over and above individuals. Rather than being a preparation for politics, for Kant fine art is a preparation for morality.

Further, Kant's conception of the necessity of beauty leads him to propose that it allows a transition from mere sensual pleasure to moral feeling.[147] Schiller takes up this refrain, and stresses the role of genius in fine art; but he combines it with Fichte's theory of instinct to argue that beauty can determine moral value. The beauty of an action ensures that the actor can be certain that his action is morally correct.[148] And while Kant tries to promote a harmony between nature and fine art because he accepts and worries about a distinction and relation between subject and object, Schiller is interested only in the development of a Third Way which, influenced by Fichte, eliminates the thing-in-itself and denies the distinction of subject from object for the sake of a harmony between sense and freedom.[149]

If the Fichtean influences which underlie Schiller's understanding of the relations between, first, nature and reason, and second, between individuals, differ from Kant's conception of those relations, then so will his understanding of culture, and fine art's participation in culture, differ from that of Kant.

Schiller claims for fine art the ability to define the distinctive nature of man, and this reveals another important difference between his thought and Kant's. This has to do with art's ability to penetrate to a transcendental reality. Schiller begins by distinguishing a material, physical, or sensuous impulse from a formal impulse in man's character, and his intention is to show that this bifurcation may be overcome in a state in which man will be neither too rational nor given over to sensuous pursuits. He wants to produce an aesthetic state which is significantly similar to Fichte's State in that it describes a relation between individuals rather than one between rational faculties in a state of consciousness. Only beauty can achieve this end-state because genius yields the only sensuous experience that is capable of gaining access to a transcendental reality.

And, here, the superficial similarity in Kant's and Schiller's attitude to culture covers very different conceptions of cultural development. Fichte's and Schiller's use of Pure and Empirical Ego and Person and Condition have already been mentioned. Schiller goes on to use Fichte's theory of knowledge as 'reciprocal action'[150] to interpret Kant's 'free play of faculties' anthropologically, as something about the activity of a developing human reason.[151] Taking the goal of the free play of the faculties to be the cultivation of a harmony between a formal and a material or sensuous drive,[152] the result Schiller leads to is not moral freedom in Kant's sense but the culture of an Aesthetic State which is seen as a 'Third Way' proper to the unity of an 'Ideal Man'.[153] Only men are able to follow the path of an aesthetic politics for they alone suffer this bifurcation between sensuous and formal impulses.

Moreover, Schiller argues that the Third Way is both distinctive of man and definitive of the Ideal Man. Thus, the Ideal Man, rather than being an individual in a community seeking to actualize moral good in this world, becomes the subject devoted to promoting a community with other objects on the basis of his or her aesthetic appreciation of man and nature.[154] And the aesthetic, playful reconciliation of nature and freedom in the aesthetic state is held up as the true state of man: 'For it must be said once and for all that man only plays when he is a man in the full sense of the word, and *he is fully human only when he plays*'.[155] Consequently, not only do subjects truly know themselves as subjects through art, but in the aesthetic state they also know themselves and others in a truly human way.

Given their separate starting-points and their different interests, it is unlikely that Schiller and Kant will agree in their understanding of fine art, culture, or man. While the former may argue that an art created by genius reconciles nature to freedom in a distinctively human way that is also exclusively and truly revelatory of our capabilities and character, Kant looks for a more wide-ranging harmony between nature and freedom. By Kant's argument, aesthetic practice is only a part of human activity, and even if it is distinctive of man, it is not satisfactorily definitive of him. That is, Kant generally does not ascribe the revelatory power that Schiller attributes to art by saying that man is 'fully human only when he plays'.[156]

Kant comes closest to saying that fine art is revelatory when he gives aesthetic ideas some cognitive import. Rational and aesthetic ideas are interrelated through aesthetic expression, and the principle cognitive use of aesthetic ideas is as a medium for exploring our subjective, human response to the rational regulative ideas which guide and organize our experience. And, in the instances that an Idea of Man orders our experience, works of art make possible our comprehension of that Idea. But Kant does not go on to make any claims to exclusiveness: fine art comprehends other Ideas as well as that of Man, and other modes of experience and thought contribute to our comprehension of men.[157]

In one instance, Kant writes of Man as an ideal for beauty, and this marks another difference between Kant and Schiller. An ideal is 'the representation of an individual existence as adequate to an idea'.[158] In Kant's argument man is the ideal because his beauty highlights those characteristics that make beauty significant to our practical lives. All 'that our reason connects with the moral good in the idea of the highest finality' can be given 'embodiment' in our experience of human beauty.[159] But in an argument like Schiller's for the exemplary value of fine art, the fact that *man* is an ideal of beauty is not of much help. The argument needs to conclude that *beauty* is an ideal for man, so that members of the aesthetic state best exemplify the characteristics proper to man. But the fact that man is an ideal of beauty has nothing to say of ideal man as such. And, in any case, what Kant says implies that man is an ideal because of his possession of a moral character—which contrasts with Schiller's ideal of an aesthetic reconciliation of moral and rational principles with sensuousness. Moreover, Kant quickly adds that an estimation according to the standard of such an idea 'can never be purely aesthetic',[160] so that it is an ideal only because it is not 'a simple judgement of taste'—which serves further to qualify any attempt to relate it to Schiller's aesthetic enterprise.

Although man's status as an ideal of beauty does not lend itself to arguments proving the aesthetic character of ideal man, it serves to illuminate other issues. It suggests that for Kant the order and interrelation of the concepts we are concerned with bears an interest that is not Schiller's. We do not seek to discover the nature of man through fine art, nor is fine art constituted by a rational order—perhaps of symbols— which is uniquely true to subjects as subjects. Instead, Kant follows an order of presentation—of man, his beauty, and thence of man's moral qualities as an ideal for beauty—which suggests that a conception of man already underlies our understanding of beauty. As we suggested earlier, other rational principles, such as those of culture as opposed to politics or morality, underlie our understanding of man and fine art, showing how we must think of both. And this too contrasts with Schiller's claim that fine art reveals all about ideal man.

Even if we accept that Kant has a distinctive starting-point, it may be argued, his conception of the nature and content of fine art's comprehension of man comes to agree with that put forward by Schiller.[161] The claim is that both want the nature of fine art and beauty to yield truths about man as he 'really' is and as other modes of thought cannot reveal. In this vein it has been argued that 'it is impossible to exaggerate the importance, for our conception of the Kantian subject', of a particular interpretation of the role of reflective judgements. 'The emergence of reflective judgement in the philosophy of Kant is not now the familiar addition of a new mediating faculty, but the *transformation of a whole philosophy*'.[162] Taking aesthetic judgements as a paradigm of reflective ones, the author argues that their use 'is tantamount to introducing an anthropological postulate, for [the] *constitution [of a] feeling which is universal* implies *a depth structure of humanity* which is, let us not forget, an individual possession or potentiality and not merely an abstract presupposition of science'.[163] Others see the entire critical enterprise as an anthropology,[164] and aesthetic judgements are put forward as the final moment of self-reflection in which men comprehend themselves in a human way.

So far as this reading agrees with Schiller in giving fine art an especial revelatory and definitive role, it will fall to the same criticisms. It would make aesthetic necessity independent of moral or cultural force, for the real expression and development of our nature will be in the aesthetic state. We could still give validity to moral or cultural activity, but they would have to serve the balance between nature and reason that is peculiar to human subjects and available only in fine art. The trouble with such readings is that they reverse the proper order of things. Culture is seen as a function of the concept of man which, in turn, is gained through aesthetic experience. Accordingly, aesthetic experience interrelates knowledge and morality in a mix which is uniquely suited to human beings in that their true character is revealed to us through the experience of fine art. And, consequently, our understanding of human nature, whose pinnacle is the 'Ideal Man', has a hierarchy which begins with fine art and beauty in which nature and reason are interrelated, and proceeds through culture and politics. However, against such a claim, and leaving aside questions of whether Kant can condone the existence of an 'aesthetic experience', we must remember that concepts like art, person, and man are themselves cultural constructs in a sense important to the argument. An explanation of culture in terms of anthropology is inadequate because for Kant the latter must itself be explained as a feature of the former. For culture is the more general relation between nature and reason, and we may expect a more general dichotomy to explain the particular variations.[165]

The enquiry conducted in this chapter suggests that the argument for aesthetic necessity will not be straightforward. Culture's mediation introduces complications that do not lend themselves to neat, short resolution. Indeed, it is not yet clear what cultural duty could consist in nor how it is related to the supreme principle of morality. Nor do we know how aesthetic practice can take on such an obligation.

This returns us to the second objection noted earlier, that it is not yet clear that cultural behaviour and artistic intention, understood as the grasp and use of meanings, are possible in the phenomenal world. Kant must be able to give some serious explanation of what it means to set rational ends in nature, for the complex account of aesthetic and cultural practice which this chapter has shown him to propose would be poorly defended if it proved impossible to conceive of objects as rational ends requiring an interpretation and understanding of meanings. In fact, Kant considers the issue in other parts of the third *Critique*, and if his arguments are successful, then we may conceive of our experience in nature as permitting a unity between subjects as subjects.

These issues are considered in the next chapter. Following that, we must examine the relation of fine art to the *sensus communis* to see what sort of necessity is in question.

IV

Fine Art and Natural Necessity

IT was proposed that it makes best sense to see fine art as a participant in culture rather than in politics or morality. Both features of fine art—its beauty and its nature as art—were essential to that participation, and their importance raises further questions. For it is not yet clear that the activities of producing and appreciating fine art are possible in the phenomenal world. We know that fine art contributes to culture through the particular use of reason that it sustains, and that it requires us to understand and interpret works conceived of as goals. That is, it is not understood fruitfully in terms of causal determinations; rather, the construction of art requires intentional rational action, and its interpretation, appreciation, and production are supposed to occur in the causally determined phenomenal world. Kant must explain this possibility, and must argue that we may conceive of rational ends in nature and that nature is not fully explicable by scientific mechanical laws—at least to the extent that it cannot exclude our rational interpretative and constructive activity. For this would go to explain what we need to know: that genius may and must be seen as a feature of the rational will that explains the intentional production of fine art in the phenomenal world.

This enquiry is essential to our argument for the necessity of beauty. There is a gap between *explaining* the possibility of fine art and judgements of taste and *justifying* ascriptions of necessity to an experience of beauty by reference to the part played by fine art in constructing a morally valuable community between rational and feeling subjects. Here, it is because we alter the very relation of nature to reason by setting a rational end in nature that we participate in *constructing* a relation between the two elements by setting rational ends. Further, it is because the end is an aesthetic one that we construct a particular sort of relation through producing and appreciating fine art, and hence contribute to cultural change. By then arguing that this cultural change is morally valuable, we will have gained a justification of the necessity of beauty as cultural activity. Clearly, the account of necessity being proposed depends for its effectiveness on at least being able to conceive of the intentional production of fine art in nature.

We may raise two doubts about an argument such as the one proposed. First, it has been argued that it is possible and sufficient to discover an epistemological guarantee for the compulsion aesthetic judgements exercise on subjects. Aesthetic judgements, the argument goes, are like cognitive ones: both are like reports about the world with which any rational and perceiving subject will agree because of the nature of the world, the mind, and its objects.[1] If this claim were successful, it could make redundant the 'cultural' argument for necessity and so make it unnecessary to argue for the possibility of fine art and its moral connotations. However, the latter would not thereby be refuted. And if we are able to explain that morally valuable aesthetic ends can be realized, we can gain a justification of the necessity of beauty that may be not only compatible with or complementary to an epistemological deduction, but will be able to explain some puzzling features of the latter. For in his deduction Kant moves from arguing that we *can* make aesthetic judgements, because the necessary conditions are satisfied, to the claim that we *ought* as a duty to agree with others' judgements. And this imperative mode stands in need of explanation. We shall return to this issue later.

The second doubt will be put forward and dealt with here by looking at the context in which the occurrence of fine art in the phenomenal world is relevant. Kant holds that although they make different ontological claims and are based on different principles, judgements about nature are synthesized with ones supposing that rational human freedom exists. The possibility of such a synthesis is guaranteed by a 'third thing'—God—who is the single 'supersensible substratum' underlying both freedom and nature.[2] Based on this synthesis, culture and fine art are said to manifest our continuing reorganization of the natural and human world, and it is the reshaping of physical and social nature that leads to the realization of morality in the empirical world.[3] But we may doubt the possibility of this general synthesis, pointing out that Kant cannot permit morality to depend on nature. And even if the proposed synthesis were possible, as in the *summum bonum*, it would be taken to concern only the interrelation between virtue and happiness in an individual. It contains no claim about a general relation of nature to human freedom.

To explain these points further we may look at two background issues: one pertains to the second *Critique* and the issue of freedom; the other concerns the nature of causal explanations and their contrast with intentional accounts of human activity. This will prepare us for other features of Kant's argument.

Reason and Freedom: Intentions and Causes

An account of Kant's moral theory can begin with the *Foundations*, where he examines the nature of morality by analyzing 'common moral knowledge'. Knowing that killing and stealing are wrong does not tell us what makes them immoral. Only by understanding *why* an act is moral do we understand the nature of morality. To explain the latter, Kant assumes that our ordinary moral claims are valid and analyzes them to see what element in them makes them valid. In this analysis we cannot rely on empirical generalizations of how we actually act. Moral claims tell us how we *should* act, and that we actually behave in one way does not imply that we should continue to do so.

Kant's claim is that the universality and necessity of moral imperatives are crucially related to the use of reason. Where inductive generalizations can only tell us how we actually behave, the a priori character of reason can give us insight into how we *should* behave. Further, for Kant reason is at the very basis of moral imperatives and action because, first, to be moral we must be free and, second, we are free in an important sense only when we act rationally. When we act rationally we exhibit an autonomy and lay claim to 'dignity'.

The relation between morality, freedom, and reason can be presented by contrast with the behaviour of animals and inanimate objects. To be moral we must be free because the ability to act morally presupposes the ability to act. Only a being who can be singled out as the source of his own choices, who can decide to follow one or other course of action, or can choose to not act, can be held capable of the acts of commission or omission to which we ascribe moral approbation or blame.

If there were no such sources of free action, we should have no justification for ascribing them responsibility. An apple may fall off a tree, or one billiard ball may be impelled to move by another, but it is inappropriate to blame either for its movements. As they are incapable of choosing to act, we cannot ascribe praise or blame to them for any act they have performed. Accordingly, if all our behaviour were compelled in the way that the behaviour of inanimate objects is compelled by external determining causes, then we too could not be held responsible for our behaviour because we should have no control over it and should not be free to do otherwise.

An objection to this proposal is that it conflates an independence from external influences with independence from all preceding determination. A being may be self-determining in the sense of being determined by its own nature, and so may be independent of external influences, yet is still subject to determination by preceding events. Thus, a person would be said to be responsible, because his action is self-determined, even though his action is not free. One part of Kant's reply to this objection is to dismiss it as a mere 'freedom of the turnspit', which, once it is wound up, follows a predetermined course. The suggestion is that we cannot describe such 'self-determination' coherently if we try to distinguish it from the factors which determine its behaviour; and where we identify this relation, we also see that self-determination is only a case of an individual being determined by, at best, its 'own nature'. Because its actions are so completely determined by its own nature, it does not possess the freedom where 'an act *and* its opposite must be within the power of the subject at the moment of its taking place'.[4]

Kant's further thesis describing this freedom can be expressed as follows. Not only must we be free if we are to be moral, but we are free only when we act for reasons. By contrast with animals, for example, whose behaviour can be explained by reference to determining instincts and responses to external stimuli, and by contrast with inanimate objects, whose behaviour is determined by other objects, to explain human behaviour we point to the reasons for action. To explain why an agent is walking along a street, we point to his reasons: that he wants to go to the bank to draw out some money. That is, his reasons for acting explain his behaviour; and on the face of it, at least, this account differs from the type of explanation we give for objects and animals that we do not think of as free or able to act intentionally. Further, our reason for acting may be to gain the satisfaction of a desire or natural, sensuous inclination, as much as it may be to gain a moral end. In both cases there is 'a rational will underlying our actions'.[5]

In Kant's earlier work the relation between freedom and reason is more restricted in that Kant thinks we act rationally only where we follow the moral law—where a free will and one following moral laws are identical. That this identification is unsatisfactory may be shown by arguing that it makes immoral behaviour impossible. If Kant holds that when we follow our inclinations, rather than pursue the moral law, we are not free because our behaviour is determined by our natural being rather than our rational character, then we are rendered incapable of being immoral. For if the actions of a being are not free, it cannot be held responsible for them at all, and so cannot be accused of failing to be moral or immoral. As its behaviour is determined when it follows its inclinations, it could not be held responsible or liable to punishment or blame. It is either moral or incapable of morality. It cannot be immoral.

However, in the Second *Critique* Kant argues that freedom is transcendentally presupposed by the moral law, and that this freedom is a capacity to follow or reject the moral law. As we can choose to follow our inclinations, we can be accused of immorality for failing to follow the moral law. Where he had formerly identified freedom with following the moral law, in the second *Critique* he provides a significantly different proposal: 'though freedom is certainly the *ratio essendi* of the moral law, the latter is the *ratio cognoscendi* of freedom'.[6]

Freedom exists and is the transcendental basis for the moral law, for we cannot pursue the latter unless we also suppose the former, but we only know our freedom through the choices we make. We cannot expect to explain the source of this sort of freedom: a causal account would be self-defeating and one in terms of freedom useless. The existence of freedom and reason is a fact we must just accept, and its nature is understood by examining its exercise in choosing ends—in our intentional behaviour.

This claim for freedom raises at least two issues: First, if we can choose not to be moral, then we can be free but not rational in so far as the moral law is rational. By making freedom include the capacity to decide to follow reason *or* desire Kant is also making moral justification more difficult. Second, we need some account of how we can conceive of human behaviour as free in the sense proposed. To be able to choose between moral law or inclinations is to have a purpose or intention. We act for a reason, and our behaviour is based on that reason even though it may not be one that satisfies the moral law. It is necessary to provide some account of this sort of explanation in order to distinguish it from explanations in terms of determining causes which, according to the first *Critique*, constitute our experience.

We shall return to the second issue later. Of the first issue: the notion of freedom was broadened to cover more than the pursuit of the moral law. But this seems to extend the notion too far. For if we choose to be determined by our inclinations, we are free because we have made a choice, yet have not necessarily acted rationally. So Kant must be mistaken in supposing that we are free only to the extent that we act rationally.

Part of Kant's answer to this is as follows. Were our actions entirely determined by inclinations, our behaviour could be merely random and, consequently, not free. We should be led by the strongest desire we experienced at any moment, become diverted by the pressure of newer inclinations, and so shift into pursuit of some other desire before the first one was satisfied because the later desire happens to be stronger. And although we could be said to be free even when we choose to follow our inclinations rather than the moral law, nevertheless, when we give in to desires and the resulting randomness of behaviour we also give up our ability to choose. We become passive to the force of natural laws and are as determined in our behaviour as animals. Thus, we do not so much exercise our ability to choose when we prefer inclinations over reason as give up that ability. We thereby defeat ourselves, and could not succeed in our intention without also failing in it. Consequently, it is only when the individual chooses his goals and accepts the business of making choices that he can be said to be free. And we may add here that it is the task of culture to promote this ability to make choices.

The second part of Kant's answer is this: desires based on inclinations and arbitrary preferences are idiosyncratic and particular to individuals. The goals involved can never be universalized even though contingently they may be generally accepted. Consequently, independence of such inclinations or freedom from such causal determinations can be ensured by adopting a maxim or principle of action which is universally valid. Its very universality ensures that it is independent of animal impulses and natural inclinations; and it establishes the agent's fully free and rational nature.

Indeed, Kant uses the universality of reason to propose a supreme principle for morality: act as if the maxim of your action were to become through your will a universal law of nature. To explain: maxims have goals or ends and a plan or means for achieving that end. Obviously the goal and means are interdependent. And we can test whether a maxim is universalizable by seeing whether it can always govern the behaviour of perfectly rational beings. If it cannot, it fails to be universalizable and so cannot be rational. Consequently it cannot be moral either.

Universality can fail in two ways. In adopting a maxim an agent adopts a goal; if the goal is adopted because it is universalizable,[7] then in accepting the maxim the agent is accepting whatever result follows from every rational being also acting upon that maxim. That is, there are really two goals: first, the goal the agent has in view when adopting a maxim as an individual, and, second, the goal he finds himself adopting when he accepts the maxim as a principle which every rational being will always follow. But the two ends may conflict: the pursuit of the second may frustrate the first. For example, the agent may make a false promise of repayment in order to obtain money quickly. If this maxim were one which every rational being were always to try to adopt, then the individual goal of obtaining money for himself by false promises would be frustrated because the institution of promising would become vacuous and he would be unable to succeed in his goal by this means.

In this failure of universality, Kant holds, the will is in contradiction with itself. Another failure occurs when the contradiction of the will is so radical that the pursuit of the second goal frustrates goals essential to human life. Then the maxim cannot be *conceived* of as a universal law of nature. Thus, what we have through the demand for universality is a procedure for distinguishing immoral from other acts. If the maxim fails to be willed without contradiction or cannot be conceived of as a universal law, it is not rational and cannot be moral.

Even as this plausibly gives us a way of identifying acts which fail to be moral, we need a more positive criterion for moral laws and ends. All ends and goals which are not self-contradictory will be compatible with each other and incompatible at least in part with self-contradictory maxims. Whereas a failure in universality gave us a procedure for distinguishing immoral from other acts, the compatibility of maxims yields a procedure for developing a moral system. Kant may be taken to suggest that an end is good if and only if it can form part of a systematic harmony of universalizable ends: if it can be part of the Kingdom of Ends.

In showing how the perfectly rational individual will behave, Kant sets out the features of our autonomy. From this perspective human beings are thought of as free agents, as possessors of a free will capable of acting independently of natural laws and animal being. It is through this that they gain autonomy, as agents neither limited to 'the freedom of the turnspit'[8] nor determined by 'alien causes'. Instead we see ourselves able to give laws for ourselves,[9] and in culture develop and realize this perception in the face of natural inclinations.

Our autonomy, the capacity for following rational moral ends, is the source of our 'dignity'. In the *Foundations* Kant acknowledges making a 'step into metaphysics', where we not only consider acts and their maxims for their universalizability but also suppose that we are explaining something about these acts by associating them with the actor—their autonomous source. And so far as he is understood to have the capacity for acting to gain universalizable rational ends, the individual has 'dignity'. He has a capacity for choice, a *Willkür*, which can be 'determined to an action *only so far as an individual has incorporated* [an incentive] *into his maxim*'.¹⁰ While he may on occasion choose inclinations, his capacity for reason must be respected as the moral law itself.

Clearly, the 'fully rational being' serves here only as a model. By contrast with this paragon who *always* behaves according to rational laws, we are capable of irrational behaviour. But although we cannot be rid of our inclinations—some, like hunger and thirst, are essential to our continued existence—their satisfaction or 'happiness', which is the state of their satisfaction, can be governed by reason. In the early works Kant presents this relation between reason and inclination as an individual possession much as autonomy, dignity, and free will are also individual possessions. Here the highest good or *summum bonum* for us consists in an individual maintaining a balance between virtue—his power to act according to moral law—and his happiness—the satisfaction of desires compatible with moral law. The moral law provides an unconditional criterion for our behaviour, whose requirements are unqualified, while happiness is conditioned by the former.

However, later the *summum bonum* is given a new character. The highest good now covers a general synthesis between reason and nature¹¹ which obviously includes individuals as well. Happiness is denied its former prominence, and Kant argues that nature in general is the empirical element involved in the *summum bonum*.¹²

Nature's relation to rational freedom is a complicated business, and it is important to give reasons for enlarging our concern from one in virtue and happiness alone to one that covers the general interrelation of reason with nature. Kant attributes to reason a striving for totality that is exhibited in moral reason as an attempt both to delineate the absolute form of moral action—among other things this required actions to be capable of being universalized—and to set out the promotion of the highest good as the supreme content of moral action. Accordingly, it is insufficient to explore only the formal, 'absolute', or 'unconditioned'¹³ element if we wish to understand a system of practical reason. We need also to conceive of a material, 'comprehensive', and 'whole' element which tells us not only how to act but, in addition, proposes what must be actualized through action. Thus, although at first Kant writes that 'in the absence of all reference to an end, no determination of the will can take place in man',¹⁴ he proposes later that it is necessary 'to conceive of some sort of final end for all our actions and abstentions, *taken as a whole*, an end which can be justified by reason and whose absence would hinder moral decision'.[15]

The suggestion is that ends cannot be conceived of piecemeal but must form an interlinked whole, and this involves two mutually qualifying claims. First, Kant holds that in the interrelation between the two elements, the formal moral law is the 'rational condition of the employment of our freedom and, as such, of itself alone lays its obligation upon us, independently of any end as its material condition'. Nevertheless, he goes on, second, 'this also defines for us a final end, and does so a priori, and makes it obligatory upon us to strive towards its attainment. This end is the *summum bonum*, as the highest good *in the world* possible through freedom'.[16]

Kant explains that the final end involves happiness, but proposes that any justification of the interconnection between reason and happiness will be a general argument justifying our conception of the world as moral nature.[17] This is essential because in so far as nature is considered as a system or totality, any relation of its parts with reason will carry implications for the whole. No one part of it may be associated with moral rules to the exclusion of other parts, and our understanding of one proposed interrelation—between virtue and happiness—will require us to comprehend the other elements.

A similar tendency to totality is manifested in actions, for we give continuity and unity to a series of actions when we talk of a moral character. As a formal law, moral reason relates separately to individual acts; but if it says nothing of the continuity between either past and future choices of agents or interrelations between the consequences of their actions, it becomes difficult to talk of moral personalities of agents. Kant proposes that in spite of the absolute freedom of the will, it is essential to integrate the discrete expressions of our spontaneity into a whole both 'within' individuals and in relation to others. And in *Religion* he argues that we must give some consideration to the consequences of our actions.[18] However, although the representation of ends or consequences is essential if men are to act, thought of consequences only accompanies a moral act without actually determining it.[19] Nevertheless, it succeeds in placing the action in a broader context of promoting the highest good.

Further, as a duty, the highest good is presented by reason 'to *all* rational beings as the goal of all their moral wishes'.[20] The system of morality becomes an area in which the greatest moral perfection is combined with the greatest degree of satisfaction in nature.[21] It establishes not just a common tendency to universalization but *a single moral end*, the highest good, which unifies all the discrete wills as their common object.[22] For if an agent is to examine the consequences of his actions in a context of duties or rules that we may expect all other subjects to be capable of accepting, this is bound to bring into focus the whole range of his actions *and* those of others.

Moreover we must interrelate the two distinct totalities of rational freedom and nature. For moral reason to be more than merely formal, we must consider the end which actions are striving towards. These actions must not only take account of our own past and future actions but also consider those of others. And if we are to take account of the consequences of our actions, it becomes necessary for us to face the problem of how far the will can act in the external world to ensure that moral law is embodied in empirical nature. As our knowledge of the latter itself forms a totality, this requires Kant to discover a relation between the two totalities. He writes of the world having a 'final end' in men 'subject to moral laws'[23] and of 'the reciprocal relation subsisting between the world and [a] moral end, the possibility of realizing it under external [that is, "outside" the individual] conditions'.[24] Thus we are led to consider 'the course of the world from a moral viewpoint'.[25]

The only guarantee that Kant can discover for such a total synthesis is one based on God who, as the substrate for both freedom and necessity, binds the two elements into a synthetic, heterogeneous unity. The claims made for such a synthesis may be questioned and qualified; it is necessary, first, to understand another of its features. For morality depends on our freedom to act. If it is to be realized in this world, we must be able to conceive of rational ends, of goals open to interpretation and understanding, in this causally determined world.

That is, the suggested expansion of the relation between virtue and happiness indicates another feature of Kant's moral theory. As we have a rational *and* animal character, we will not *always* behave rationally. And as imperfectly rational creatures, rational action exerts a *compulsion* upon us, or lays an obligation on us, which is contrasted with the conflicting pull of inclination. Perfectly rational beings would not feel this compulsion or necessity because they are unable to behave in any other way. Only creatures who can be led by their inclinations *or* their reason will know the pursuit of rational action as an obligation.

The recognition that moral law imposes a requirement not on a rational being but on one who is both rational *and* animal is developed in and after the second *Critique*. Although the contrast is present in the

Foundations in the form of the holy and moral wills, Kant there develops the distinction in relation to the moral law rather than in terms of our human character. Only later does he show that the highest good is not to be realized in some transcendental ahistorical reality. Freedom is meant to be actualized in the sensible world.[26]

The question of how such realization can take place involves the issue we raised earlier: of the contrast between causal and intentional accounts of human activity. If freedom is to be realized, we must be able to recognize actions and ends in this world. Kant has an account of how this is possible, which we will present shortly, but it may be useful to set out just what the contrast is.

Kant had argued in the First *Critique* that our experience was necessarily causal. All the objects and events in the world of experience and knowledge must be causally determined and capable of being ordered under determinate and necessary natural laws. And so far as we are ourselves members of this phenomenal world, our behaviour must be understood as subject to the same laws and determinations. But this seems to exclude the possibility of our ever knowing ourselves to realize our freedom in this world. And that, in turn, makes moral demands vacuous because causal explanations of our experience seem to leave no room for intentional accounts. In so far as our experience is causal, it cannot be intentional; therefore, it cannot be said to be rational, or free, or moral. Yet Kant's moral theory needs our sensible character: if we cannot account for intentions in this world, we cannot coherently incorporate our sensible character into Kant's moral theory.

The contrast between intentional and causal account may be presented as follows. There is a distinction to be made between on the one hand the motion of our bodies, such as our reflexive blinking at bright light or jerking our knees when struck, and on the other our intentional behaviour. The latter involves something more than bodily movement. By raising his arm, for example, an agent may be engaged in pieces of behaviour as diverse as saluting, bidding at an auction, voting, testing the direction of wind, or touching the ceiling. Accordingly, it may be possible to give a causal explanation of his bodily movements, perhaps even citing the flow of neurophysiological impulses in the brain, so that we have a complete description of the law-governed and causally determined movement of objects, yet still have failed to explain what it means to vote at an election, to go into a bank to cash a cheque, or to perform any of our many intentions. This is because the same bodily movements can have a number of different meanings, and explaining the first need tell us nothing of the second. To explain human behaviour we must show what its purpose is, must point to the intentions and reasons of the actor engaged in it, and so give the physical movements a meaning. As the latter is something more than a set of physical changes, we cannot hope to explain how people behave in following out their intentions if we restrict ourselves to explanations of bodily movements in terms of causality alone. From the physiological explanation of an arm's being raised we cannot infer the meaning of an agent's intention of voting.

The two sorts of explanation seem to be very different. One sees its objects and events being determined by preceding forces which, perhaps, can be specified in terms of, say, spatial and temporal magnitudes, the relation of bodies, regularity of association between events, and various law-governed constants. The other sees agents with purposes who act for reasons and follow, or intentionally subvert, norms. For the former, the self-conception of objects is at best irrelevant to explanations of their behaviour and at worst introduces confusion. Explanation can consist basically in showing that events are instances of well-supported regularities and natural laws, and no special status is accorded to agents when they are the objects being examined and their behaviour is the event being explained. There may be a greater degree of complexity involved, but agents do not differ in kind from other physical mechanisms. The explanation of their 'behaviour' needs only the sort of magnitudes mentioned above, and while we may be ignorant of all its details, with the advance of science in physics, chemistry, biology, and some sorts of psychology, we will be able to discover the natural laws or regularities governing and determining agents' behaviour. At that point we will see that talk of agents' self-consciousness, intentions, and reasons for actions does not point to anything in their actions that cannot be explained completely by using the natural sciences.

To some extent, at least, Kant seems to put forward claims similar to the latter case when he argues that all our experience must be causally determined. For that does not allow for any exception in the case of human actions. But he also comes to accept that we may give other sorts of explanations, and proposes that we can *conceive* of some objects as the result of intentional actions by agents. And, in any case, scientific explanation itself presupposes some purposive order in the world—in spite of the fact that the experience given order in science is causally determined.

The distinctive context and concepts involved in intentional accounts of human actions are signified by Kant when he says of human actions that we always presuppose a 'rational will underlying actions'. And in this context we accept certain justifications for actions which point to the ends individuals are trying to attain, whose pursuit or attainment need not be predicted and need not be subject to nomological laws. In explaining their behaviour we could consider their intentions: rather than seek to show they are instances of well-supported regularities which are determined in a law-like way by preceding causes, we could seek to identify an agent's goal and to interpret the meaning any piece of behaviour has for ourselves and for the actor in relation to the goal. We look not for determining external causes but for the agent's reasons for action. And the relation of instance to generality involved will differ accordingly, as we shall see.

These distinctions obviously have implications for our concern with the possibility of culture, for works of art are produced intentionally. Aesthetic judgements make a demand for universality over autonomous subjects in experience—rather than being mere generalizations about people. We could not hope to appreciate, in common with others, the simplicity of Titian's *Man with a Blue Sleeve*, and to participate in a community with others through such appreciation, if our response were capable of being nothing more than a general but contingent effect caused by the work. Clearly, this requires us to conceive of free agents acting in this world, who are capable of changing themselves. And if the practical necessity of aesthetic judgements is to be justified, it is in order to legitimate the demand it makes on us as members of this world. To show that they are possible, we may examine the possibility of cultural action generally.

The Possibility of Cultural Action

The First *Critique* had argued that freedom and determination were compatible. But a morally viable culture seems to require more, for its development should enable man to liberate himself from the natural forces which both form and pervert his intentions, so that he can realize his freely chosen goals. This requires Kant to show that nature can be conceived of as responsive to human reason and action in that it must be capable of being reshaped as we intend. Otherwise progressive culture is impossible;[27] moreover, cultural duty would be vacuous if its demand could never be attained. At the very least, we must be able to show that we can conceive of rational ends—the objects of human rational activity—and that they cannot be reduced to mere causal mechanisms. And, for our own argument, we must be able to show the possibility and indispensability of conceiving of some objects as works of fine art—as the products of rational activity, which are goals open to interpretation and understanding by rational and feeling subjects, and which can lead to the formation of a morally valuable community.

In the later part of the *Critique of Judgement*, the *Critique of Teleological Judgement*, in the context of objective finality, Kant deals with issues relevant to the existence of fine art. In the Analytic, Kant examines the nature of finality and the different nature of things, including art, considered as ends; the second part of the text is devoted to presenting and resolving an antinomy between mechanistic explanations and teleological accounts of objects in nature. This presentation is taken to show that teleological conceptions are indispensable, and this conclusion could be a step in an argument for the indispensability of our interpretation and appreciation of fine art. First, we must look to the deduction of finality presented in the Introduction to the *Critique of Judgement*.

As we saw, in the Transcendental Dialectic of the First *Critique*—especially in the Appendix, in the Doctrine of Method—and most clearly in the Introduction to the *Critique of Judgement*, Kant argues that in addition to the order gained for experience by deducing a system of categories, we must give to our knowledge of nature an order gained from a 'regulative employment of ideas of pure reason'.[28] The need for the latter is presented in Section V of the *Critique of Judgement*, where Kant deduces 'the principle of the formal finality of nature' as a transcendental principle of judgement.

We know from the deduction that we must use the concept of causality, among other concepts. But we do not know which particular causes will be present in experience.[29] For actual objects, in addition to the characteristics they share merely because they are objects at all, also have distinctive natures, which, consequently, will be determinable in diverse ways. Therefore, each of these empirical objects and its characteristic determinations may be expected to 'have its rule, which is a law, and, consequently, imports necessity'.[30]

In respect of these empirical regularities and rules, Kant thinks that we must consider them as a unity.[31] For in the absence of unity we would understand very little: we would have a fragmented set of experiences of diverse events but be unable to explain them, to give them more or less importance, or to see the relation of one event to another or to all others.

Some order or unity is necessary for empirical understanding, and given that the transcendental deduction has guaranteed a uniform objectivity for all our experience, we may expect that all our knowledge of nature can form a *single* system made up of diverse but interconnected events under natural laws.[32]

The system must be constructed by ordering particulars, but in some cases we do not know which law, principle, or rule is instanced by a particular event.[33] All we have is the event which we couple with an impetus toward systematization: we suppose that the event must be capable of being part of an explanatory structure. Now, in some cases we know which rule will explain a particular event, and, by subsuming the former under the latter, we go some way toward systematization because we know the place of that law within the system. Judgement, as a 'faculty for thinking the particular under the universal',[34] is *determinant* here, having to deal only with given particulars and universals. However, the large variety of possible determinations in nature introduces the possibility that determinant judgements may fail because it is not clear which rule is applicable in any instance. In such cases, it is necessary for judgement, as it were, 'to give itself a rule'. That is, our judgement is based on the supposition that although we do not know which rule is instanced, some rule must be. Such *reflective* judgements are 'compelled to ascend from the particular in nature to the universal' and, in order to succeed, they 'stand in need of a principle'.[35]

In accounting for this principle, we know it is necessary to suppose that there is an empirical order if we are to have empirical knowledge of nature.[36] Further, we must suppose that the order is one we can understand. Moreover, we have seen that although in some cases we know how events fit into that order, there will always be ones where we do not know which universal covers the particular events. In these instances, where reflective judgements must be made, Kant suggests we suppose that we *can* understand events even though we may not do so as yet. But Kant goes on to give a particular slant to the requirement that some order or unity is necessary for our explanation of empirical events. For he proposes that reflective judgements are based on a principle according to which undetermined empirical events and laws must be thought to belong to 'a unity such as they would have if an understanding (though it be not ours) had supplied them for the benefit of our cognitive faculties, so as to render possible a system of experience according to particular natural laws'.[37] The principle is adopted by us in making reflective judgements, and is not derived from either things themselves or some actually existent mind that gives nature its order. But, unless it is true that the natural order is rational, we cannot hope to achieve the knowledge of objects and events that we seek. Thus, in our investigation of nature, we must suppose it true that nature is structured for or 'shows some regard' for our cognitive faculties. Only this supposition and its assumption that the natural order results from the working of some mind like ours, Kant holds, allows us to go beyond the contingency of undifferentiated nature to arrive at empirical laws based on the minimal coherence obtained for our experience through the transcendental deduction of categories.[38]

We must, therefore, see the order of nature as purposive or directed toward certain ends—in this case toward the end of our comprehension of it. We must apply reflective judgements and 'must regard nature' in their application 'according to a principle of finality for our cognitive faculty'.[39]

Having distinguished determinate from reflective judgements and having argued for the transcendental necessity of a principle for the application of the latter, Kant goes on to divide reflective judgements into those which have to do with ends in nature and those which have an end in a particular harmony of faculties in the judging subject. That is, he distinguishes teleological from aesthetic judgement.[40] In aesthetic judgements we suppose that the end or purpose of order is to suit a particular state of mind of the subject. In teleological judgements we suppose that the *object* must be purposive in its relation to other objects or its parts must be purposive in relation to the whole. That is, in teleology, the order and arrangement of the parts, for example, are explained by reference to their ability to bring about the whole.

It could be, of course, that an object's order has as its mechanism, or as the agent of its order, not nature but our actions.[41] Such objects are instances of art, 'where we realise a preconceived concept of an object which we set before ourselves as an end'.[42] These too will be understood teleologically, so far as they may be conceived of as rational ends. But before looking at this possibility in any detail, we must consider other issues in Kant's account of teleology.

By deducing the principle of finality Kant shows that teleological judgements are possible. We may legitimately conceive of nature in terms of ends,[43] and where an object is thought of as an end, the conditions for its existence cannot be determined without prior conception of the result they are expected to gain. The object, taken as an end, 'points out the appearances and problems to which the causal principle

should address itself'.[44] It is as if the conception of the object is
necessary to its existence in the sense of being the cause of its parts
coming together to form the object.[45] Where 'the object itself (its form
or real existence) as an effect is thought to be possible only through the
concept of it, there we imagine an end'.[46]

In summary, the order we give to our knowledge of nature supposes
that events are causally interrelated. The transcendental deduction of
categories has shown the necessity of causality; but it does not tell us
which causes will be instantiated in empirical nature. In our attempt to
order the diversity of empirical events, we are led to accept the principle
that we 'must *estimate* the possibility of all events in material nature . . .
on mere mechanical laws',[47] and to use causality and its embodiment in
mechanical laws as a principle of organization for empirical events.[48]
However, while this principle may be necessary for giving order to our
knowledge of nature, we cannot infer that the unity of empirical
knowledge is a consequence of the unity of things in themselves. By
accepting the latter we would overstep the critical limits of thought and
mistake something true of our approach for something true of objects.[49]

This order of our knowledge of nature cannot admit of a free causality
in nature, and all events are thought of as determined according to
mechanical laws. However, Kant goes on to argue in the *Critique of
Teleological Judgement* that the development and nature of this order
cannot *show* that *all* events are causally necessary and determined
according to mechanical laws. It is a principle *we adopt*, and will not be
proved by the order it makes possible. Thus, to say that we must explain
events in nature 'on mere mechanical laws' is not to 'assert that they are
solely possible in this way, that is, to the exclusion of every other sort of
causality'.[50] By accepting mechanical laws as a way of 'estimating the
possibility of all events in material nature' at best we indicate 'that I *ought*
at all times to *reflect* upon these things *according to the principle* of the
simple mechanism of nature, and, consequently, push my investigation
with it as far as I can, because unless I make it the basis of my research,
there can be no knowledge of nature in the true sense of the term at
all'.[51] But we may also, when the occasion presents itself, 'follow the trail
of a principle which is radically different from explanation by the
mechanism of nature, namely the principle of final causes. For reflection according to the first mechanism is not thereby superseded'.[52]

In putting forward this last claim, Kant depends on his resolution of
an antinomy between mechanical and teleological principles.[53] Both
mechanical and teleological principles give us ways of talking about

order in the world, and apply only to appearances.[54] We cannot assert that the use of either leads us to misdescribe the world of things in themselves.[55]

Further, of the two principles, explanations in terms of mechanical laws may be given priority because their use depends on a mechanism that the transcendental deduction has validated. As our use of causality as a principle of order and explanation is based on its constitution of experience, 'we may and should explain all products and events of nature, even the most purposive, so far as in our power lies, on mechanical lines—and it is impossible for us to assign the limits of our powers when confined to the pursuit of enquiries of this kind'.[56]

However, we also discern numerous instances of the inadequacy of mechanistic explanations. This is not simply a consequence of the extent of contemporary scientific knowledge. In the case of works of art it could be argued that intentional descriptions are indispensable for investigation, and cannot be displaced by causal and mechanistic explanations.[57] This is because works of art are ends in the natural world whose structure and design calls for explanation by reference to rational agents[58] and cannot be explained satisfactorily by causal determinations.

To develop this account further, we must show at least that explanations along mechanistic lines cannot provide a satisfactory account of rational, intentional ends. An argument put forward in this context is as follows. It denies that the 'causal idea' can be 'the means to a true insight into the [first] and absolute grounds of organised life' because, it claims, 'within phenomena themselves the infinite complexity which every organic natural form possesses for us points to the limits of the powers' of mechanical explanation.[59] The suggestion is that a causal explanation of ends will never be entirely satisfactory: because there is such an infinite complexity in the number and sorts of events involved, we cannot hope to provide a causal explanation of organisms, their coming into existence or their behaviour. As intentional ends are similar to organisms in being conceived of as ends,[60] by showing that the one cannot be explained mechanistically we also show the inadequacy of mechanistic explanations of intentional, rational ends.

However, *this* stress on infinite complexity does not work, for it is not clear either that there is infinite complexity or that nature cannot be understood because of it. Natural laws allow for infinite application— this is part of what is involved in saying that natural laws are generalizations which go to explain events—and the possibility of infinite complexity in natural events does not show the limitation of causal mechanistic laws because these general rules may well be capable of application to an infinite number of cases while themselves being simple. Consequently, the possibility of infinite complexity in nature is meaningless as a basis for denying the power, range, or possibility of mechanistic explanations. The assertion merely denies the comprehensiveness of causal explanations without argument.

Nor can it be claimed that the inadequacy of causal explanations is simply a consequence of our inability to rationalize the 'inner possibility' of things. By *this* account, although we may be able to explain events as the result of preceding events in nature, we do not go outside experience by retracing the sequence of causal connections. One event may precede and determine another and its occurrence may explain the occurrence of the later event, but their 'inner possibility', or why these rather than other phenomenal objects exist or relate to each other, is not something we can expect or seek to explain. It seems that we must simply accept their existence and nature as a fact. Further, such passivity is supposed to signify a limitation of our reason and ability to explain events. We are brought to explain events because they are objective. This means that their behaviour and order is distinct from our perceptions of them or our desires or intentions towards them. *We* must explain them in order to understand their behaviour whereas, by contrast, a divine intelligence may create what it perceives. For such an intelligence a distinction between perceiving something and creating the order perceived does not exist. It is only because of the passive nature of our capacity for reason that we need to explain events. And just because of those limitations we will never be able to understand their 'inner possibility'.

But if this is successful as an argument for the insufficiency of causal explanations, it also proves the insufficiency of teleological ones because it points to the limitation of our reason generally. If we cannot explain 'inner possibilities', we cannot explain them teleologically or causally, and this feature does not serve to distinguish causal explanations, on account of their power, from other judgements. After all, teleological judgements do not provide answers either, unless the very existence of a design leads us to ascribe it to a designer—an ascription that violates the critical limitation of teleology by wrongly denoting reality as purposive when it should be our conception of reality that we denote.

Perhaps the indispensability of teleological judgements may be treated as a specification of the general deduction of reflective judgements. These were necessary if we were to have a system of science, for the latter required us to suppose that the order of nature generally was suited to and directed at our understanding. The principle of finality that is accepted here is capable of being used in other contexts,[61] we might argue, and becomes necessary in considering physical ends because only its use allows us to form a content that is to be given a mechanistic explanation. That is, though we should attempt to explain all events on mechanical lines,

we must never lose sight of the fact that among such products there are those which cannot even be subject to investigation except under the conception of an end of reason. These, if we respect the essential nature of our reason, we are obliged, despite those mechanical causes, to subordinate in the last resort to causality according to ends.[62]

Thus, we may understand Kant to contend that there will always be objects that need to be identified as ends before we can begin to give a causal account of them. In such instances, even if a causal account is intended to be comprehensive, it cannot be proposed without first identifying the end that must be explained. Consequently, the vocabulary of purposes and ends, and the judgements in which we express it, is indispensable. And while we may explain how the parts of an object causally interact and what caused them to come together to form the object they did, we cannot dispense with identifying their end—the object formed.

   This conclusion is based on two other claims: first, as we are ignorant of things in themselves, 'we are ignorant of how far the mechanical mode of explanation . . . may penetrate':[63] second, the physical end has, 'as far as any empirical laws go, a *contingency* of the form of a thing in relation to reason'. It is supposed that Kant explains the second claim by saying that

reason in every case insists on cognizing the necessity of the form of a natural product, even where it only desires to perceive the conditions involved in its production. In the given form mentioned above, however, it cannot get this necessity. Hence the *contingency is itself a ground* for making us look upon the origin of a thing as if, just because of that contingency, it could only be possible through reason. But the causality so construed becomes the faculty of acting according to ends—that is to say, a will; and the object, which is represented as only deriving its possibility from such a will, will be represented as possible only as an end.[64]

   However, this merely says that we use teleological judgements only where events are contingent with regard to mechanistic laws and then only so far as it is necessary to comprehension. That is, reason insists on comprehending the object and ascribes its creation to a will; but it does this only because of the contingency of the object with regard to mechanistic laws of nature. Yet this contingency is itself, at best, a contingent factor. And ignorance of the comprehensiveness of the mechanical mode of explanation is no guarantee of contingency, even if it is based on the supposition that both mechanistic and teleological modes apply to appearances only. For mechanistic explanations are taken to aim for comprehensiveness there, and to provide a system for all our explanations of experience. Ignorance of how far they may penetrate does not validate the supposition that they must be limited. And while at least one judgement according to ends is necessary—by which all nature is taken to have an end in our rational understanding of it—this does not show that physical ends, works of art, and the vocabulary of our reference to and understanding of them, are indispensable. The latter may yet be replaced by a purely mechanistic account.

Although the arguments just given fail, each of them points to something important, and their reformulation yields a version of the argument that succeeds in showing the possibility and indispensability of purposes, goals, and the vocabulary of interpretation and understanding essential to the construction of art generally and fine art in particular. The mistake made in the earlier arguments was to begin with experience and to try then to introduce rational ends. In these claims, contingency and a commensurate infinite complexity *in nature* were supposed, wrongly, to provide a reason for concluding that it was necessary to use concepts of ends. Instead it is more fruitful to begin with reason and to see contingency as something true of *reason* when it is considered in *relation to nature*.

The latter approach is suggested in the following quotation, in which Kant considers the case of someone coming upon a hexagon in an apparently uninhabited country.

His reason would . . . forbid him to consider the sand, the neighbouring sea, the winds, or even animals with their footprints, as causes familiar to him, or any other irrational cause, as the ground of possibility of such a form. For the contingency of coincidence with a *conception* like this, *which is only possible in reason*, would appear to him as so infinitely great that *there might just as well be no law of nature at all* in the case. Hence it would seem that the cause of the production of such an effect cannot be contained in the mere mechanical operation of nature, but that, on the contrary, a conception of such an object, *as a conception that only reason can give* and compare the objects with, must likewise be *what alone contains that causality*. On these grounds it would appear to him that this effect was one that might without reservation be regarded as an end, though not a natural end. In other words, he would regard it as a product of art—*vestigium hominis video.*[65]

There are a number of claims contained in this passage. First, we use reason to comprehend the natural event. Second, reason would not be satisfied by pointing to 'irrational causes' to explain the event. This is because, third, the use of reason is to be contrasted with laws of nature. *Where* a conception is only possible in reason, it is one that does not fall under natural laws: 'there may just as well be no natural laws' or 'the production of such an effect could not be contained in the mere mechanical operation of nature'. That is, fourth, the inadequacy of natural laws in dealing with rational ends seems to be a consequence of factors other than the contingency of natural events. And rather than serving to explain the differences between them, contingency seems to be a mark or symptom of the difference between rational and mechanical explanations.

We may explain the relevance of these points to the issue of the possibility and indispensability of conceiving of some objects in nature as works of art, as the understandable goals of rational activity, by putting forward a counter-argument. Thus, one way to deny the possibility of rational ends such as culture and art in nature is to argue that science is comprehensive—that empirical events are 'solely possible in this way'[66] and all else may be reduced to mechanistic explanations. Thus, the validity we may wish to give culture, art, or fine art, by treating judgements upon them as rational and universal, can be made redundant by giving, of our response and creation of these objects, a scientific explanation based on mechanistic causal laws. By doing so, it may be argued, we substitute scientific generalizations for the rational ends and universalizable judgements of fine art and culture.

However, against such a claim we may argue, first, that science claims apodictic necessity of a sort that culture cannot manage and, second, that an explanation based on scientific generalizations cannot be substituted for the interpretative understanding of goals or ends that culture involves.

A defence of interpretative activity is that as science itself depends on such activity, we cannot hope to eliminate it in favour of scientific, non-interpretative, mechanistic explanations. Kant affirms the necessity of interpretation and of understanding ends in the construction of a scientific system when he distinguishes the faculty of understanding from that of reason and assigns to the latter the task of conceptualizing the order of empirical knowledge. Reason's interest in gaining an order is promoted through reflective judgements and, as we saw, the latter operate on the principle that nature has a rationally comprehensible order. Accordingly, reflective judgements and their part in constructing a system can be taken to characterize the rational perceiving subject and his nature in that the mode of comparison validated in Kant's deduction of the finality of nature is validated for such subjects. What this shows, however, is that the reflecting subject itself is not characterized as an object of science, but is presupposed in the enterprise. Thus, when science tries to replace common sense or contingent experience with a systematic order of nature, the existence of scepticism about the possibility of constructing a system leads Kant to argue for a principle that legitimates making comparisons between ends and orders of objects—a comparison of the sort necessary to interpretation, and one which a rational subject carries out. That is, those comparisons must be understood by a rational subject who is not himself an object of science. Thus, the scientist must set out his analysis of events in a manner that at least takes himself to be a rational, interpreting, and understanding subject. Even as we try to substitute a non-rational, causal explanation of an event, we must see that the very expression of that intention, and its pursuit, are a matter of interpretation and of understanding meanings. And for Kant this places the enterprise of science outside the domain which science investigates.

Even where science consists of determinate judgements alone, so that there is no need to apply reflective judgements, the gap between the faculties of reason and understanding embodies that distinction between, on the one hand, constructing a rational order of our knowledge of nature and, on the other, the nature which is the object of science. That is, in this case too the capacity for comparison and interpretative activity is indispensable to science, and in neither case of reflective or determinant judgement can we hope to substitute scientific explanations for the practice of understanding and interpreting those very explanations.

An examination of the differences we are concerned with can be centred on a contrast between scientific generalizations and the universality of aesthetic judgements and culture. Kant accepts that we can refute generalizations in science by presenting counter examples. Natural laws are not a priori, although at some level they are based on the a priori categories of understanding that make objective experience possible. A natural law is a generalization covering the behaviour of an object in different circumstances, and is falsifiable in that we can formulate circumstances in which we would reject the hypothesis: perhaps the object fails to behave as we would expect and no satisfactory *ad hoc* hypothesis explains that behaviour as a single aberrant instance. Here, the generalization itself is at risk, and counter-examples force us to abandon or at least revise our general claim in order to accommodate a recalcitrant experience.

Cultural and interpretative understanding cannot be refuted in this way. A counter-example does not require us to revise the generalization in order to accommodate a recalcitrant experience. At most we may be forced to admit that our claim about a particular work of art or an instance of behaviour does not fit under a proposed generalization about either works generally or human behaviour. This is the case because we do not arrive at both the interpretative understanding of works or actions and scientific generalizations in the same way. In the latter case, generalizations are hypotheses used to explain the occurrence of an event; in the other, generalizations identify what we are concerned with. In the second case, of understanding and interpreting goals, works of art, or human behaviour, we can only use generalizations about human reason and artistic practice or some notion of normal human reason. And we cannot explain how reason comes to exist if the only vocabulary available to us consists of the rules which constitute the use of reason.

Kant asserts at least as much in his statements about the fact of reason, and his claim can be extended to cover more than practical reason alone. Our ability to exercise reason just does exist, and it is in its nature to provide universal principles applicable to all individuals. There is nothing else we can say to explain how it comes into being, although we can articulate the implications of this conception of reason. And while empirical generalizations may be refuted or must be revised in the face of counter-examples and once our ingenuity in formulating *ad hoc* hypotheses fails us, interpretative generalizations about works of fine art and human action cannot be refuted in a similar way, for we do not prove ourselves irrational whenever we make mistakes. At best, generalizations about them may be thought inadequate to a situation and their particular inadequacy may require us to discover an alternative principle. But we cannot be asked to revise the generalization itself on the ground that it does not account for an example of art or an instance of behaviour. In applying the generalization we do not put it at risk because we do not seek to explain the existence of a state of affairs but only to understand it by seeing which, out of a whole body of generalizations about the use of reason in art or human actions, are applicable. It is this difference that Kant seeks to grasp by saying first that there is a rational will underlying all our actions—our behaviour is intentional and its rationality a fact—and, second, that rational ends in nature are not effects that can be 'contained in the mere mechanical operation of nature' because they 'depend on a conception only reason can give'.[67]

The different status each has results from the distinctive connection between principle and instance. Natural laws and scientific explanations suppose that a sound explanation articulates the causal regularities operating in a particular instance. The antecedent is a sufficient and necessary condition of the existence of the consequent.[68] If the connection between intention and action were like that between a scientific generalization and its evidence, then we could never attest to the appropriateness of an action to an intention because there is an infinite variety of actions in which an intention is realized. No single piece of behaviour would be a sufficient and necessary condition for us to ascribe an intention to an agent in the way that the behaviour of an object can be sufficient and necessary as evidence for us to classify an event as an instance of a scientific generalization.

Further, if there were an evidential relation in such understanding, then the existence of particular conditions but the absence of the action could imply that our generalization about human reason, on which our understanding of the action was dependent, must be revised. The absence of an action would count as a counter-example that must lead us to refuse universality to the principle. But such a conclusion is not warranted in the case of understanding human behaviour because we do not possess sufficient and necessary criteria. We may hold on to a principle because short of seeing that an appropriate action is performed, there are no sufficient and necessary criteria whose satisfaction would ordinarily lead us to expect the occurrence of the action. If there were necessary and sufficient conditions, then we may have expected counter-examples where conditions were satisfied and the consequence failed to appear. Instead, all we have is the supposition of rationality, in which a capacity for rationality is possessed altogether or not at all, together with various cues for interpreting the behaviour in question. And we have a whole range of principles of rational behaviour to apply in understanding. Whereas the most ingenious *ad hoc* scientific hypothesis must acknowledge the possibility that we can be forced to reject an empirical hypothesis, in the case of understanding behaviour we would seek alternative principles, more clearly adequate to behaviour, rather than seek to reject the original principle. Rational principles are not at risk in the explanation. To accept that a piece of behaviour is rational is to accept that we must consider an agent's beliefs and past actions in order to understand present behaviour, for example. The principles we consider are just those involved in supposing an agent to be rational.

As it is independent of the sort of explanation according to necessary and sufficient conditions that we use in scientific explanation, rational behaviour and the interpretation of goals cannot be substituted for by scientific explanation. Rational principles articulate what it is about a piece of behaviour or a work that makes it an action or object that deserves to be understood. And to treat a principle as we would an empirical hypothesis is to expect an explanation of the fact of reason. But obviously this explanation cannot be given in terms of the rational principles which characterize our behaviour as an object of our understanding. Nor can we ignore these principles if we are to suppose that some behaviour constitutes action or is the result of it. So if scientific explanation is to have application at all, it must take the behaviour or goal seriously as rational action or as the result of such action. All we can do is to consider a series of possible accounts of the action to discover the set of principles that is most clearly adequate.

The differences between scientific generalizations and interpretative understanding must be specified further if we are to show not only that the latter cannot be eliminated but that the sort of interpretative understanding we wish to defend will suffice to account for our responses to fine art or natural beauty.

Aesthetic Judgements and Realism

Our concern with rational ends in nature is for the sake of explaining our participation in culture through the creation and appreciation of fine art. The possibility of the latter, as art, is defended by pointing to the indispensability of conceiving of rational ends. But that leaves open the possibility that aesthetic judgement and beauty, as participants in culture, may yet be excluded. Although we have shown how the production of fine art is a matter of producing a particular sort of work of art, so that a defence of art is also a defence of fine art as art, it is still open to a realist to argue that the state of mind that results in our experience of beauty is 'pursued as an actual (intentional) *end* of nature (or of art)'.[69] To explain our aesthetic judgements we must conceive of nature as having ends; and, rather than understand beauty as denoting the subject's assessment of the object's suitability to his pleasurable state of mind, we may see the latter as an end of nature. That is, one of the ends in nature is to produce the experience of beauty. Consequently, we may *deduce* rules for beauty from the beautiful object because its beauty is a characteristic of the object, the realist may argue, and idealism is mistaken if it supposes that *we* apply the ends to objects. Rather, from our experience of the beauty of particular objects we may deduce which characteristics will lead generally to an experience of beauty; and while it may be indispensable to conceive of rational ends in the phenomenal world, aesthetic ends are not rational ones. For if this realism is correct, then our experience of beauty, whether of natural objects or of works of art, cannot be part of our self-development in culture because, at best, it manifests an end of nature and so cannot be a measure of our reason or its intercourse with nature. The contrasting case of idealism in aesthetic judgement holds that the 'forms which nature produces in accordance with particular laws' may well suit the mind and enable it to make judgements of taste, but the accord between nature and mind is 'one that is independent of an end [of nature], spontaneous and contingent'.[70]

The contention of realism is supported by a great deal of evidence. Nature exhibits considerable regularity in providing beautiful objects, and we can discover innumerable instances of natural beauty where 'the elegance of animal formation of all kinds, unnecessary for the discharge of any function of their part', seems to be chosen 'with an eye for our taste'. Nature's organization is so regularly and consistently directed toward our pleasure that objects of beauty exist even where men rarely go: beautiful formations from the depths of the sea sometimes appear on the surface of oceans, and beautiful flowers bloom in the most depopulated and desolate places. There is a variety and harmony of colours which,

inasmuch as they touch the bare surface, and do not even here in any way effect the structure of these creatures—a matter which might have a necessary bearing on their internal ends—seem to be planned entirely with a view to outward appearance; all these lend great weight to the mode of explanation which assumes actual ends of nature in favour of our aesthetic judgement.[71]

Accordingly, given that explanations of the occurrence of objects and events must be consistent, the abundance and variety of examples of beauty must motivate us to expect and seek an account in which nature has an objective end in our aesthetic pleasure.[72] The regularity and necessity underlying the lawful production of beautiful objects makes it an easy next step to suppose that beauty is evidence of nature's end.[73]

Kant's main argument against this conclusion, and for the idealism of taste, depends on Occam's Razor[74]—and is unsatisfactory. It may well be a principle of reason that we use the least number of principles possible to provide an explanation; and, for this reason, Kant wants to exclude the possibility that nature tries to satisfy our ability to make judgements of taste. But it is equally possible to argue that although we do not know why or how natural beauty affects us or causes us to feel pleasure, when we have completely systematized all knowledge of nature we will see that aesthetic pleasure is as causal as that of the agreeable and no more suitable as a vehicle of our self-development in culture than the latter. Consequently, given both the evidence we gain from nature and the obtundance of Occam's Razor in this instance, we may be led to accept the realism of taste.

However, if these arguments are unsuccessful against realism, there are other factors which must be considered. These centre on problems with realism itself. For if a realist account of beauty seeks to relate nature generally, in terms of its ends, to a particular exercise of mind, it would have to derive that exercise from the form of objects judged beautiful. But such a derivation would fail to get off the ground. First, to judge the beauty of an object we rely on an a priori principle which supposes that our judgement can legitimately claim a general validity—the very subjective principle which realism seeks to deny and replace. Thus, to discover a relation between nature and beauty we have to presuppose a transcendental principle—without which we would be unable to distinguish the beautiful from the agreeable, from our cognitions, or from the good—in order to know that we are discovering a relation to beauty. Kant's argument for aesthetic judgements does not seek to constitute pleasure, for pleasure already exists, but to establish that in certain cases, because we follow an a priori principle, we are justified in claiming universal validity for our subjective experience and in calling the object beautiful. If realism were to deny this principle, then the distinction between beauty—our experience of a universally valid pleasure—and the agreeable—where we cannot make a claim to universal validity—would collapse; and as we would no longer have an experience of beauty, we would lack a candidate to explain by relating to nature. To deny the a priori principle in order to substitute a realist derivation is to deny the conceptual scheme in which it is meaningful to make the effort to judge things beautiful. And no experience of beauty can be derived from nature because the possibility of beauty rests on the a priori principle just denied in order to substitute the realist account.

Thus, the search for an explanation based on objective ends would not be able to begin—unless some other realist account of beauty were given.

Second, this relation cannot account for the subjective validity of taste which distinguishes the latter from agreeable judgements. Kant maintains that 'just as the *ideality* of objects of sense as phenomena is the one way of explaining the possibility of their forms admitting of *a priori* determination, so also, idealism of finality in estimating the beautiful in nature and art is the only hypothesis upon which a *Critique* can explain the possibility of a judgement of taste that demands a priori validity for everyone'.[75] The analogy between objective finality and empirical idealism (or idealistic realism) indicates that just as scepticism is the logical consequence of supposing that 'real' things must exist independently of the mind, the consequence of supposing objective ends in nature is scepticism about the possibility of beauty. Because of his own starting-point, the aesthetic realist is unable to acknowledge that the experience of beauty depends on certain conditions and, instead, tries to deduce or argue from objects in some way 'outside' us to an experience 'in' us. His move suffers the fate of scepticism and can be rescued only by acknowledging the subjective conditions of beauty and the 'idealism of the finality of nature'.

Aesthetic Judgements and Idealism

The argument for the idealism of taste remains incomplete. We have not yet considered the claim voiced earlier that pleasure, even in aesthetic judgements, should be explained in causal terms, as a matter of fact, rather than as a demand that must be satisfied. To explain why we judge a work beautiful, it is claimed, we may provide a descriptive generalization of how any agent would behave in particular circumstances. The explanation is merely factual, and any question of 'understanding' another person or work is at best a heuristic device which cannot form part of an explanation of our response to the object.[76] Description and interpretation are not complementary, then, but exclusive.

An explanation of the existence of an object and of our pleasure in it makes redundant all our attempts to understand it, and so makes vacuous any justification of aesthetic necessity that is based on participation in culture. So long as explanations of empirical events can claim necessity only on the basis of causal determinations—a thesis that Kant seems to argue for in making the categories constitutive of experience—all other necessities are at best regulative and at worst must have causal regularities substituted for them. The notion of 'understanding a work' is excess baggage, although we may be misled to suppose that agents attempt to do so when they defend their claims about works of fine art by proposing comparisons with other examples.[77]

However, to argue in the way outlined above, we may say, is to misunderstand the event to be explained. To begin to explain the fact of an agent's judgement it is necessary to accept that it is a case of a judgement of taste. That is, the event which is being passed off under the guise of descriptive generalization cannot be identified except by using a vocabulary in which it is possible to express and talk of our intentions and make normative claims. If this vocabulary were not accepted, then the effort to substitute a causal account would be unnecessary because the object, which is rational and understandable as a norm, would be unrecognizable. But once the vocabulary is taken to be sensible enough to identify an object for all concerned, it also becomes unavoidable. For to eliminate it we would need a methodological argument that causal explanation is all embracing in that empirical events 'are solely possible in this way'.[78] And that, we have seen, is not forthcoming.

This does not as yet complete an argument for fine art in the phenomenal world. The account given so far does not yet exclude the possibility of a causal explanation of aesthetic judgements. To maintain that the aesthetic use of concepts is concomitant with interpretation and understanding is to take too much for granted, it may be argued, because we also need to show that aesthetic judgements can be distinguished from the agreeable. For if we could not do so, then the necessity of taste will be no more than a causal determination of subjects to the experience of pleasure, and aesthetic practice will have no right to claim any validity in the cultural self-development of humanity.

This reasoning depends on comparing aesthetic and agreeable judgements on the basis of the pleasure they occasion. Allegedly by contrast with the former, the latter are directly causal: an object causes pleasure in us, and we are interested in the existence of the object because it causes us pleasure. And it is possible to argue that for all we know our pleasure in aesthetic judgement is caused in the same way. Their only difference is that in agreeable judgements we know what is causing pleasure and why, whereas in aesthetic judgements we do not. Our ignorance of the causal relation between an object and the pleasure we experience leads us to a false belief that no object causes our pleasure, and thence to the conclusion that aesthetic pleasure is not bound up with the existence of the object which initiates the causal chain that ends in our experience of pleasure. Our ignorance and mistake, as it were, become institutionalized in our claim that aesthetic pleasure results from a particular use of mind in judgement—that it is a pleasure which could be occasioned also if only the representations conducive to our judgements were present to the mind, and the object, whose representations they are, were itself absent. In reality, the argument goes, in some as yet incompletely understood causal chain, an object is causing us pleasure. So any arguments for the necessity of aesthetic judgements are mistaken in principle if they are content to seek a *justification* of the demand that subjects should *agree* with judgements. The only justification likely to be successful will be based on the supposition that pleasure is caused by an object, and it will consider agreement to be a fact that is stated rather than a demand that is satisfied.

As this line of reasoning stands, it must defend its claim that all our experiences in principle can be reduced to causal relations between ourselves and objects or events. And it is not clear that this reduction is a real option. Further, it ignores important features of our aesthetic judgements and experience. Even if we accept that in principle aesthetic pleasure, like the pleasure we experience with agreeable judgements, must be explained in causal terms just as every other event or experience is, there are yet other ways of distinguishing the beautiful from the agreeable. Instead of considering the two simply in terms of pleasure, we may explore them as judgements about things and give *reasons* for pleasure in our judgements. That agreeable judgements have an interest of sense may then be explained by saying that when an object causes pleasure this gives us a reason for judging it to be agreeable. Given Kant's association of interest and existence, when we judge the agreeable object to exist, the judgement gives us pleasure for the reason that we know the object causes pleasure in us. By contrast, the pleasure associated with aesthetic judgements depends only on the activity of judging. Aesthetic judgements are pleasurable neither because of the existence of the object nor because nature causes a harmony of faculties but for *no reason at all*. No further use to which an object can be put will explain our aesthetic pleasure. Thus pleasure is not predetermined: an interest in gaining an experience of beauty does not determine which objects we will find beautiful. At most, our interest follows on from making a judgement. And a similar contrast can be made with moral judgements. In their case, we judge that something is morally good and then, when we find that the object or event exists, we are pleased for the reason that it exists. Thus, whereas no interest gives us reason for the pleasurable judgement that an object is beautiful, either an interest of sense or an interest of reason determines pleasure in agreeable or moral judgements.

In one instance at least Kant appears to think that our aesthetic experiences can neither be determined by nor found an interest. But his claim that 'judgements of taste do not even set up any interest what-soever'[79] is prefigured by the qualification that they do not give rise to an interest 'by themselves'. And although no interest determines which objects we will find beautiful, we can have a moral or other interest in beauty.[80] As Kant argues, we may propose a need for beauty. And this does not decide which particular or variety of objects we will judge beautiful—because a reason for seeking beauty is not a reason for finding some one particular object rather than another beautiful, nor for finding something beautiful rather than thinking it aesthetically uninteresting.

That a judgement lacks reason—in the above sense—does not preclude us from justifying and defending it by pointing to the structure, complexity, expressiveness, and so on, of a work. But this only supports the contention that an aesthetic judgement is subjective, involves a purposiveness which we attribute to objects, and is singular. For we cannot, from judgements, *deduce* the sort of characteristics which will be found beautiful. Our defence of judgements will be a matter of adumbrating the features of a particular piece in demonstrating by example and comparison how its unity is achieved. And such an explanation cannot be applied equally to other works as if it were a generalization about objects on the basis of their empirical character-istics, for all we have here is a principle for estimating an 'inner finality in relation to our mental powers' in particular.

All this goes to establish that the activities of producing and appreciating fine art are possible in the phenomenal world in spite of the validity of causal explanations. We may conceive of objects as works and of works as fine art. Further, the claim that interpretation and understanding of the sort necessary to appreciating fine art may be reduced to causal generalizations was denied by arguing that understanding and appreci-ation differed from causal explanation and could not be substituted for by the latter. In addition, we argued against other reasons for denying the claim that our aesthetic judgements and activity allowed us to participate in culture and self-development.

The Critique *and Other Texts*

This examination supports the contention that aesthetic necessity may be justified by reference to fine art's participation in culture. It also raises at least two other points. The first issue is a textual one: the emphasis on fine art in culture and community seems to receive more support from outside the Third *Critique* than from within it. We need to clarify the relation between these different texts, to show whether the emphasis can be shown to rest clearly on the *Critique* itself or whether sources outside this work provide us with one interpretation of it. And this leads to the second issue: in the text Kant develops his theory by arguing that the proposed conception of cultural action remains unjustified unless physical teleology is given a particular association with moral teleology. Yet it is not clear why this claim can or should be accepted.

Although culture is mentioned infrequently in the *Critique of Aesthetic Judgement*, we have seen that it has a salient location in the Introduction and that the claims for culture and fine art which Kant makes in this text square fully with the claims he makes in other writings. Further, although culture is not mentioned explicitly or frequently, its surrogates, effects, and related practices are amply represented in the first part of the Third *Critique*. Given that Kant is proposing a theory of culture, this diversity should not be surprising, for a theory will seek to juxtapose and relate apparently diverse phenomena. Thus, culture appears on few occasions, but Kant discusses and interrelates not only the concepts of genius, necessity, and imperative modes, but also of sensibility, nature, and morality, of symbolic relations to moral good, of fine art, communication, taste as a *sensus communis*, cultivation, *humaniora*, beauty in relation to social spirit and to our animal and rational character, and interest in beauty. All of these, we have seen, are crucially part of culture, and their interrelation helps us to give aesthetic substance to the more general practical and moral claims Kant makes.

His moral theory seems to use different sets of concepts, but related issues are involved in both. Their relation is not always presented in the sort of detail we might have liked, but this is partly because Kant's interest in the first part of the Third *Critique* is in understanding and clarifying the nature of aesthetic judgements. And the interrelation between concepts is suggested without drawing out every implication here, partly because Kant's theory presupposes a complex background which cannot be fully developed in this work: and that, in turn, is because Kant has already set out its details in other works.

The usual epistemological interest in aesthetic judgements merely institutionalizes the emphasis on judgements and so fails to attend to these cultural features even though they explain the relation of experience to morality, as it were, from the side of the former. Moreover, perhaps because of the chronological sequence of Kant's writings, the deduction of taste is taken to be no more than that. Accordingly, Kant's deduction of the principle of finality is generally treated only as part of the argument for aesthetic judgements. What is often ignored is that by means of this deduction and his development of teleology, Kant is providing the critical underpinning for his account of cultural and historical development. For if we can or must think of nature as ends or finality, then we may not only conceive of objects as the result of goal-directed actions, but can think of all such objects and events in terms of a larger goal-directed order—providence or the development of civic community as the unintended consequence of our egotistic actions[81] and a community 'under moral laws' in the case of actions directed towards rational ends. Further, we might expect, if this is indeed the case, that following a deduction of finality Kant will go on to provide some sort of 'metaphysic' or application of this way of thinking. And, as we see, having defended this way of conceiving of nature, Kant goes on to provide a systematic presentation of purposive thought and behaviour in nature: to account for cultural development[82] as something which follows in theory from conceiving of a teleological order of nature generally.

This is not the appropriate place to develop such architectonic detail, and the arguments given above do not entirely depend on it. But given that the *Critique of Aesthetic Judgement* is concerned to deduce the validity of aesthetic judgements; that Kant relates this issue to various surrogates and features of culture; that this deduction is placed within the context of a deduction of a principle of finality which seeks to provide a critical underpinning for Kant's conception of culture and history; and that this presupposes a complex background already explored in other works, it may be suggested, first, that although Kant expresses himself in the Third *Critique* by using a vocabulary which seems to be different from the one native to his moral theory, nevertheless, once we recognize that the same issues are being considered, we can see that the *Critique of Judgement* is the source of our thesis that the necessity of beauty is a practical cultural one, and second, that the interrelation between the issues described in the different texts is so close that it is not so much the case that the latter provide an interpretation of the Third *Critique* as it is

the case that the *Critique* attempts to justify and give content to the
claims Kant makes in the other works. That is, the Third *Critique*
provides a critical foundation for some of the claims made in the
historical and cultural texts and developed further in *Religion*, and seeks
to give a more substantial content to features of his moral theory. As
these claims are related to the Third *Critique* in critical theory and form,
rather than ask whether we are exploring what is already present in our
text or interpreting that text by reference to other works and sources, we
must recognize that they are all directed towards clarifying the same
theory of culture and moral action in its different facets. In this sense,
when we read the *sensus communis* as a practical ideal or understand such
claims as the symbolic relation of beauty to moral good and the interest
associated with aesthetic judgements on nature, or clarify matters of
expression and community, of *humaniora* and social spirit, and see them
all as part of an aesthetic theory, we are taking seriously Kant's
intention, expressed in the Preface, to link theory with practice and
cognition with moral action. Thus we may use other texts to clarify or
support his conception of aesthetic judgements; but it is only because
these practical issues, which are already present in the Third *Critique*,
have been ignored for the sake of an epistemological interest, that it
becomes necessary to regain such moral connotations by explicitly
explaining Kant's references to the complex background of the two
preceding *Critiques* and the other 'lesser' works.

Further, as we are to take the text itself seriously, when we turn to the
sections on culture we see that Kant goes on, from his account of the
ultimate end of creation, to argue that culture, and, by implication, the
necessity of beauty, cannot be justified satisfactorily unless physical
teleology is encompassed by a moral teleology. We must now consider
this part of Kant's claim. As we shall see, Kant's argument here is
unsuccessful and, in any case, is unnecessary to justifications of
aesthetic necessity.

Phenomena and Moral Teleology

The place of morality in a theoretically understood reality is to be seen in
cultural and historical development towards the highest good of which
we animal *and* rational beings are capable. As the ability to do three
things—'to use nature both internal and external'; to 'determine the will
independently of nature'; and 'to develop the capacity for reason'—
culture requires that nature be capable of an organization suited to
gaining human ends. Kant thinks that ultimately this suitability can only

be justified by showing that moral teleology encompasses physical teleology.

Physical teleology allows us to conceive of ends in nature, but their order and relation to each other is arbitrary. Objects in nature may be seen as means to the ends of man 'and the multifarious uses to which his intelligence teaches him to put all these forms of life'.[83] But equally, for no better reason, we may follow 'the chevalier Linne' and see man as only a means to gaining 'a certain equilibrium between the productive and destructive forces of nature'. After all, nothing in nature suggests otherwise: 'External nature is far from . . . having preferred [man] to all other animals as the object of its beneficience'.[84]

Kant justifies choosing man as the end of the order of purposes in nature by looking outside nature and beyond man as a physical end. And, in order to legitimate culture as the manipulation and organization of nature, Kant thinks it necessary to look to its participation in the struggle for perfection. What gives man a special status is that he is 'the single being upon earth that possesses understanding and, consequently, a capacity for setting before himself ends of his deliberate choice'.[85] But this is 'always on the terms that he has an intelligence and the will to give to it and himself such a reference to ends as can be self-sufficing independently of nature'.[86] Where there are ends in themselves which man must and is able to pursue because of his rational character, there, in developing culture, he may use nature to suit his purposes as an end in himself.[87] Without man's position as a final end, one justified by practical reason independently of nature, the organization and use of nature have no more justification than any other ordering of ends. It is not that anything is possible and every sort of organization acceptable; rather, if we are without a final end then nothing is permitted.

Kant thinks he needs to argue further that purposes or ends in nature cannot be ordered in relation to each other with man as a final end except under a conception of all creation being directed to a fulfillment of man's rational moral objectives. Ultimately, it is faith in God, whose purpose is also the final end of man, that gives a systematic, purposive, and moral unity to the world.[88] Just as physical teleology supposes that the systematic theoretical order of nature results from its creation by a divine understanding for our understanding, similarly a moral teleology supposes that nature has a systematic, purposive, and moral unity where the attainment of man's final end is guaranteed.[89] It is faith in God that gives a point of unity between nature and moral action, apparently supplementing a physical teleology by encompassing it within a moral teleology.

For Kant, such an addition becomes necessary because man's final end is the '*summum bonum*, as the highest good *in the world* possible through freedom'.[90] The *summum bonum* is only a 'synthetic' unity between the separate elements of virtue and happiness and between reason and nature: happiness does not cause virtue; nor does virtue alone cause happiness. Their unity cannot be 'conjoined by means of mere natural causes, and also conformed to the idea of a final end' because that would exclude freedom. 'Accordingly,' Kant goes on, 'if we do not bring the causality of any other means besides nature into alliance with our freedom, the conception of the *necessity* of such an end through the application of our powers does not accord with the theoretical conception of the *physical* possibility of its effectuation'. That is, the pursuit of virtue can cause happiness only if the natural conditions for the latter are already present.

As an agent in the developing relation of reason to nature and the progressive liberation of the will from natural inclinations for the pursuit of virtue, it seems that cultural activity too must suppose that a unity between reason and nature is possible. Further, if the unity between reason and nature generally is not to seem merely accidental, Kant thinks he needs to provide some assurance of their providential relation. Not just happiness—the state of satisfaction of desires—but also the use and manipulation of nature must be guaranteed if culture is to have hope of ultimate success. And for him this implies that any instances which are alleged to exhibit cultural development must be capable of being understood as a unity of physical and moral teleology. The physical end must be shown to be in unity with moral purpose—otherwise its occurrence cannot have much to do with cultural advance towards the *summum bonum* in the natural world.

To gain this assurance Kant finds it necessary to go beyond nature to suppose a world cause who guarantees the co-operation of nature and reason. Faced with apparent evidence that the two components lack any connection, culture ultimately relies on faith in God, who brings about the final end of man, in order to sustain its attempt to gain unity between nature and culture or moral action and between natural and moral purposes. God is the 'third thing' that brings about a synthetic unity between the disparate elements of nature and reason and guarantees nature's satisfaction of moral demands. Culture can continue to strive for unity despite evidence suggesting that the realization of moral aims is impossible in nature.[91] We can be certain that we are not simply deluded when we discover evidence of their morally satisfying unity.

Although a unity between physical and moral teleology is thought necessary, it is also unlikely. While physical teleology must be supplemented by a moral teleology, it is difficult to see how there might be a unity between them. Each has a justification independent of the other; and the use of each is carefully restricted from intruding upon the other.[92]

In the *Critique of Teleological Judgement*, at Sections 86, 88 and in the General Remark on Teleology, Kant suggests a positive relation between the two teleologies. He asserts that natural beauty gives 'to the ideas produced by pure practical reason an incidental confirmation in physical ends'. We are led to inquire after 'the incomprehensibly great art that lies behind [natural] forms'.[93] Understood after an analogy with art, natural beauty evinces nature's regard for reason and man's rational ends. Similarly, in the Remark Kant asserts that

admiration for beauty and the emotion excited by the profuse variety of ends of nature . . . have something about them akin to a *religious* feeling. Hence they seem primarily to act upon the moral feeling (of gratitude and veneration towards the unknown cause) by means of a mode of critical judgement analogous to the moral mode . . . .[94]

The suggestion in both is that experience of ends in nature leads us to suppose that God's purpose as exhibited in nature is also the final end of man. Through physical teleology, the theoretical knowledge of nature 'does attain an accession' to the objects of practical reason[95] and to moral teleology.

In both cases the turn to God is not a matter of chance. Kant is clear that it 'is a waste of labour to go burrowing behind these feelings for motives'. They are not to be explained away as general but only psychological needs contingently exhibited by men. We are concerned not with pathology but with the moral condition of men, and these feelings are 'immediately connected with the purest moral sentiment: *gratitude, obedience,* and *humiliation* . . . being special modes of mental disposition towards duty'.[96] Natural beauty, for example, leads men to feel gratitude towards someone. 'In a word, [men] need a moral intelligence'. Here 'it is at least possible . . . to form a representation depicting a pure moral need for the real existence of Being . . . whereby our morality gains in strength or even obtains . . . an extension of an area, that is to say, is given a new object for its exercise'.[97]

Neither case is satisfactorily argued. In the General Remark Kant claims at first that ends in nature 'act upon the moral feeling', then admits that beauty's role is to '*affect* the mind by *exciting moral ideas*. It is then that they inspire that admiration which is fraught with far more interest than mere theoretical observation can produce'.[98] Natural beauty is effective, then, only through its expression of moral ideas. But a justification based on this is unsatisfactory. Kant's stress on the expression of moral ideas leads to an exclusion of most works of fine art and does not clearly include natural beauty. For artistic beauty is not concerned to express only moral ideas, and the Finality of Nature that natural beauty is taken to express is not clearly a moral idea. Hence the proposed relation of nature to reason through beauty becomes more an exception than the rule.

Even if Kant's stress on the expression of particular moral ideas is ignored in order to emphasize 'an analogy with the moral mode that allows beauty to act upon the moral feeling' or the aesthetic 'mode of critical judgement analogous to the moral mode',[99] the relation of nature to reason is still not clearly established. The occurrence of natural beauty shows that there is something to be explained and perhaps also suggests where we may look. Its existence is taken to suggest that natural forms are created for our understanding. But this suggestion needs to be explained and justified. It is supposed that beauty shows God's plan because 'there is in our moral habits of thought a foundation for so doing'. But to justify this association of beauty with moral habits of thought we would already have to know how the

moral destination of man's existence supplements the shortcomings of theoretical knowledge, by directing us to join to the thought of the final end of the existence of all things ... the supreme cause as endowed with attributes whereby it is empowered to subject entire nature to that single purpose and make it merely instrumental thereto.[100]

Natural beauty itself is what needs to be explained, it is not part of the explanation. Not all natural forms are beautiful and there are other cultural products apart from works of artistic beauty. And by Kant's account we may expect that an explanation of all their roles in practical reason is gained only if a unity between physical and moral teleology generally can be justified. The occurrence of natural beauty does not argue for supposing that there is a unity between the two teleologies; rather, an explanation of the latter would justify the significance given to the existence of natural beauty.

Further, the existence of natural beauty is explained by reference to a supposed creator. But their connection is too close to talk of the former as confirming the existence of the latter. It leaves open questions of whether it is possible for natural beauty to occur or be understood at all without the supposition of God's existence and of whether and how anything in nature can confirm or disconfirm claims about His existence. It also fails to answer questions about whose existence is confirmed or denied—the moral or the physical creator of the world. Yet these were the questions it was supposed to resolve by showing how moral and physical purposiveness are united.

It may be that in the passages just quoted Kant is trying to do no more than argue for a rational faith that supports our human effort to gain the *summum bonum*. The existence of natural beauty and ends in nature suggest a positive relation between moral and physical teleology by proposing that we may have rational faith in the coincidence of a moral purpose that God attributes to nature with a physical teleology and our own final ends. It gives 'strength for one's moral disposition'.[101] Faith answers an 'existential need', not a psychological one. As one commentator has it, what is necessary to the 'moral disposition should not be translated into what psychological incentives may be needed by weak and pathologically effected men; it is part and parcel of the moral condition of responsible man'.[102]

This rational faith is far from justified by Kant. On the contrary, he seems to admit that moral and physical teleology are entirely separate. If it is a rational faith, based on an existential need, it is one which is successful despite contrary evidence. Indeed, as faith it seems unnecessary, because the moral argument itself is successful in spite of a failure of the physico-teleological argument. The moral argument for the existence of God 'does not, strictly speaking, merely as it were simply *supplement* the physico-teleological proof so as to make it a complete proof. Rather, it is a distinct proof which compensates for the failure of the latter to produce conviction'. What the moral proof requires 'is so essentially different from anything that is to be found in or taught by physical conceptions that it requires a special premise and proof entirely independent of the foregoing'. Indeed the moral proof 'would, therefore, continue to retain its full force were we to meet no material at all in the world or ambiguous material for physical teleology'.[103]

Nor can the link be established from the side of natural teleology. If a rational faith is to be effective it must allow us to suppose that the organization of nature according to physical teleology suggests a moral author of the universe. But the two teleologies yield different and unrelated concepts of God. Physical teleology provides no basis for inferring anything about the God whose determinate characteristics are gained through the moral proof. Physical teleology ends by 'subordinating the mechanism of nature to the architectonic of an intelligent author of the world'. It yields a 'conception of an intelligent world-cause', without 'any other attributes belonging to it than those which experience reveals as manifested in its operations'. And this conception does not 'lift us above nature' even though it is easy to suppose, wrongly, that it does.[104]

Thus, Kant recognizes that 'God, regarded as a moral author of the world', cannot 'be substantiated by means of physical ends alone'. He goes on,

Nevertheless, when the knowledge of those ends is associated with that of the moral end, the maxim of pure reason which directs us to pursue unity of principles so far as we are able to do so, lends considerable importance to these ends for the purpose of reinforcing the practical reality of that idea by the reality which it already possesses from a theoretical point of view for judgement.[105]

But this emphasis on reason's preference for unity also stands in need of explanation. By distinguishing practical from theoretical reason Kant has made just that unity problematic. The distinction is repeated in his examination of physical and moral teleology; and Kant's statements about these weaken any assertion of their unity, making it difficult to see how the one may justifiably strengthen or encompass the other.

Understanding the world as a morally ordered purposive whole does not give any support to seeing the natural world as a system. The moral conception of God 'is not necessary for the extension or rectification of our knowledge of nature or, in fact, for any theory whatever'. The moral argument satisfies only in the 'moral employment of our reason, from a practical point of view. Speculation does not here display its force in any way, nor does it enlarge the borders of its realm'.[106] We cannot gain any theoretical knowledge of God from the moral argument. Thus, there seems to be no interaction between the two teleologies. Kant has not shown that they are capable of the unity he earlier suggested was necessary for culture. His argument depends on God's purpose, but even He cannot create an impossible and indefensible unity between the two realms.

It may be that what God cannot do, man is expected to attain.

What God guarantees is not the realisation of the Highest Good but only its ontological possibility . . . . Since there is a God, namely, since there is one 'suprasensible substratum' of the whole of creation, the synthesis of the highest good is possible. But the realisation of this possibility, its translation from potentiality to actuality, is the duty of man and not the action of God. At most God helps us help ourselves.[107]

Or, from the side of nature, as man must make himself free, nature's effectiveness is necessarily limited. Nature must 'compel men without destroying their freedom'.[108] It confines itself to 'posing the problem to be solved; but does not solve it. Man himself both can and must give the solution. He must give it, because nature does not give it, and because the problem, unless solved, will destroy him'. Perhaps, then, physical teleology cannot interact with moral teleology because it would destroy human freedom, forcing men to behave in a particular way. As the two teleologies are not incompatible, if moral teleology is to interact with physical teleology, this must be brought about by men who, possessing insight into their final end, organize nature to gain those ends.

However, this would require nature to be manipulable in a quite radical sense, and the only guarantee we are given that nature will suit man's moral needs is based on the purposes ascribed to God as the moral creator of the world. Without this guarantee, cultural progress remains accidental, and physical ends cannot be recognized to belong to a moral teleology. But where their interrelation remains accidental, there cultural progress fails. Kant does not seem to accept that cultural activity towards the *summum bonum* should be continued, even where it is contingent, just because there may be some chance that nature will show itself subservient to moral expectations. Indeed, it is only because he thinks it defended by a *rational* faith that Kant is prepared to overlook appearances suggesting that moral aims cannot be realized. Really, contingency could not occur 'without doing injury to moral sentiment'.[109]

Where the necessity of beauty is based on the relation of moral to practical teleology, the lack of unity and interaction between the two teleologies leaves beauty only a very tenuous claim to necessity. The latter results from participation in a culture that claims legitimacy. But that legitimacy, in turn, is made to depend on a unity between nature and reason which is not successfully defended. Lacking assurance of an interaction between them, cultural activity can no longer proceed on the expectation that nature will gain a synthetic unity with reason and virtue. Nor is it clear that our activity can proceed any better on the assumption that nature and reason may not always be opposed. For in that case unity would still be contingent.[110]

If Kant's account of culture and the progressive emancipation of a rational humanity in culture and history is to be useful, it must allow for the possibility of man's nature being affected by reason and for human activity and intention to be conceivable and expressible in the phenomenal sensible world. Yet the interrelation of moral and physical teleology leaves it unclear how this might be possible.

In a sense this is to be expected, for we do not need to show the relation of moral to physical teleology in order to show that human activity is conceivable in the phenomenal world. The former relation is unnecessary to Kant's account of aesthetic necessity. We have seen that moral reason must be effective in nature and that for Kant the concept of freedom included the ability to follow moral law or to reject it for the sake of our natural animal inclinations. As part of that context, Kant has already proposed that the moral law is effective in this world and, first, has argued that freedom and determinism are compatible and, second, has shown that we must be able to conceive of action toward rational ends in nature. Consequently, he does not need to argue the further thesis, that purposes or ends in nature can be brought into relation to each other if we conceive of all creation as directed toward fulfilling moral objectives, nor to defend this thesis by showing that moral teleology encompasses physical teleology. He has given an a priori argument to the effect that rational—including moral—action is possible and that nature is compatible with morality. He need not then fear that any instance where moral or cultural progress occurs is merely contingent. It is not the latter because its possibility has been guaranteed by the a priori arguments for compatibility and indispensability.

It may be argued that contingency is still involved because although our moral and physical lives are compatible and each indispensable, nature may just not present occasion for cultural progress and moral action. So we may know that the two are compatible, yet simply because of the way nature is have no instance where the issue arises. However, even if this claim were acceptable, it would not justify Kant's further claim that we must either show all nature subservient to moral purpose or give up cultural activity toward the *summum bonum* because we do not know whether it can be gained. So long as there may be instances where we can develop our moral capacity, we may say, we are obliged to pursue our cultural development. Nor will contingency disrupt our efforts; this is because it is only contingent: we know a priori that any instance of physical nature may be compatible with rational freedom; and no appearance can succeed in showing that moral aims cannot be realized. Consequently, we cannot suppose that there will be no more instances where cultural progress is possible: nature and reason cannot always be opposed and we cannot know that it is impossible to attain the *summum bonum*. Therefore we do not need to argue for a unity between moral and physical teleology in order to defend the claim for aesthetic necessity and a morally directed culture. We have seen that man's nature can be affected by his reason and that human action can be conceived of in this world. The unity between teleologies could not, in any case, have accounted for what we need; at best the argument shows that the two are compatible; and we shall go on to provide the account of necessity we want.

First, we may clarify some features of the relation between cognition and aesthetic judgements.

From Consciousness to Community

Kant may have failed to argue that moral and physical teleology have a positive unity, but we may proceed to develop his account of aesthetic necessity.

The emphasis on fine art's involvement in constructing a community brings to attention two of Kant's aims. It stresses, first, a unity between theory and practice or nature and reason, and second, a unity between individuals in a community. Kant wants to justify an aesthetic necessity which is cognizant of both unities. Accordingly, aesthetic judgements are supposedly made by autonomous individual subjects on the basis of a felt subjective necessity that is universalizable over all equally rational and autonomous subjects. Individual and community are thought to be reconciled and united through judgements of taste. Further, fine art is supposed to reconcile theory with practice: a judgement using cognitive faculties needs to take account of subjects as ends in themselves. If these claims are acceptable, then a satisfactory understanding of works of art will allow subjects to participate in cultural activity towards the realization of the *summum bonum*.

In Kant's critical system, culture is based on a synthesis of reflective judgement with practical postulates. On the one hand, if we suppose that purposeful human activity exists in the phenomenal world, we are committed, first, to the ontological claim that rational human freedom exists and, second, that its existence is such that nature is responsive to intentional human activity. On the other hand, the products of rational freedom are understood by using reflective judgements. The latter have a particular place in Kant's critical theory: reflective judgements do not make any constitutive claims about the existence of freedom. They presuppose only the purposiveness of nature generally when it is necessary to comprehension. Accordingly, Kant says that although the existence of freedom cannot be justified to be true, where the occurrence of an object or event is contingent according to natural causal laws *and* a teleological account cannot successfully show that an object is an organism, there we can assume that the object may be 'determined by an intelligent cause'.

Fine art's participation in culture specifies this claim further. A judgement of taste is not an assertion of fact of the sort that science and cognition consist of, in one understanding of science. Taste carries an irreducible reference to subjects as creators and recipients of a work. As we saw, it is our practice to conceive of the object as a product of human activity and as something that must be understood *as a goal* rather than simply explained as the result of causes. This goes to make the exercise of taste part of the process of human self-understanding that proceeds through our production and intersubjective response to cultural objects.

In the *Critique of Pure Reason* Kant argues that to have empirical cognitive experience is to gain a unity or organization of representations that cannot be described except by using concepts of an objective world. Concepts are applied to representations to constitute objects possessing various qualities, and an explanation of their characteristics must proceed by pointing to the causal connections which precede and determine them. Cognitive judgements are objective and testable, and report on something which is 'just there' independently of any particular perceivers. They claim agreement with the world, carrying truth and empirical necessity where they fit the world.

The predicates applied in cognitive judgements are gained from a language that can be formalized in science to give univocal meanings to predicates. Scientific natural laws formulate regularities governing the determinate behaviour of objects. These generalizations may be falsified by recalcitrant experiences, but their truth value will not be determined by any considerations of how natural objects conceive themselves to be acting. Scientific natural laws are not norms that may or may not be followed correctly.

What Kant says can be used to contrast this case with that of aesthetic practice. An object is judged beautiful for its appropriateness to the subject, not for its subsumption under any concept. And the autonomy of aesthetic judgements makes it impossible to dissolve disagreement simply by dismissing one claim as a false belief. Instead, it is necessary to persuade a dissenter that his inability to judge a work beautiful is perhaps a consequence of his failure to consider some aspect of a work or the influence of charm or sense on his judgement and so on. Similarly, the object is seen not for the physical causes of which it is an effect but as a meaning that must be understood. We may give a detailed account of a work, of its size, weight, material, colour, and method of construction, without understanding that this object—Maillol's *Seated Nude*—results from an intended primitivism and that the figure is heavy in a way that has nothing to do with the weight of its material.

The search for agreement and dialogue essential to fine art's participation in culture evinces the importance of understanding particular meanings. Such understanding cannot accept the restrictions whereby a scientific explanation of the behaviour of objects pays no heed to the intentional actions of the objects it is trying to describe. Not only are aesthetic 'regularities' norms that may or may not be followed and may consciously and consistently be offended against, but we cannot identify them without having some conception of what it is for a rational will to follow a norm.

The act of bringing norms to consciousness will itself effect their status. While cognition describes regularities without any fear that its objects will be effected by the explanation it offers of their behaviour, cultural practice is reflexive in the sense that a part of its effectiveness consists in just this ability to change practices by making us conscious of them. Thus, while cognition and science allow an individual to explain the occurrence of an object by reference to empirical causes, natural laws, and the relation between objects, aesthetic practice in culture requires us to understand an object as a particular meaning proferred by another subject; and an individual must know what it is to participate in a dialogue between autonomous subjects concerned to gain a unity, between themselves, in reason and feeling.

If Kant can characterize our cognitive activity as seeking an agreement with the world and aesthetic activity as engagement in a dialogue with other subjects, then the latter represents a shift in emphasis from a concern with consciousness to one with community. The cognitive synthesis of a perception, in which the self gains its objects, puts an emphasis on the individual consciousness in its relation to objects. The judgement that an object is beautiful, in which a subject seeks to appreciate an object, involves an individual's relation to others in a community and a dialogue aimed at interpreting and understanding the work.

In spite of these differences, cognitive and aesthetic judgements can be seen to be complementary to each other in culture. In explaining the cultural nature of fine art Kant wants to reject the fragmented collection of individual perceptions and habits of thought that actually obtain in unreconstructed common sense. These form an arbitrary series and lack rational guiding principles, consistency, or unity. By contrast, the community is a unity whose public standards are drawn from and respect the human capacity for reason and feeling. It precludes arbitrary relations between monads seeking individual satisfaction in opposition to each other, and replaces them with a unified, intersubjective and persuasive dialogue between autonomous individuals. This community has to be constructed, and works of fine art are comprehended in the context of this cultural development toward the community.

However, although works of fine art differ in the sort of questions and considerations relevant to understanding them, they do not differ *as such* from empirical objects. Works of fine art are also objects in the world, and our experience of them must depend on the transcendental necessity of the categorical system that is constitutive of empirical consciousness and the experience of nature.

The categorical system may be seen as a core of concepts that must be presupposed for any objective experience to be possible, and their use in judgements also requires a unity of representations in the mind. Communication would be impossible if this categorical unity were absent, and even individuals who are to disagree must presuppose its validity. Those who share these presuppositions are the possessors of consciousness between whom communication is possible. As Kant thinks that the categories are necessary if experience is to be possible at all, communication in principle includes all those who are capable of experience. And, as Kant talks of experience in terms of the relation of rational faculties, we may expect that those capable of using rational faculties to gain and communicate knowledge are capable of effecting the relation of faculties involved in both aesthetic and cognitive judgements. Accordingly, our cognitive experience generally may be said to be complementary to aesthetic judgements.[111]

To defend this claim we must look more closely at aesthetic judgements. And this not only to justify the distinction from science and cognition suggested above; but also to show that the epistemological deduction of taste leaves room for us to ascribe a practical necessity to our experience of beauty. We bring to attention accounts of aesthetic necessity which are based on the nature of aesthetic judgements rather than on the cultural nature of fine art. What we hope to show is that the deduction of taste leads us to look to the cultural role of fine art and beauty to explain our ability to demand that others should agree with our judgements. This will also give substance to Kant's intention to link theory with practice in an 'intimate unity'.

Only when we have dealt with these issues will we be in a position to provide the promised justification of aesthetic necessity.

PART II

AESTHETIC JUDGEMENTS AND AESTHETIC NECESSITY

V

The Necessities of Taste, Fine Art, and the *Summum Bonum*

IT is in the Fourth Moment of the *Critique of Aesthetic Judgement* that Kant explicitly attends to the modality of aesthetic judgements. But what he says of 'necessity' there must be treated with caution, for the concept covers a number of senses in this *Critique*, depending on the epistemological or logical features of aesthetic judgements and their basis in an experience of pleasure. Among other things, it depends on whether we are concerned with the transcendental possibility of such judgements, with particular attempts to make them, with claims to success in judging, or with the legitimacy of our demand for agreement from others.

In the Deduction itself Kant shifts attention from necessity to subjective universality, arguing that the need to provide a deduction arises 'even where [judgement] requires subjective universality'.[1] And this shift seems to have led some commentators to claim that universality and necessity are always identical.[2] Consequently, it is thought that the deduction of the former would satisfy the requirements of the latter, and the Fourth Moment need be seen as only adding some features to a consideration of universality.[3]

If this were true and the deduction successful, then it may become unnecessary to consider any other sort of necessity. For the deduction would secure judgements against sceptical doubts, and, instead of providing further stages of critique, we would only need to produce rules for appreciating and criticizing fine art. If we can give some account of necessity apart from subjective universality, however, this reading would have to be discounted; and it becomes clear, once we identify the distinctive nature of aesthetic judgements, that it is essential to develop other senses of necessity. For the deduction legitimates the general transcendental possibility of making aesthetic judgements but, because of the subjective, singular, and autonomous nature of aesthetic judgements, this leaves open issues of the nature of attempts to make, and success in making *particular* actual judgements. Consequently, distinctions between transcendental, subjective, and objective necessity come into play and, as we shall see, correspondingly varied senses of a 'common ground' are also deployed, all of which must be understood if we are to understand aesthetic judgements with any completeness. Moreover, the epistemological uselessness of one of these distinctions suggests the need to bring in a practical compulsion to justify the force of aesthetic judgements. We may approach these distinctions in the following way.

The Analytic of the Beautiful sets out our expectations of judgements of taste, clarifying the character of our experience in the vocabulary of critical idealism and thereby also locating the areas where justificatory arguments will be needed. We learn that judgements must be disinterested and formal in order to ensure that they are singular but subjectively universal and necessary. To understand this fully, we must examine the distinction between appreciation and cognition in terms of the ideas of objectivity, subjectivity, and intersubjectivity. What makes the universality of aesthetic judgements subjective is that it attaches to a mere feeling, and the feeling is universal in that we expect it to carry more authority than an expression of merely personal preferences. Phrased in this way, subjective necessity does not refer to any other subjects: were a subject alone on the earth, his aesthetic judgements would still have the legitimacy guaranteed by a transcendental deduction. But whether he would or could make particular judgements is another matter, for, first, an interest in making aesthetic judgements is a consequence of living in society and, second, it is always possible that in spite of his self-reflection he only mistakenly believes that a particular judgement is one of taste. To account for the latter case, we need criteria by which to assess our self-reflection. And we will see that communication governs judgements: although inessential to justifying the transcendental basis for making aesthetic judgements generally, it plays an important role in considerations of the role and behaviour of particular actual aesthetic judgements.[4]

This, in turn, requires different senses of *sensus communis*. Whereas the deduction of taste depends on a 'common ground', whose possession warrants the possibility of taste, in other contexts the *sensus communis* is treated as 'the idea of a *public* sense'—not a sense like hearing or sight or taste, but a 'critical faculty' we use to avoid mistaking personal preferences for universal and communicable judgements. For in a putative actual judgement we may erroneously confuse particular aesthetic judgements with pleasure occasioned through ignorance, charm, emotion, pleasure in communication, interest, or confusion of aesthetic with cognitive judgements or ones of the sublime. The occurrence of any of these would more than show that our judgements were mistaken, they would show they were mere idiosyncratic claims and not aesthetic judgements at all. Consequently, we need criteria by which the success of our actual judgements is assured. And Kant proposes that we assess whether particular justifications are successful, and our preferred subjective responses universalizable, by considering whether others can gain our experience. As to justify an aesthetic judgement is to enable another subject to gain the same experience, a successful judgement must also be one that is communicated. Here, we rely on the *sensus communis* as a regulative ideal of satisfactory communication, and by means of this ideal seek to ensure the *success* of our actual particular aesthetic judgements. However, as this is an extension of the original epistemic use of a 'common ground', which legitimated the *possibility* of aesthetic judgements, it must be given its own justification.

As we said: only when we have a way of dealing with the empirical fact of these actual judgements—ours and those of other subjects—can we make full sense of not just the claim that others *can* make the same judgement but the claim that they *should* agree with our judgements. The deduction must show the possibility of a locution setting out what others 'should do', but because it does not allow us to derive conclusions about the validity of the response and claims we actually make, we need to understand further the justifications of the success of particular aesthetic judgements, of the claims we may make of others, of the reason why others should participate in the same activity. Just as Kant acknowledged the need for an additional justification of the necessity carried by empirical cognitive judgements—one additional to the necessity deployed through the deduction—we may insist that in addition to the force aesthetic judgements exert on the basis of their deduction, we need a justification of the demands particular aesthetic judgements make upon us. Kant seeks to justify the necessity of aesthetic judgements by arguing that the pursuit of beauty through understanding, criticizing, and evaluating fine art is a morally important activity. This is because actual judgements are governed by the idea of the *sensus communis*, and as an ideal for fine art the latter is dependent on Kant's expanded notion of the *summum bonum*.[5]

However, as the basis of aesthetic judgements lies in a subjective felt pleasure, it requires us to distinguish subjective from objective necessity in their case. As we shall see, a subject's aesthetic judgement may carry a rational conviction for himself, based on his own experience of a pleasurable state of mind, which, if the judgement is correct, will have intersubjective validity; but as it may be mistaken, its claim to intersubjective validity must be questionable. And the only guarantee of the success of a particular judgement, then, is that another subject makes a similar autonomous judgement, based on his own reflection on his pleasurable state of mind. Until such concurrence is gained the judgement has only subjective necessity—being based only on an autonomous judgement on his own state yet carrying a conviction that is more than merely psychological—but is unable to compel agreement from others. Once it is certain that the judgement is a successful one, and that it is correctly based on the *sensus communis* which a subject possesses in common with others, it may make a claim to objective necessity. However, the latter is only '*like* an objective principle' because its basis remains subjective and the judgement is only exemplary.

There is a paradoxical air to these claims—one which is more marked if the *sensus communis* is seen as an epistemological ideal. It suggests that whatever additional force its objective necessity may seek to give a subjectively necessary judgement, that compulsion must be otiose: as an ideal for successful judgement the force of objective necessity is felt only when it is unnecessary because agreement has already been reached. By contrast, a subjective necessity is unable to compel agreement or guarantee success in judging. However, if the *sensus communis* is seen also as a morally valuable ideal, then, as we shall see, the epistemic status conferred on an aesthetic judgement by describing it as objectively necessary involves a practical compulsion also. And it is just because of this dual role of the *sensus communis* that beauty combines theory and practice in an intimate unity.[6]

The points sketched out above need to be considered in more detail,[7] since they will clarify the relation of beauty to culture, showing how the early part of the *Critique of Aesthetic Judgement* fits with its later parts, and also placing the *Critique* in the context of Kant's other works. We may begin by looking at the ideas of objectivity and subjectivity, to show that cognition and appreciation are distinctive. This will lead us to the matter of aesthetic necessity.

Cognition and Appreciation

It is in the Analytic that Kant characterizes aesthetic judgements prior to abstracting their logical or epistemological features and providing their deduction. The Analytic has recently received serious attention, and in many ways the account given below follows the line mooted by others. Thus, it seems most fruitful to suppose it is constructed to provide analytic and explanatory arguments, where universality and necessity define the status a feeling must be given for it to ground an aesthetic judgement, while disinterestedness and finality are criteria 'by which particular feelings of pleasure may be decided to have the requisite status for justifying a judgement of taste'.[8] Further, our understanding of the *Critique* is best served by interpreting judgements of taste as the outcome of a double process of reflection, both producing pleasure and evaluating it.[9] And what is presented below is in the main compatible with these theses. Differences arise, however, because some features of Kant's thought are insufficiently stressed and their consequences drawn out incompletely.[10] The best way to clarify this issue is to contrast cognitive and aesthetic judgements.

Kant holds that cognitive judgements are objective, involve a determinate relation between the faculties of understanding and sensibility, and are capable of truth or falsity. Consequently, they are intersubjectively valid and carry a compulsion based on their relation to objects. By contrast, aesthetic judgements are subjective, depend on our feelings, and require communication between subjects rather than bearing truth or falsity by reference to objects. Consequently, they are intersubjective in a distinctive sense and require a commensurate necessity.[11]

All judgements are subjective in one sense because they depend on the existence and nature of the subject making judgements. But judgements which are ontologically subjective can be objective in epistemological and moral terms. Where the nature of the subject forms a necessary condition for judgements on objects or actions generally; or where agreement between subjects depends on the nature of the objects or ends, as where a subject's experience provides knowledge of phenomenal objects; or where a subject's intention or maxim can be universalized over all subjects, there we describe judgements as objective although they depend, ontologically, on the subject. For although a subject's response is involved, it is the validity of this in relation to objects that is at issue. The categorical structure of experience, for example, sets out the necessary conditions for our experience of objects and, therefore, is epistemologically objective. In basing himself on the categories a subject does not merely report on representations he has. He also commits himself to how his representations are interrelated and ordered; for the categorical system tells us of our experience of objects generally, and Kant's argument is that we cannot be conscious of the content of our minds as ours unless we are able also to conceive of some part of that content as perceptions of objects existing independently of our perceptions of them. So that although in a sense it depends on our nature as subjects who live in a world not entirely of our making, its business is to tell us of our experience of objects. Similarly, subjects of a given sort have intentions and goals; but by examining the nature of their goals we may arrive at conclusions about how they must act if they are not to deny their rational character. Moral theory may be said to be objective in that it concerns the discovery of ends which we must all have.

To develop the notion of objectivity we can use Kant's distinctions between the modalities of possibility, actuality, and necessity.[12] The possibility of experience requires satisfaction of the formal conditions which are set out in the categorical system as a conclusion of a transcendental deduction. If experience is to be at all possible, if our ordinary empirical claims are to be made legitimately, then those formal conditions must be satisfied and the categorical system is transcendentally necessary. Accordingly, an account of the possibility of judgements sets out the necessary conditions for epistemological objectivity generally.

However, knowing that judgements of experience are possible does not validate particular actual judgements. Clearly, when we actually make a particular judgement, we postulate—or take it as a proposition which is presupposed as immediately certain in our action[13]—that the conditions necessary for experience generally are satisfied; yet our judgement may be false. That is, actual judgements postulate their own possibility, but still need to be validated and shown to be true or false. And this brings us to a second sense in which judgements are epistemologically objective: actual judgements provide us with knowledge of ordinary phenomenal objects. Subjects have experience of objects, which they express in actual objective judgements which will depend on the nature of objects.

In making these actual judgements, the subject is neither entirely passive nor irrelevant. For Kant, empirical judgements involve a determinable relation between the faculties of sensibility and understanding. The first is essentially a passive, recipient capacity through which we gain the content of our minds—the sensory state, perceptions, representations, and so forth: intuitions ordered in time and some in space also. These are the materials of our experience, whose elements are organized—classified, discriminated, compared, and interrelated—under concepts by the understanding. In describing an object, we give the intuitions order or bring them 'under a rule' provided by the concept. The concept, that is, identifies the determinate order of our intuitions. In terms of faculties the understanding orders sensibility, and for the concept to be applied again, the material it brings under a rule must have the same determinate order. In this context, transcendental conditions do not tell us which particular cases or predicates and representations will be found in actual experience. For although the latter must satisfy the general conditions set out, empirical concepts will identify the determinate character of the object 'yielded by experience'. The objects are known through a posteriori judgements.

Clearly concepts are used to make objective judgements—which can be true or false, depending on whether they correspond to the way the world is. As the truth of a judgement depends on its agreement with an object, in an important sense agreement with other subjects does not provide objective judgements with any greater validity. First, Kant's deduction is directed at individuals' experience. It shows that an individual—any individual—must give the content of his or her mind a particular order: self-consciousness of a sequence of intuitions depends on experience of an objective realm. But the need for, or satisfaction of, these conditions does not depend on the existence or experience of other individuals. The question of other minds is dealt with by Kant some time after the deduction, and it does not show that intersubjectivity is a necessary condition for experience to be possible. Second, empirical judgements are similarly individual possessions in that a subject's experiences of an object do not depend on any other subject. A lone observer would still make true or false judgements about the world.

Nevertheless, empirical judgements are public in that the observer commits himself to something about the order and sorts of actual intuitions he *and others* would have were they to behave in relevant ways in relation to observed objects. He brings his intuitions 'under a rule' which will be followed by others. Consequently, in an important sense empirical judgements are intersubjectively valid: they must be 'valid at all times and equally for everybody, for if a judgement agrees with an object, all judgements about the same object must agree with one another, and thus the objective validity of the [actual] judgement of experience means nothing other than its necessary validity [for everyone]'.[14] Validity does not depend on the existence of other individuals, but has consequences for their judgements on the same objects in that it compels their agreement. Others cannot accept the grounds for a judgement yet still refuse to be convinced of its truth, for the former possesses an evidential force which leads us to accept the latter.

Further, feelings—say of pleasure or displeasure—play no part in justifying the truth or falsity of cognitive judgements. That a subject does not like heavy stones or that they can cause him pain is irrelevant to ascertaining the objective properties of the stone. Cognition involves subjectivity and understanding but it does not depend on the subject's psychology. Feelings of pleasure or pain, for example, tell us nothing of the object and vary from subject to subject, depending on their particular physiology. Further, they do not allow us to infer any general predicates of the object as if we could ascribe pleasurableness as a concept to the object. As Kant says, 'from concepts there can be no transition to the feeling of pleasure or pain'.[15]

Actual cognitive judgements postulate a transcendental necessity and intend to report on what is in the world independently of any particular perceivers. Where they agree with the state of things they claim validity. A true judgement is valid for all subjects, and compels agreement because it agrees with the state and explanation of events and objects. Where cognitive judgements are ordered and unified in science, there natural laws formulate determinate regularities governing the behaviour of objects. Coherence within the system gives cognitive judgements a necessity they would otherwise lack; and while their compulsion is derived from incorporation into the system, if they could not be shown to agree with and explain the state of objects, they would be falsified. The objective state of affairs would continue to subsist regardless of whether particular individuals believe it so.

Although we have referred to true judgements in explaining the nature of objective cognitive judgements, it should be clear that their truth does not determine whether they are judgements at all. To be judgements they need only postulate the necessary conditions Kant sets out in the deduction. Nevertheless, it should be clear that Kant also has criteria for success in actual cognitive judgements. For the latter may be true or false depending on whether they fit the world and our explanation of its events. Accordingly, a successful cognitive judgement is one that is true and so coheres with the set of explanatory statements and generalities incorporated into a scientific system. But a false judgement is no less a judgement: it asserts that some state of affairs obtains. In either case, judgements depend on agreement or disagreement with objects and with the system of scientific explanation. Even a system of science, in theory at least, can be constructed by a single individual by examining objects. His knowledge does not need other subjects even if he must treat himself as he would any other rational interpreting subject.[16] Nevertheless, true cognitive judgements can compel agreement from others.[17]

In all these features, aesthetic judgements differ significantly from cognitive ones. And accounts of Kant's aesthetic theory are likely to be mistaken where they try to apply the epistemological model of the First *Critique* too quickly to the Third *Critique*. Clearly, many of the concepts involved figure in both *Critiques*, but as their roles are different, we must treat the subjectivity, autonomy, basis in feeling, and intersubjectivity of actual aesthetic judgements as recommendations and require a distinctive necessity of them—one gained through cultural development.

A judgement is epistemologically subjective when it is 'incapable of becoming an element for cognition'.[18] It tells us nothing of the object and depends only on changes in the subject. Pleasure and pain, as states of the subject, Kant thinks, are entirely subjective. As they are based on feelings of pleasure, aesthetic judgements are subjective, able neither to provide knowledge of particular objects nor a necessary condition for the experience of objects generally. They depend on changes in the subject that cannot legitimately be understood as properties of things; and although it is usual to talk of beautiful objects,[19] strictly, aesthetic value does not belong to them.[20]

Yet aesthetic judgements are intersubjectively valid and not subjective in the further sense that responses to effects will so vary with subjects that they cannot claim any validity. A preference for sweet or sour tastes cannot make a legitimate claim to general validity because by nature it is particular to individuals. To explain his preference for apples a subject need say no more than that he likes their taste. Whereas he cannot expect others to appreciate apples merely because he does, even though the pleasure at the basis of aesthetic judgements may tell us nothing of objects, it is still intersubjectively valid. Individuals expect their aesthetic judgements to be valid and capable of being agreed to in spite of the fact that they depend ultimately on a change in the subject.

However, Kant is not claiming that aesthetic judgements involve a distinctive sort of pleasure:[21] instead, he holds that for various reasons experiences of pleasure can sometimes be given a particular status and the judgements based on this experience can claim to be valid for all subjects. Accordingly, his deduction is not directed at constituting an object. By contrast with the transcendental deduction of objective experience, which shows what conditions must be satisfied if we are to talk of objects at all, the deduction of aesthetic judgements does not suppose that the existence of pleasure needs to be justified or explained by setting out its necessary conditions. Rather, it seeks to show what conditions must be satisfied for some of our experiences of pleasure to claim validity for all subjects, showing they are intersubjectively valid even though our experience of pleasure gives us no knowledge of objects.

Kant justifies the validity of aesthetic judgements by reference to a pleasurable relation of cognitive faculties in a subject. Because the judgement is pleasurable, it is not available for the 'determination of the object (for the purposes of knowledge)'.[22] Nevertheless, as it results from the harmony of cognitive faculties, which we possess in common with others, and whose exercise characterizes us as rational and knowing creatures, we may expect that others can experience our pleasure in a similar exercise of their faculties. As this pleasurable judgement turns on a relation between faculties, its transcendental justification seeks to warrant its validity by reference to the faculties as a 'subjective factor which we presuppose in all men'.[23]

We shall examine Kant's deduction of taste later, after we have considered further the distinctive subjective nature of aesthetic judgements. Two features, their singularity and autonomy, are important to showing a third feature—their necessity. In the case of cognitive judgements it makes sense to dismiss a contrary judgement as false or irrational. We make assertions about objects on the basis of having grounds for our beliefs about them, where the grounds have evidential force in that we cannot agree with the grounds for a belief yet reject the belief itself. This does not require us to have the same experience of the object, as if we could not accept another perspective on it, nor that we have the same sensations, as if only the ability to distinguish colours by sight allows us to identify an object as red. Rather, it is necessary that we have the same beliefs about the object, based on adequate evidence for those beliefs. However, where evidence is inadequate, for example, the belief will be unjustified, and assertions can be shown to be false by showing the inadequacy or misconstrual of grounds. In the case of cognitive judgements organized in science, where we might offer to explain events by reference to nomological laws, it makes sense to dismiss a counter claim by showing that it fails to instantiate the law. Accordingly, judgements may be true or false, depending on their agreement with the object, and where a judgement fails to agree with our own judgement on or explanation of an object, there it makes sense to dismiss one of the contrary judgements because it is false.

Aesthetic judgements are based on a pleasurable relation of faculties in judgement, and can neither be dismissed as false nor be subject to the usual ways of generating assent. As they depend on the subject and his experience of pleasure, and not on the object's determinate properties, they cannot be dismissed for failing to agree with the object or with an explanation of its existence and behaviour. The character of the *subject's feeling* is crucial in their case, in that it must be pleasure arising from a relation of faculties for it would otherwise fail to be universalizable. That is, the judgement is subjective; and because our concern is with an experience of pleasure, denoting not the generally explicable nature of the object but the relation of faculties occasioned in our response to a particular, the aesthetic judgement is singular. As our state of mind is at issue while the nature of the object is not, our pleasure does not depend on the general predicates which characterize the object. We would say 'this flower is beautiful';[24] and we may even use a concept to identify the object—'this tulip is beautiful'[25]—yet not infer its beauty from the general concept. The claim that an object is beautiful depends only on the pleasurable judgement, and so cannot be inferred or deduced from any general quality of the object: no general rule applicable to the latter relates it to our individual experiences of pleasure in beauty.[26]

It may seem we have not yet shown that aesthetic judgements differ from cognitive ones in their 'intersubjectivity'. Just as what is discovered to be true by one subject must be true for all other subjects, we might say, so too aesthetic judgements are claimed for all subjects. Consequently we may expect both sorts of judgement to dismiss contrary claims as false. However, the subjectivity of aesthetic judgements makes them autonomous in a way that precludes compelling agreement from other subjects in a similar fashion. Just as the transcendental deduction of objective experience was addressed to the individual alone, setting out the conditions which must be satisfied for any individual to have self-consciousness, similarly the deduction of aesthetic judgements addresses the state of the subject, setting out the conditions which must be satisfied for a subjective experience of pleasure to be able to claim universal validity. As in the first case, the satisfaction of these *necessary* conditions does not depend on the existence or experience of others.

Further, cognitive judgements are autonomous in a similar way: we can only make judgements for ourselves. Autonomous cognitive judgements claim intersubjective validity for agreeing with an object. Here our judgements can have evidential force because the character of the object is of concern. But the autonomy of aesthetic judgements leads us to claim a distinctive validity, and their ground cannot count as evidence nor deploy a similar force. Aesthetic judgements are subjective for depending on an experience of pleasure. An experience of pleasure from a harmony of faculties is a ground for claiming universal or intersubjective validity because the state of mind is valid for all subjects: the same faculties must be possessed by all those who are capable of our ordinary experience. Here, however, a judgement is autonomous in that it has to be made by a subject for himself because he has to experience for himself a pleasurable relation of faculties. Another person's experience of pleasure cannot lead us to agree with him, for agreement requires us to have adequate evidence for the same beliefs, yet the only ground for this belief is the occurrence of a similar pleasurable relation of faculties.[27] And no one else can experience a subject's pleasure for him.

Nor can an experience of pleasure be compelled. A contrary cognitive judgement can be dismissed or supported by considering the object and evidence for a given belief, and we could deduce or infer other judgements from the nature and concept of the object. Aesthetic judgements are subjective in that our concern is with the subject's experience of pleasure, not with the object, and agreement can only be given by subjects making their own pleasurable judgements. The frequency, conviction or facility with which they are made by others cannot form any evidential basis for a subject's assent because the only ground for his judgement is the pleasurable judgement of taste. Thus, he can agree only if and when he makes the same judgement. And as his own judgement cannot be compelled by appeal to the fact of others' judgements or to induction from the nature of objects, he cannot expect to compel agreement from others.[28] And so we cannot dismiss a contrary judgement as false either, for the fact that pleasure is not occasioned in that case does not show the ground for our claim, and that someone judges an object beautiful does not compel others to make a pleasurable judgement, since their own judgements are the only ground for agreement.

At best, then, a subject puts forward his aesthetic judgement as an intersubjectively valid pleasurable relation of faculties, but cannot compel agreement in the way he might compel agreement with cognitive judgements, because aesthetic judgements are subjective, singular, and autonomous. That is, the claim to universal validity must be addressed to the subject and his experience of pleasure rather than to a principle or rule which covers the object because of its nature. Consequently, the expectation of universality is a relation between subjects or is an intersubjective validity. And as the aesthetic judgement is subjective, singular, and autonomous, it will exert a distinctive and, by comparison with cognitive judgements, a limited compulsion. As we shall see, however, other subjects' judgements do have an important role to play in confirming *actual* judgements of taste even though their judgements do not provide any evidential basis for a subject's own judgement.

We may further explain this feature of aesthetic judgements in the following way. Autonomy leads us, in aesthetic judgements, not to making assertions but to recommending a viewpoint and anticipating others' agreement on the basis, first, of our own postulation that aesthetic judgements are possible, and second, our conviction that ours is an instance of such a judgement. Conviction is based only on our experience of pleasure. And this shows us why actual judgements are vulnerable, being intersubjective in a sense which calls for a distinctive necessity. As we have said repeatedly, aesthetic judgements are concerned with the subject and his state rather than with the nature of the objects or the purposes they serve because of the type of objects they are. Moreover, cognitive and moral judgements are not concerned with the process of estimating or judgement, only with the objects judged to belong to one class or another. Cognition is concerned to establish the rule under which intuitions may be given a determinate order, and the process of judging is not itself a part of our concern with the object. By contrast, aesthetic judgements treat the object or its representation as an example of a 'universal rule' denoting a pleasurable state of mind experienced by subjects. And, in order to establish the universality of pleasure, in these judgements we first estimate or reflect on the suitability of an object to a pleasurable state of mind *and*, second, reflect or assess whether the resulting pleasure is universalizable. By contrast with cognitive judgements, which are constituted by applying a rule to a given material, aesthetic judgements are concerned with their own origin and their own application. They involve a pleasurable estimation of a representation *and* a reflection on the source of our pleasure.[29]

Kant clarifies this aspect of aesthetic judgements by treating them as recommendations.[30] To understand aesthetic judgements we must not only explain what the source of our pleasure is, but also 'anticipate' others' judgements by seeing that the source of our judgement is a common one. That is, we try to show that pleasure arises from a particular relation of cognitive faculties—one which all subjects can attain: that pleasure is not subjective and idiosyncratic like the preference for apples over elderberries. Because pleasure is something a subject must experience for himself, aesthetic judgements are autonomous, so that a subject's reckoning that his is a universalizable pleasure does not provide a basis for predicting what others will do. But he may *anticipate* what may happen if other subjects judge the object on the same grounds as underlie his judgement. At best, here he imputes or attributes this pleasure to others on the basis of his conviction over his own case. Nevertheless, he is unable to predict that they will try to gain or succeed in gaining the same pleasure. He can only hope to propose from his own case that with such and such a use of rational faculties such a pleasure results. Aesthetic judgements, although they cannot compel others, in effect propose that they can adopt a viewpoint like the subject's because the latter's is a claim about the rational and feeling nature of subjects as exhibited in the act of judging. Thus, others 'ought' to follow and make the same judgement for themselves.[31] But from the rationality of this act it does not follow that a subject can predict that other subjects will adopt it. By contrast, if we could treat cognitive judgements in a similar way, then from the rationality of cognitive judgements it would follow that we can predict and compel agreement to a true judgement.

We shall return to this issue when we treat aesthetic necessity later in this chapter. Here, the subjectivity, singularity, autonomy, and recommendatory nature of aesthetic judgements leads us to see that they seek a distinctive confirmation—one which makes the matter of their actual success an important issue.

Aesthetic Judgements: Confirmation and Communication

To understand the distinctive confirmation meted out to aesthetic judgements, we must recall the claim made in the Analytic, that disinterestedness and finality are criteria 'by which particular feelings of pleasure may be decided to have the requisite status for justifying a judgement of taste'.[32] That is, to evaluate whether our pleasure is universalizable and thereby to decide that ours is an aesthetic judgement, we consider whether our actual pleasure may not have been caused by an object rather than being the experience of a judgement and its relation of cognitive faculties. If the judgement is disinterested—if our pleasure arises from the judgement alone and so is free of an interest we may have in an object because the latter causes pleasure in us—then we may identify ours as a disinterested aesthetic pleasure rather than as a pleasure caused by the object in question because of its characteristic effect upon us. That is, our actual aesthetic judgements are made on the basis of this reflection on disinterestedness and finality; it is a reflection we must carry out for ourselves and which recommends itself to others rather than compels agreement. This suggests that we need to consider actual instances further, to show how subjective and autonomous judgements can be confirmed or what it is for a recommendation to be made so that it can be accepted. For we may justify the validity of judgements, showing that they are transcendentally possible and that it is rational to make them, yet, because of the nature of reflection, not have justified our dealings with their actual instances.

The latter is more than a matter of psychology. It is possible that a subject is unable to make aesthetic judgements because, for reasons having to do with traumas over feeding which he had as a child and whose memory he has subsequently repressed, he is unable to distinguish between a displeasure caused by seeing apples and the absence of disinterested delight in Cézanne's *Still Life with Apples*. In the case of this psychological difficulty, we may be able to make him amenable to responding disinterestedly to Cézanne's painting by bringing the memory to consciousness and treating it. By contrast, our concern is with whether and how our actual judgements could be thought successful at all. Because judgements are subjective and autonomous and depend on the subject's consciousness or reflexion on his own state, we also seem to lack satisfactory criteria for the validity of particular actual judgements in spite of knowing that such judgements are possible.

It is because judgements of taste are subjective and autonomous that a subject's certainty in his own case becomes a crucial issue. Kant acknowledges this difficulty when he writes it is possible that 'for himself [a subject] can be certain [that he is making a judgement of taste] from his mere consciousness of the separation of everything belonging to the agreeable and the good from the delight remaining to him', but adds that this is 'a claim, which under these conditions, he would also be warranted in making, were it not that he so frequently sinned against them and passed an erroneous judgement'.[33] But he does make mistakes in actual instances, sometimes confusing charm, emotion, sensuality, pleasure from communication, moral interest, and other sorts of approbation with the universally valid pleasure of aesthetic judgements. For disinterestedness and formality are not self-evident characteristics of objects or experience. Disinterestedness does not appear to us in consciousness in the way our experience of pleasure or pain does, and the aesthetic judgement, whose exercise is transcendentally justified yet can actually be mistaken, needs some criteria by which its disinterestedness and formality can be assessed in the actual case. Otherwise we may never be able to know whether ours is an aesthetic pleasure or one whose source is psychological.

If we are unable to identify disinterestedness in our experience and cannot directly claim validity for actual judgements on the basis of our own reflection, then we are unable to defend the claim to have a universalizable pleasure. Further, even if we could indirectly identify disinterestedness and were to set out the viewpoint of our own judgements and, so, to hold that the necessary conditions for judgements have been satisfied, we would in any case be unable to *assert* the judgement or compel agreement because, at best, it is only a recommendation made on the basis of our own autonomous experience. As it happens, our reflection on our experience may itself be mistaken, and here we need criteria for certainty about our autonomous subjective judgement and self-reflection. Accordingly, Kant proposes that only another's experience of his own aesthetic judgement can go to confirm a subject's own singular judgement.

As judgements depend on our subjective consciousness and are autonomous, Kant is led to assert a programmatic statement toward the end of Section 8: that 'nothing is postulated in a judgement of taste but the idea of a *universal voice* in respect of delight . . . ; consequently, *only* the *possibility* of an aesthetic judgement capable of being at the same time deemed valid' has been acknowledged.³⁴ In making a particular judgement of taste on the basis of the transcendental deduction, the subject claims that given the legitimacy of ascribing universality, and because of his viewpoint, his pleasurable experience is one capable of being universalized. That is, if his own actual judgement is based on conditions which others can attain, they too should be able to agree with his judgement.

The last claim, we know, can be mistaken; and Kant goes on to link the possibility of error in actual judgements with the need for communication. At best, in aesthetic judgements we can only *impute* agreement to everyone, on the basis of various assumptions about the nature, psychology, and rationality of ourselves and others as subjects, and are led to treat the putative aesthetic judgement as 'an instance of the rule in respect of which it looks for confirmation not from concepts but from the concurrence of others'.[35] For the only way to confirm an aesthetic judgement is to bring another subject to gain the pleasure felt by the judging subject. That is, given that a putative judgement may be mistaken despite the subject eradicating interest from it, the only way he can support his claim for the rightness of his own judgement is by enabling another subject to make the same judgement; for if others can make the same judgement, if we can succeed in communicating it, it goes to confirm that our own reflection and pleasure are universalizable and that our actual judgement is not mistaken.

This illustrates that Kant is not relying on a defunct theory[36] when he writes that 'it is the universal capacity for being communicated incident to the mental state in a given representation which, as the subjective condition of the judgement of taste, must be fundamental, with the pleasure in the object as its consequent'.[37] Kant's claim is that if we are to know that pleasure in actual instances is intersubjectively valid, the relation of faculties from which it arises cannot be incapable of being public or 'must have a universal capacity for being communicated'.[38] To show this, we need only recall that the possibility of error—in which we would wrongly impute agreement to others on the basis of our own viewpoint, judgement, and pleasure—is raised by saying that judgements and pleasure seek the concurrence of others. We are mistaken when our pleasure turns out to be mixed with charm, emotion, or is merely psychological—and the presence of such confusion explains the nature of our mistake. Though we may not recognize our mistakes through our own reflection, we could do so when our judgement is unable to gain concurrence—when it fails to be communicated because the judgement cannot claim universal validity.

The last may seem to conflate concurrence with communication: it is not clear that the one requires the other. Certainly, one sense in which concurrence is prepared for is that by pointing to its conditions in himself, a subject, in making a claim to universal validity for his judgement, also indicates the viewpoint and conditions which must be satisfied in others if they are to make the same judgements. But while this may lead to concurrence, there seems to be no clear need for communication. That there is such a need in actual particular cases becomes clear when we remember that considerations of disinterest and formality by themselves are inadequate to establishing universality in the actual case. Consequently, we need some other guarantee that ours is an aesthetic judgement. And we are assured of the validity of actual judgements only when we are able to communicate them: when we enable others to make the same actual judgement. In the absence of communication we would not know whether another subject's pleasure were arbitrary—a sheer coincidence in which pleasure is accidentally induced by irrelevant factors rather than the result of his making the same judgement as ourselves. And as we cannot *assert* our judgements, we *recommend* them on the basis of the viewpoint we have taken up in our judgements, and seek confirmation through their successful communication.[39]

Communication thus turns out to be fundamental to assessing our actual particular judgements of taste. However, communication is not the ground for reflective pleasure, and it does not make aesthetic judgements transcendentally possible. Although we may use its communication as a measure or mark of the universality of the actual case, we do not suppose that our pleasure is universal simply *because* it has 'subjective universal communicability'. That much is implied by saying that the 'mental state' is the object of our concern. As Kant is quick to point out, the 'universality of the *subjective conditions* of estimating forms the *sole* condition of this universal subjective validity of the delight . . .'.[40]

Kant also says of communication that its 'pure subjective [aesthetic] estimating of the object . . . is antecedent to the pleasure in it, and is the basis of this pleasure in the harmony of faculties'.[41] This suggests that an assessment of communicability is the basis of an harmonious and pleasurable relation of faculties. This would contradict his earlier claims were it not that Kant is here concerned only with particular actual judgements, and there is an important sense in which particular actual successful communication results in a universalizable pleasure. For our communication of pleasure in the beautiful is successful when others experience pleasure for themselves. That is, success in communication gives rise to universalizable pleasure in the beautiful in other subjects because they make the same universally valid judgement as ourselves. Similarly, so far as the conditions we consider in ensuring that our pleasure is intersubjective are those which ensure that it is universally communicable, we could say that the intersubjectivity of pleasure arises from the conditions of its communicability. This is the point of Kant's comparison of the 'universal capacity for communication' of aesthetic judgements with the universal communicability of 'cognition and representations such as appurtenant to cognition'.[42]

Moreover, we must mean successful communication here, rather than mere 'communicability' (so far as the latter does not bear reference to successful communication). 'Communicability' is an unsatisfactory criterion because it depends on the sort of reflection which was shown capable of erroneously claiming universality. And it is no guarantee of universality, for we can assess it only by reference to ourselves, in our own autonomous judgements, by which we may at best recommend and impute agreement to other subjects if we could be sure that we had not made a mistake in our reflection. Here we add nothing to our understanding of or dealing with actual aesthetic judgements. Because communicability is entirely dependent on the fallible reflection in which we can mistake an experience of pleasure for a judgement of taste when it is no such thing at all, we cannot be sure that our particular recommendations are justified, and we have made no progress in warranting any actual instances of them.

What we need to do then is to bring in considerations of success. Actual judgements of taste are in a peculiar position. For while the possibility of judgements may be justified, and one sort of scepticism refuted, another sort of scepticism, directed at whether we can at all know putative judgements to be actual judgements of taste, is left unanswered if, in making such autonomous and subjective judgements, we can only rely on a reflection which is by nature corrigible, which lacks criteria self-evident in reflection, lacks reference to an independent object and, in the case of communicability, cannot depend on any other subject either. The only satisfactory standard by which to judge whether an actual pleasure is universal, therefore, is to see whether others can experience it. That is, we must see whether it can be communicated, whether others are able to bring their rational faculties in the same relation and so make the same aesthetic judgement. And while we may *explain* the communicability of a judgement by saying that these subjective conditions must be fulfilled, this will not satisfy our claim that an actual particular instance of pleasure is an aesthetic judgement. For we may be mistaken in our judgement of whether they are fulfilled. Only its successful communication will show that we have succeeded in making an actual judgement of taste. Accordingly, Kant's claim that taste may be conceived of as the 'faculty of estimating what makes our feeling in a given representation *universally communicable*'[43] must involve considerations of success and of 'concurrence from others'.[44]

We have seen that aesthetic judgements are intended to be subjective, autonomous, pleasurable, and intersubjectively valid, but unable to compel agreement. They can be treated as recommendations of a particular viewpoint, and their communication is crucial to actual judgements. Consequently, we may also expect, first, that their necessity will be similarly distinctive and, second, that an explanation of the possibility of taste will take account of its special character. And in the next section we will look at the nature of necessity before turning to the *sensus communis* and the possibility of taste.

The Fourth Moment and Necessity

Being aesthetic, judgements of taste have to do with pleasure. But whereas there are contingent relations possible between consciousness, objects, and pleasure, in judgements of taste the relation is necessary.[45] Thus, an object may actually cause us pleasure, and so lead us to judge it agreeable, or it is at least possible that every representation or content of consciousness happens to give rise to pleasure. But in both cases, the association of delight with the object is contingent. By contrast, in aesthetic judgements we take pleasure to have a necessary connection with our consciousness, and it is the apriority of such a relation between pleasure and some feature of our consciousness that needs to be proven.

However, such a proof must aim for a distinctive apriority and necessity. It cannot be 'a theoretical objective necessity', like that we depend on in cognition, by which we might 'cognize *a priori* that everyone *will feel* this delight in the object that is called beautiful by me'. In cognitive judgements we describe objects, applying concepts of an objective world to organize our representations. Our consciousness and our awareness of the external world stand or fall together, and our consciousness that objects have a particular property can legitimately lead us to dismiss contrary claims as false. But the claim that an object is beautiful was seen to denote a pleasurable state of mind; it is not a classification of the object for having a nature of a certain type. Consequently, pleasure is not like a concept applied to the representation. We might expect every rational subject to agree with a cognitive judgement on the nature of an object, so that if pleasure were similarly associated with objects there we would know that our judgement will be agreed to by everyone just as if it were a cognitive judgement. But as aesthetic judgements are distinctive, we cannot expect an exactly similar necessity.

Nor is aesthetic necessity simply like that of moral judgements.[46] The latter would also require us to classify an object under a particular concept or objective rule. While cognitive judgements use objective theoretical concepts, practical judgements construe objects as satisfying or failing to satisfy a practical rule by virtue of the nature of the object, and our pleasure in it would be determined by its ability to satisfy a moral demand. Hence satisfaction of a moral compulsion may stimulate pleasure, but that denotes the object and its satisfaction of the objective law. It does not denote the subject, as aesthetic judgements do.

In summary, Kant proposes the following contrasts.[47] First, aesthetic judgements denote subjects and are not determined by the type of the object being judged. Both cognitive and moral judgements, by contrast, concern themselves with the nature or type of object. Second, aesthetic necessity cannot be an analytic one, based only on the relation between concepts, for it is based on an experience of pleasure rather than on whether the antecedent of a judgement 'contains' its consequent. Nor, third, is aesthetic necessity something about which we can make an inductive generalization based on the a priori conditions of experience generally: for then it would be merely contingent or a posteriori, and could not claim a priori universality and necessity.

Instead, aesthetic necessity 'can only be termed exemplary. In other words, it is a necessity of the assent of *all* to a judgement regarded as exemplifying a universal rule incapable of formulation'.[48] The qualifications that exclude cognitive and moral judgements, which show that the experience of beauty is not constituted in the way the other two might be, result from trying to ascribe necessity to aesthetic reflective judgements. Necessity attaches to our state of mind and its pleasure. And it depends on the order and relation of faculties occasioned by the particular, not on the general nature of the object itself—neither on how well it suits moral requirements nor on 'the nature of the internal or external possibility, by this or that cause, of the object'.[49] Necessity 'can only be termed *exemplary*' because our judgement that an object is beautiful is a claim that the particular 'exemplifies a universal rule'. It is an example because it is the object of a singular reflective judgement, which proceeds to examine and assess our state of mind in relation to a particular; and it is exemplary because the order and relation of faculties occasioned results in a pleasure which we expect *all* other rational and feeling subjects to appreciate. We do not seek to abstract a rule under which that object and all others of that type must be classified for us to describe it as beautiful, for what is of interest is the intersubjective validity of our state of mind in responding to it. As the judgement assesses the particular object by reference ultimately to the state of mind of the subject, its necessity attaches to the subject and his state of mind, not to the object for the sort of object it is.

Further, Kant clarified the nature of aesthetic judgements by treating them as recommendations. To understand aesthetic judgements we must not only explain what the source of our pleasure is, but also 'anticipate' others' judgements by seeing that the source of our judgement is a common one. A subject may *anticipate* the result which will follow if other subjects adopt the same viewpoint as underlies his judgement; but he is unable to predict that they will try to gain the same pleasure. An aesthetic judgement, accordingly, in effect proposes that they adopt such a viewpoint. That is, aesthetic judgements recommend that other subjects 'ought' to adopt such a viewpoint and act by making that judgement. Kant writes that 'everyone *ought* to give the object in question his approval *and* follow suit in describing it as beautiful',[50] where the 'ought' is basically a claim about the rational and feeling nature of subjects, as exhibited in the act of judging, and anticipates how others would judge the object.

Cognitive judgements are not anticipatory in quite this way.[51] The recommendation in aesthetic judgements denotes the subject's pleasurable state of mind. Any necessity this involves attaches to what is revealed of the subject, for the judgement proposes that such and such an act be seen as an exemplification of the rational and sensuous nature of subjects. To accept it is to take it that *this* is how subjects are: it shows at least that we are not indifferent to what we take subjects to be. By contrast, cognition emphasizes a relation to the object. Necessity attaches to our claims about the object or, in science, to the order of our knowledge of the relation of objects to each other: and the subjective nature of the percipient is not our immediate concern.

By pointing out why it makes sense to say one *ought* to judge in such and such a way, Kant is clarifying one aspect of the necessity of aesthetic judgements. This sort of recommendation is an example put forward by the subject to show how his rational and feeling nature is engaged in gaining a pleasure which he thinks is intersubjectively valid, and which, consequently, carries a compulsion for him which he claims also has validity for others.[52] That is, any compulsion involved in the latter, its recommended viewpoint, is a subjective necessity, based on the subject's own state, and addressed to other subjects and their state. But it is still only a recommendation, and not a basis for prediction. For there is no guarantee that the subjective basis will be assented to by others in the judgements they make.

We saw that to make a judgement is to accept that the nature of the subject is not a matter of indifference. It not only shows how subjects would act if they were like ourselves, it is also a claim about what we should look for in subjects for them to be suitably like ourselves. This is why in making a judgement of taste its subject is also recommending a point of view from which to regard subjects. That is, in making an aesthetic judgement a subject supposes, first, that his judgements are 'in accordance with all the requisite data for passing judgements': he supposes that his judgements are proceeding by reference to the relevant features of the representation and his response. Second, he supposes that this way of making judgements, this exhibition of what is important in the subject, is legitimate and so may be recommended to others. Hence the necessity of these judgements is 'still only pronounced conditionally',[53] for implicit in them is the claim that we should look at subjects in such and such a way. 'We are suitors for agreement from everyone else'[54] because we propose to attend to particular features. Consequently, the force of necessity is qualified and subjective in that as yet our concern is with the subject's proposal, based on his own judgement, that such and such a feature in the subject is what we should focus on.

At this point we may introduce a sceptical note, whose resolution points to the need for another sense of necessity. For while we had been concerned with the subjective necessity of particular judgements we saw that we must also consider the matter of their success. Kant says 'we would be able to count on this agreement' from other subjects to our judgement and its implicit proposal of how subjects are to be regarded if we could be sure our judgements were correct—'provided we were always assured of the correct subsumption of the case under that ground as the rule of approval'.[55] Whereas we were formerly suitors for agreement to particular judgements which claimed subjective necessity, now to 'count on this agreement' is to be more than a suitor. It is for the subject to have his suit accepted, where a condition for such *success* is the '*assurance* of a *correct* subsumption'. While we may know that we can recommend our judgement to others and ascribe subjective necessity, whether any particular such proposal is successful is a different issue. As we saw, it is possible to be mistaken in our actual judgements, and so we must use communication as a criterion for success in judgement, by which we are assured that a given subsumption is correct. And we may expect that a communicated and confirmed judgement will carry a distinctive necessity. Such necessity may be termed 'objective' in order to distinguish it from subjective necessity.

Kant also claims that the possibility of making such judgements, proposing which features of the subject we must attend to, is dependent on the supposition that there is 'common ground' which we all possess. It seems that we are bold enough to be suitors for agreement, and so claim that intersubjectively valid pleasure is possible, 'because we are fortified with a ground common to all'.[56] We presuppose that the particular feature which judgements recommended us to attend to is one that all others may be expected to possess. This possibility of taste will sustain the legitimacy of our recommendation of how subjects are to be regarded and of our anticipating that they should judge objects in the proposed way. But the supposition that there is a ground common to all leaves other doubts about the comprehensiveness of Kant's theory,[57] for we need to account for the *success* of particular judgements and so must understand their necessity in relation to the common ground.

We shall turn to this in the next section. First, it is appropriate to remember that Kant thinks that aesthetic judgements, or the feelings on which they are based, are capable of being required of other subjects 'as a duty'.[58] The imperative connotations of what we 'ought' to do or the 'recommendation' we make in judgements may also be given a more substantial meaning, it seems, and may accordingly claim a moral force or necessity which must be shown to cohere with the senses of necessity we have already presented. Whether this ascription of moral value is possible or necessary we shall consider later, after we have become clearer on the epistemological necessities we are presently considering.

The Necessity of Taste, A Common Ground, and the Sensus Communis

From what we have seen of necessity, we may suppose Kant's assertion at the end of the Fourth Moment, that the beautiful 'is cognized as object of a *necessary* delight', is ambiguous between subjective and objective necessity. And as he himself later deduces only the subjective universal validity of judgements generally, we may take it that the Fourth Moment sets out three distinctive senses of necessity. Accordingly, given the need to provide grounds justifying ascriptions of necessity, we may expect to discover different but related grounds for the three senses of necessity involved—for transcendental possibility, subjective, and 'objective' necessity.

A distinction between necessity and possibility that we pointed to earlier was that while communicability was inessential to justifications of possibility, it could be seen as a criterion by which to consider the actual aesthetic judgements we make, to justify their compulsion. This distinction gives us a clue to what Kant wants to propose. We may expect that possession of a 'common ground' is the justifying basis for the possibility of taste, while the particular judgements of taste we actually make, which stand in need of separate criteria because we cannot derive conclusions about their necessity from their transcendental basis, will be ordered by reference to communication. The latter, in turn, may be guided by an idea such as the *sensus communis*, which allows for a distinction between attempted and successful communication.

When we turn to the *Critique of Judgement* this is indeed what we find.[59] The first conception of 'common sense' appears in Section 20, where it is treated as a subjective principle by which we assess whether our own response is universally valid. If we are able to show that in common with other subjects we possess a ground which is the source of a pleasurable response, then we may be justified in believing that other subjects will also be able to feel a similar pleasure and, so, in the case of a harmonious relation of cognitive faculties, we will have an a priori principle for the universal validity of a judgement of taste.

In introducing the common sense as a subjective principle, Kant also prepares us to accept that a subject's recommendation in a judgement seeks to refer representations of the object not to a determinate relation of faculties under a concept but to their pleasurable harmony. Were the judgement based on a 'definite objective principle' or no principle at all, either it would lead to an order of representations which subjects would have to accept by virtue of the nature of objects, or it would lead to a situation where we were unable to provide an intersubjectively valid order. In the one case, a subject would recommend it as an order on the basis of objects being taken to be of particular types, and in the other case he would have no justification for recommending it at all. Similarly, ordinary common understanding is guided by 'obscurely represented principles', which are conceptualized even if the set of concepts and principles is not always internally coherent. Obviously each of these cases differs from that of aesthetic judgements. And Kant associates judgements of taste, their subjective principle of a common sense, and a feeling of pleasure, by saying that the judgement of taste 'depends on our presupposing the existence of a common sense [or common ground]'.[60]

But this introduces a second use of 'common sense'. For Kant adds in parenthesis that the common sense 'is not to be taken to mean some external sense but the effect arising from the free play of our powers of cognition'. And this effect can be nothing other than pleasure or 'feeling of life'. So the common sense is now taken to be a feeling, which results from a relation of faculties that we can expect of every subject. This new meaning of 'common sense' is related to the first use, compatible with it, and required by Kant's present concern with particular empirical aesthetic judgements and the claims we can make on their behalf. For by characterizing the common sense as a feeling that is an effect of a reflection, Kant is shifting attention away from transcendental possibility to the actuality of judgements. And the shift is necessary here just as it was in the case of science. The knowledge that aesthetic or cognitive judgements generally are possible does not do anything to validate the particular judgements we make; rather it raises the issue of how the particular examples of judgement are to be ordered. In the case of objective knowledge, on the basis of causality as an idea or principle of organization, we were expected to organize our experience into a systematic and explanatory science where coherence with the system gave its elements an empirical necessity. By contrast, as aesthetic judgements are singular, autonomous, and subjectively universal, coherence with objects or with judgements on them can add nothing to their acceptability. But their communication does provide for a community among subjects. So if particular judgements, or the feelings of pleasure which are occasioned in them, are considered by reference to an idea of a common sense or *sensus communis* as a community of feeling, then we gain some order for the particular judgements we make and provide them with a compulsion they would otherwise lack.

The common sense as a feeling or effect of a reflective 'free play of our cognitive powers' differs from its use as a transcendental condition because the former concerns an actual judgement of taste and serves as a rule for its order and organization. Of course, this use of common sense as an idea must depend on its deduction as a priori principle for the universal validity of aesthetic judgements generally. Therefore the second may be expected to be compatible with the first. However, the reference to communicating actual judgements does add something to the deduction, because even if an aesthetic judgement were universally valid, the a priori principle which legitimates this conclusion must be supplemented by considerations covering what it means to convey our pleasure in the sense of another subject experiencing that feeling. This requires something more than the addition of a pragmatic element, for although the communication of judgements is not essential to deducing their possibility, other doubts about actual judgements are resolved through considerations of communication.

In any case, when Kant comes to consider the common sense as an idea, he is merely using it in the definition of ideas he will provide later[61] but already has in mind. In this context, the common sense as an idea is a principle by which particulars are ordered, where the order, first, is subjective in being brought about by reference to the pleasurable state of mind of the subject and, second, may be seen as an effect of or as seeking to communicate and maintain an intersubjectively valid pleasure.[62] That is, judgements of taste recommend that we ought to order representations of objects in accordance with the principle that we seek to maintain an intersubjectively valid pleasure arising from all subjects' states of mind. Consequently, the 'ought' of particular aesthetic judgements depends on an idea of a common sense, and 'only under the presupposition . . . of such a common sense, are we able to lay down a judgement of taste'.

To 'lay down' a judgement is to make a particular judgement,[63] and when Kant goes on to characterize his argument as the claim that 'the universal communicability of a feeling presupposes a common sense',[64] both phrases emphasize his concern with particular actual judgements.[65] As it remains 'a matter of uncertainty whether a person who thinks he is laying down a judgement of taste is, in fact, judging in conformity with the idea',[66] we still need to be assured that assent is gained and deserved. And in the section entitled 'The necessity of the universal assent that is thought in a judgement of taste, is a subjective necessity which, under the presupposition of a common sense, is represented as objective',[67] Kant uses the idea of a common sense to argue to their 'objective' necessity. His concern is no longer simply with the possibility of aesthetic judgements or with the nature of actual judgements as recommendations. It is with the *assent* given to the recommendation made in a judgement of taste.

And this raises a third meaning for 'common sense', which Kant often denotes by calling it a *sensus communis*. The second use of common sense was as a feeling; the third sees it as a faculty or ability; it is 'the idea of a *public* sense, that is a faculty of estimation'.[68] It is a *sense* in that the order of representations and the organization of particular judgements is based on a felt pleasure, and public in that the order may be appreciated and the organization conducted by all those who accept the recommended basis in a common sense.[69] But Kant is now identifying the common sense with the ability to make such assessments. Indeed, he goes on immediately to suggest that *taste* is a public sense, so that the common sense is both the feeling shared *and* the ability to judge that the feeling *is* shared. Of course, this sense still depends on the first use of common sense as a subjective a priori transcendental principle; and it extends the second use by bringing in the ability to consider the *successful* communication of judgements. Further, obviously this use introduces the element of empirical necessity or its aesthetic equivalent, and while it does not change the task of the deduction,[70] it does qualify its role by raising questions about particular aesthetic judgements. For the ability to estimate our particular judgement, it now appears, must be guided by some conception of what is to count as *successful* communication, of how it governs the judgements we actually make, and for which we claim necessity.

This last use of common sense will be considered further later, but some points may be made here. As we saw, Kant raises the issue in terms communicating judgements. Where a judgement claims 'objective' necessity, the subject contends, everyone can and must correctly subsume the case 'under that ground as the rule of approval'[71] because his own judgement is such a correct subsumption. In 'all judgements by which we describe anything as beautiful, we tolerate no one else being of a different opinion'.[72] Our certainty about our own subsumption leads us to claim of our feeling that it has other and more authority than can be claimed by arbitrary pleasures in tastes, colours, sounds, and so on.

The involvement of the *sensus communis* and its reference to success-ful communication in aesthetic judgements gives these a particular sort of necessity. In making the judgement, in reflecting on our estimation of the object, and by separating out 'everything belonging to the agreeable and the good from the delight remaining to me', we let our judgement serve as 'an example of the judgement of the common sense'.[73] Consequently, it can have only 'exemplary validity' because it works by exhibiting its satisfaction of the common sense rather than by a classifying or subsuming an instance under a rule or concept. That is, the common sense as an idea cannot be met in experience, but when in aesthetic judgements we consider objects for themselves rather than as belonging to a given class, every successful judgement exemplifies the common sense, as if this individual case were adequate to the idea. As Kant holds that where a particular example is adequate to an idea, there it is an ideal[74] and functions as an exemplary or ideal norm, for the particular exemplification of the common sense in a beautiful object to be adequate to the idea is for it to be an ideal and to have a commensurate 'exemplary validity'.

Further, the necessity by which we demand universal assent will only be '*like* an objective principle'.[75] First, if our judgement satisfies the *sensus communis*, where the latter is understood as successful communication, then as the *sensus communis* can only be an idea, it will exercise its normative force as an ideal: as an instance adequate to an idea. It will not have the force commensurate with our conceptualizing a maxim or rule for action that is universalizable; and it will not work as, say, a categorical imperative demanding that individuals do such and such, but will be seen as a valuable example of what individuals attempt and attain through appreciating an object. Second, necessity is only *like* objective necessity in that it relates to a feeling of pleasure, and so is subjective in the special sense Kant suggests by saying that pleasure can never be part of our knowledge.[76] Accordingly, it 'determines its object *in respect of delight* . . . with a claim to the agreement of everyone, just *as if* it were objective',[77] but not as an objective principle.

We have already mentioned the other contrast of such a quasi-objective necessity: an actual judgement is still subjective in that it is based on a subject's assessment of his own feeling. While he himself assents to it, in the sense of separating out everything that he thinks might disrupt its intersubjective validity, and so sees it as a successful judgement for himself, its necessity is still subjective in that only he has assented to it. If judgements make us suitors for agreement, then, in reflecting upon his estimation for himself, the subject supposes that because it is based on his rational faculties, and is not merely a matter of psychology, the judgement carries some authority. Were the judgement actually based on the common sense, and free of error, its necessity would be 'represented as objective' in the sense proposed above.[78]

We may conclude from the present discussion that the transcendental possibility of judgements of taste and the validity of attempts to make such judgements may be distinguished from questions of our success in making them or the necessity they possess through correctly recommending their subjection to the *sensus communis*. Further, the subject's own certainty that such is their basis, the subjective necessity of taste, is distinguishable from an 'objective' necessity that is ascribed when they are actually so based. Moreover, both subjective and 'objective' necessity must be exemplary, so that the latter is only like an objective principle, and the *sensus communis* serves as an ideal norm that we try to attain by making aesthetic judgements. It is an ideal norm in reason *and* feeling, and to understand Kant's account further, we must first examine the deduction to show that we are justified in presupposing a common sense and an a priori validity for our judgements. As we shall see, Kant goes on to argue that taste must be seen as a *sensus communis*— it is neither just based on a common sense nor simply exemplifies it— and, second, its necessity must be understood accordingly.

The Possibility of Taste

In Section 31 Kant shows again that although he has shifted from talking of necessity to proving 'subjective universal validity', his concern is still with transcendental possibility.[79] For a deduction is necessary even where judgement claims only 'subjective universality' because the latter has an a priori basis. That is, although the judgement involves pleasure, nevertheless, its source is in our rational activity, and an explanation of its occurrence may be expected to show that it is rule-governed in a way that will be applicable to all subjects.[80]

However, as aesthetic judgements are based on the subject's pleasurable state of mind, they must have a particular form and their deduction will differ accordingly from the one in the First *Critique*. First, the deduction must legitimate the 'universality of a *singular* judgement' by showing that it is valid for all subjects even though it addresses the pleasurable state of mind which each subject gains for himself.[81] Second, as we may expect, because an assessment of this subjective experience must be made by the subject himself, any explanation or deduction we provide will have a peculiar efficacy. For a while such a judgement may have transcendental necessity,[82] it is not one which can 'enforce the assent' we seek. We cannot hope to deduce the validity of judgements which are able to compel others to agree with our judgements by the force of argument or by methods of proof that do not depend on an actual experience of a pleasurable state of mind. The latter cannot be brought about by, say, providing inductive generalizations from other cases, or by giving reasons as if these entail the existence of that state of mind in particular cases.

Both peculiarities are conditions that judgements must satisfy if we are to have the experience of beauty that the Analytic has presented. If the pleasurable state of mind of the subject's judgement on an object is to have a status that distinguishes it from pleasure that is merely idiosyncratic and arbitrary, we must be able to explain its occurrence— to show that it is transcendentally possible for a singular judgement to have universal validity. Our task then is to legitimate the peculiar universal communicability of our pleasurable state of mind by showing that there is a logical form for affirming its occurrence.[83] That is, 'the solution of these logical peculiarities'—our ability to show what their distinction from cognition consists in—'will of itself suffice for a deduction of this strange faculty', because our experience of pleasure already exists and need not be constituted: the only question is of how we explain its source and status.

Such universal but subjective validity concerns the a priori necessity of judgements, not the subjective or objective necessity we were concerned with in earlier sections of this chapter. The latter concern the specific recommendations we make in a particular judgement and the assent we gain for that judgement. As with cognitive empirical judgements, where necessity relates either to the transcendental conditions that all such judgements must satisfy or to the order of our knowledge of nature, similarly, aesthetic judgements are necessary either because of their transcendental conditions or in a sense related to their particular instances in our experience. And the particular instance is one that is transcendentally possible: a subject can make his recommendation in a particular judgement of taste only because such recommendations are possible generally.

Further, as we suggested, Kant supposes that a subjectively necessary judgement can 'demand universal assent *like* an objective principle, *provided we are assured of our subsumption under* [the common sense] being correct',[84] because, first, the general possibility of such judgements must be justified by showing that the grounds for our judgements generally are ones we may expect of all others; second, that in making a particular judgement a subject recommends that its basis be seen, as it were, to participate on those grounds in that he proposes that his judgement is based on something that may be expected of all other subjects; and third, that his recommendation is in fact accepted because it is actually based on these grounds. We might be thought to mean that if a judgement *is* based on such universally possessed grounds, then it has objective necessity regardless of whether or not others agree with it. But the inference does not follow because: we know that we can be mistaken, that judgements are singular, and that they are autonomous. The subject cannot be certain that his judgement is based on such grounds, and so 'looks for confirmation . . . from the concurrence of others'[85] through *their* estimation of a particular object. This claim is not a psychological one nor a concession that we have not avoided sceptical doubts; it can be made because, by the nature of aesthetic judgements, a subject's estimation of an object is one he can make only for himself, and so it postulates an *agreement* that *he* must *give*. Consequently, the judgement can only be *like* an objective principle because its compulsion is effective in a particular manner. Thus, questions of what necessity there is are left open by the deduction, although some constraints are imposed.

These constraints are imposed by the logical peculiarities of the judgements; and they serve to make the deduction distinctive. To repeat: that universality is of a *subjective* judgement suggests that agreement cannot be compelled even though our judgements are well founded; and that universality is claimed of a singular judgement suggests that we must look for validity through our own rational faculties—whose use has already been legitimated in the *First Critique*, even if only indirectly.

Consequently, in the face of their singularity and subjectivity, Kant's talk of a 'principle' for judgements of taste may seem a misnomer. At best we have a general expectation that our claims are not irrational, and this expectation is exhibited in diverse singular judgements. Nevertheless, what the deduction provides must count as the constitution of taste. For without it we would associate pleasure with a state of mind but have no right to claim it of others and consequently no reflective judgement of taste *at all*.[86]

In any case, in the deduction Kant's concern is to show the possibility of making judgements by showing that these are based on conditions we may expect to be satisfied in all those who can have empirical knowledge. A presupposition of such likeness will not only legitimate our attempt to make aesthetic judgements, it will go to explain how the latter enter into the construction of a community. We may then produce maxims[87] for their exercise much as the organization of our knowledge of nature into a science depends on maxims about the continuity of nature and so on.

The substance of the deduction is contained in the footnote and Remark following Section 38. We know Kant wants to conclude that 'the accordance of a representation with [a given] condition for the judgement must admit of being valid a priori for everyone'.[88] This condition is the 'subjective condition of judging generally'.

As 'beauty is not a concept of the object', we do not have to prove that the order of our representations or perceptions is that of a particular object existing in space and time independently of us and that ours is a cognitive judgement. In the latter case, Kant distinguishes between some parts of our explanation of how knowledge is gained, which have to do with applying particular concepts to given representations to show that an object is one among others like itself, and some parts which have to do only with the operation of the mind in judgement regardless of the particular judgement made. The conditions for judgement generally—Kant talks of 'cognition in general'—may be the same in all subjects if the particular judgements they make are objectively valid; and if so, then we may be assured of a similarity in all subjects even though we make judgements that only claim intersubjective rather than objective, concept-dependent validity. Consonantly, all that a judgement of taste 'holds out for is that we are justified in presupposing that the same subjective conditions that we find in ourselves are universally present in every man, and further that we have rightly subsumed the given object under these conditions'.[89]

But this makes our task much more difficult in the case of aesthetic judgements. For where we might have argued to a necessary set of concepts if cognitive judgements are to be possible, shown which empirical concepts are applied in a judgement, and so avoided having to argue separately for some intersubjective validity on the basis of the conditions present in the subject, our aesthetic subsumption is clearly tied to a subjective basis, where validity has to be proved, and where individual and subjective subsumption 'may easily prove fallacious' in a manner that casts doubt on its very possibility.

Kant's answering claim is put forward in the footnote to Section 38 and in Section 21. Universal validity must be possible even for subjective aesthetic judgements, he maintains, because they are rational; and if we did not assume that we had the same 'subjective conditions' as all others, we would be unable even to communicate our knowledge. Aesthetic judgements, therefore, are possible, and the intersubjective validity of an experience is constituted, because these depend on something that must be true if knowledge is public—which it is. That is, 'in order to be justified in claiming universal agreement for an aesthetic judgement merely resting on subjective grounds it is sufficient to assume: (1) that the subjective conditions for this faculty of aesthetic judgements are identical with all men in what concerns the relation of the cognitive faculties, there brought into action, with a view to cognition in general. This must be true, as otherwise men would be incapable of communicating their representations or even their knowledge.'[90]

However, the footnote suggests that our claim that an object is beautiful does not depend solely on the transcendental conditions for experience but on the conditions necessary for *knowledge to be communi-*

cated. If we did not possess the same subjective conditions, it seems, we would be unable to claim we shared a single set of concepts when we made cognitive judgements. As Kant is addressing not the transcendental deduction of categories itself—the claim that there is a single set of concepts which must underlie all experience—but the use of the latter in making particular objectively valid claims about empirical objects, we need to understand what are these conditions for communicating knowledge and how they differ from, while being related to, conditions for the transcendental possibility of experience generally. Further, we must see what makes them necessary.

Clearly these conditions for communicating knowledge cannot be the maxims of science. The latter are needed only to organize our knowledge of nature, not for communication with other subjects, and are in any case not strictly necessary. Further, if anything, the maxims of science can only be applied if knowledge can be communicated.

Nor could these conditions, it seems, be those of the deduction itself, for that only points out the necessary conditions for experience to be possible. But Kant's claims in Sections 21, 38, and in the *Critique of Pure Reason* suggest a closer relation between the conditions for experience generally and for the communication of knowledge. Communicability is essential in cognition if we are to suppose that our judgements tally with their putative objects: that if they were not universally communicable 'a correspondence with the object would not be due them'. As it is 'cognitions and judgements' that must, 'together with their attendant conviction, admit of being universally communicated',[91] the suggestion is that we see the deduction of categories in terms of the legitimation of judgements and of mental operations rather than as a proposal about the general characteristics of objects. Moreover, such a claim about the communicability of knowledge must be implicit in the First *Critique*, where the conditions for knowledge are examined.

Indeed the claim *is* implicit in the First *Critique*.[92] Thus, Kant claims as the highest principle of synthetic judgements that all concepts and principles, including those which are possible a priori, 'would yet be *without objective validity*, senseless, and meaningless, if their necessary application to the objects of experience were not established'.[93] That is, apart from this relation they have no objective validity.[94] This principle of significance[95] pronounces that our interest is in empirical knowledge, that it is there that objective validity is relevant, and that the deduction by itself does not yield knowledge, only its possibility. Indeed, '*there can be no* a priori *knowledge, except of objects of possible experience*',[96] where possible experience refers us to empirical intuition and knowledge.[97] Implicit in these is the claim that the subject's intuitions and their order must be party to the claim to objective validity or, conversely, that the legitimation of objective validity involves a claim about the communicability of the subject's state, and hence the expectation that the same faculties in similar relations are present in all subjects. That is, objective validity *is* a particular sort of intersubjectivity: it is the universal communicability by which subjects know that their experience is similar to that of others. And the possibility of aesthetic judgements rests on the validity of this claim.

In the First *Critique* it is not thought necessary to argue explicitly to this conclusion because that text questioned whether the order a subject gives to his representations—his subjective experience—is one that all other subjects must give if they are to have the sort of experience we all claim to have. As the search is for objective validity, the subjective conditions for experience are not brought into direct focus. We all have representations, and it is their validity that is in question: and the latter is established by establishing the set of concepts we must use to order representations. The subjective conditions are implicitly treated as if they were the same in all subjects, and by arguing to the necessity of certain judgements we defend just that implicit claim, for only scepticism would raise the possibility of different subjective conditions in order to argue against universal validity.

In this context Kant does concede something, for he accepts that the modes of intuition that we possess are only contingent in that 'we cannot judge in regard to the intuitions of other thinking beings, whether they are bound by the same conditions as those which limit our intuitions and which are for us universally valid'. But to concede this contingency is far from yielding to scepticism over the unity of subjective conditions, and Kant clearly does not do so. His principle of significance points to the subject's capacity for responding to the world, to those conditions in the subject which, within the limits of critical idealism, refer not to the psychology or physiology of subjects but to their rational capacities. Consequently, as we shall see, he can argue that the subjective conditions for knowledge must be the same in different subjects because they are formal, and must be the same as those in aesthetic judgements because they are involved in any judgement.[98]

Thus, categorical universality and the objective validity of any knowledge claim are dependent on the conditions for cognition in general— the possession and use of faculties necessary for objective experience.

What we have prior to the categories is not experience; but nor is it enough to have the categories, for we must have the capacity for experience. And whatever is involved in this capacity is needed for cognition in general, and may be available even if it is not involved in a knowledge claim. That is to say, the subjective conditions present in a cognitive judgement must be present in all subjects, and may be present in a non-cognitive judgement because they are conditions for judgements generally, not just for particular cognitions. And Kant's presentation of these conditions follows just this line. For he writes that for *judgements to be made* the categorical principles are grounded in or have as a necessary condition 'the unity of consciousness that alone constitutes the relation of representations to an object, and therefore their objective validity and the fact that they are modes of knowledge'. Indeed, upon this unity 'rests the very possibility of the understanding'.[99] The unity of consciousness 'is a condition under which every intuition must stand in order *to become an object for me*':[100] that is, not just the categories but, in a judgement that conforms with the categories, the unity of consciousness is needed for an object to be judged and for any subject to have experience. Without these conditions, he does not have any judgements on objects, and consequently, no experience, even though the general conditions for experience may be satisfied.

Moreover, the conditions necessary in a subject for *cognition in general* are necessary for anyone who makes that judgement. And we can know this by seeing that subjects do make the same judgement. This is because the unity of consciousness must be present in whoever is to make a judgement. It is a formal identity, not one limited to a particular subject, and so necessary for any subject who is to make a judgement— although in the case of empirical judgements its content will be determined by the concepts applied—and involves the use of the same faculties, for these are necessary for the unity of every single consciousness. As Kant phrases the point, 'the "I" . . . is [an] absolute (although merely logical) unity'. It is not itself an experience 'but a formal condition'; and the 'I think' here 'belongs to and precedes every experience; and as such it must always be taken only in relation to some possible knowledge, as a *merely subjective condition* of that knowledge'.[101] It is a 'formal condition, namely the logical unity of every thought',[102] and in justifying the possibility of making claims to validity, we begin with consciousness,[103] treating 'I think' as the 'vehicle of concepts',[104] though the subjective conditions have a wider role than that in cognition alone. And it is only because we can make judgements at all, because the subjective conditions for cognition in general are satisfied, that we can use categories claiming objective validity. Consequently, we are able to use a common set of categories because the same subjective conditions for judgement are satisfied in all subjects. And the latter must be satisfied, for unless they bore some relation to empirical intuitions in us—'to actual or possible experience'—judgements and cognitions 'would yet be without objective validity'.[105] These subjective conditions, then, are necessary to our communication of knowledge or for the objective validity of judgements, for without them either 'concepts are empty' or we have nothing but 'a rhapsody of perceptions'.[106] Therefore, we may be assured that aesthetic judgements are possible, for they are based on faculties—in a relation which gives rise to pleasure—that can be shown to be possessed in common with others because without them objective validity and knowledge claims would be impossible.

The second condition Kant puts forward for the possibility of aesthetic judgements is

that the judgement has paid regard merely to this relation (consequently merely to the *formal condition* of the faculty of judgement) and is pure, that is, is free from confusion either with concepts of the object or sensation as determining grounds. If any mistake is made in this latter point this only touches the incorrect application to a particular case of the right which a law gives us, and does not do away with the right generally.[107]

This is clearly concerned with particular judgements, requiring that we are able to reflect on our estimation of the object or its representation to ensure that it attends only to those features of it that are capable of being part of an a priori claim: the judgement must be disinterested, based on a finality of form, and so forth.

Kant also says of this relation between faculties that not only must we have the same faculties but in an aesthetic judgement there must be one best proportion which everyone accepts.[108] If this is the condition to be fulfilled, then we must be justified in expecting not only that every one will have the same faculties in responding to the same objects, but that in particular judgements they will respond in exactly the same way. Yet Kant seems to justify the latter only by saying that in cognitive judgements people do respond with the same proportion of faculties in making knowledge claims. And this assertion is clearly inadequate.

But Kant does not repeat the requirement of one best proportion in other instances.[109] Nor does he need to, for he needs to guarantee only the possibility of 'universal agreement'. As the conditions for making a universally valid judgement are those which must be satisfied for it to be communicated, we may examine universal agreement not as a judgement which can claim universality but as a judgement whose pleasure can be communicated. There, the communicability of the sensation of pleasure attendant on the state of mind is guaranteed, first, by its depending 'for everyone on the same conditions, seeing that they are the subjective conditions of the possibility of a cognition in general' and, second, on the fact that 'the proportion of these cognitive faculties which is requisite for taste is requisite also for ordinary sound understanding'.[110] If we think of empirical judgements as a relation of faculties, then aesthetic judgements, dependent on the same thing, must also be possible. But no claims for their possibility need to be tied to a single proportion. All that must be universally communicable is this feeling, 'and that, too, without the mediation of concepts',[111] so that is all that is necessary is for another subject to have the same feeling on the basis of a relation of faculties in his judgement on the object or its representation. That is, the only necessary condition for possibility is that subjects have the same subjective conditions and are able to reflect on their estimation of the object to avoid the confusions that could arise from agreeableness, morality, and so on.

Now this claim may give reason to doubt the validity of Kant's deduction in that unless we can know that the same best proportion is gained, the same pleasure need not be. However, we might respond to this claim by charging that it would be plausible only if we could show that the sameness of a proportion must be known for us to have the same pleasure. And we might argue then that as the only criterion for the existence of that proportion is the occurrence of pleasure, this requires us to be able to compare pleasures by themselves. Although sceptics must be able to make this comparison, it is difficult to see what sense there is to it. If we treat pleasure merely as a sensation, the only related comparison that seems to be possible is one through the subjective conditions being present. But that is just the requirement which makes judgements possible and, as we have seen, it can be satisfied. But still, doubts remain, for we may not be able to know that we do not have the same pleasure; but what we need to know is that we do. And if it is impossible to know we do not, then neither can we really claim to know that we have the same pleasure. So we have not made any progress: we may know generally that aesthetic judgements are possible, but do not have any way of dealing with particular judgements.

Two points need to be made here, one to clarify the requirement of one best proportion and a second to develop another aspect of taste.

First, the question of one best proportion is not about the possibility of judgements of taste. The second condition for aesthetic judgements, if it is seen as expressing a need for one best proportion of aesthetic judgements, really concerns the *success* of their particular instances. To raise it as an issue in the context of a deduction is at best to ask whether judgements capable of being successful in such a way are transcendentally possible. And the answer to this question is that so far as subjective conditions are concerned, judgements which can be successful in this way must be transcendentally possible for the same reasons: their basis is in a common ground. That is, so far as success requires a single best proportion, the subjective condition that must be satisfied for such successful judgements to be transcendentally possible is just that condition which we have argued is necessary for the possibility of aesthetic judgements: the possession of a common ground. Naturally, there are conditions for the success of particular actual judgements in addition to conditions for their possibility, and we can argue that the *sensus communis* provides us with the relevant guidelines, but those conditions concern particular actual judgements, and are a separate issue from that of the possibility of aesthetic judgements generally. In any case, so far as these judgements generally are possible, this is shown by the first condition, and Kant cannot raise the second condition in this context as one of the success of judgements, for its satisfaction does not constitute a judgement: that it is not satisfied 'only touches the incorrect application to a particular case of the right which the law gives us, and does not do away with the right generally'.[112]

Given that a claim that there must be one best proportion refers to conditions for the success of judgements rather than their possibility, it is not surprising that Kant raises the issue of a single best proportion only in the Fourth Moment and is content everywhere else to speak merely of a 'proportion of these cognitive faculties' with no more specification than that contained in talking of their relation. For in the Fourth Moment, of course, the issue of necessity is related to questions of the 'idea of a *sensus communis* or public sense' and, so, to successful judgement.

The second point that needs to be made is that the 'formal condition' of the possibility of an aesthetic judgement may be expected to allow for expression in beauty. For the faculties we have in common, which we use in reflecting on our estimation of an object or its representation, may evoke the pleasurable relation of faculties in ourselves through what might be called an aesthetic use of concepts. This reflection by a subject on his own estimation, or what in an actual judgement is the evocation of the pleasurable state of mind in himself, and the aesthetic use of concepts or expression which serves as a vehicle for others in gaining their own judgement, have been shown to be part of the 'formal conditions' of judgement. And as they depend on the subjective conditions we all have in common, their possibility too is deduced.

This leaves us with the problem of accounting for the 'one best proportion' of faculties; and, having considered the deduction, we need to look to the *sensus communis* again, to see how it enters as a condition for successful judgement.

The Sensus Communis *and the Necessity of Taste*

It is tempting to suppose that the transcendental possibility of aesthetic judgements may be understood in terms of *sensus communis*. The judgement depends on a similarity in subjective conditions to make its claim to universality—these conditions, the relation of cognitive faculties, being directed to 'feeling with pleasure the subjective bearings of the representation'.[113] If judgements of taste are possible, then this pleasure has intersubjective validity in that a subject has a priori justification for supposing that others are able to gain the pleasurable state of mind that he attains. And so far as common possession of these conditions leads us to see that pleasure is intersubjectively valid, we may speak of the ability to make such a use of faculties as the possession of a 'sense', for that is the name 'often given to judgements where what attracts attention is not so much its reflective act as merely its result'.[114] Accordingly, the order of our representations may be seen as the result of, or as seeking to maintain a particular pleasurable relation of faculties. Moreover, as the order of representations is assessed or reflected upon to establish whether we may expect on a priori grounds that others will be able to obtain it, we may talk of this sense as a public one to mark our interest in universality. Hence, within such limits, we may consider the subjective conditions, the common possession of which makes aesthetic judgements possible, as a *sensus communis*, and so see possession of the latter as a necessary condition for the transcendental possibility of aesthetic judgements. The necessity of taste then adds a pragmatic element, to tell us of the use which might be made of the *sensus communis*.

However, even such limits as these do not allow us to think of the *sensus communis* as a condition for the possibility of judgements of taste. Simply, by Kant's account we may talk of a sense only where the result is achieved. The mere possibility of a judgement does not license our ascribing a 'sense of truth . . . of propriety . . . or of justice, . . .'.[115] Only success in application does so; and we would confuse Kant's notion of *sensus communis* if we were to understand it to refer to the common sense or common ground whose existence is a necessary condition of the possibility of judgements.[116]

And to understand the role of the *sensus communis* we must consider our actual successful judgements. Here it may help to summarize the conclusions we have arrived at. We have seen that the deduction of taste only shows the universal validity of pleasure by pointing to its source in a common ground. Accordingly, it only legitimates our making aesthetic judgements which are subjective but intersubjectively valid; autonomous and singular; may be treated only as recommendations; and seek confirmation through communication to other subjects. Further, as judgements are autonomous and only recommendations, aesthetic judgements cannot enforce assent in the way cognitive judgements might be able to.

Although the deduction may have legitimated aesthetic judgements, it is the nature of deductions only to validate the general possibility of making judgements. Accordingly, we stand in need of criteria by which to assess the success or failure of actual judgements. Given that actual judgements were expected to be universally valid but could be mistaken in particular instances and could not be enforced, it was proposed that we could assess the particular judgement by seeing whether it could be communicated. For if a judgement could be communicated, that would go to show that it was universally valid.

It was in the context of such validation that we left the idea of a *sensus communis*: as the ideal norm for aesthetic judgements—a norm which actual aesthetic judgements satisfy when they involve both a feeling which can be shared and our claim that we are able to judge that the feeling *is* shared. For where these two conditions are satisfied, the judgement of taste exemplifies the idea of a common sense. Here the judgement is confirmed because we know that the feeling is shared and is therefore universal. If the feeling could not be shared, it would not be universalizable and, consequently, would be merely an experience of pleasure rather than a judgement of taste. Therefore, it could not make any claim to legitimacy. On the other hand, if the judgement satisfied the *sensus communis*, we would 'be assured of a correct subsumption'[117] and could *demand* others' agreement to our judgement, and would claim it exemplified a '*necessary* delight'. Or, as Kant writes, the 'necessity of the universal assent, which is thought in the judgement of taste, is a subjective necessity which, under the presupposition of a common sense, is represented as objective'.[118] We *demand* assent to the recommendation made in the aesthetic judgement.

By this account, the *sensus communis* is an epistemic ideal governing aesthetic judgements. Because of the special nature of judgements, subjects making them may follow certain maxims and thereby gain a facility for assessing whether their actual judgements are aesthetic and universalizable. That is, Kant uses the idea of the *sensus communis*, a standard for successful communication, to provide maxims which will guide our attempts to make judgements of taste.

Unfortunately, although the *sensus communis* can serve as an epistemic norm, it is not clear that as such it can demand assent in the manner appropriate to aesthetic judgements. To explain: the reflection involved in making aesthetic judgements was said to proceed in actual judgements of taste by the criterion of communication. Accordingly, the order of representations of a particular object, which gives rise to a pleasurable state of mind, is assessed or reflected on to consider whether others would be able to gain a similar order and pleasure. And aesthetic judgements are communicated when, for the same reasons as mine, other subjects gain the same pleasurable state of mind. Thus, the deduction shows that judgements are possible. But to justify our particular attempts at judgement, we need to consider their communication, to gain some account of what it is to be successful in our actual judgements. If we could be certain that we were correct in our judgements, and that they satisfied the idea of a *sensus communis*, we could claim an 'objective' necessity for them. But so long as they do not satisfy the *sensus communis* we may only claim a subjective necessity. Here the judgement is 'in accordance with all the requisite data for passing judgement', and the subject's conviction that such is the case is not based only on psychological observation but on the satisfaction of necessary conditions. That is, a 'private feeling' is put forward as carrying authority and, on the basis of our own reflection, in good faith, we recommend our judgements to others. In effect, the judgement proposes what we should attend to in the subject if we are to experience the same pleasure and so make the same judgement.

It is clear that communication is a criterion for dealing with actual judgements rather than their transcendental possibility. Particular judgements of taste must be communicated to be successful. And Kant is thought to claim that they are validated when they, as it were, participate in the *sensus communis*. By the *sensus communis* Kant means 'the idea of a *public* sense'; and its use as a standard for communication involves its sense as 'a critical faculty which in its reflective act takes account (a priori) of the mode of representation of everyone else'.[119] By assessing the public nature of their own pleasure, subjects consider whether its source is one that all subjects can possess; and in doing so, they 'weigh [their] judgements with the collective reason of mankind'. Those elements that evoke a pleasure in a subject may be expected to do so in all others, and while communication is successful only when others make the same pleasurable judgements, a subject may still assess its likelihood guided by some conception of what it is to succeed.

This is accomplished by weighing the judgement, not so much with actual, as rather with the merely possible, judgements of others, and by putting ourselves in the position of everyone else, as a result of a mere abstraction from the limitations which contingently affect our own estimate.

Again: a subject cannot impose his judgement upon others, but his claim that his judgement satisfies the ideal of a *sensus communis* grounds his demand that other subjects should make the same judgements. And to make this claim, he has to feel his way into 'the position of everyone else'.[120]

That is, the *sensus communis* contains an ideal norm, one that we try to gain in every judgement of taste we make. Its use does not constitute aesthetic judgements but governs the particular judgements we make, providing a standard by which we assess their successful communication. Its viewpoint is the one recommended in particular aesthetic judgements, indicating how we should look at subjects. When a judgement does participate in the *sensus communis*, Kant says, our aesthetic judgements 'could, in what concerns the conscious of different judging subjects, *demand* universal assent like an objective principle, provided we were assured of our subsumption under it being correct'. Here we have, in effect, found that one best relation of faculties that others may also gain, where the particular participation in the *sensus communis* serves as an *ideal*. We propose that our judgement gains it when it participates in the *sensus communis* and, consequently, we 'cannot tolerate' anyone being of a contrary opinion.

However, all this fails to advance our understanding of aesthetic judgements if we want to justify their claims to a quasi-objective necessity but consider only their epistemological features. We know that judgements of taste can be deployed as a recommendation to other subjects; but as such they are unable to compel agreement.[121] In this case, at best, their necessity is subjective. However, by introducing the *sensus communis* as an epistemic norm, we may seem to have changed the situation. Now it may seem that judgements would be objective if we could be sure of the correctness of our claim that a judgement exemplifies the ideal of a *sensus communis*. For, then, the communication of judgements would be assured, we would vindicate our recommendation that subjects be thought of in such and such a way and so be able to demand it, and a community between subjects would be gained in the way proposed.[122]

Unfortunately, the situation is not so straightforward, and it is not so clear that actual aesthetic judgements are able to make an epistemic demand for agreement. For we can make mistakes but do not have a satisfactory way of correcting them. As Kant writes:

for himself [the subject] can be certain of the universality [of the judgement] from his mere consciousness of the separation of everything belonging to the agreeable and the good from the delight remaining to him; and this is all for which he promises himself the agreement of every one—a claim which, under these conditions, he would also be warranted in making, were it not that he frequently sinned against them, and thus passed an erroneous judgement.[123]

But the subject does make mistakes, and consequently, for this and other reasons, the only criterion we have proves inadequate to our purpose of justifying the quasi-objective necessity of aesthetic judgements. Our difficulty is that we are given only one way of ascertaining the communication of judgements: by assessing whether our subjective state can satisfy the ideal of a *sensus communis* or *public* sense. But, at the same time, not only is our estimation or reflection fallible, but also we do not know what it is to satisfy this idea except that the judgement be communicated. For, first, given the fallibility of our reflection, we will discover whether we have justifiably claimed that our judgement exemplifies the ideal only when others make the same judgement. Certainly Kant proposes other measures or maxims: for example, the attempt to 'take account of others' or 'put ourselves in the place of others' depends on our 'letting go the element of matter'.[124] But, second, these measures too are unsatisfactory: they lead us away from the pitfalls of idiosyncrasy, yet, because of the autonomy of judgements and the nature of the *sensus communis*, do so without showing that our subsumption under the *sensus communis* is correct or that we can demand agreement. For aesthetic judgements are, in some sense, formal in being dependent on the relation of faculties rather than on the determinate content. And it may be thought we could ensure that our judgements were universal if we showed that they were independent of the determinate character of the object. But if Kant were to claim this was a sufficient guarantee, he would be confusing explanation with justification. That is, we may explain why a judgement can be communicated by pointing to the subjective conditions which must be fulfilled, but this need not justify a particular claim to have satisfied the *sensus communis*. For not only have we still not escaped fallible reflection, but the only satisfactory justification we could have would be a successful, communicated judgement. Consequently, in the absence of communication, the judgement possesses only subjective necessity and cannot, 'in what concerns the consensus of different judging subjects, *demand* universal assent like an objective principle'.[125] And so long as it remains a subjective necessity, subject to a fallible reflection, its claim to being an aesthetic judgement at all is open to doubt.

When expressed in this way, the epistemic norm of a *sensus communis* is seen to be otiose or unsuccessful. If to communicate a judgement is to satisfy the idea of a *sensus communis*, and if only satisfaction of the idea gives judgements a quasi-objective necessity,[126] then the demand made in objective judgements is idle. For as a demand for universal assent it can be made only when it is unnecessary to make it because as a demand it can be deployed only when others make the same judgement and communication has already been successful. So the only time we would be able to demand that others agree with us is in just those instances where they actually do so. Certainly, being able to claim that a judgement has quasi-objective necessity will tell us something, for it shows the epistemological status of agreement in judgements. But it is no use as an epistemic *demand* for agreement because it can be made only when agreement in judgements is reached. And, if we cannot justify that, it is not clear how we could go on to justify 'exacting' the feeling in a judgement of taste *as a duty*.[127]

This conclusion may seem to prove the absurdity of taking success in communication more seriously than mere communicability. That is, we may propose, instead, that a claim to have satisfied the idea of a *sensus communis* can be justified not by reference to successful communication but by reference to what explains communicability. Thus, we could say, to gain the conditions which make a judgement communicable is to satisfy the public sense, and it permits us to demand assent.

But this raises other problems for aesthetic judgements and the distinction between subjective and objective necessity. For it makes it difficult to see what subjective necessity might be except a judgement of which the subject claims that it postulates a 'universal voice' yet is prepared to admit the possibility that his claim might be mistaken.[128] For an aesthetic judgement that postulates a universal voice is one that '*looks* for confirmation . . . from the concurrence of others'.[129] Accordingly, a subjectively necessary judgement is one which postulates a universal voice but still *seeks* an agreement, which only others can give, and only *imputes* agreement to everyone. By contrast, presumably the quasi-objective judgement *demands* agreement because the subject is certain of the correctness of its subsumption under a *sensus communis*. But it is difficult to see what justifies the epistemological difference between subjective and objective necessity which allows one to make a demand and the other an imputation. For, by hypothesis, the grounds of both sorts of necessity are the same because we are considering the case of a *sensus communis* where to gain the conditions which make a judgement communicable and 'objective' *is* to satisfy just those subjective conditions which make it an aesthetic judgement at all, rather than a merely contingent experience of pleasure, and allow it a subjective necessity.[130] If this were the case, then the possibility of error would become a merely psychological matter and would fail to explain epistemological differences between subjective and objective necessities.[131]

Thus, the *sensus communis* governs either the successful communication or only the communicability of judgements of taste. If it governs the first, then it cannot provide an epistemological demand for agreement because, first, it is only fulfilled, and the ideal gained, when communication has been gained, and second, the demand it contains cannot be effective until it is fulfilled. If it governs only the communicability of taste, then there is no justification for saying that it is epistemologically different from subjective necessity or the idea of a universal voice that imputes but cannot demand agreement. We may make aesthetic judgements for ourselves, yet be unable to assure ourselves of their actual universality.

One way to have both objective necessity as a demand and as something different from subjective necessity is by seeing the *sensus communis* as both an epistemological ideal that governs the communication of judgements *and* as a practical ideal which can demand agreement. Subjective and objective necessity may then be epistemological, though neither is able to demand agreement. Our postulation of a universal voice, on grounds which are independent of merely psychological conviction and carry more authority than the contingent occurrence of pleasure, gives to our judgements, first, a subjective necessity that allows us to impute agreement and, second, where they participate in the *sensus communis* so that communication is gained, an objective necessity which shows what epistemological justification there was for the claim. However, nothing about the demand we may make of other subjects through judgements of taste can follow from this epistemic necessity, for it cannot compel actual agreement by virtue of its correctness or valid grounding: each subject has to make his own judgement.

Nevertheless, we may suggest that we can also see objective necessity as a practical necessity, and can see the idea of a *sensus communis* as deploying a *practical* demand for agreement from other subjects. Accordingly, successful judgements of taste may be seen as making a practical *demand* for agreement even though its subjective necessity can be only a claim about its epistemic status in relation to the *sensus communis*. That is, objective necessity based on the *sensus communis* may be said to involve both a practical demand and an ascription of an epistemological status while subjective necessity is only an epistemological claim. This needs to be explained further.

To justify the practical demand made by aesthetic judgements, Kant suggests that if we could 'assume that the mere universal communicability of our feeling must of itself carry with it an interest for us . . . we should then be in a position to explain how the feeling in the judgement of taste comes to be exacted from everyone as a sort of duty'.[132] But at that point he also says this is an assumption 'we are not entitled to draw as a conclusion from the character of merely reflective judgement'.[133] However, it could be said that both the suggestion and the denial are true, for it may be possible to combine an interest with judgements to give them a quasi-objective necessity which, under the guidance of a *sensus communis*, does allow us to exact agreement as a sort of duty. We do not draw this interest from reflective judgements, but show how it may be combined with them to complete their task. This may be suggested in the following way.

We have seen that universality is assured where other subjects are able to make the judgements we do. For the possibility of error, in which we would wrongly impute agreement to others on the basis of our own judgement and pleasure, has been raised in terms of comparing our judgements and pleasure with those of others in order to gain assurance of a correct subsumption. Now, in one sense whatever is necessary for us to know that our judgement is a pleasurable reflective one is also what is necessary for its communication, for in pointing to its conditions in himself, the subject points out the conditions that must be satisfied by others if they are to have the same pleasure. Further, if these conditions are recommended to others, in my judgement, as a common ground, then successful judgements would be ones in which other subjects experience the same pleasure when they accept the recommended view of subjects.

What we need to do then, in order to avoid the sort of doubt that arises when we wish to be assured that a given subsumption is correct, is to give value to the *sensus communis* and the recommended viewpoint of the subject that it implicates. For by this means we may secure *confirmation in judgement* of the correctness of our subsumption. That is, if we were to give value to the *sensus communis*, it would require subjects to take seriously the viewpoint implicit in every judgement and to assess it by making their own judgement of taste. That is, by giving value to the point of view recommended, we give value to the pursuit of beauty through understanding, criticizing, and evaluating objects, and thereby avoid scepticism arising from an absence of confirmation, because others following the viewpoint implicit in a judgement, so far as that judgement is correct, will gain that pleasure which confirms our own subsumption, which is itself based on a claim about the rational and sensuous nature of subjects. In doing this, of course, we give particular judgements a distinctive necessity, but there is reason to suppose that Kant can give this value to the *sensus communis*.

These reasons will be examined later, after we have said something of the relation of beauty and fine art to the *sensus communis* and to culture. And we end this section by recalling our claim that aesthetic judgements differ significantly from cognitive ones. We must be careful how we apply the epistemological model of the First *Critique* to our understanding of aesthetic concepts. Of course many of the crucial ideas originate in the earlier work and find application in the later work, but we have seen also that the epistemology of aesthetic judgements may be supplemented by an account of their practical character. While too much must not be made of the contrast between an epistemological and a non-epistemological account of aesthetic judgement, for the former is an important part of aesthetic judgement, too little should not be made of it either, for that would risk ignoring the peculiar character of aesthetic judgements and may leave us unable to give proper credence and weight to the practical value of beauty and fine art. Indeed, even if the account just given were mistaken in thinking we could not justify an epistemological demand for agreement, and even if such a justification were given, it would not invalidate the claim made for the practical value of the *sensus communis*. Nor could it show that the justification of practical aesthetic necessity, which we shall give, is inappropriate or inapplicable. Even after explaining the epistemic validity of the *sensus communis* we would be left with the task of justifying 'how the feeling in the judgement of taste comes to be exacted from everyone *as a duty*'.[134]

Beauty, *the* Sensus Communis, *and Culture*

Having proposed that we should ascribe value to the *sensus communis*, we shall leave consideration of Kant's justification of the practical, quasi-objective necessity of aesthetic judgements for the next chapter ('Culture and Morality: Aesthetic Necessity'). Here we may consider the grounds for ascribing a practical character to the *sensus communis*. By defining the *sensus communis* as a public sense Kant already indicates this practical turn. In the *Anthropology* he suggests that the 'one universal characteristic of madness is loss of *common sense* (*sensus communis*) and substitution of logical *private sense* (*sensus privatus*) for it'.[135] And, as we saw earlier, he contrasts it also with ordinary human understanding.[136] In both instances, a fragmented, unsystematic mode of thought, in which individuals are set apart from each other and insensitive to each other as rational and feeling creatures, is contrasted with a unity among individuals, where 'a regard to universal communicability is a thing which everyone expects and requires from everyone else, just as if it were a part of an original compact dictated by humanity itself'.[137]

There are various explanations for the fragmentation and disunity between us, among which we may point to impositions on our behaviour and thought stemming from tradition or force,[138] provinciality,[139] the misuse of reason,[140] ignorance, radical evil,[141] and so on. More than modes of thought, these are patterns of behaviour and relations between individuals. And where Kant contrasts this fragmentation with 'that which forms the point of reference for the harmonious accord of all our faculties of cognition—the production of which accord is the ultimate end set by the intelligible basis of our nature',[142] the 'harmonious accord' is equivocal between the accord of a subject's faculties and an harmonious accord between individuals that is based on their faculties. For only through the concurrence of other subjects and their experience of an intersubjectively valid pleasure can a subject confirm and communicate his own judgement of taste. Consequently, so far as our experience of beauty exemplifies our human—animal *and* rational—character, it is only with other people that a subject can feel himself to be a person, as only they, being persons, are able to treat him as one like themselves.[143]

In this unity between individuals, they present themselves publicly with a claim to universal validity. This contrast of 'publicity' is with something being secret. The universally valid claims we make may be proposed publicly,[144] for they and we do not threaten the humanity of another subject. The contrasting case is of a desire or claim that must depend on a 'maxim which I cannot divulge without defeating my own purpose [and which] must be kept secret if it is to succeed'.[145] And a subject must be prepared to countenance using others as means where he cannot succeed to his goal by rational persuasion. Yet in a unity between individuals we cannot accept a distinction between those who do and those who do not share secret maxims: 'no member should be a mere means, but should also be an end, and, seeing that he contributes to the possibility of the entire body, should have his function in turn defined by the idea of the whole'.[146]

Kant's association of universal validity, publicity, and a reciprocity by which a person's contribution to the whole is the basis for defining his role and position in it, may be understood as a matter of having a certain viewpoint. Publicity, universal validity, and the proposed reciprocity require subjects to make judgements from a viewpoint which encompasses those of other subjects. Given that 'the entire body' is made up of individuals, the suggestion is no one individual's position may be delineated without also defining how other individuals are to be placed. This is not to deny that there are psychological and other personal differences between individuals; it is to recognize the irrelevance of such personal differences as arise merely from 'the capacity to be conscious of the identity of one's self in the various conditions of one's existence'.[147] For as a moral personality the individual is intrinsically valuable, and shares his moral identity in the whole with all other individuals.

Or so the *Foundations* proposes. A contrast may seem to be proposed in the *Doctrine* where, as a person is someone to whom blame or praise may be imputed, we may ask how well or badly one individual has behaved, and cannot hope to ignore differences between morally responsible agents. Differences allow us to assess the personal achievements of individuals, and so, it may seem, the individual's function or position can be delineated without reference to the whole. However, in this case too, our assessment must be from a viewpoint that includes all others in the whole. For while there are personal differences and differences of moral personality, the supreme principle itself urges the adoption of a universal viewpoint, and we assess differences in the moral personalities of agents by considering their satisfaction of universaliz-able maxims.

In the context of this supreme principle—and the criteria of con-sistency, of universality, validity, personality, and reciprocity,[148] that it subtends—in this context 'publicity' may be seen as the exemplification of the a priori moral demand in our actual political, legal, cultural, and aesthetic lives. The 'public' then denotes a relation between imperfectly rational subjects, who are capable of entering into discussion, of making decisions, and of having feelings. In this relation they are treated as agents who are ends in themselves. Publicity in political relations sets out the conditions that must be preserved if persons are to pursue moral laws without hindrance from the merely private individual interests of others. In legal, civil, and international relations, 'all actions affecting the rights of other human beings are wrong if their maxim is not consistent with being made public'.[149] The 'form of publicity' is what remains if we 'abstract from all the material of public law (i.e., abstract from the various empirically given relationships of men . . .)'.[150] Similarly, by comparing judgements of taste with a public sense Kant brings our subjective lives into the domain of duty and right. Where we might have thought our subjective lives must be merely personal and idiosyncratic, not only incapable of rationality but also the source of our isolation from others, by showing the universal validity of aesthetic judgements and their comparison with a public sense Kant shows them capable of value.

Through such association he draws out the implications, of the recommendation made in aesthetic judgement, that the subject be perceived in a particular way. For such a recommendation may be shown to have value where its publicity exemplifies a moral demand. Thus, our reflection underlies our attempts to 'put ourselves in the position of everyone else'. And it makes an aesthetic judgement one in which, commensurate with its subjectivity, we recognize subjects as subjects, just as legal and political relations involve a recognition of others as litigants and citizens. The *sensus communis*, then, as an ideal norm which guides our reflection on the possibility of an aesthetic judgement, has a value and compulsion that is moral in form, and is linked at least formally with law, politics, and morality.

Further, in making aesthetic judgements, in considering the subject from the viewpoint proposed in them, we change ourselves. We consider ourselves in relation to 'the merely possible' judgements of others, abstracting 'from the limitations which contingently effect our

own estimate'.[151] Kant provides maxims for such reflection because
there cannot be laws governing the 'application of judgement'.[152] And
these propose: first, that we should think for ourselves, without being
prejudiced or prejudging a case because of what others claim or of what
we ourselves may have felt in the past; second, that we should 'think
from the standpoint of everyone else', detaching ourselves from our own
habits and context to the extent of being able to compare ourselves with
others without giving an unargued priority to opinions or conceptions
merely because they are ours. By being detached in this way, we show
ourselves capable of an 'enlarged mind' that thinks 'from a *universal
standpoint* (which [we] can only determine by shifting [our] ground to the
standpoint of others)'.[153] Third, we should think consistently, to provide
a coherence for our opinions that comes from unprejudiced thought
gained from a universal viewpoint, so that they are consistent both
internally and in relation to others. Thus, in making aesthetic judgements, as we said earlier,[154] the subject judges not only an object but, in
accepting a recommended viewpoint, also judges himself by considering
his adequacy to the object as he does its suitability to himself and an
intersubjectively valid feeling. By judging in this way, he changes
himself, discovering the different ways object and judgements sustain
and promote a unity between individuals. Further, in changing himself
through such reflection, he also changes the conditions for future
judgements and thereby ameliorates the ill effects of merely subjective,
personal tendencies. Consequently, beauty 'interferes' with the very
condition which made the particular judgement possible. And it is these
features, by which a judgement operates in following the ideal norm of a
sensus communis, that allow aesthetic judgements to participate in
enculturing rational and animal creatures like ourselves. And they
involve the very features which, we noticed earlier, underpinned
beauty's analogy with morality.[155]

Fine Art, The Sensus Communis, *and the* Summum Bonum

Fine art is beautiful art: a work of art that satisfies a judgement of taste by
evoking an intersubjectively valid pleasure in which the *sensus communis*
is an ideal norm. Both beauty, as our experience of judgements of taste,
and genius, in the production of works, must be grasped if we are to
understand their synthesis in fine art. Together they foster a relation
between individuals and to nature that explains fine art's participation in
progressive culture. For each by itself is inadequate to the latter. While

art in general may lead to the development of a civic community, the formation of the latter does not prevent us from being led by our animal nature and is compatible with the existence of iniquity and inequality between individuals. Similarly, while our experience of beauty may go to ameliorate the ill effects of our sensuous inclinations, it fails to explain the activities of judging *and* of producing which are essential to progressive culture.

The possibility of each aspect of fine art must be understood independently of the other. Earlier we explained the production of art generally and fine art in particular by genius, presented Kant's concept of culture, and, by showing how the latter relates to natural necessity, we accounted for the possibility of fine art. We have examined the possibility of taste now, and proposed that a successful justification validates an experience that sustains a mutual treatment of individuals as rational and feeling subjects. The latter obviously contributes to culture, and by justifying the possibility of taste we show where a cultural necessity, if there is one, finds room or is located in our experience of beauty.

These steps may be seen as part of an argument for the necessity of beauty that will be provided presently by justifying the moral demand made of culture, and, so, of fine art and our experience of beauty. It is important, for this argument, to consider the possibility of taste and our experience of beauty. For Kant's deduction has been seen as an argument conducted in epistemological terms only, and his claims for beauty are supposedly open only to a commensurate justification.[156] A judgement of taste involves the use and order of cognitive faculties, of the operation of the mind, so that if aesthetic judgements have necessity, it is claimed, it is an epistemological one.[157] But even if such a view of necessity were accepted, it would not make redundant any derivation of necessity based on the *sensus communis* as a morally justifiable ideal norm nor invalidate fine art's participation in culture.

In any case, when we turned to Kant's deduction of taste, it was to discover that it concerned the possibility of subjective universally valid judgements. Although the Analytic acknowledges that aesthetic judgements carry necessity, the deduction, as we might expect, proves only their possibility as subjective but valid judgements. Evidently, a validation of their possibility generally is not a justification of their necessity in particular instances, and the latter was found to involve the *sensus communis* as an ideal norm—but not as a norm capable of epistemological compulsion. Just what that necessity might be is left open by the deduction,[158] though some constraints are imposed on it by virtue of the nature of aesthetic judgements. Thus, whatever else necessity might be, it must be capable of being deployed through the reflective relation of faculties that is legitimated by the deduction and of being associated with our experience of beauty. These constraints are satisfied by the *sensus communis* as an ideal epistemological regulative norm, though we must remember that as such the *sensus communis* cannot make any *demand* for agreement from everyone.[159]

Of the proposal that the *sensus communis* and the judgements of taste it sustains be given a practical justification, it may be claimed that we go further than Kant's writings warrant. For in them, it may be said, there is no clear indication of what sort of necessity we should provide. When talking of aesthetic judgements, Kant says a subject '*ought* to give the object in question his approval and follow suit in describing it as beautiful'.[160] But the use of this imperative mode does not imply that the necessity of aesthetic judgements is moral. In discussing reflective teleological judgements also Kant uses the same locution in reference to science. The deduction of causality as constitutive of experience leads the subject to suppose 'that I *ought* at all times to *reflect* upon the order of natural events *according to the principle* of the simple mechanism of nature'.[161] That is, given both a distinction between empirical and a priori necessity and the need for reflection in constructing the order of our knowledge of nature, Kant uses an imperative mode to describe the operation of reflective judgements generally. The principles guiding reflection are gained from reason, and the rational compulsion guiding their use is expressed in terms of 'ought' and 'should' in relation to *our* ordering our knowledge of nature. It may be that Kant uses a similar imperative mode of aesthetic judgements because they too are reflective. That is, given the constitution of our experience and the nature of reflective judgements generally, it is possible to ascribe to the latter a compulsion that we express in an imperative mode. And as aesthetic judgements are reflective, they too may be ascribed an imperative mode.

Although this locution fails to explain what sort of necessity is called for, a comparison with teleological judgements may tell us more. Of these, Kant claimed that reflection ought to proceed along causal lines because the deduction has shown causality to be constitutive of our experience. Reflective judgements, then, are based on that original deduction, and while aesthetic judgements are proved separately their proof is based on that original deduction. Thus, an imperative mode used in either context depends on the same sort of necessity—or at least is epistemological in the same way.

However, this claim is not warranted. A similar locution was possible because there was a deduction that was constitutive of experience: because there was an underlying deduction claiming necessity. But freedom can also be deduced in some similar way. Hence, the deduction allegedly supporting the imperative mode characteristically applied to reflective judgements may be one of free will and not of natural causality. Consequently, the imperative mode, if it is at all indicative of the sort of necessity that is needed, is ambivalent between cognition and morality.

Nor can we give cognitive necessity more weight because we happen to be dealing with an experience which occurs in the phenomenal world and depends on a use of cognitive faculties. It may be claimed that, as the whole account of transcendental necessity is dealt with by showing that judgements of taste allow us subjective general validity for cognitive faculties in response to empirical objects, only epistemological and not moral connotations are important. However, this wrongly diverts attention from the subject. Judgements of taste and experiences of beauty are dependent on the nature of the individual subject and tell us of him in important respects. Earlier we also showed how our experience of beauty may be related to culture; and there seems to be little reason to exclude the moral connotations that may be ascribed to these features of judgements of taste.

Rather than look to see whether the necessity involved is cognitive or moral, and the deduction epistemological or something else, we should look to see if the deduction, and the imperative mode governing the judgements which it legitimates, are compatible with both morality and epistemology. After all, Kant is trying to bridge the gap between reason and nature, and the *Critique of Judgement* deepens the deduction of determinate, objective experience by pointing to the common ground, possessed by all subjects, that justifies the deduction of aesthetic judgements. Moreover, the *sensus communis* is an *ideal* for subjects, and may be capable of development. That is, it is dependent on subjects' actions for its construction, and that may make it capable of being a moral as well as cognitive ideal. By being such, it also provides a ground for transition, telling us about subjects themselves *and* their capacity for action in the world they know. In an important sense, because of the way the success of taste relies on a common ground and on a *sensus communis*, the latter may be seen as the location of a unity between the *summum bonum* and our knowledge of the world—between our capacity for rational action, for thought, and feeling.[162]

This relation between *sensus communis* and *summum bonum* in its different aspects is more clearly seen in fine art.[163] For fine art as art makes an ontological commitment to the existence of freedom. The commitment was shown to raise a number of problems, the most important of which, concerning the relation of rational freedom to nature, was raised by asking how the experience of a causally determined nature can be reconciled with the existence of human agency and the claim that some objects are the products of human action. An understanding of the possibility of fine art can provide a reference to our moral enterprise because works depend on the rational will that is ordered by moral law, but the reference needs to be completed by giving an account of beauty in art. Only by clarifying the nature of beauty do we explain the specific role of fine art in uniting our capacity for rational action with our capacity for cognition—freedom and nature—in Kant's expanded notion of the *summum bonum*. For if the *sensus communis* can be shown to be a practical ideal, then the ontological commitment to the existence of freedom made in a work of art is directed toward satisfying a moral demand by constructing an object which satisfies a relation of cognitive faculties.[164]

For Kant, in art an ontological commitment to the existence of freedom is presupposed. Thus, an object cannot be understood as a work except by reference to intentions or to a rational will; but this work exists in phenomenal nature, and is judged by the use of cognitive faculties under a practical imperative. After all, as Kant insists of nature and freedom, 'the latter is *meant* to influence the former—that is to say, the concept of freedom is meant to actualize in the sensible world the end proposed by its laws'.[165]

Such compliance between nature and reason is the domain of the *summum bonum*. As we argued, Kant's original understanding of this concept as the relation between virtue and happiness is expanded to cover the relation between our natural and rational character generally. The highest good comes to cover a general synthesis between reason and nature, and no longer refers to a separate realm in which alone virtue is realized. Not only happiness but our natural character generally is the empirical element to be synthesized in the *summum bonum*. Earlier we gave reasons for this expansion, showing that any justification of the relation of virtue to happiness must be seen as a general argument for conceiving of the world as moral nature.[166] So far as nature is thought of as a totality, and moral actions are taken 'as a whole', to that extent the *summum bonum* must be seen as 'the highest good *in the world* possible through freedom'.[167] This involves a 'reciprocal relation subsisting between the world and [a] moral end, the possibility of realizing [the latter] under external conditions'.[168] And, as we saw, the compatibility of nature and reason permits us to expect that moral ends may be realized in nature. It is unnecessary to argue that a physical teleology must be comprehended within a moral teleology.

In the present context, first, pleasure being a feature of our nature that itself arises from our use of (phenomenal) cognitive faculties which, second, are guided by the moral idea of a *sensus communis*, and third, as the work which is the object of aesthetic judgements is taken to exist in the phenomenal world even though, fourth, it is seen as the product of a rational will, then we may suppose that fine art, because of its participation in progressive culture through the *sensus communis*, depends on the possibility and nature of the *summum bonum*—of the synthesis we achieve between moral reason and nature. It depends on it because the object, to be a work of art, must depend on the existence of a will which can be ordered by practical reason—in this case an order effected through the practical and epistemological ideal of a *sensus communis* governing the intersubjectively valid pleasure we feel.

The association between *sensus communis* and *summum bonum* should not be surprising. We said that fine art contributes to progressive culture, and went on to clarify that claim by showing that judgements of taste, whose experience beauty is, are governed by the idea of a *sensus communis*. This idea of a public sense, we showed, through its association with universal validity, publicity, and reciprocity, is linked at least formally with morality, politics, and law; and by exploiting this formal similarity Kant is able to make plausible our attempt to bring our subjective lives, as exemplified in aesthetic judgements, within the scope of duty and right.

Of course, this depends on being able to justify the practical necessity of aesthetic judgements. And Kant hints that we might be able to do so if we could

assume that a mere universal communicability of our feeling must of itself carry with it an interest for us (an assumption, however, which *we are not entitled to draw as a conclusion from the character of a merely reflective judgement*) for we should then be in a position to explain how the feeling in a judgement of taste comes to be exacted from every one as a sort of duty.[169]

Knowing what we do about a synthesis between reflective judgements and judgements making an ontological commitment to the existence of freedom, we may expect that fine art's participation in culture through the *sensus communis* will go a long way to explain how fine art can claim a practical 'exemplary validity'.[170] Further, knowing that the idea of the *sensus communis* is a moral ideal, we can also explain how their synthesis allows us to say that judgements on fine art can 'be exacted from every one as a sort of duty'.[171] This is because the promotion of culture makes claims upon us as agents capable of morality, where judgements may recommend just this view of the subject. This matter depends on our ability to explain how fine art participates in culture—an account we have presented—but it also depends on whether we can justify the claim that the *sensus communis* is a moral ideal. And we have shown that in relation to culture the *sensus communis* may be seen as a part of progressive culture because, for example in fine art, it is something we are all able to gain as subjects. Consequently, to satisfy its ideal is to promote our human powers for setting rational ends; and it is this character of these ends that makes us a moral species.

What we need to show now is that Kant can justify a cultural duty, derived from the supreme principle of morality, which would succeed in making the *sensus communis* a moral ideal extending over fine art and its intersubjective unity between reason and feeling. What we know already is that its practical justification is compatible with the epistemological role that it plays.

VI

Culture and Morality:
Aesthetic Necessity

KANT holds that the transcendental possibility of aesthetic judgements must be distinguished from the necessity of beauty. An argument for the former will not explain the moral or dutiful character of the latter.[1] Indeed, aesthetic judgements possess a peculiar necessity: they may be transcendentally possible, but subjects cannot be compelled to accept them in the way that they must accept cognitive judgements; and moral compulsion cannot lead to the experience of aesthetic judgements.[2] Rather, Kant prefers to describe the experience of beauty as one in which 'the theoretical faculty gets bound into unity with the practical in an intimate and obscure manner'.[3]

Kant may be accounting for this unity when he describes beauty as a symbol of the moral good. And his claim that symbolic relations are based on analogies may suggest that beauty's homology with morality is constitutive of aesthetic necessity. It is as if an isomorphism between our aesthetic and moral activities is itself sufficient to guarantee aesthetic necessity. Perhaps at some level of abstraction there are similarities between the two practices that warrant our deference to both in their actual employment.[4]

However, this sort of account must strike us as merely mechanical and abstract. It is an abstraction to think that symbols depend only on a homology between two elements. As Kant makes clear, we rely on a symbol when its object cannot speak for itself. In this instance, as moral experience is impossible in the phenomenal world, and because aesthetic judgements are similar to their moral counterparts, we treat the latter as symbols of moral good. But to explain this relation we need something more comprehensive than an account of their similarity, to show not only that moral experience is impossible but also that beauty can be a surrogate for the former.

The issues raised by the last point indicate that to rely on an abstract symbolic relation alone is to propose a merely mechanical relation between beauty and morality. For we have seen that Kant's writings put forward a complex account of the relation between nature and reason, and that aesthetic activity plays a complicated part in the intricate interrelation of moral, political, and cultural actions that constitute our human existence. Consequently, while the 'intimate and obscure' unity that obtains between theory and practice in aesthetic judgements may ultimately gain its rational force from moral reason, the relation between moral good and beauty is mediated by culture and the general relation of reason to nature. That is, for example, fine art does not merely evoke an imaginary and ideal solution to present problems through the content expressed in aesthetic ideas. Rather, it participates in the cultural processes that make up our self-determining attempt to create a community between finitely rational subjects. In this comparison, to emphasize the content of ideas expressed in fine art would be to see the latter as 'an imitation of reality'. But the 'second nature' that is constructed in fine art is woefully inadequate as an image or representation of reality. Images must differ from reality if they are to be images, and they must be constructed if they are to be similar. However, if they are important as images of *reality*, so that they bear significance for their closeness to their model, then their only virtue derives from the suppression of their nature as images. Or, if the fact of their being *images* of reality is the vital feature, then aesthetic judgements cannot claim any virtue. For a correspondence between image and reality must postulate a separation between them which renders fine art incapable of participating in cultural progress: that is, no subject succeeds in participating in culture if his only access is to an unreal image. Thus, to present fine art in terms of images of reality is to define it by its similarity, and our appreciation of fine art will come to turn on judging its conformity to reality. Not only does this sin against the disinterestedness and autonomy of aesthetic practice, but an argument in its favour, explaining why it is valuable to construct images of reality, must be able both to compete with an alternative argument, which contends that fine art participates in culture, and to show how our passivity in the face of reality can be reconciled with the expectation that we are moral agents active in reality. Although these points do not make the argument by themselves, the claim that we seek only to provide images of reality seems implausible in the context of Kant's accounts of aesthetic judgements, fine art, and their participation in culture.

We must replace such abstract and mechanical conceptions with one cognizant of fine art's complex involvement in moral and cultural practice. Rather than merely seeking to link the two discrete orders of nature and reason in some purely external homology, fine art has a distinctive role in creating the moral species. It is a role based on its part in culture generally. And where beauty is a symbol of moral good, it is so because its necessity is based on fine art's promotion of a moral species.

An explanation of their symbolic relation must show that fine art and moral good claim a similar compulsion and reality, but we must also understand how the first differs from the second. That is, first, we must understand the special role of aesthetic activity in culture—a goal we have pursued in past chapters by examining art and aesthetic judgements. Second, we must investigate the relation of fine art, as cultural activity, to the development of a community of individuals and to moral necessity. And, here, while we are unable to justify the necessity of beauty if we rely on a mechanical and abstract conception of the symbolic relation between beauty and morality, once we have understood the complex relation between fine art and cultural activity in the development of a moral species we can go on to construct a justification of aesthetic necessity through fine art's participation in a morally legitimate culture.

Cultural progress is assessed as an advance in enlightenment and self-determination, where the latter are ends determined by practical reason. And it is practical reason that we must consider first.

Practical Reason and Cultural Duty

Kant's investigation of practical reason extends over the whole range of his critical writings. We have examined some part of it in the past few chapters, where we saw that in the *Foundations of the Metaphysics of Morals* and in the *Critique of Practical Reason* Kant sets out the 'unconditional command of practical reason'—the categorical imperative and its variations. The first text examines the nature of a supreme principle of morality and seeks to justify its validity. Next, the supreme principle is interpreted and placed in different contexts: maxims must be in keeping with natural laws; people must be treated as ends in themselves, never merely as means; and, in behaving morally individuals must act as members of a Kingdom of Ends.

Kant's principle proposes that rational moral agents should act according to maxims which it is possible for all others to have. In thinking of a course of action we can articulate a maxim or general rule that action instantiates, which consists of both a goal or end and a scheme for attaining that end.[5] The rule may then be considered as a course of action not only for us to follow but one which 'every rational being is *always* going to act upon in relevantly similar circumstances'.[6]

This yields a procedure by which we may distinguish immoral acts, for their maxims are self-defeating. And the procedure is formal or a priori in that it does not itself depend on any substantial moral judgements.[7]

Further, Kant's formal principle abstracted from all ends. It said only that rational moral agents should act according to maxims of ends which can be universalized. Having examined the supreme principle and its variations, in the *Critique of Practical Reason* Kant goes on to argue that it is possible for men to act according to that principle. Only in the *Metaphysics of Morals* does the *Doctrine of Virtue* finally show which intentions or ends are obligatory for men. These are put forward by Kant as conditions of inner freedom.[8] And, in keeping with man's dual nature, the obligatory ends or duties derived from the categorical imperative include obligations to men as both animal and rational beings: we are subject to duties of developing our own perfection and promoting the happiness of others.[9]

Clearly Kant's formulation of duties is not 'pure *a priori*': it depends on empirical propositions about men as imperfectly rational beings. Nevertheless, it can be maintained that Kant's considerations are a priori in a sense because not only are men characterized at such a general level that his conclusions are applicable to them all in spite of not being strictly a priori,[10] but, more importantly, the compulsion governing maxims of the will is not derived from experience. The duties Kant derives are binding upon all men as such; they are not modified by empirical circumstances.

In any case, Kant's writings imply a teleological conception of perfection. Men are required to be adequate to some end, and perfection depends on the suitability of an individual to that end.[11] As Kant seems to take human perfection to require self-development,[12] to satisfy the duty of perfection is to 'promote' or 'realize to the greatest possible extent' the abilities man possesses. And as men are imperfectly rational animals, these abilities include both natural and rational characteristics. That is, although his capacity for intentional actions is partly constitutive of man's rational nature and distinguishes him from animals,[13] Kant does not exclude the physical powers necessary to realizing rational ends. Men are to treat the humanity in their person as ends in themselves, and must work as much for 'the cultivation of those powers (or natural capacities)', which enable them to attain physical ends, as they work for those which enable them to choose rational ends.[14] And the latter includes cultivation of our will in the sense of our readiness to fulfil our duties because they are moral.

If the fulfilment of duties is itself a maxim which individuals must make their end, and if culture is our aptitude or ability to set and gain ends, then in arguing that men have a duty to attain natural and moral perfection, Kant is proposing a justification of cultural obligation. We have a duty 'to make ourselves worthy of humanity by culture'.[15] Consequently, culture becomes the 'cultivation of all one's *power* for promoting the ends which reason puts forward'.[16]

It seems, further, that the ends put forward by reason are derived from the supreme moral principle through moral law and, therefore, are ends in themselves. This introduces a complication which may be explained as follows. Kant has asserted that an end is 'an object of free choice, thought of which determines choice to an action by which the object is produced'.[17] It must be set by a rational will and is 'an act of freedom on the agent's part, not an explanation of nature'. As the power to set an end is characteristic of man, he can contend that 'the perfection of man consists precisely in *his own power* to adopt ends'.[18] But Kant now goes on to talk of perfection as a person's 'power to adopt his end *in accordance with his own concept of duty*'.[19] And this suggests that the humanity which becomes an end in our search for perfection characteristically adopts only the ends which are proposed as duties. In the struggle to gain perfection, then, culture is no longer just the aptitude for setting any, arbitrary ends.[20] Rather, cultural obligation applies only to the aptitude or ability to set and gain moral ends: particular ends in themselves which are derived from, and need no other justification than that provided by rational moral law. So only when culture is devoted to ends determined by moral law can we be obliged to promote it. The general ability to set ends, which is explored in the *Critique of Judgement*,[21] it seems, must be qualified by a cultural obligation that consists of a limited engagement in promoting man's nature towards moral ends and perfection. It may be called moral culture to indicate that restriction.

A consequence of this reading is that if fine art and beauty were to claim necessity through participation in a moral culture, they would come to be determined by cultural duty. Judgements would be able to claim necessity only so far as they realized to the greatest possible extent the ability to adopt particular moral ends. As a result, a particular moral end would, in some way, become an end for the beautiful; and to judge the latter it would not be enough—or even necessary, perhaps—to point to a harmony of rational faculties; it would also—or, only—be necessary to point to the moral concept by which it is determined. Fine art, then, could no longer be the object of judgements which are both necessary and disinterested. If they are necessary, they must be part of the attempt to satisfy moral culture and must be judged according to the criteria of moral cultural duty rather than only according to aesthetic criteria. Conversely, if we were to deny that fine art were a part of culture, we would contradict Kant's contention that it participates in culture and would complicate hopelessly the justification of objective necessity that is gained through participation in a *sensus communis*.

Thus, it seems that either we can succeed in justifying the necessity of judgements of beauty only by giving up their disinterestedness or we can persevere in taking fine art to be disinterested but must give up looking for an account of necessity in terms of culture and morality. And this could force us to fall back on an epistemological account of aesthetic necessity. Naturally, there is a third possibility: we use cultural duty to justify aesthetic necessity but deny that thereby fine art is morally determined. And it is this possibility we will consider.

Moral Culture and Culture In General

The objection is that if the necessity of beauty follows from its participation in culture, then beauty comes to be morally determined because for Kant cultural necessity covers only the ability to gain moral ends. That is, only moral ends carry any obligation, and we are obliged only over those cultural developments that promote our capacity for moral ends because these are ends in themselves.

The objection will not work in this form. The claim is that we are obliged to promote culture only where it leads to an increase, to the greatest possible extent, in our capacity to set moral ends. But it is difficult to use this as a criterion to distinguish cultural activity that is necessary, where it fulfils such an obligation, from cultural activity that does not. It could be argued that any setting of ends is a promotion of rationality and therefore is necessary simply because, in some way, it promotes our capacity to recognize and choose moral ends. Thus, fine art and our experience of beauty are eligible for ascriptions of cultural necessity even though they are merely 'general' rather than 'moral' ends.

Such a defence may be worked out for Kant by reference to later sections of the *Metaphysics of Morals*. There, he proposes that we may distinguish the pragmatic value of culture from the value of culture itself and can derive a duty to set ends generally rather than set moral ends alone. This may be called a duty of 'culture in general' to distinguish it from moral culture.

Man possesses both animal and rational capacities by nature. These natural capacities form a substratum and necessary condition for his moral being and perfection. Further, the demands made on our actions by moral perfection cannot be ones which men are incapable of accepting and fulfilling. Considering man's animal nature, Kant acknowledges that we are subject to the compulsion of our inclinations or instincts. Some compulsions, like hunger and thirst, are essential to the very continuation of our lives; but not all of them are necessary. Kant argues that it is possible to decide which desires are permissible by looking to morality for guidance in order to arrive at a balance between reason and nature in ourselves. Here, to look to morality is to seek maxims which are goals for our actions. And to be able to set ends is to have developed man's natural perfection—his power for promoting ends[22]—by freeing it from total subjugation to inclinations. That is, the cultivation of natural perfection is necessary to moral perfection; without the former, man would be unable to attain the latter.

This suggests an asymmetry in Kant's treatment of the animal and rational features of our nature. Men have an obligation to take their own perfection as an end: to 'the cultivation of all one's powers (or natural capabilities)'. But this perfection must be located in 'whatever man can bring into being by his own actions, *not in the mere gifts he receives from nature*; for otherwise it cannot be a duty to make perfection an end'.[23] It includes the development of 'understanding, the power of concepts, and so too of one's will'. Thus, Kant cannot suppose that natural perfection is only the cultivation of animal being—this would be the search for happiness—but must include the development of the capacity for reason.[24]

Kant goes on to contend that natural perfection is an end in itself; it is not simply a means to the end of moral perfection. The claim that natural perfection 'is the cultivation of all one's powers for promoting the end which reason puts forward' may seem to imply that it is only a means to bringing about particular moral ends. But, Kant goes on to argue,

that natural perfection is a duty and so an end in itself, and [that] the cultivation of all our powers, even without regard for the advantage it brings, has an unconditional (moral) imperative at its basis rather a conditional (pragmatic) one at its basis, can be shown in [the following] way. The power to set an end—any end whatsoever—is characteristic of humanity (as distinguished from animality). Hence there is also bound up with the end of humanity in our person the rational will, and so the duty, to make ourselves worthy of humanity by culture in general, by procuring and promoting the power to realize *all possible ends*, so far as this power is to be found in man himself. In other words, man has a duty to cultivate the crude dispositions in human nature by which the animal raises itself to man. To promote one's natural perfection is, accordingly, a duty in itself.[25]

This reference to culture in general adds a different sense to quotations already used. An end is an object of free choice determining action to production of that object. It depends on a rational will and on a freedom from nature.[26] By Kant's argument here, we have a duty to promote the perfection of man: and that is to develop to the greatest possible extent his power to set and gain ends. The promotion of this power is, by itself, in accordance with the concept of duty. Thus, if we have a duty to promote humanity as the power to realize ends generally, among the ends we would be justified in developing to the greatest possible extent is the very capacity for gaining ends.

The humanity that becomes an end is characterized by the possession of a rational will able to do two things: to free itself from animal nature and to adopt the ends proposed as duties. Kant does not intend that natural perfection should have value only in so far as it is a basis for moral perfection—which would make culture only a moral culture. Rather, our capacity for reason or our rational nature has value in itself.

One set of objections to this claim may be expressed in the following way. So far as it is necessary to reject the supposition that there are two actually existing worlds, one of which—the intelligible world—is a largely unknowable domain of rational intelligences, it also becomes doubtful that we can claim that our rational nature exists as an end in itself.

We may explain this further by looking to the *Critique of Judgement*. There, the suggestion is that there are two ways of legislating over phenomena or two orders according to which human actions, for example, are to be understood.[27] The first involves natural causes and the second supposes men capable of motivation by reason. And, as imperfectly rational beings, men try to attain to the ideal of acting as a perfectly rational will would behave. However, if moral rational behaviour is an ideal to which we attain, it is not clear why our 'rational nature', as the capacity to behave according to moral laws, should be an end. If we are but imperfectly rational beings trying to gain an ideal sort of behaviour, we can act on the principle that the cultivation of our capacity for rational behaviour is an end in itself. But this still leaves questions of why or whether we should, as *imperfectly* rational beings, value our *rational* capacities in this way.

Kant himself admits that the 'subjective impossibility of *explaining* freedom of will is the same as the impossibility of finding out and making comprehensible what interest man can take in moral laws'.[28] In accepting this, he seems to give up the possibility of justifying our valorization of rational capacities. Just as we cannot explain the interest we have in the moral law, so too we cannot make comprehensible why we should take an interest in or value our capacity for reason and moral behaviour. Both evade explanation in other terms—an empirical causal account of the freedom of the will would be useless, for example, and an account in terms of a capacity for free action would be unilluminating.

For Kant it may be answered that our rational nature, just like the Fact of Practical Reason,[29] needs no 'justifying grounds' but *shows* itself in the choices we make in that we are there already engaged in an activity over which moral reason claims legislative authority. It does not need any further explanation of how we come to be involved in this way. We *see* the dependence of practical reason on that activity. The Fact of Reason is not a condition for our being morally active but *is* that activity ordered and clarified by reason. The validity of the idea of reason depends on our maintaining it in practice, and the rule for following the categorical imperative is maintained only by the rule being followed. Similarly, where our rational nature is the ground of moral behaviour, our valuing it as an end in itself cannot then be given a *further* explanation, as if in answer to a question of why we should value rational nature. To value it *is* to behave morally; to possess it is already to be capable of engaging in activity that can be judged by moral standards.

One attempt at a further explanation of the sort just said to be unnecessary is made by saying that natural perfection supports moral perfection. To develop natural perfection only for its contribution to moral perfection is to use the former for the advantage it brings. However, Kant disallows such a development.[30] It is not always possible to say where its benefits may lie. In fact it may well be disadvantageous to cultivate the power to set an end independent of nature. For example '(according to Rousseau's principles) the advantage may turn out to be on the side of man's crude natural needs', where instinct provides a more reliable guide for action than does cultivated reason. It is 'a command of moral practical reason and a duty of man' to cultivate his power for setting ends, not a matter of the advantage it brings.

Thus, moral culture would require, say, the judgement that certain ends are proper to moral perfection together with the development or subjugation of natural instincts which, it is judged, will assist or hinder that particular end. Natural perfection emphasizes instead man's relative freedom from natural inclinations, but it does not give us an interest in gaining moral perfection by seeking particular moral ends. By promoting man's power to set ends generally, it makes possible the realization of the ends proposed as duties. But this culture in general, this exploration of man's reason and capacity for setting ends, has a value of its own. As beings capable of rationality, we will the cultivation of our potential for rational action for itself. There is 'bound up with the end of humanity in our person . . . the duty to make ourselves worthy of humanity by culture in general by promoting the power to realize all possible ends, so far as this power is to be found in man himself'.[31]

Its generality appears to make such a claim useless to Kant's conception of culture. As a rational will underlies all our actions, to will the cultivation of our potential for rational action as an end in itself may well be to make every action a duty. And the derivation of a duty attached to every action is hardly a gain in refinement. However, Kant's argument is more restricted than this suggests. A rational will underlies but does not determine every one of our actions. In some cases, we choose to let our actions be determined by sensual and natural inclinations which are not qualified by reference to our needs. In the instances in which we choose to follow inclinations, it is more correct to say that actions are determined by our animal nature. As we saw earlier, Kant talks of the activities which constitute culture as skill as the pursuit of private, sensual interests rather than rational ends.[32] And here, the duty to culture in general must be restricted to disciplinary or progressive culture, for an important contrast with skill is that the former concern our ability to reason about ends.

But even in the development of culture as skill, it can be argued, our capacity for reason is being promoted because in order to gain the rational ends we decide upon, it is essential to develop our skill in using various means. We can attempt to rescue the distinction between rational and natural ends by arguing that skill involves only means and our ability to attain ends in relation to particular empirical situations. It does not concern our potential for rational action in the sense of our ability to reason to the conclusion that the will should be determined to certain ends. But this claim in turn leads to another problem. For it is difficult to see how we could arrive at rational ends which were not also moral. That is, when we restrict the duty of culture in general to a concern with gaining rational ends, we arrive at a culture in general that is not very different from moral culture. This is because rational conclusions carry a compulsion that must be accepted by all subjects who claim to be rational. While the search for private, sensual ends leads to conflict because similar desires are combined with a truculent egotism and result in rivalry between subjects, rational ends permit us to treat subjects as ends in a community of rational feeling beings. And it may be argued that only moral ends can satisfy the criteria for membership of this community between individuals.

But it is illicit to move without argument from the conclusion that rational ends are the basis of a community between rational beings, to the further claim that the only duty we can ascribe here is that of moral culture. For the latter restricts itself to our ability to set moral ends, and it is not necessary that every rational end be a moral one. Indeed, the importance of fine art and the community of taste, like the unity based on religious belief, is that we hope to construct a unity, based on subjective feeling rather than rationality alone, that yet still contrasts with culture as skill.

Culture in General and Aesthetic Necessity

In past sections we have urged that fine art participates in culture, and proposed also that we are subject to a duty to culture in general. We shall argue further that fine art gains necessity through its satisfaction of our duty to culture in general. Accordingly, fine art is a participant in culture's task of developing man's capacity for reason in relation to nature through the *sensus communis*. An object of taste, existing in empirical nature, occasions an accord between reason and nature whose emphasis, in the case of natural beauty, is on the extent to which nature sustains an accord with mind, and whose emphasis, in the case of artistic beauty, is on the extent to which reason may be developed in nature. In the first, so to speak, reason tries to fit itself to objects found in nature while, in the second, reason tries to fit nature to its own potential for constructed forms and rational order.

Other points must be made. Both natural and artistic beauty develop man's capacity for reason and the choice of ends, but the latter also leads to an emphasis on the relation between subjects capable of rationality. It was shown that a subjugation to nature and to its concomitant contrast between nature and reason turned into a conflict between individuals in pursuit of their exclusive, selfish desires. Fine art resolves that conflict by relating nature, whether external or internal, to reason in a manner in which all subjects may participate communally. Individuals participate in a *sensus communis* and its ideal norm of unity between individuals in reason and feeling by making autonomous, persuasive, and intersubjective judgements on works of fine art. Because works of fine art provide instances of an accord between rational and feeling individuals which is also an accord of reason with nature, judgements of taste are put forward as examples of the construction of a community. On the basis of participation in the *sensus communis*, our obligation to cultural duty in general warrants certain expectations we have of the force of our own judgements of taste: it justifies the exemplary necessity that Kant claims for aesthetic judgements. This may be explained as follows.

Evidently, Kant holds that the beautiful work of art promotes our capacity for reason by manifesting a harmony between nature and reason that other subjects are also able to attain. This contention is expressed in a number of ways. It is said that judgements of taste involve a response to an empirical object where the interrelation between cognitive faculties can be entertained by all other subjects because they possess a common ground and rely on a *sensus communis*. Similarly, in positively developing a particular relation of cognitive faculties to each other and to nature, it develops our humanity through a practice in which we treat each other as subjects who are ends in themselves and capable of rational persuasion. Alternatively, cultural duty obliges men to promote their own humanity, and our experiences of fine art are instances in which others can participate because they possess the faculties essential to satisfying the ideal of a *sensus communis*. Basically, Kant's arguments in the deduction of the *Critique of Judgement* are intended to justify the supposition that all other subjects can make the aesthetic judgements which we make; and if we have an obligation to promote humanity through aesthetic judgements, then other subjects are obliged to seek to assent to our claims about particular works of fine art. All these formulations lead to the same conclusion: the necessity of culture in general justifies or warrants claims made for works which are judged beautiful. First, all rational individuals have an obligation to promote their humanity by developing their capacity for reason and for setting ends. Second, works of fine art and our judgements upon them provide instances in which subjects make judgements, based on an accord between reason and nature, that can develop every individual's capacity for reason. Third, it is possible for all individuals to make these judgements because they too possess the necessary rational faculties. Therefore, fourth, a subject making a judgement is justified in thinking to be warranted his claim that every other rational individual *should* assent to his judgement about the beauty of an object.

Indeed, this is what exemplary necessity consists in. First, it involves our humanity, possessed of both an animal and a rational character, and the promotion of our capacity for reason and ends. Second, works of fine art are significant only to humanity, and our judgement of beauty is said to promote our capacity for reason and for the determination of the will to rational ends. Moreover, judgements of taste have universal validity, being based on a relation of those rational faculties that are possessed also by all those who are capable of empirical experience. We are not concerned with a development of reason or a promotion of a capacity whose possession is contingent or restricted to particular individuals. Advances in enlightenment and self-determination do not occur only through the agency of some particular especially gifted individuals, who alone, unlike the rest of mankind, can participate in this activity. Instead, it must be seen as the promotion of humanity generally: the development of individuals and their capacity for reason is through participation in an activity which, by its nature, is open to all. And in making aesthetic judgements we are recommending just such a view of imperfectly rational feeling subjects united under the idea of a *sensus communis*.

Third, the judgement is exemplary. It is a claim that it provides an example of an accord between reason and nature that requires the relation of subjects to each other as subjects. And a successful judgement provides an example which is an ideal because it satisfies the *sensus communis*. Kant maintains that examples may count as proof: they are individual cases of practical rules in so far as these demonstrate the feasibility or impracticality of an action.[33] Exemplary works serve as proof that it is really possible to act in a particular way. Good example or exemplary conduct, for instance, involves 'not comparison with any other man whatsoever (with men as they are), but comparison with the idea of humanity (what man ought to be)'.[34] Similarly, a judgement of taste is a claim made for a work, asserting that it shows how a persuasive and autonomous experience may be gained. Consequently, works of fine art are 'models' or 'exemplary'; they serve as 'a standard or rule of estimating'.[35] In this, judgements invite comparison with something similar to the 'idea of humanity (what man ought to be)' which the duty to culture in general obliges men to try to attain. Here the accord between man's animal and rational being reflects nature's satisfaction of a relation of rational faculties in which the animal character of individuals is no longer conflictive. Instead, while remaining subjective, it is seen to be capable of participating in a harmony involving other individuals.

It is this exemplary necessity, characteristic of judgements of taste, that allows a judging subject to demand and expect all others to assent to his judgement. The duty of culture in general warrants his claim that others should assent to his autonomous, persuasive, and intersubjective judgement on a work—a work which is therefore exemplary. In this way, the demand made of others, that they assent to our judgements, is warranted by an obligation arising from the duty of culture in general.

We can explain this in more detail.

The Critique of Judgement *and Unity*

We have suggested how Kant could justify aesthetic necessity and so have given an account of the claim that 'the theoretical faculty gets bound up into unity with the practical in an intimate and obscure manner'.[36] Just as a 'synthesized imagination'[37] yields an experience which is an organization of representations that cannot be described except by using concepts of an objective world, similarly, taste requires the use of cognitive faculties to gain an experience whose unity cannot be described fully except by using concepts drawn from practical reason.

Judgements of taste are based on a relation of the cognitive faculties[38] whose distinctive employment in aesthetic judgements can be characterized by means of a contrast between community and consciousness.[39] For the unity of faculties in aesthetic judgements admits of argument and discussion in a way that treats men as rational, feeling, and acting subjects. Here a unity of faculties is also a unity between individuals capable of sharing a judgement of taste. Consequently, the search for a unity of faculties is invested with a practical value because it leads to a unity between rational and feeling individuals. Further, the practical value of fine art was justified on the basis of its participation in culture. This accounted for the unification of theory with practice, indicating, in turn, how the *Critique of Judgement* acts as a bridge between the *Critique of Pure Reason* and the *Critique of Practical Reason*.

However, if the *Critique of Judgement* is a bridge, it is one suspended between the first two *Critiques*. And as the *Critique of Judgement* rests on conclusions drawn from them, its purchase on both must be shown to be secure. But this raises various problems. For example, the necessity of beauty depends on Kant's moral theory; but the latter has been criticized quite fully, both for its detailed argument and for its general outlook.[40] And it seems we must defend moral theory in order to defend his aesthetic theory. But as that would be inappropriate here, we may instead concern ourselves principally with aesthetic theory and the necessity Kant ascribes to our judgements on works of fine art.

In one sense, the proposed account of necessity leaves things as they are.[41] A justification of necessity does not put a stop to disputes about works by providing a set of rules whose successful application will yield fine art. Thus, Ruskin's strictures against the use of blue as a central colour in a painting, for example, are no more acceptable to Kant than they were to Gainsborough when the latter produced a portrait of a child dressed in blue. This is because any attempt to issue instructions about the use of particular rules leads to problems about their application. To 'instruct is to impart rules, and if judgement could be taught there would have to be general rules by which we could decide whether or not something is an instance of the rule; and this would involve a further inquiry to infinity.'[42] At best judgement can be exercised and become well practised; it cannot be instructed and trained.[43] If moral reason guarantees the necessity of beauty it cannot be the application of particular rules governing the construction of fine art that is shown to be necessary. Necessity leaves aesthetic practice as it is.

But the role of judgement shows also that the necessity ascribed to beauty, in an important sense, does not leave things as they are. Kant's arguments for the transcendental possibility of aesthetic judgements are intended to show that an expression of preferences for fine art is defensible in a way that a preference for, say, sweet or sour tastes does not stand in need of justification. Further, given the nature of aesthetic judgements, Kant contends that our experience of beauty and reflection on it become a part of practical reason and the cultural self-development of subjects. While moral reason will not guarantee the truth of judgements of taste, it does justify aesthetic practice and ascribes necessity to the need to enculture oneself. Accordingly, discussion and argument over works of fine art are meant to change those who participate in them.

Aesthetic practice is given a critical cultural role based on a negative use of an ideal unity. It is free of any positive conception of a system of history—such as Hegel's—but confronts present reality with the ideal norm of a community. Comparing inadequate local generalizations with a conception of a universal community of rational and feeling subjects, aesthetic judgements become part of the demand that things should change. Through criticism and self-reflection individuals reject the domination of private sensual interests, abandon attempts to dominate others in thought or act, and seek to give all participants an equal status, supposing them equally capable of putting forward justifications, interpretations, or refutations that satisfy public and intersubjective criteria. Public discussion and argument between individuals possessing equal status should guarantee the universality of judgements. Thus, in a realm from which set rules are absent and where discussion is rampant, where participants cannot claim knowledge based on some correspondence between judgement and the world but, nevertheless, do not have arbitrary preferences, there is still room for necessity because discussion and agreement are important to morality in our self-conscious and rational practices. While moral reason does not make necessary the application of particular rules in creating and judging works of fine art, it does permit us to ascribe necessity to the practice of understanding, appreciating, and defending our opinions of those works and the cultural developments which they portend.

Of course, we can question a number of points in Kant's theory. For example, his claim that the appreciation and creation of fine art participates in cultural progress, and so counts as a practice because it leads to a transformation of our own behaviour as well as our relation with the work, may be questioned on the ground that cultural 'practice' does not really change. We do not produce entirely new forms of relation between nature and reason so much as merely produce ones which are classed under the general, apparently unchanging relation which the concept of culture has always circumscribed. Indeed, Kant holds that culture is a permanent feature of our human character, and cultural progress is never progress out of culture to politics or morality. It may be argued that, consequently, to call culture a practice is either redundant or a misnomer. It is either a practice only in a way in which all activity will count as practice or it misrepresents the ultimately static state of our being in the world, in which no essential transformation occurs.

However, it is not clear that such objections are very serious. This is because they raise issues pertaining to conclusions which are peripheral and, even if successful, do not cut very deep into the theory. In this case, the objection may be answered by legislating over the use of 'practice', and accepting the limitations which accrue to culture, without having to give up any important part of Kant's theory of culture, for his conclusions do not depend on this unsatisfactory notion of 'practice'.

Similarly, we may doubt the adequacy of Kant's distinction between culture and politics. He suggests that the problem cases which confront us will not change the basic categories of culture, politics, and morality used to classify different practices. The only problem is one of deciding on the natural home of problem cases, and perhaps even accepting that some will not be completely happy in one category. But it can be argued that problem cases present us with a deeper question—about the wisdom of thinking of them as distinct groupings. For we must recognize that culture may itself be political in that cultural progress is constituted by changes in the relation between subjects which, in turn, can effect their relation as citizens. Similarly, politics may interact with culture in that coercion can determine that some of the possible relations between subjects and of individuals to nature are thought to be illegitimate. And perhaps a more adequate understanding of culture will be gained by considering the diverse ways in which different social groups represent their various interests rather than by raising questions about the sort of obligations individuals can and should accept.

Such an objection may well be true. Certainly, as we shall see, Kant's theory may well need to be developed to take account of such an issue. However, this is not the appropriate place to consider this issue because it does not so much show that Kant's theory cannot be developed without contradiction as it depends on an alternative theory about the relation between culture and politics to make a point about Kant's theory. So to understand the point we would have to examine that theory. Rather than pursue the alternative theory, here we may more usefully raise questions about the unity or coherence of different parts of Kant's system, for this will allow us to develop Kant's theory and to raise issues which are more central.

The Moral Determination of Culture

We may develop Kant's theory by showing that not only have we excluded moral culture, but that although aesthetic necessity is derived from the duty of culture in general, taste is still free of a moral determination.

Although culture in general differs from moral culture in that it does not legislate over the particular ends we must gain, it still imposes an obligation on individuals to promote the capacity for reason and ends generally. And as the duty to culture in general warrants a demand for others' assent to a judgement that a work is beautiful, it could be argued, other subjects are obliged to promote their capacity for reason by also judging a work to be beautiful. However, this can be taken to assert that an individual must judge a work beautiful in order to satisfy an obligation that arises from cultural duty and so warrants aesthetic necessity. But no judgement made to satisfy a moral obligation could be disinterested. Assent would be obtained through the obligation to agree to a judgement and because of a duty to culture in general. And its disinterested aesthetic character would be either irrelevant or contradicted by the moral demand.

A straight forward and correct answer to this objection is to deny that works of fine art are judged beautiful for the sake of an obligation. It is because we judge a work beautiful that we ascribe necessity; we do not find it beautiful because of an obligation. The latter does not determine what, if anything, we will judge beautiful. Further, individuals must make the judgement for themselves. Only when a work is found beautiful does our experience of beauty enter into a system of obligation and exemplary necessity, and only there can its claim to assent be warranted.

But it is also possible to be mistaken. While 'in what concerns the consensus of differing subjects' judgement may 'demand assent like a universal principle', others can only agree 'provided we are assured of our [judgement] being correct'.[44] A judgement may fail to be universalizable because it is influenced by charm or sense; and in so far as the judgement of taste is a claim that a cultural obligation is present because of the beauty of its objects, the claim will be unfounded where a judgement depends on the indefensible—because irrational—premise that we are charmed or pleased by the object. No rational defence by example and comparison can be given in such cases, for charm and sense have a merely psychological or physical base. Consequently, we cannot impose a cultural duty on others to judge the object beautiful.

Only a misunderstanding of general cultural obligation leads us to pose an alternative between necessity or disinterestedness. Kant would contend that the necessity of the beautiful is a result of a disinterested judgement. In judging an object beautiful an individual supposes also that our appreciation of the object promotes our humanity. To find an object beautiful is to gain an end that develops our capacity for using reason in a way open to all, and this makes it valuable to culture in general and its concomitant duty. Further, only the beautiful permits us to make a claim to everyone's assent: only once an object has been judged beautiful can a cultural duty be ascribed. And a subject is not obliged to judge the work beautiful merely because it satisfies the duty to culture in general. For moral compulsion cannot occasion the subjective experience that makes taste autonomous, persuasive, and intersubjective. Rather, cultural obligation requires subjects to assess an individual's claim for the beauty of an object in a particular light because this judgement is a claim that it is the attainment of an end that promotes our capacity for reason and universality. It requires other subjects to attend to the object and to judge it because a successful judgement itself constitutes a promotion of humanity. But we cannot extend the obligation to say that subjects must gain the end on moral grounds. For what is of interest is the aesthetic character of that end. We can gain the end only by satisfying aesthetic criteria, and a consequence of that may be that we also satisfy moral standards. That is, the judgement is one of taste, and is made according to relevant standards. It is morally valuable to attain those standards, although the judgement of taste itself is not successful if made in order to and for the reason of satisfying moral values.[45]

Further, the argument proposed above against moral determination is successful even if aesthetic practice are considered part of moral culture. That is, Kant also writes of the aesthetic character of moral feeling and of the development of a moral disposition through our experience of beauty.[46] Both of these are derived from the supreme principle and are ends in themselves which a moral culture would attempt to fulfil. But their fulfilment is based on the need to satisfy aesthetic criteria. It is because of the beauty of the object that its appreciation will satisfy whichever moral end is proposed. Thus, subjects may judge objects in order to fulfil an obligation to moral culture, but their claim that an object is beautiful will be based on aesthetic considerations, not on moral grounds.

However, even if the disinterestedness of judgements is compatible with a duty to moral culture, so that beauty seems to suit both culture in general and a moral culture, nevertheless, fine art is more appropriately a feature of culture in general. This is because beauty's title to association with moral culture is unclear. To consider beauty in terms of moral culture is to ignore a great many features of the production of fine art which can enter into our appreciation *except* if we are concerned only with beauty as an end. For the production of fine art involves skill—the search for, testing of, and rejection or acceptance of techniques, all of which a moral culture does not concern itself with—and is part of the construction of a unity based on subjective feelings which are not experienced as moral feelings. If we consider fine art as subject to moral culture alone, we drive a wedge between features of our experience of beauty—such as the distinction of artistic from natural beauty and between different art forms.

As we continue to develop Kant's theory, we shall see the different contexts in which fine art must be understood and appreciated, and the different features it possesses.

Aesthetic Necessity and the Sensus Communis

It is necessary to clarify other issues in the relation of beauty to cultural duty. Kant holds that the necessity of taste is constitutive of beauty. That is, to say that an object is beautiful is to make a judgement claiming necessity. But given that cultural necessity is ascribed only when an object has been judged beautiful and for its beauty, it is not clear how beauty is discovered in the first place. We need some idea of what sort of beauty an object possesses and of how the judgement is constituted so that necessity is ascribed to it.

Kant argues that beauty possesses not only necessity gained through cultural duty, but also a subjective necessity which, through the *sensus communis*, becomes *like* objective necessity. His account of subjective necessity is an explanation of how we first gain judgements of taste, and it was considered earlier. Rather than repeat that account here, we may develop Kant's theory by considering an objection to it. This is the claim that subjective necessity is similar to the compulsion involved in cognitive judgements about some objective empirical fact—that any 'necessity claimed by aesthetic judgements [is] ... similar to the necessity claimed by cognitive judgements'.[47] The implication seems to be that just as cognitive judgements are true or false depending on the state of the world, similarly the correctness or incorrectness of aesthetic judgements can be established incontrovertibly. Just as we can dismiss a cognitive judgement because it is false, it seems, we may refute a subject's claim that an object is beautiful. Clearly, this claim goes against the conception of autonomous, subjective, and singular aesthetic judgements which we have presented all along,[48] which cannot but be persuasive and intersubjective rather than objective.

We can begin to defend Kant against this objection by reiterating the distinction he makes between subjective and objective necessity. Kant asserts that 'the necessity of universal assent that is thought in a judgement of taste, is a subjective necessity which, under the presupposition of [a *sensus communis*] is represented as objective'.[49] By presupposing the *sensus communis* we guarantee that the judgement of taste as well as the delight in the object expressed in the judgement, is rightly converted into a rule for everyone. For the principle, while it is only subjective, being assumed as subjectively universal (a necessary idea for every one), could, in what concerns the consensus of differing judging subjects, demand universal assent like an objective principle, provided we are assured of our subsumption under it being correct.[50]

Subjective necessity thus, attaches to the claim that ours is a correct subsumption. And where the beautiful is an experience of a singular, autonomous, intersubjective, and persuasive judgement, there subjective necessity stresses the aspect of autonomy.

Subjectivity implies a basis in the subject; but rather than being a reference to an individual's psychology,[51] this concerns the transcendentally necessary conditions for having and communicating experience. As judgement is based on a generally available relation of faculties, it is possible for all subjects. And to claim that others could make the same aesthetic judgements, Kant holds, is to affirm that judgements are made according to standards which have other and more authority than a claim about the individual himself. Only this regard for formal capacities allows us to argue, defend, reflect, and develop our judgements as something more than an expression of merely personal inclinations. It stresses that the judgements we make are a matter of agreement with a universal norm, not just a case of liking something in common with others. Further, while a judgement of taste is autonomous, it is also an appeal for agreement. And, although it springs from a subject's consideration of his own faculties, nevertheless, it carries authority for other individuals such that their agreement will be more than a matter of chance without being any the less autonomous.

If a judgement, as an appeal to others, merits their agreement, then it participates in the *sensus communis*. That is, where an appeal is successful, there we gain agreement and unity between individuals in reason and feeling. Further, where a judgement participates in the *sensus communis*, it serves to promote our humanity; and where it promotes our humanity there it has a necessity that is like objective necessity. That its participation in the *sensus communis* is an expression and promotion of humanity generally is explained by the fact that only in the *sensus communis* is our judgement a general end or the increase of our capacity for reason generally, for all rational individuals. Anything less than participation in the *sensus communis* would have less than 'objective' necessity. As an appeal it would not merit agreement because of its subjugation to sense or charm, for example, and would be merely the expression of a particular individual's preference—even though we may explain it as a general characteristic of people that they are capable of gaining a pleasure of sense. However, where a judgement does partici- pate in the *sensus communis*, its appeal for agreement is based not on personal preference but on standards applicable to all those who are capable of the experience that the *Critique of Pure Reason* shows to be legitimate. It possesses necessity, and is no longer just an appeal for agreement. Indeed, its participation in the *sensus communis* allows the judging subject to do more than impute agreement to others.[52] For participation in the *sensus communis* gives the universality of judgement the character of a promotion of humanity, and it gains a necessity drawn from cultural duty that makes it like objective necessity and warrants the demand for other's agreement.

Evidently, only a successful appeal to agreement, one which partici- pates in the *sensus communis*, can rely on an obligation drawn from cultural duty. So it may well be redundant to assert that a judgement claims a necessity that is like a practical objective one. For such a judgement is merely necessary and one which others should make. By contrast, a 'subjectively necessary' judgement merely seeks 'the consen- sus of differing subjects'; and through the judgement an individual appeals for agreement on the basis of his use of commonly accessible standards in his own judgements. He is a 'suitor for agreement from everyone else';[53] but his *appeal* for agreement remains merely subjective, so long as it is void of participation in the *sensus communis*, because it lacks necessity. And the necessity of taste, which is derived from cultural duty, can be titled 'objective' to distinguish it, as a claim which is warranted by its participation in the *sensus communis* and can *demand* agreement from others, from a subjective claim by an individual, which remains an *appeal* for agreement to a judgement, based on a felt suitability of object to mind, that participates in the *sensus communis* if it is successful.

Thus, in summary, subjective necessity is characterized as an appeal for agreement that is not yet warranted because its participation in the *sensus communis* is questionable and, so, its title to an obligation based on the duty of culture in general remains unclear. Rather than ascribe validity for all others to a judgement about the beauty of an object, if we treat subjective validity as an appeal, we can see it as our submission of a judgement to others in order to test its claim to necessity. It tries to 'think from the viewpoint of everyone else' and seeks to establish its univer- sality. A judgement claiming subjective necessity is the autonomous individual's appeal, made in good faith, for the agreement of all others to a judgement made according to standards that possess other and more authority than personal preference.

In clarifying the claims made for judgements of taste Kant also characterizes the objects of taste: these objects are met in the empirical world. But it has been objected that the nature of subjective necessity exposes taste for being nothing more than a quasi-cognitive judgement about objects. A subject assesses an object in the case of a claim to subjective necessity, it is said, according to a relation of rational cognitive faculties. But on this basis, any agreement between subjects will be similar to agreement in cognitive judgements over stating what is the case in the world.

However, we have shown that judgements of taste must be distinguished from cognitive or factual judgements. Subjective necessity too is ascribed to judgements of taste and, similarly, has to do with an autonomous, intersubjective and persuasive judgement that is contrasted with cognitive judgement. But, in addition, subjectively necessary judgements are concerned to understand their object as a goal of human activity, and they require us to understand meanings and to conduct a detailed interpretation of a work perceived as a goal rather than an object to be explained on the basis of its preceding and determining causes. So its validity does not make a subjectively necessary judgement of taste more like cognitive judgements. It remains part of a dialogue between subjects rather than the assertion of a 'fact' that possesses or lacks correspondence with the world. Further, a common response is explained by reference to a common ground and the idea of a *sensus communis*. Agreement over fine art will depend on acknowledging that a similar participation in the *sensus communis* will determine the communality of subjects' pleasurable response to a work. And the more the work itself interacts with and transforms the mutual self-understanding, appreciative abilities, and common experiences of subjects acting upon the world in engagement with each other, the more will all individuals be able to share in a joint response. To repeat a point made earlier: progress is the participation of an ever-increasing number of individuals in a common experience of the beautiful. And that clearly contrasts with the case of cognitive judgements.

All this serves to re-emphasize a concern with community. Subjectively necessary judgements are involved in a dialogue between subjects. Kant's concern with the autonomy and universality of judgements evinces his interest in arguing to the possibility of an experience which all subjects may gain as subjects. By contrast with a distaste for 'the ignorant multitude' which is expressed by Burke and implicit in Hume, Kant sees the value of fine art and beauty in their public nature. Where Hume thinks that only a few experts are capable of deciding what is or is not beautiful,[54] Kant argues that all those who are capable of having and communicating experience are also able to appreciate beauty and understand works of fine art. Where Hume and Burke would seem to reduce an appreciation of beauty to the ability to respond to a particular sort of sensation, Kant insists on the rational, intersubjective, and active nature of our aesthetic practice. And he is able to comprehend fine art and the appreciation of beauty as active agents in a universal cultural progress. For in making a judgement a subject abstracts from limitations contingently affecting his own estimate and seeks, instead, a universalizable experience of beauty and aesthetic practice to develop our capacity for reason, for making judgements and participating in activities which are open to all rational and feeling subjects. They bring with them a cultural duty that warrants a demand for the assent of others.

Another issue that can be raised here is one we touched on earlier. Kant says that the necessity of taste can 'demand universal assent like an objective principle provided we are assured of our subsumption under it being correct'.[55] The account of necessity we have provided may seem to argue that aesthetic necessity is objective, and, so, may appear to reject the proviso that the demand is only '*like* an objective principle'. This appearance is mistaken. Certainly there is cultural duty; and so far as it is derived from the supreme principle of morality, it is objective. That is, our experience of beauty does gain necessity from satisfying that duty; but the demand made is only *like* an objective principle because of the nature of the experience to which it applies. Its demand can be made only if the object is judged beautiful; the moral demand does not evoke an experience of pleasure. And by contrast with the usual case of moral necessity, which is independent of all feeling, the necessity of beauty is dependent for its realization on a feeling of pleasure. Moreover, as we shall see in the next two sections, the subjectivity of our experience of beauty puts limits on the way in which cultural duty is realized through our appreciation of fine art. Each of these goes to show why the demand for 'universal assent' is only *like* an objective principle.

However, the claim to being '*like* an objective principle provided we are assured of our subsumption under it being correct', may be taken to have another sense. Perhaps correct subsumption makes the demand an objective one because it is sufficiently like an objective principle once we are 'assured of our subsumption under it being correct'. If this is how the claim must be understood, then a moral or cultural duty may be superfluous as long as we have an account of what is a correct subsumption. Once we can show that an experience of pleasure has a basis in the *sensus communis*, that should be a sufficient guarantee for our demand for assent from other subjects. However, this conflates different necessities. As we argued in 'The Necessities of Taste, Fine Art, and the *Summum Bonum*', we must distinguish the transcendental possibility of taste, which is legitimated by the presupposition of a common sense, from the necessity ascribed to actual judgements. All that can be shown by a correct subsumption under a principle based in the common sense is that others must be *able* to make the same judgement. But the transcendental possibility of making pleasurable, autonomous, and singular aesthetic judgements does not compel others to make that judgement themselves. Yet it is the latter compulsion that must be argued for. Thus, even if it is possible to claim subjective necessity, it was shown that it is not an objective principle, and it fails to account for the relevant demand that everyone *ought* to agree with us by making their own judgements.

But this raises another issue, of the relation between subjects and their obligation to cultural duty.

Cultural Duty and Other Subjects

The proposed justification of aesthetic necessity may be found wanting because we have not explained fully the relation between subjects on which it depends. Although we have considered the subject's response to a work, and while this shows how his expectations of other subjects may be justified, it does not go far enough in understanding the participation of other subjects in a community. Because the argument seems to be that a judging subject's expectation of assent from others is a demand that they should do their duty—that they should agree with a judgement for that is their duty—it can be objected that while the subject judges a work on aesthetic grounds, he seems to expect agreement from others about an object's beauty on the grounds of their cultural duty and not on the basis of their judgement of its beauty.

This objection is based on a misunderstanding. For it is not simply cultural duty that leads to agreement. Our obligation is to the promotion of our capacity for reason, and the subject makes what he considers to be a well-founded claim that the appreciation of the object promotes that capacity. Kant is not arguing that others have a cultural duty to assent to a subject regardless of what agreement is about. So that we do not have to agree for the reason that a subject asserts a claim. Kant argues that we may expect agreement in the experience of beauty; and this can only be gained if others do make the same judgement. Thus, the necessity of beauty is not an obligation to agree because of the subject who is making the judgement but an obligation resulting from the experience of beauty which the subject claims to have.

Were agreement to be one with the subject, we would have to assert that it is a duty to promote another's perfection—for only on that ground can we demand another's agreement with ourselves. Rather, the only obligation arising from an aesthetic judgement is one which each subject must gain for himself by making the judgement and so promoting his own perfection. In considering aesthetic necessity Kant focuses on the judging subject, but this is not because he thinks that others are morally obliged to judge an object to be beautiful. He says little about others because he takes them also to be potential judging subjects themselves, all possessing a *sensus communis* and participating in the community.

It is in this way that Kant is able to maintain that aesthetic practice is a cornerstone of intersubjectivity. An individual may claim of others that they find the object beautiful because his own judgement is not idiosyncratic or exclusively personal. A beautiful object provides an example of the promotion of our capacity for reason. But others have to judge for themselves that the work is beautiful. Where it is a duty to promote culture in general, and as we develop culture by making the judgement of taste, other subjects can satisfy their duty by judging the beauty of the object. But this is in no guise an expectation that others will agree because they have a duty to do so and regardless of whether they think the work beautiful or not. While subjects, at most, must satisfy the duty to attend to an object and to judge it, they cannot have a duty to think the object beautiful if they do not do so. And an assessment of its beauty cannot be inferred from any other principle. For there is no other way of satisfying the cultural duty to promote our capacity for reason through aesthetic activity and our experience of the beautiful except through aesthetic activity and our experience of the beautiful. And that practice and experience have their own criteria.

Thus, Kant considers us all as potential judging subjects. For us, necessity does not depend on who ascribes it but on the nature of the judgement and our experience of beauty. Necessity becomes available because of the object's beauty, not because of the particular subject making the judgement. Nevertheless, it is available only because it involves subjects and the development of humanity.

However, the possibility of development introduces another issue into Kant's justification of aesthetic necessity.

Progress and the Claim to Aesthetic Necessity

An important issue in Kant's derivation of aesthetic necessity is the nature of the value of beauty. Cultural development is underpinned by moral reason, and Kant refuses to make some permanent, ahistorical moral order of purposes the goal of rational development. He argues that the end prescribed for man is virtue, which 'is always *in progress* because . . . it is an ideal which is unattainable'.[56] And in our striving for this goal, culture changes continuously as we put forward different solutions to changing problems in our progress toward self-determination. But where the necessity of beauty is justified through participation in culture, if culture is itself developing, then it is not clear how the beautiful may participate in a changing culture while also, as Kant wants, having permanent value.

Kant favours a resolution of this problem in which we identify a fundamental motivation underlying and uniting the superficially differing patterns of cultural development. Not only is the heterogeneous collection of activities united under the obligation to cultural duty and, so, to moral reason, but these different activities participate in our collective and universal struggle to wrest a rational order out of nature and its necessity. Past practices and cultural objects are not seen merely as occasions for an abstract historical interest, but may be placed within the unity of our human struggle towards the highest good. Thus, cultural history consists in discovering signs and clues of that struggle and thereby restoring and promoting the complex presence of that fundamental motivation in its objects; and it is to liberating men to create a moral world that cultural practice is directed.

Kant considers beauty's relation to a changing culture in at least two places in the *Critique of Judgement*. In both, the issue of whether beauty can have permanent value is raised in terms of a contrast and relation between nature and reason. In one instance, the products of genius—a creative *natural* endowment—are given stability by taste—which requires our capacity for reason—and qualified for 'permanent and universal approval, for being followed by others, and for a continually progressive culture'.[57] In the other case, Kant affirms that while cultural progress 'will cause nature to recede further into the background', nevertheless we must always be 'sensible of [nature's] proper worth'.[58]

Both instances carry the suggestion that nature and reason are two opposing poles, each necessary for any appreciation of the permanent value of beauty. In the second case, there is the further suggestion that regardless of how far the refinement of techniques and prescriptive rules—for example in schools of art and thought in a developing community of taste and in society—may grow away from their basis in genius and become more expressly social and less natural, it is still necessary to invoke their relation to genius and nature in some direct or disguised manner in order to understand fully this increasingly social culture.

Kant gives as an example the way pupils are taught fine art. Given that fine art depends on genius, it is taught by exciting the pupil's imagination rather than by prescribing rules. Prescription results 'in genius being stifled' and imaginative freedom being lost. Without this freedom, 'fine art is not possible, not even as much as correct taste of one's own for estimating it'.[59] That relation between genius and taste exemplifies the claim that the rational social relations which men enter do not excise their natural being. And in the tension and harmony between nature and reason lies Kant's hope of ascribing a permanent value to fine art and the beautiful in a progressive culture.

We need to consider this further in order to explain the claim to universality made for fine art and to answer doubts about its part in human progress.[60] In this context, nature refers to human nature, which can be seen as a repository of individual creativity and choice—the will (*Willkür*) underlying actions which can, but need not, follow the moral law (*Wille*). Further, human nature includes our animal *and* rational being. The first, in turn, includes both the pleasure we gain in making universalizable but autonomous aesthetic judgements and the pleasure we gain from satisfying exclusively individual and unreasoned ends. The second feature of human nature—our capacity for reason—is developed in relation to other persons, is often opposed to what an individual may desire for himself, and may disregard whether the ends of our action are pleasurable or painful.

Both nature and reason are essential to the value of beauty. To emphasize human nature as spontaneous action while placing a minimal stress on our capacity to be motivated by rational norms to change our behaviour is to make existing social conditions seem 'natural' and incapable of change. But these conditions may be illegitimate because they are based only on one individual's search for unreasoned and irrational ends. Thus, to accept them as intractable features of our lives is to suppress the realization that our actions have a basis in a rational will. It is to forget that we must choose to let our actions be determined by sensual desires. Consequently, it gives up the possibility of gaining moral freedom through cultural progress. It is to accept that people are selfish by nature, for example, so that a demand that they universalize the maxims by which they act must seem obviously inapplicable. Yet such a general claim cannot be based merely on empirical data and must be grounded on some unargued methodological principle that allegedly altruistic actions are in truth selfish. And it is difficult to see how this principle can be defended, in the face of actors' apparently sincere claims to the contrary, except by relying on the sort of account of actions precluded in the last chapters. Conversely, to emphasize the continuous development of social institutions—such as schools of art and thought based on prescriptive rules—is to suppose that the historical process is essential and to lose sight of human nature and aesthetic autonomy.

By contrast with positions which emphasize either reason or nature to the exclusion of the other, for Kant culture includes both human nature, as the basis of aesthetic pleasure and production, and the capacity to satisfy a rational demand for universality—both individual and community. Neither one may be given up entirely just for the sake of the other, for it is a permanent tension everywhere underlying human development. And if fine art presents us with examples or models of the relations possible between reason and nature generally, for all subjects, these will have a permanent value. 'Hardly will a later age dispense with these models.' Where social determinants appear to have replaced natural ones, it is primarily through the use of models from past struggles to regulate and comprehend nature that we will become conscious of our natural being. Without examples from the past 'a future age will scarcely be in a position to form a concept of this happy union . . . of law directed constraint belonging to the highest culture with the force and truth of a free nature sensible of its proper worth'.[61] So that while the past does not determine our future behaviour in every instance, the fact of our natural existence can be ignored only at the risk of making our hopes for the future into a merely vacuous, irrational faith with no basis in reality.

In this context we must understand the creation and appreciation of fine art as a search for and construction of a harmony between nature and reason. An emphasis on reason—the prescription of rules—stifles a subject's creative imagination and leads him to sterile repetition. And while the cultivation of genius leads us to explore new possibilities, an overemphasis on originality has its natural end in incomprehensibility. Further, the history of fine art contains a continuity like that which is enacted in culture generally. Not only is fine art engaged in the human endeavour that makes up cultural progress, but it participates as fine art. While there are homologies between the history of art and that of culture, their interrelation incorporates a mutual determination that extends beyond any simple comparison between their structures.

In any case, in order to preclude the denial of either nature or reason Kant again proposes that we look to morality and its relation of nature to reason to discover what is a proper balance between the two. Morality signals the unique situation of men: it is an expression of humanity caught between the demands of reason and nature.[62] Kant argues that the highest good provides 'that mean [or balance] between higher culture and the modest worth of nature, that forms for taste also, as a sense common to all mankind, that true standard which no universal rule can supply'. If that balance is accepted, he holds, then the refinement and progression of social forms cannot eradicate individual creativity and spontaneity; and reason will be unable licitly to extend its influence over all natural being.

Thus, the fundamental motivation for our actions is the human adventure of constructing a moral rational community among individuals who possess a rational and animal nature. And whether considering the past or the present, our use of the two opposing poles of nature and reason gives continuity to our cultural activity. Whether their relation is more or less sophisticated, now or earlier, and is discovered in fine art or elsewhere, the use of this opposition makes possible an appreciation of works. It gives them a permanent value in the task of cultural development from primitive ritual, designed to articulate our hopes of changing seasons, through icons, representing the passions of Christ, or through figurative designs, which are celebrations of human unity under Islam, to more recent concerns with the nature of cultural and political intervention.

By virtue of its engagement in this task, the value of fine art need not be restricted to the society in which it was created nor tied down to the conditions of its genesis, but can exert an influence over the development of humanity. By insisting that fine art is determined by the manner of its appreciation, and given its part in cultural development, we deny the possibility of some single, complete and final assessment of a work or its part in culture. Works are reproduced, so to speak, in a progressing culture. They exemplify individual spontaneity in relation to social and rational rules, and it is possible for us to reunderstand works by placing them in their historical or cultural context and so making them continuous with our present project. We do not detract from the value of a work by doing so; we are better able to appreciate it and can invoke the urgency it possessed for earlier protagonists in the collective human adventure we even now pursue. It is to claim particularly by emphasizing the historical position of a work and its relation to us rather than to seek some ahistorical universality whose possibility, in any case, is doubtful. A development of our capacity for reason comes about through the relation and presentation of new unities, and the more thoroughly a work explores that relation between reason and nature, now or earlier, aiming at some central and unavoidable conception of ourselves as human beings, the more deeply it participates in cultural progress toward unity, and the better it begets a permanent enrichment of humanity.

Or so Kant might hold; and fears of a loss humanity, which usually dog progress theories, might also be accounted for. Part of the reason that he is able to avoid overemphasizing some progressive social rationality to the detriment of individual spontaneity, autonomy, and nature, is that he does not try to develop a dialectical view of rational development, such as that constructed by Hegel, which sees reason as necessarily being mediated by empirical history. Whereas Kant's argument, that reason makes itself known in history, applies only to the history of the subject, Hegel asserts that the progress of *Geist* gives to empirical history a determinate rational order, so that natural events are stages in the progress of the self-consciousness of a Reason that includes what Kant would take to be Nature outside man. Hegel contends that the real is rational and the rational is real; Kant does not make a similar distinction of subject from object or of reason from nature. For Kant argues that the idea of history is merely regulative— that it does not determine empirical events. Accordingly, progress is not conceived of as a continuous linear development, where events could not have occurred in any other order.

Kant's rejection of linearity and a necessary order is a corollary of the importance he accords to moral individuals and the permanent value he ascribes to culture. In relation to the first, when Kant questions whether the human race is constantly progressing, his answer supposes progress to consist in the increasing self-consciousness of subjects about their own actions. And this is not simply a form of consciousness but becomes a real historical force that seeks to be effective in social and cultural activity. For progressive culture and history do not formulate predictions and prognoses for future events. Rather, they yield guidelines for actions which are dependent on human will; and progress involves an increase in our self-consciousness as beings capable of moral behaviour. Thus, the sympathy which the French Revolution was able to evoke gives us reason for confidence about man's future: it is a mode of thought that 'manifests . . . a universal yet disinterested sympathy'. Kant goes on to suggest that 'owing to its universality, this mode of thinking demonstrates a character of humanity, at least in its predisposition, a character which not only permits people to hope for progress towards the better but *is already itself progress in so far as its capacity is sufficient for the present*'.[63] The revolution may fail, it seems, but it has already succeeded in showing us what man is capable of doing. Events following the revolution can be regressive, showing it to have too high a price at present because they cause an increase in barbarity—so that later events are not better for being later. While we should not condone these immoral events, the revolution is progressive in providing a model which exhibits man's ability to pursue the good. For even though Kant fails to show how empirical conditions sustain particular varieties of self-consciousness, he argues that the model will guide later attempts to realize the highest good in the world while avoiding any evil effects that might have occurred previously.

Further, in his understanding of progress Kant refuses to countenance evil or suffering as an unfortunate but necessary path over which reason must progress. Consequently, the development of history does not have a justifying meaning when it leads over the suffering and misery of individuals. The closest Kant comes to arguing for such a justification is in his use of the notion of providence. His consideration of this notion occurs in the context of a general examination of nature's suitability to our human interests. But even here he does not so much argue that a moral state is inevitable as put forward a negative thesis, which is worked out in works such as 'Old Saw', 'End of All Things', and other writings on history, that our conception of nature does not preclude the realization of the highest good. Kant must defend such a claim because according to his moral theory we can have an obligation to do only what it is possible for us to achieve: if a moral pessimist were correct to contend that morality cannot be realized because nature inevitably conflicts with our moral expectations, then moral claims would lose their validity for us. And Kant defends his moral theory by arguing that history may be understood regulatively, where its 'natural' features are compatible with our moral desires. In the context of this discussion, we do not exclude the possibility or necessity of understanding morality to denote individuals and their behaviour rather than historical and natural developments. At the same time, his entire moral theory may be seen as an essay on the importance of individuals *as individuals* to the moral community. Clearly, Kant would not tolerate their suffering and misery for the sake of some supra-individual morality.

Fine Art and Culture in General

The necessity of beauty may be justified through the duty of culture in general, but fine art remains only a part of the task of cultural and historical development toward a good and moral life. Many other cultural objects, artefacts, and activities seem to be more effective and essential to our progress than fine art and the beautiful. However, the proposed justification of aesthetic necessity provides the basis for explaining beauty's symbolic relation to morality. This, in turn, makes beauty special, and allows it to play a distinctive role in cultural progress. Its distinction may be formulated as follows: beauty symbolizes moral good because it is *like* the latter. We may explain this further.

A symbol represents one thing by means of another.[64] By contrast with an allegory—where representation is achieved by relating the *content*, through its meaning, to something else—in a symbolic relation one thing represents another not through its meaning but by virtue of being itself. Thus, Titian's *Allegory of Prudence* (1560) uses a visual image invested with philosophical connotations to provide an allegory. Its three portraits, of the artist himself, of his heir, and of an adopted grandson,[65] in left profile, full face, and right profile respectively, placed above a three headed figure of Prudence as a *Serapis* monster and below a motto—'From the experience of the past, the present acts prudently, lest it spoil future action'—is allegorical because its juxtaposition of the three human and animal heads is clearly intended to be understood, and is meaningful, through the relation of its content to its motto. Further, its theme is emphasized through its aesthetic qualities. The distribution of colour and line, of light and shade, give less substance to the old man and the youth than to the face in the centre. But the first is obscured by shadow rather than, as in the case of the youth, blurred by an excess of light. Moreover, the allegory is successful because of its symbolic content. The faces symbolize past, present, and future, typified through old age, maturity, and youth. And so the individual portraits must be seen not only as particular persons but as representations of something universal. While an allegory is successful through the meaning of its content, the analogies between elements in a symbolic relation are given significance and 'meaning' through their relation. For a symbol invokes a connection between the representation and what it symbolizes. It is not simply a meaning to be correctly and exhaustively understood.[66] Yet although the example used above is of a representational picture which is also a symbol, symbols need not be pictorial. The representation of a dog in Dürer's *Melancholia* may be a symbol of 'a darker aspect of the melancholic complexion',[67] but not through its pictorial or representational qualities.

By this account, beauty is a symbol of moral good not because of what is beautifully represented but because of the very nature of beauty. It is significant because it *is*: individuals recognize each other as subjects through the experience of beauty, and its necessity, independence from determination by interests, its freedom, general validity, autonomy, persuasiveness, intersubjectivity, and unity, all make an experience of beautiful works of art of special interest because the work occurs in the phenomenal world and yields an experience which is a surrogate for that experience of moral freedom which is never possible for man. By contrast with other cultural practices, which also gain legitimacy through cultural duty, our experience of beauty is analogous to a conception of moral experience. Thus, while non-aesthetic cultural practices may depend on conceiving of other subjects as morally responsible persons, only beauty can claim, in addition, to provide a milieu in which all subjects recognize each other as subjects. And this invests beauty with a power to initiate cultural developments in a way that other artefacts and activities cannot generate.

All this points to further differences between Kant and Schiller. For Kant may argue that the symbolic relation of beauty to morality shows the human significance of aesthetic reflective freedom. But he does not argue that this justifies aesthetic necessity. By contrast, Schiller gives a major role to symbols in justifying aesthetic necessity. We may mention two contrasting features of their positions. First, while Kant explores the nature and operation of symbols in aesthetic judgements by understanding beauty's relation to moral good, Schiller holds that the use of symbols is central to and perhaps definitive of artistic beauty. Indeed, a 'beautiful object serves as a symbol for an idea', and its access to an otherwise unknowable reality gives to beauty its task and, hence, its necessity.[68] Second, Schiller bases his account of the aesthetic education of man on the analogy between moral good and beauty. Given their similarity, for him beauty provides a 'Third way' between the demands of reason and nature.[69] While Kant argues that cultural activity is determined by the end of establishing the rule of reason over nature, so that our artistic production and appreciation of beauty develop nature for the sake of reason and show the harmony possible between reason and nature, for Schiller beauty is its own end in the special sense that it seeks to fuse nature and reason into a harmony that defines man's proper station. Thus, what Kant could take to signify the tragic fate of men—that they are bound, by radical evil, to fail whenever they attempt to act like purely rational beings—becomes, for Schiller, the desired end. His Third Way sees as its positive goal the attainment of a harmony between nature and reason in which each must be given its due. By contrast, for Kant, men must resign themselves to living a life balanced between nature and reason and perpetually under threat of surrender to nature because of their imperfectly rational character. Further, consonantly with these distinctions, for Schiller, beauty's symbolic relation to morality takes on a greater moment than it has for Kant. Because it is symbolic, fine art gives us access to a reality beyond appearance and so goes to define the positive end, task, and necessity of beauty. It is also the only reliable access we gain, and the pursuit of beauty is the most important part of the Third Way. For Kant, beauty's symbolic relation to moral good makes the former distinctive among other cultural products, but it neither justifies its end nor gives it its necessity. Nor does it show the pursuit of beauty to be the most important among our activities.

Comparisons of Kant with Schiller raise another issue. Schiller holds that to understand particular works fully we must relate them to the real world beyond appearances. But for all the arguments showing that for Kant aesthetic necessity must be justified through fine art's participation in culture, we do not yet know how that argument affects our understanding and appreciation of fine art. Some indications were given in saying that by placing works from the past in the context of a continuing struggle for reason out of nature we are able to recapture the urgency they hold for past protagonists. But we need to know more than that. The argument connecting fine art with culture cannot be simply a priori in that all works are related to culture even where we are not conscious of the link. This would not permit our cultural development to enter into our appreciation of particular works. For if fine art is to aid us in the cultural task of constructing a community of rational individuals, our experience of fine art must move us consciously toward recognizing other subjects as rational ends. Nor can this development be limited merely to 'placing a work in its social context' if that fails to exhibit the nature of our engagement in culture through an experience of fine art. Kant's a priori arguments show that it is legitimate to make aesthetic judgements and that we may demand assent to them. But it is the business of the subject to argue that a work satisfies an aesthetic judgement and to explain how it contributes to the development of culture.

Kant does not set out how we are to justify particular judgements except to say that we may produce a science of criticism. His negative characterization precludes the influence of charm or sensual pleasure on our aesthetic appreciation. But apart from the suggestion that we must argue by example and comparison, a few curious remarks in praise of verses authored by the King of Prussia, and the reasoning he gives in support of a hierarchy of fine arts, Kant does not give us many examples of how we are to articulate our response to works. Some remarks addressed to the creative work of genius cast more light on this matter, but these remain quite unsystematic if considered from the point of view of a critical theory. Partly this is a consequence of the abstract level at which Kant is writing. His concern is with the a priori features of our aesthetic practice: its transcendental conditions and the nature of its necessity. Kant's work is intended to show the reasoning we may engage in over works of fine art. The defence we actually provide for our judgements on particular works is a further matter, based on the justifications he has provided of the status of aesthetic judgements and artistic works. In spite of Kant's apparent reticence, however, we may suggest some of the features we must attend to in appreciating fine art. For although Kant does not conduct lengthy analyses of examples, in the process of considering aesthetic judgements and their part in progressive culture and rational history, he provides a number of suggestions.

Kant clarifies the nature of fine art initially by examining the operation of genius in the construction and consumption of aesthetic objects. Works are texts or constructed objects which must be explained and understood as goals open to interpretation. Kant's account of expression and presentation explores how works are made intelligible, and how our understanding gains unity through a concentrated study of particular objects. The particular works, further, have continuity with others in the history of art, and part of our study can consist in discovering traces of the latter in the present work. Moreover, as we proposed earlier, the works we consider do not possess an unchanging and fixed essence. Rather, judgements of taste and our experience of beauty involve a relationship between subjects which works of fine art may realize in different ways in history.

In this way Kant relates aesthetic judgements and objects to the practical task of culture. Aesthetic judgements are free of determination by any interests but, rather than being precluded by the disinterestedness of aesthetic judgements, an association with moral interest is essential to the necessity of taste. However, to admit to our interest in beauty is to change our understanding of the aesthetic cultural object. We are no longer concerned merely to understand or interpret it but must consider the part its experience plays in the construction of a real community. In effect, our understanding and interpretation of works must be reconsidered in terms of their engagement in constructing a society. A sociology of art or literature may go the extent of associating a work with particular social groupings on the basis of various homologies between the content of a work and the patterns followed by society. But we have already suggested that this approach is merely abstract and mechanical.[70] By contrast, Kant conceives of fine art as an active principle in culture: our understanding of fine art, as it were, is itself an instrument of cultural progress. And this differs markedly from a sociology of art or culture in which two elements are compared and related on the basis of a method whose logic and rationale seem to be qualitatively distinct from the appreciation of works of fine art or engagement in cultural advancement. For Kant, in order to conduct enquiries into the cultural or communal involvement of art we must apply the very concepts which were excluded by aesthetic autonomy and disinterestedness. That is, we must investigate works in terms of their part, as works of fine art, in constructing or regaining a social unity between individuals.

Further, culture is but one mode of a relation between reason and nature which man also enters through politics, science, and morality. And any comprehensive exploration of our engagement in cultural development must also consider its difference from other practices. Rather than merely assert the autonomy of culture from politics, science, or morality, however, we must also consider their interrelation. For while Kant's ultimate objective is to gain a unity between nature and reason under moral laws, in so far as this is possible for an imperfectly rational creature like man, he also avoids the pitfall of attempting to impose a homogeneous unity on the distinctive forms which creativity and spontaneity can take. By thinking in terms of increasingly wider contexts, beginning with judgements of taste and our experience of beauty, through aesthetic activity as an intervention in cultural development, to nature's part in uniting reason with nature, he makes it possible to assign each mode its due. Only if their distinction *and* interrelation are not respected will fine art either gain some etiolated 'purely aesthetic' life separate from reality, or suffer an iniquitous absorption into morality or politics. Instead, for Kant, aesthetic activity may be seen as an arena in which distinctive social and cultural problems are resolved.

However, although Kant wants to insist on the reality and unity of individual and community of reason and nature, as part of his claim to unite theory and practice, it is not clear that he can do so.

Autonomy: The Impossible Unity

The necessity ascribed to beauty warrants an individual's demand for agreement from others about a judgement on a work or object. To be successful, this agreement must be based on valid reasons and the shared experience of a judgement of taste. For otherwise it could be merely a coincidence of pleasures, perhaps occasioned by a similarity of interests. But as Kant only sets out merely formal and negative criteria for taste, makes the individual's own experience a basis for judgements of taste, yet holds that the universality of taste is guaranteed by agreement with others possessing a common ground and a *sensus communis*,[71] it is not clear that the necessity of beauty allows, as it must, if it is to be consistent, for a clear distinction to be maintained between warranted and unwarranted agreement or disagreement. For by this account it is open to an individual to hold that his own judgement is correct even though others fail to judge the work beautiful in the way he does.

Thus, faced with Wesselman's *Great American Nude, No. 44*, a subject may point to its composition to argue that because the detail from Renoir's *Gabrielle à la Rose* contained in the painting uses warm colours to portray a woman, it must be contrasted unfavourably with the nude figure beside it, which uses similar colours but has different tones and lacks substance. He can choose to emphasize a particular juxtaposition of elements in the painting in order to argue that Renoir's conception of the task of portraiture was misguided because it idealized its subjects. There are other aspects of the work he can point out to justify his interpretation and to defend his assessment of the work's success. And he may judge the work's aesthetic merit for these reasons. The features he stresses lead him to disagree with others, who emphasize the flatness of the nude figure, point out that it is only a silhouette, empty of any human presence and represented as painted on one wall in a room heated by a radiator, and who see the work as an unfavourable comment on the limitations encountered in present-day portraiture. Thus, in the final analysis, the individual may argue, all he can do is to give reasons which show that his judgement is free of moral, cognitive or other interests, point to the work being judged, and stand by his own judgement—even if others are unable to judge the work well for his reasons.

The difficulty raised by this autonomy of judgements is exacerbated by Kant's reference to *potential* consciousness or *possible* consciousness in a community of individuals, each of whom may claim to be guided by a *sensus communis*. A subject may defend his own judgement by dismissing others' disagreement as an empirical accident and by maintaining that others *could* share the judgement. Defenders of Picasso and Braque, for example, behaved consistently in valuing their work for reasons which have become more generally accepted. And it seems justifiable to hold to those valuations in spite of a lack of general agreement, for it is difficult to concede that an actual general agreement or disagreement proves judgements correct or incorrect. This should be a matter of the reasons given and their reference to the *sensus communis*, regardless of their general acceptance. If the reasons are universalizable and, based on possible consciousness, anticipate agreement in the *sensus communis*, then, even if general agreement is not actually gained, the individual may hold to his judgement and his experience of beauty.

Further, because his judgement does anticipate agreement with others possessed of a common ground and guided by a *sensus communis*, the individual may also claim aesthetically 'objective' necessity. That is, it seems that in spite of a lack of agreement with others, the individual may hold to his judgement and also advance the demand that others assent to it by making the judgement themselves.

But if this claim to objective necessity is permissible, then it is not clear just when a judgement is right or wrong. If necessity no longer depends on an actual agreement but can fall back on an anticipated consensus, it is difficult to see what criteria to use in adjudicating over a disputed judgement. For while disagreement is warranted if a judgement can be shown to be determined by interests, there are no rules setting out the basis for agreement. Positive points are found only through making a judgement. Yet even others' inability to make the judgement—that is, their failure to find such positive points—still allows an individual to claim necessity and demand assent. Yet surely this is inadequate. It is strange to claim that others should assent to a judgement merely because they cannot disagree with it as it is not determined by charm or interest. If others are unable to judge a work favourably, surely they should be able to dismiss an individual's judgement whenever it fails to provide a clear reason for accepting it.

But this sort of dismissal is not available to Kant. His stress on the individual's autonomy in making judgements, together with his emphasis on the need for cultural progress, suggests a methodological prejudice. Where an individual makes a judgement, and claims that its being grounded in a common sense and following the *sensus communis* promotes culture, others are also required to judge the work. There are no limits to the cultural demand for agreement made by the individual's judgement except that it must not be determined by an external interest. A failure by others to judge a work beautiful may simply be 'their fault', requiring them to rethink their approach. And this rethinking will continue until they either share the individual's judgement in the anticipated *sensus communis* or discover it to be misguided for some reason. That is, others must continue to take the individual's judgement seriously until they actually discover some error in it. But this need never occur, and the former means that others may have to continue their reassessment indefinitely. The demand of cultural duty for the creation of a community, in this case one following the ideal of a *sensus communis*, requires them to continue an indefinite search for the positive points which may be the basis for another's judgement and whose acceptance will allow them to share the judgement that a work is beautiful and so a participant in cultural progress. They are unable simply to dismiss an individual's judgement for the reason that it does not provide a clear justification for accepting it. For Kant, the onus is on others to try and understand the individual's judgement; yet there is no point at which agreement or disagreement is reached.

An alternative to this endless search may be sought, for Kant, in a pluralism where there is agreement between *some* individuals. It may be possible to concede that some individuals find an object aesthetically valuable for the reasons they give even though these reasons do not have the same force for other subjects. The defenders of that judgement take it to be universalizable and necessary because others possessed of rational faculties may also, in theory, judge the work beautiful. The judgement, it may be said, has a status of universality even though aesthetic argument fails to show that it is generalizable in the sense that not everyone finds that reasoning equally compelling.

Such a pluralism may be acceptable within Kant's scheme. Indeed, it seems that cultural progress through aesthetic discussion depends on something like it actually obtaining. Progress consists in an increasing number of individuals making the given judgement on a work: at some time they did not all accept the claim to universality made by a particular judgement. While those who judged a work beautiful claimed universality and necessity, those who detracted from the judgement were unable to accept the claim to universalizability—not because they thought the judgement wrong but because for them it lacked the same force. Thus, even if aesthetic necessity shows only that our experience of beauty and discussion of works are valuable but does not adjudicate between the particular rules used and reasons given, it may be possible to warrant agreement by reference to the group which gives due weight to the reasons given in defence of a judgement. Although only members of that group actually judge the work well, the claim is that others *could* agree. The judgement is universalizable in that it refers to a possible consciousness.

However, not only do we lack criteria for membership of this group, but, if such a pluralism were accepted, it would become increasingly difficult to distinguish it from an individualism where a single individual makes a judgement which, in theory, anticipates agreement with other participants in a community, but which he stands by even though others, in fact, fail to make that judgement. Further, the absence of membership criteria shows that the proposal is part of the problem rather than the solution. For to assert that we possess satisfactory criteria we must be prepared to countenance an intimate relation between our aesthetic experience and our social lives on the basis of which we go on to claim that aesthetic value may be understood by reference to a social group within the whole community. But it is just this claim and this relation that we are presently trying to justify by considering whether individuals can be in harmony with the community.

Further, if in spite of a lack of agreement by others the individual may claim that his judgement is correct, this only leaves unanswered doubts about what warrants agreement or otherwise over judgements of taste. In spite of the rational nature of judgements and the requirement of universal standards, it seems that aesthetic judgements are little better than expressions of personal preference. For the individuality which marred claims for sensational or simple pleasures is also present in aesthetic judgements. The individual's preference is indisputable in both cases. In one, his expression of preferences cannot be refuted because it is like a preference for sweet over sour tastes; in the other it is indisputable because it bears reference to some anticipated *sensus communis* but cannot give reasons which are strong enough to motivate others to share the judgement.

The points made above indicate that the shift in emphasis from consciousness to community leaves open a number of questions about the relation of individuals to each other. It seems that there remains an irreducible tension between, on the one hand, the individual's autonomy in making judgements and, on the other, the community to which these judgements may be addressed. By Kant's account, both are necessary and each is supposed to use mutually acceptable criteria. Thus, judgements are based on criteria which have general validity and other and more authority than a confession of personal preferences. It is a validity that, in principle, admits of justification, discussion, and agreement with others in a community. Judgements are 'other-directed' in that argument and agreement or disagreement with others is supposed to test the generalizability of judgements. In the explanation, defence, and discussion of works, subjects are treated as rational and feeling ends, each capable of making and sharing judgements.

However, even while they stress this relation to community, there is a corresponding stress on the individual and his judgements. No one else can make a judgement for him; nor can others legitimately impose agreement upon him. The individual makes his own judgement; and even if he uses criteria which, in principle, carry authority for others—so that their agreement is not simply a matter of chance or unreflective experience—their inability to accept his judgement does not, by itself, require him to give up that judgement. That it fails the test of actual general acceptance does not lessen his claim to its universality. And there seems to be no way, within Kant's scheme of aesthetic necessity, to adjudicate between such opposing claims by individuals in a community.

This tension between the individual and community, in turn, suggests a problem with affirming that fine art and culture forge a unity between theoretical faculties and practical reason. Beauty was supposed to exemplify a unity between individuals. It shows that a subjective experience need not generate conflict between reason and nature or between individuals. Instead, it promotes a unity between them because it is an experience open to all and claiming necessity. To promote such a unity is to develop culture through individuals' possession of the *sensus communis*, their participation in a community, and the satisfaction of cultural duty. But as we are dealing with an *anticipated* unity, a preference for a work of fine art for its promotion of unity cannot be shown to be spurious by arguing that the judgement lacks agreement from others. To concede this is to accept that the search for unity between individuals through aesthetic judgements remains inconclusive. If it is not clear how to adjudicate between an individual's claim to universality and others' lack of agreement, then the construction of a unity between individuals is also problematic. For the differences between them remain unresolved: discussion, argumentation, and agreement are the only means of resolving differences, but they are evidently inadequate to the task of gaining unity.

If taste no longer gives reason for supposing a unity between individuals, this weakens the claim that it unifies theory with practice. It may be thought that a unity between theoretical faculties and practical reason is affirmed simply by arguing that cognitive faculties are used to make aesthetic judgements which admit of intersubjectivity, discussion, and justification—procedures which are important to practical reason. But no satisfactory argument for unity can be gained if it cannot also be shown how necessity is ascribed and requires that others *should* make that judgement, for without the latter the relevance of aesthetic practice to moral reason remains unargued. At best it shows that practical reason is not incompatible with theoretical faculties in aesthetic use; but it fails to show why or how their unification occurs.

To ascribe necessity we would have to argue that cognitive faculties are used to satisfy a demand of practical reason. In this instance we could claim that beauty, an experience of unity between rational faculties, satisfies cultural duty by promoting unity between individuals treated as rational subjects. But because this unity is explained in terms of an anticipated agreement grounded in the *sensus communis*, it is not clear that any unity is achieved. As it is possible to hold to judgements despite failing to gain agreement from others, the claim that a judgement is grounded in the *sensus communis* does not clearly promote unity between individuals. If its claim to being grounded in the *sensus communis* cannot be shown to be spurious by showing that others do not share that judgement, it is not clear what real force is attached to the claim to unity itself. If the claim to unity remains unclear, then so does the claim that the judgement promotes cultural progress and satisfies cultural duty. As it fails to promote culture, the judgement cannot be said to evince a unity between theoretical faculties and practical reason because the latter unity depends on judgement creating a unity between theoretical faculties which is *also* a unity between subjects treated as acting subjects and as rational and feelings ends.[72]

However, at the same time as we question Kant's claim that theory is unified with practice by denying that it is satisfactorily grounded in an individual's *anticipation* of a future or presently displaced community, we are also forced to acknowledge that Kant sees the individual rather than general culture as the agent of change and of the construction of a community. The individual, so to speak, is the point from which we view culture's task of criticizing present reality.

It is the subject who experiences an opposition between the forms taken by common human understanding and the *sensus communis*. The former consists of the unargued and fragmentary responses which are inculcated in us by habit, force, and domination, or the arbitrary development of an irrational culture. Its parts are unlikely to cohere with each other in a single consciousness and certainly will not cohere in a social whole. A *sensus communis*, by contrast, is a unified individual consciousness which is united with others in some perhaps unrealized community.[73] And part of a subject's procedure in the latter case is to persevere in following the demands of a consciousness that goes against the grain of common sense.

Unless we are to grant that an ideal community has been achieved, the rational individual as the source of that uncommon thought must be given due weight. And as Kant holds that this ideal is 'always in progress', there seems to be no point at which an individual counter-consciousness can be ignored altogether. A rational individual, then, is the source of the discussion, appreciation, and interaction between subjects that make up the community. And we cannot absorb individuals into the community without also giving up the hope of a rigorous account of communality. In other words, the individual may be distinguished within the society he lives in, but he remains the source of a rational, public consciousness that constitutes the community. And given that his construction of a community proceeds by contrast with present reality, he must be able to anticipate a future or presently displaced unity with other subjects in order to claim the assent of others. Thus, it must be clear that Kant's theory of culture cannot do without the given accounts of autonomy and the possibility of anticipating participation in a *sensus communis*.

But Kant's stress on subjects leads to other problems for his claim to unity. This has to do with another sense in which the subject is the source of an as yet unrealized community. For it is not clear which subject is the source and repository of the 'consciousness' that participates in the community; whether it is the empirical ego, with its contingent and, strictly, disunited collection of images, and so forth, or the transcendental ego, with its real spontaneity and creativity. And regardless of which one we make a claim for, we will have to show also how the other is related. But we cannot avoid making a claim; and whichever it is for, it seems, the other will be excluded. Here the procedure Kant describes is one of gaining clarity about the order and proper motives of our engagement with nature and other subjects. We expect to attain some moment when all individual subjects are fully conscious of their own motivations and the extent of their determination by nature. At that moment the conditioning that makes us susceptible to common sense is dissolved and our clarity about ourselves gives us full access to the unity between individuals in reason and feeling. However, such clarity must be impossible because the transcendental ego, the source of spontaneity and action, is outside our experience. Yet if fine art is to participate in a unity between theory and practice, and between our empirical experience and moral demands, it is in our actual experience that we must gain the lucidity that empowers us to join a community which, through its basis in the *sensus communis*, manifests our satisfaction of a moral demand. And if the transcendental ego is outside our experience, it is not clear that we can become transparent to ourselves—as we must in order to participate in the community. But further, if such clarity is unattainable, then because Kant will not permit that there can be rational moral demands which subjects are unable to fulfil, the necessity of beauty loses credibility.

It is necessary for Kant to clarify how the demand for unity may be met through being grounded in the *sensus communis*. Until it is clear what sort of unity, what extent of agreement, and between whom, are necessary before a work may be said to promote culture, the proposed unity between theory and practice remains doubtful. The unresolved tension between individual and community raises doubts about the unity of theory with practice that Kant seeks in the *Critique of Judgement*. Thus, as moral reason only justifies the necessity of aesthetic judgements generally, and as Kant does not give a clear account of the positive basis for a consensus about works, his argument for the unity between theory and practice may be thought to be incomplete. Thus, although the *Critique of Judgement* depends on conclusions drawn from moral theory, its purchase upon the latter, which provides the substance of practice to be unified with theory, seems far from secure.

In spite of the thoroughness with which it seems to have been shown that it is impossible to gain a unity between individuals and between theory and practice, this account seems more to misconstrue the nature of Kant's claims than to have shown their inadequacy. For example, by raising questions about the relation between transcendental and empirical egos it does not show that Kant's account of necessity is any less credible. What it claims to require—that if fine art is to participate in a unity between theory and practice, and between our experience and moral demands, it is *in our actual experience* that we must gain the lucidity that empowers us to join a community which, in turn, through its basis in the *sensus communis*, manifests our satisfaction of a moral demand—is just what we have argued actually obtains. Chapter IV proposed that moral action must be actualized in *this* world *and* may be conceived of as realized. In so far as the transcendental ego is taken to be the source of our free and rational actions, its products are manifested in our experience.

Kant's theory recognizes the need for, and tries to satisfy, the claim that moral laws can be realized in this world. It neither wants nor needs to accept without qualification the claim that we may expect to attain some moment when all individual subjects are fully conscious of their own motivations and the full extent of their determination by nature. Kant's theory, it must be understood, turns on conceiving of our self-development as a continuing process, not one having an end in a static perfect state beyond history or change. And as we can never escape our animal nature, our motivations need never be so clear to us that we escape the latter entirely.

However, the point raises another issue. Given that we can develop ourselves in and through our lives in this world, under moral laws, we need to know how this could proceed. We have already proposed part of the answer. Cultural progress proceeds as we come to act rationally in situations which seemed to be subject merely to causal determinations, because we see that a rational will underlies this part of our behaviour. Behaviour once thought of as a part of our animal nature, for example, or such hindrances to our lawful behaviour as are really a result of the 'neglect of pure ideas',[74] come to be seen as within our control, and the action and its ramifications are reordered on the basis of our better understanding of their source and nature.

So, for instance, works of art provide us with examples, which give occasion for the exercise of judgement.[75] Each exemplifies the general rule of an intersubjectively valid judgement, as it were providing a schema for our humanity and yielding not contingent a posteriori generalizations about individuals but exhibiting our *capacity* for participating in a universally valid activity. And, further, in understanding particular works, the very activity of producing fine art counts as an 'external witness' by indicating which products might count as works while also showing where and how the range of possibilities may be expanded and the practice of producing works itself may be changed. It both permits and limits the production of works by providing resources, such as criteria we can use to give meaning to the properties of objects, which artists may draw upon, while also imposing constraints on how those objects must be used in order to bear meaning.

As these criteria regulate the production of fine art although they do not necessarily act upon the artist in a conscious way, by understanding their role we can also bring them under our control.

As conventions, these criteria provide a general background which determines the creation of particular works without specifying every one of its characteristics. Such a determination need not be intentionally followed by the artist in that he need not describe his own actions in terms of following the conventions of art. So it cannot be the reason for his action. But it does contribute to an explanation of his decisions—to follow through the actions he had addressed to paint and canvas—by qualifying his intentions and locating for us the particular impact of the practice of producing fine art. In such cases, we may think of the conventions as a force whose effect is understood in terms of causality rather than reason. For it is commonplace that our actions are not transparently rational. Here, while we accept that in principle our actions need not be reduced to merely causal terms, particular examples of behaviour may still be understood more completely if we consider them in terms of quasi-causal relations rather than as examples of practical reasoning. And in becoming conscious of their force we may redescribe the artist's intentions and so explain the latter by showing how they are responses to an inclination issuing from the widespread acceptance of or apparent force exercised by the practice of fine art. Consequently, once we recognize their nature as norms, we may also bring these conventions under our control.

Kant says little about *this* procedure of understanding and interpretation, though scattered remarks suggest he may have a consistent position. It is possible to suggest what the procedure might be. We might point out the inappropriateness of, or the presence of *non sequiturs* in an author's or a subject's conceptions and the conventions he follows, or show that the latter is not applicable to the object, and discover other factors—perhaps psychological, social, or political ones—that *caused* the author or the subject to fail to recognize the rational gaps in his conception or deluded him into thinking that *non sequiturs* existed where there were none. By understanding these different factors, we gain a greater self-understanding as well as a better appreciation of the object.

Thus, although the general laws of understanding alone fail to explain the influences on producing or appreciating fine art, when taken together with other rules they make an important contribution as 'external witnesses' by leading us beyond the artist to the objects and institutions he is working with. This move may even be considered necessary: works of art and other cultural objects may lack the facility for being given univocal meanings in a system of science, but they are meaningful and we must try to understand them—even if to do so we have to rely on something like the quasi-causal explanation referred to in showing how conventions provide 'external witnesses'. By analysing the background to our aesthetic judgements we show also how something which seemed to determine the artist's intentions, and so to be a cause rather than an intention, could actually be chosen or offended against, and is capable of being part of our rational activity rather than being an unconscious and external determination of our prodution of fine art.

Other examples of such development have already been given: in the role of the French Revolution as a model for us; in the way we may analyse inconsistencies of behaviour to discover their cause and so perhaps remedy our behaviour. Thereby we increase unity between individuals in reason and nature.

And this returns us to the objection that individuals are not united by aesthetic judgements and so there cannot be a unity between reason and nature in feeling. The criticisms made misconstrue Kant's theory or, at least, place requirements which Kant could not accept without changing the nature of his theory. For example, Kant recognizes that the relation of individual to community is an issue likely to engage us indefinitely. And rather than seek to give either pole of individual or society more prominence, he prefers to show that they can be united without one being subsumed under the other. Thus, in his moral theory, the individual is the source of action, but this action is universalizable and directed toward the community. Similarly, in history and cultural development, Kant proposes we must recognize man's 'social unsoci-ability': this is a permanent tension in our lives, where the individual may be overpowered by others treating him as a means to their own ends, and it can lead to an inequitable society.

We are subject to impulses of both society and individuality. But that does not mean that we live an impossible contradiction which can be resolved only by the victory of one principle over the other. Instead, Kant wants to maintain both poles, and, it may be suggested, will be more tolerant of individual differences. Thus, it is right to point out, as we have done, that there seems to be no way, within Kant's scheme of aesthetic necessity, to adjudicate between opposing claims by individ-uals in a community. As we shall see, this does raise an important issue concerning how our interpretations are validated, and requires us to develop Kant's theory further in one respect. But the need for validating interpretations need not be taken to exhibit the failure of Kant's scheme. For one thing, there are two different issues: an account of how interpretations are validated may still leave open the possibility that we cannot adjudicate between conflicting interpretations. All that is shown by the absence of adjudication mentioned above is that Kant's schema is more individualistic than others, and that the community within which such individuals exist does not have as determinate a unity as others might. Nevertheless, it is still able to boast unity: it is wrong to claim that it leads to arbitrariness and that consequently aesthetic judgements cannot be distinguished from more sensational pleasure. The individ-ual's preference is indisputable in the latter case because it is capable of explanation but not of justification. But aesthetic preferences do not work in this way. They are capable of justification and defence, as we have seen. They are not arbitrary, but must have reasons, and they explore our rationality in relation to others. In making them we must treat ourselves and others as rational and feeling ends in themselves. And our adopting this stance toward each other may suffice to warrant our considering subjects as the members of a unity between individuals. That is, without obtaining a determinate unity by showing in each instance precisely why or how others should agree with judgements on a particular object, we may still propose the relevance of aesthetic practice to moral reason. For the sort of discussion we must engage in when considering whether a particular work is beautiful provides the sort of unity between individuals engaged in aesthetic activity and discourse that may be brought to moral reason. Their defence may not be able to exert the sort of compulsion which can be exerted, say, in legal relations, and they carry a demand to which others must feel they can *give* assent. But neither of these factors shows that a unity is unobtainable. All they show is that it will be a unity with a particular character.

Not only can we continue to suppose that taste gives us reason for expecting a unity between individuals, but a more individualistic unity is not any less capable of unifying theory with practice. For once we recognize that discussion, reflection, and agreement may be deployed in providing justifications for our judgements, and in thereby gaining a unity between individuals, we may then ascribe necessity because beauty, an experience of unity between rational faculties, or the search for such unity, satisfies cultural duty by promoting unity between individuals conceived of as rational subjects. We will treat individuals as ends, and do so not only by providing some determinate unity, where we all find a work beautiful, but also by allowing for a range of individual choices in the way individuals exhibit their rational and feeling character. That they do not always agree does not show that they have no value, and our possession of rationality does not fail if we do not always come to the same answer. To expect or accept less would impose the wrong sort of restraints on culture. For not only does Kant's account refuse to countenance any or every arbitrary claim, but it succeeds in reminding us that a diversity in judgements is neither always futile nor irrational.

The suggestion is that the issue is inadequately understood in terms of a contrast between individual and community. Rather, we must see it as a concern with the nature of agreement and understanding. The former contrast may look to the individual as a source of the validity of judgements. But this is not a satisfactory procedure, for a concern with the necessity of aesthetic judgements is served by pointing out that agreement *must be given*. That is, the nature of the demand made in aesthetic judgements is clarified by showing the importance to it of giving assent. By saying this we not only set out the relation between individuals which is sustained by fine art, we show that it does unite theory with practice. For to deny that such unity is gained we would need to point to the irrelevance of assent (from the subject) as a way of showing that the subject was not being treated as an end. Pointing to the source of this assent—the individual—need not further explain the necessity of aesthetic judgements.

Of course, there are other issues raised here which concern the individual. For example, if judgements of beauty must be seen as a mode of active participation by the individual in creating a community by giving assent, we need to know more about how the individual decides to give assent. It seems that Kant has argued for the general possibility of aesthetic judgements and accounted for the character of the demand implicated in particular aesthetic judgements, but has not yet fully explained the validity of particular cases. For once we see that aesthetic judgements are possible and that their legitimacy is of a sort where agreement must be given, the problem of how that agreement is reached becomes an issue. Here we may propose that for Kant this agreement can be explained by seeing fine art and beauty as expressive and open to interpretation. And the way in which this agreement is reached, the sort of criteria we need to account for the validity of expression and interpretation, concerns issues separate from those of the possibility and practical necessity of judgements. To clarify this we may return to the issue of validation which was raised earlier.

The Problem of Validation

Even if we are satisfied with such a relation between individual and community, other problems threaten Kant's theory. It may be possible to deny the proposed unity between theory and practice by questioning the relation of taste and expression to theoretical knowledge. It was said earlier that intentions underlying fine art must be realized in the causal and mechanistic order of empirical nature.[76] However, even if, because of teleology, we are able to recognize objects as works, it is also necessary for us to understand works of fine art as meanings. Yet meanings are not observable; they are not phenomena to be picked out by empirical observation. Nevertheless, if the subject is to understand a work, he must be able to distinguish and establish meanings. It was suggested that it may be possible to argue that for Kant meanings are established in dialogue between subjects.

However, it may be claimed that if we succeed in showing that aesthetic judgements, with their stress on community, must be distinguished from cognitive judgements and their stress on consciousness, we thereby also show the inadequacy of Kant's deduction of taste. The latter rests its justification of the possibility of aesthetic judgements generally on supposing that others possess the rational faculties necessary to having and communicating knowledge and cognitive experience.[77] Given our distinction of aesthetic from cognitive judgements, that justification at best provides a necessary condition for taste. But it is not a sufficient condition because there is the additional problem of arguing to the possibility of understanding meanings—meanings which, we have seen, are essential to expression in fine art and natural beauty.

The deduction shows that if all others are capable of our ordinary experience, then they can perceive the object being judged. It satisfies the criteria of being an object in the world. Thus, faced with Hamilton's *Just What is it that Makes Today's Homes so Different, so Appealing?* (1956), they will be able to recognize a picture, cut out from a physique magazine, of a body building enthusiast carrying a giant lollipop with 'POP' written on it, and other pictures of a nude female figure, a television, and so on. They may be able to compare the colours in the work, recognizing that some are lighter than others or yellower. But if they can only make cognitive judgements, they may be reluctant to give validity to the claim that one shade is more garish than another or flatter, preferring to describe this as a subjective response over which no one person can claim more certainty than another. Their ability to recognize objects and colours does not show that they can enter into dialogue about the intention—the search for 'popularity, transience, expend-ability, wit, sexiness, gimmickery, and glamour'[78]—that juxtaposes elements of the work. The ascription of intention and meaning seems less than objective because it is an interpretation resting on our subjective response, and not a statement of fact.

It is necessary to argue that agreement, defence, and interpretation are possible. Such procedures are necessary for the dialogue character-istic of aesthetic judgement and discussion. In addition to justifying the ability to use concepts to cognize objects, it is necessary to justify the recognition and interpretation of expression and meanings. For we cannot assume a priori that every one capable of cognition will also be capable of the operations necessary to agreement and disagreement in aesthetic considerations. By this account, aesthetic dialogue remains illegitimate where it claims to be more than description or subjective and emotional response.

This criticism evidently neglects other features of Kant's work—such as his deduction of reflective judgements. But these too are not clearly adequate to the task assigned to them. Reflective judgements, it is claimed, allow thought according to ends, permitting just that com-parison, appreciation of connections, and juxtaposing of elements that is necessary to explaining a work as a meaningful goal. Certainly, the use of reflective teleological judgements seems inadequate here. The teleolo-gical alternative is only another sort of casual explanation, we may claim. Knowledge is still conceived of in terms of ordering casual connections into a system in order to explain what happens. Thought is still tied to pointing out the mechanisms whereby ends are achieved. However, reflective judgements, and their concept of finality, can support the possibility of discovering meanings. That is, the possession of cognitive faculties is only part of what is necessary for the possibility of universally communicable aesthetic judgements. The use of faculties in under-standing ends and goals can be seen to legitimate the discourse occurring in our understanding of works of fine art.

But even this may be considered an inadequate explanation of the character of our appreciation of fine art. This is not because of the correct, but general, criticism of Kant that reflective judgements conflate functional explanation with ascriptions of purpose and design. Rather, it is because showing the possibility of reflective judgements provides only necessary and not sufficient grounds for aesthetic judge-ments. And it is necessary to explain how recognizing ends in nature allows us to gain the meanings of these ends in expression and through dialogue with each other.

However, the force of the contrast between aesthetic and cognitive judgements makes it pointless to look for such a deduction of the former. A contrast between aesthetic reflective judgements and cogni-tive judgements is that the latter are constitutive of experience while the former are only regulative. For Kant this means that in principle all explanation must be, ultimately, determinist and casual. Only this can claim apodictic explanatory necessity. Although the use of reflective judgements allows us to organize experience according to ends so that some objects may be understood as if they were the result of an intention, this remains a heuristic device.

In aesthetic considerations human goals are topics of detailed inter-pretation. Works of art are the result of some communicable intention. This is the basis of their participation in culture. Works of fine art are understood as goals rather than in terms of the mechanisms of their achievement, and we are not concerned with whether those mechanisms are casual or teleological. In considering natural beauty, too, interest centres on how nature must be conceived for its objects to be seen as part of a communicable intention. Yet because of the contrast between cognitive and aesthetic reflective judgements, the latter's concern with understanding works, rather than merely explaining their existence, seems pointless. If reflective judgements generally are merely regulative and if concepts of purpose, intention, and design are merely heuristic devices, and if all these, in principle, with the advance of science, are to be reduced to cognitive judgements, then the vocabulary of aesthetic argument, agreement, and judgement has only a very tenuous hold on us. Not only is it difficult to develop aesthetic sensibility but there seems to be every reason to suppose it unnecessary to do so because that sensibility is constantly threatened with a redundancy which, in principle, is unavoidable. Aesthetic judgements, a variety of reflective judgements, are not really possible except in a way that, in principle, is illicit.

It is not just that reflective judgements are possible, but cannot claim objectivity because they are not cognitive knowledge claims. Were they possible they may have been able to claim objectivity through their relation to morality and in spite of not being knowledge claims. Rather, aesthetic judgements are not really possible because their existence is questionable in so far as the only defence of their possibility rests on the necessity of cognitive and reflective judgements. These go some way toward providing necessary conditions but fail to provide sufficient conditions and so fail to guarantee the irreducibility of aesthetic to merely cognitive or moral judgements. And to accept that the necessity of aesthetic judgements should be explained through understanding the participation of art and beauty in culture, which Kant wants to argue, shows also that his epistemological argument for the possibility of aesthetic judgements is inadequate.

An objection to this argument is that it forgets that for aesthetic purposes reflective judgements are constitutive, being validated by the deduction of judgements of taste. A reply to this objection takes longer to state. We may ask just what is constituted and what conclusions can be drawn from such constitution. Just as the deduction of categories constituted our objective experience in the First *Critique*, showing that a series of subjective representations had an order that must be described by using concepts of an objective world, similarly the Third *Critique* argues that, in spite of the subjective nature of pleasure, where it is associated with a particular use of cognitive faculties in experience of an object, there that pleasure may be imputed to all other subjects whose minds are similarly disposed toward the object. Just as experience was more than merely subjective in that the organization of our representations was owed to something other than and separable from the sequence of their occurrence in ourselves, similarly pleasure is universally valid in spite of being a subjective experience. Thus, just as the first deduction constituted the experience expressed in cognitive judgements, similarly the third deduction legitimates the universality of our pleasurable experience of aesthetic judgements.

By this account, then, judgements of taste cannot be reduced to anything else because they are constitutive of the universality of some of our experiences of pleasure. And so far as beauty is this pleasurable experience, all might be well. But Kant is quite clear that beauty must be both expressive and presentational. Thus the deduction must guarantee expression too. Yet the validity of the latter raises a number of issues that the deduction of taste does not deal with satisfactorily. Expression involves at least thought, interpretation, and some measure of the use of concepts. Here, we need to know how conflicting interpretations can be resolved, and whether they can be given so as to be more than arbitrarily compatible with the particular use of cognitive faculties characteristic of aesthetic judgements.

The last point needs to be explained further. If beauty is to be expressive, then expression must be shown to possess universal validity through the pleasurable aesthetic judgement it occasions. For example, the thoughts involved in expression, and associated with the state of mind, could vary from subject to subject—different thoughts occasioned by the same object could be compatible with a harmony of faculties and so give rise to a 'universally valid' pleasure. But if this were the case, then beauty would not be expressive because the universality of its pleasure would have nothing to do with the thoughts evoked in expression. Thus, in so far as beauty is universally valid, it would not be expressive. Or, if it is to be expressive, then the expression must itself be universalizable. That means that conflicting interpretations, differing thoughts, arbitrarily achieved harmonies, must be subject to adjudication, and the standards we use here must be legitimated. But Kant's deduction does not provide for such legitimization, even though he says repeatedly that beauty, whether natural or artistic, is expressive.

Nor is it clear that the deduction can provide for a non-expressive universality of pleasure. It may be thought that the relation of faculties— 'the form of which constitutes a judgement of taste'—can be justified, so that even if beauty is not expressive and universal, it may be universal and formal. As we argued earlier, the distinction between form and content cannot easily be made for Kant, for to gain form is to succeed in expressing something in an object.

Further, Kant's attempts to adjudicate over expression by appealing to ideas of reason as the 'depth structure' of aesthetic ideas, cannot succeed, for their deduction is subjective at best, and, while it points to the important place of the subject in organizing expression, it fails to govern the varied responses subjects may have to the same object. That is, ideas may raise the possibility of communication between subjects through the creation or understanding of expressive works and objects, but their deployment does not account for the different ways we may respond to works because it fails to provide a means of comparing conflicting interpretations or arbitrary responses.

Moreover, Kant's failure to justify expression renders him unable to explain the existence of expressive freedom. Nevertheless, it is only in this sense, of failing to guarantee expression, rather than any other sense, that Kant fails to account for freedom in art. It is sometimes supposed, especially by those who take Schiller and Hegel at their word, that if art is identified with an exercise of the mind's freedom then we need to provide it with a richer sense of freedom than that argued for by Kant. But for Kant expressive freedom is based on real freedom;[79] and the latter, we have seen, is possible in the sense that some objects can be conceived of as the result of human actions. Kant's failure is not as Schiller thought, that he could not account for the real freedom behind expressive art, but that his deduction fails to account for expression in art because it is unable to show that expression cannot be arbitrary to a universally valid relation of faculties.

What is missing from Kant's account of the deduction of aesthetic judgement is any attempt to put forward what might count as a process of validation. In the absence of insight into the latter, his conclusions about expression and the nature of aesthetic ideas become at best a set of reflections on the power of pleasure, while his deduction of aesthetic judgements shows only that such power can be exercised. The important matter of *understanding* expressions and the use of metaphors, images, idioms, and other imaginative products, yields to a concern with delineating the force of the imagination itself. Thus, we can no longer interpret and appreciate works: we simply succumb to their influence. But to succumb in this way is not to participate in the development of culture.

Indeed, to move from the abstraction of a deduction of taste to concrete proposals for interpretation, it may be we would have to recognize the limitations of a critical enterprise such as Kant's. For Kant recognizes that interpretation is intersubjective in being something more than an exploration of subjects: the bond between subjects, and objects, between artist or audience and work, is broken at least to the extent that we recognize that individual actions occur against the backdrop of the conventions with which they are engaged and which they may misunderstand. It is in order to overcome this break that Kant deploys the idea of a *sensus communis* as a rational and feeling ideal unity that *has to be constructed*. But the deduction of reflective judgements does not tell us anything about this development, and the other deductions address only some parts of the problems raised. The deduction of reflective judgements tells us that the conditions that justify our making particular sorts of statement have been satisfied, but supposes that this means that we know the conditions under which statements of aesthetic preference and interpretation are valid. The deduction of the First *Critique* tells us that the conditions for making true or false claims about the world are satisfied but says nothing about the validity of aesthetic judgements in so far as these are expressive. And the deduction of the Second *Critique* at most applies to aesthetic judgements in the assertion that our responsiveness to the power of the experience of beauty shows us to be suitable as moral subjects, but fails to give any account of the way that response may be validated in the use of imagination, understanding, and reason. Yet because aesthetic judgements depend on a suitability of objects to a rational state of mind, one which is universalizable over other subjects, the question of the validity of interpretation is not a merely empirical matter but must be given some sort of deduction.

Nor is that all. For the notion of expression proposed by Kant does not militate toward the desired unity of theory with practice. Kant intends to argue that expression has general validity. In this it is comparable to cognitive judgements: just as we describe and so understand physical objects and events in cognition by applying concepts, similarly we interpret fine art by understanding what is expressed. But to undertake only the critical transcendental task of legitimating judgements of taste is to leave unconsidered a number of other important issues involved in expression. Thus, in this context, Kant's work on aesthetics may be included among those writings which are concerned to discover, or recover, meanings contained in a text or a constituted object. Through his arguments detailing the validity of judgements of taste Kant answers some of the important questions we might ask about the possibility of establishing meanings in our consideration of texts or of works open to interpretation. That is, his critical enterprise goes some way toward justifying our expectation that comprehensible meanings are present in works. The argument for aesthetic necessity shows that we should seek to understand meanings so far as it is necessary—and clearly it is essential—for our appreciation of works of fine art. But apart from sceptical doubts about the possibility of aesthetic judgements, Kant sees little or no problem in our becoming conscious of meanings.

In other words, the difficulties that prevent us from making aesthetic judgements are a consequence of interference in our reflective self-consciousness by, say, our moral or physical nature. This takes the form of aesthetic judgements becoming determined by sense, charm, or moral interest. But Kant does not think that there are any special problems with expression itself; and the latter is supposedly clear to the subject who possesses it. Here, even the proposal that we use the *sensus communis* as a critical standard to assess present reality is no more than a claim about how to recover meanings from obfuscation in local and inadequate generalizations. For, to Kant, we face no special problems in our attempts to gain access to the meanings of constructed works.

Kant does not raise the radical problem of interpretation—of a '*science of meaning, irreducible to the . . . consciousness* of meaning'.[80] It may even be unfair to expect him to consider something lying outside his transcendental-critical enterprise. But Kant's inability to frame these questions about interpretation within the context of consciousness may be symptomatic of a deeper limitation in his method—because he holds an unhistorical view of consciousness and the development of reason, according to which actual historical conditions do not enter into determining consciousness. Instead, our understanding of history is determined by the nature of reason. Indeed, when Kant contends that speculative metaphysics is a disease of *reason* itself, he thereby converts the development of reason in history into a problem for an ahistorical reason. His concern is no longer to explain how men came to think the way they did in history but to examine the fault in their capacity for reason. Questions seeking to understand the genesis of a problem become identified with ones asking about the validity of modes of thought. By contrast, the recovery of meaning which we are talking about is grounded in historical reality and in the discovery of a developing and changing tradition.

Further, because Kant's argument is put forward at a very general level, he is able to attempt a stringent proof whose success makes possible generally our attempt to apply concepts in ordinary experience and our aesthetic or moral thought. A recognition of the way in which thought is exercised in expression would involve a concomitant acknowledgement of the issue of contingency: particular meanings, as it were, must be constructed out of the variety of objects presented to us. Kant goes some way toward dealing with this issue, but not far enough. For though he was seen to argue that aesthetic judgements convince by 'comparison and example', once their transcendental deduction is secured, he fails to provide any argument showing how we may adjudicate between conflicting interpretations for expression in aesthetic judgements. We do not yet know how audiences can establish either that there is a lack of alternative readings or that a given reading is plausible.

Clearly this last criticism only asks for a more complete account and does not necessarily suggest that Kant's theory is incoherent. And if Kant developed this part of his theory unsatisfactorily, there are hints strewn throughout the Third *Critique* which would help others to produce what he did not: an account of how expression can be analysed and understood. In the previous chapters we suggested how these hints may be construed and expanded on.

In this chapter we have clarified Kant's explanation of aesthetic necessity, showing how it fits with different features of his theory. In the last sections we examined two objections to that account, and argued that the first really characterizes the nature of the unity which fine art procures, while the second indicates where Kant's theory needs to be developed. It may be, as suggested, that because of his starting-point Kant cannot give a satisfactory account of expression; but the latter claim depends on a further argument, which we will not consider here, to the effect that a transcendental-critical enterprise must always be unable to explain and justify the conclusions presented in a 'science of interpretation'. But even if it were successful, this sort of claim would only serve to characterize the nature of the unity which fine art constructs, it need not show it is impossible to use aesthetic judgements to establish a unity between theory and practice.

Kant's Theory of Fine Art and Cultural Necessity

The unity of theory with practice that aesthetic judgements were intended to establish has been examined in some detail. Aesthetic judgements are based on our '*mode of cognition*', but are still able to claim necessity through participation in a culture that satisfies moral reason. In these pages the proposed relation of aesthetic judgements to cognition has been questioned and defended. And the claim to necessity made by aesthetic judgements through fine art's participation in culture has been justified by showing how culture claims necessity. Further, by examining fine art and beauty in the contexts of moral culture, cultural duty, and other subjects, in terms of historical development and by reference to the autonomy of aesthetic judgements, we have defended and explained the account of fine art in culture presented in Part I. This goes to make good the promise of justifying aesthetic necessity through cultural necessity. For if it were unable to provide this justification, the explanation and understanding of fine art's participation in culture would be inadequate to Kant's interest in discovering a unity between theory and practice.

This, then, explains Kant's justification of aesthetic necessity. The inadequacy of his account of the discovery of meanings may weaken the claims made for fine art and culture, but it does so by requiring us to develop his theory.

Aesthetic activity has a critical social role. Kant holds that it is meant to change those who participate in it. Our understanding and appreciation of fine art will increase our sensitivity to other rational subjects and to nature. Beauty promotes enlightenment; reason itself is an actual and sufficient practical motive, and the appreciation of fine art is not simply a form of consciousness but has a real impact on our lives. The importance Kant gives to consciousness may be seen in his understanding of the creation of and response to fine art, both of which he takes to require similar exercises of imaginative freedom and understanding because a qualitative difference between the artist's creation of fine art and the audience's response to it would have serious implications for beauty's effectiveness in bringing about rational enlightenment. A qualitative difference in the nature of the consciousness and intellectual activities of artist and audience would interfere with claims that universal enlightenment is embodied in aesthetic, cultural, and historical reality.

By arguing that moral action may be realized in this world, and by proposing ways in which we liberate ourselves from natural necessity, social compulsion, prejudice, and habit, and change ourselves by doing so, Kant hopes to have shown the effectiveness of real enlightenment. For rational decisions and changes can be embodied in experience, and changes in consciousness can be expressed in empirical terms as changes in persons and in their relation to each other in society.

The problems which engaged Kant are still vital. Even if his arguments only justify a particular conception of the role of beauty in unifying theory with practice or individual with community, his study of aesthetic judgements and practice remains important for what it attempts. One important feature is that Kant stresses the continuity between aesthetic and cultural practices. The creation of fine art and a sensitivity to beauty are part of the transformation and development of social life: they are intended to be social and individual events. And Kant avoids the pitfall of ascribing some permanently valuable aesthetic essence to objects: he acknowledges that an object's beauty is based on its suitability to judgements. Our aesthetic appreciation may then be seen as an estimation which can develop and change as our relation to each other and to things in the world develops. Aesthetic experience is not bound to the general qualities possessed by objects but can be recognized as a human activity in which we strive to liberate ourselves from arbitrary and avoidable compulsions in order to become responsible for our own actions. Without denying the autonomy of fine art—its satisfaction of aesthetic criteria—Kant uses the social parameters of aesthetic activity to reveal an intimate relation of individual to community and nature. Here, solidarity with a community does not imply that an individual is absorbed and lost in some larger whole. Kant's insistence on individual autonomy in aesthetic practice and judgement affirms the social and political value of subjectivity, imagination, and creativity. Fine art and the experience of beauty contribute to changing the consciousness and motivations of people; and people, in turn, can change the world. Nor is the autonomy of fine art permitted to obscure its basis in cultural practice. Kant insists that fine art is but one important feature of cultural practice. So we cannot expect to understand the nature of culture by concentrating on our dealings with fine art alone. For the latter are based on our ability to make aesthetic judgements at all and on the social life in which that ability is exercised. An overemphasis on aesthetic autonomy leaves us unable to explain the value of fine art, while a stress on the moral determinants of culture ignores fine art's participation in our creation of a human culture. Fine art possess a cultural necessity, which is ultimately a practical necessity based on moral imperatives; but to stress the fact of morality is to impoverish the quality and variety of our practical lives, while an emphasis on aesthetic autonomy impoverishes our understanding of actions by obscuring the interconnections between different features of our struggle for a good life.

We should not be satisfied by much less than the goals to which Kant wanted to argue. And we may suggest where reconstruction might begin. Thus, we may accept that Kant is correct to distinguish aesthetic from cultural, political, and moral practices. But his distinction adheres too closely to the supposition of an essential difference between them. Although Kant does not attribute to objects an essence that makes them beautiful, he does suppose that aesthetic activity is qualitatively distinct from others. His concern is still with defining the essential, permanent, and unchanging differences between experiences that are aesthetic and those that are not. So even while he recognizes that aesthetic judgement may become cognitive, as when he argues that pleasure becomes 'fused with cognition',[81] it seems that the only problem this raises is an empirical one of deciding under which rubric to place judgements. And he fails to attend to the many ways that a relation between subjects, engaged in constructing an aesthetic, cultural community, will have implications for the relations between subjects as citizens. Artists and audience are the subjects who also constitute a polity, and whose conscious intervention in their relation to each other, to institutions, and to nature, make up our striving toward enlightenment. In part, Kant's search for a priori answers results from his identification of the problems in terms of mental capacity and of the quasi-moral duty that covers our aesthetic experience. And his acknowledgement that 'aesthetic' correctly applies to judgement rather than to objects can only go so far in fully recognizing the cultural and political nature of aesthetic activity. Were we to begin with the changing ways in which what is 'aesthetic' has participated in the struggle to wrench human freedom from natural necessity and from the corruption of an irrational domination of individuals by each other or by social and natural forces, we may be in a better position to see both the relation of fine art to practices like religion, play, or education, as they have existed in the past, and to other features of our present social existence such as politics, culture, and morality. Instead of asking what is the nature and limit of our obligation to others, we may seek to discover how we represent and make conscious to ourselves our engagement in nature and with others. We would need to recognize and understand different aesthetic media, such as painting, literature, and film, and the relation between individuals fostered by the creation and appreciation of objects using these media. And this requires, at least, consideration of the *political* implications of aesthetic activity. We may further be forced to examine the object of our appreciative judgements, to see also if its unity is preserved in its continuing participation in cultural struggle. This does not imply that culture becomes political, only that it can have political implications which we may discover in our reading of objects. To stretch the concepts of politics to cover the characteristic intersubjectivity involved in aesthetic considerations is to overextend it by including both our public, generalized role as well as our particular intervention in social practice. It fails to establish the specific characteristics which the latter possesses. And while it is essential to clarify the nature and extent of fine art's intervention in our social practices, we will not understand our aesthetic practice if we fail to acknowledge its specific character.

It is to these issues that a consideration of Kant's theory of fine art and cultural necessity must lead.

Notes

I. Introduction

1. Section 59, 224/253.
2. See below, 'Culture and Morality: Aesthetic Necessity'.
3. J. Fisher and J. Maitland, 'The Subjectivist Turn in Aesthetics: A Critical Analysis of Kant's Theory of Appreciation', *RM* 27 (1974), 726–51.
4. J. Maitland, 'Two senses of necessity in Kant's aesthetics', *BJA* 16 (1976), 347–53.
5. P. Guyer, *Kant and the Claims of Taste* (Cambridge, Mass., 1979).
6. R. K. Elliott, 'The Unity of Kant's "Critique of Aesthetic Judgement"', *BJA* 8 (1968), 244–59.
7. Maitland, 'Two Senses of Necessity in Kant's Aesthetic Theory', 34–8.
8. D. W. Gotshalk, 'Form and Expression in Kant's Aesthetics', *BJA* 7 (1967), 250–60.
9. See Salim Kemal, 'The Importance of Artistic Beauty', *KS* (1980), 488–507; R. Aquila, 'A New Look at Kant's Aesthetic Judgements', *KS* 70 (1979), 17–34; H. Osborne, 'On Mr. Elliot's Kant', *BJA* 8 (1968), 260–8; D. Maill, 'Kant's *Critique of Judgement*: A Biased Aesthetics', *BJA* 20 (1980), 135–45; and R. C. S. Walker, *Kant: The Arguments of Philosophers* (1979).
10. See A. C. Genova, 'Kant's Transcendental Deduction of Aesthetic Judgements', *JAAC* 30 (1972), 459–75; Guyer, *Kant and the Claims of Taste*; D. Kuspit, 'A Phenomenological Interpretation of Kant's A Priori of Beauty', *Philosophy and Phenomenological Research* 34 (1974), 551–9.
11. K. Ameriks, 'Kant and the Objectivity of Taste', *BJA* 23 (1983), 3–17; Aquila, op. cit., 17–18; Osborne, op. cit., 261; H. Blocker, 'Kant's Theory of the Relation of Imagination and Understanding', *BJA* 5 (1965), 37–45; Guyer, op. cit., 68–119; and A. Hofstader, 'Kant's Aesthetic Revolution', *Journal of Religious Ethics* 3 (1975), 171–91.
12. Fisher and Maitland, op. cit., and K. W. Cooley, 'Universality in Kant's Aesthetic Judgement', *Kinesis* 1 (1968), 43–50.
13. D. W. Crawford, *Kant's Aesthetic Theory* (1974), Ch. 1.
14. Maitland, op. cit., 348–50; Ameriks, op. cit., 3–4.
15. Maitland, op. cit., 349–53.
16. Maill, op. cit., 135.
17. Crawford, op. cit., 146–9.

18. Guyer, op. cit., cf. 351 and 373, for example.
19. Section 18, 81/236.
20. Section 40, 154/296, italics added.
21. B165: 'Special laws, as concerning those experiences which are empirically determined, cannot in their specific character be *derived* from the categories, although they are one and all subject to them. To obtain any knowledge at all of these special laws, we must resort to experience'.
22. Kant argues this as early as the Introduction to his First *Critique*. He writes of our need to appeal to experience—an appeal whose validity is guaranteed by the necessity of transcendental categories. In empirical 'judgements, I must have besides the concept of the subject something else (X), upon which the understanding may rely if it is to know that a predicate, not contained in this concept, nevertheless belongs to it.' (A8) This X, the '*complete experience of the object* which I think through the concept A—a concept which forms only part of this experience', is based on the categorical system.

    Thus, first, we must 'mark out all this [categorical] knowledge, which forms a genus—*by itself*. . . in a system [of categories], with completeness, according to its original sources.' (A10) It is of the character of such a system that it have some sort of lawlikeness and that its elements possess necessity within the system. But in order to 'advance into the limitless field of [empirical] knowledge *yielded* by pure understanding' we need something more. For our knowledge and experience possess a lawlikeness and necessity unlike that exhibited in the transcendental system of categories which makes possible experience in general.
23. B860/A832.
24. N. Rotenstreich, *Experience and its Systematization*. 2nd edn. (1972).
25. This interest is evinced in cosmical concepts: transcendental ideas which 'refer to the absolute totality in the synthesis of appearances' (A407/B434).
26. A321/B378. Accordingly, reason 'occupies itself solely with the employment of the understanding, not indeed in so far as the latter contains the ground of *possible experience* [but] . . . in order to prescribe to the understanding [as it gains empirical knowledge] its direction towards . . . unity . . . in such a manner as to unite all the acts of understanding into an *absolute* whole.' (B383/A326; italics added.) Indeed, 'human reason is by nature architectonic. That is to say, it regards all knowledge as belonging to a possible system, and therefore allows only such principles as do not at any rate make it impossible for any knowledge we may obtain to combine into a system with other knowledge.' (B502/A474.)
27. A307, italics added.
28. A644/B672. Or: 'It is the business of reason to render the unity of all possible empirical acts of the understanding systematic, just as it is of the

understanding to connect the manifold of appearances by means of concepts and bring it under empirical laws.' (A664/B672.) In the *Critique of Judgement* Kant again refers to the analogy and distinction between understanding and reason in gaining experience and organizing it into a system. In the Introduction he affirms that in respect of the form of things of nature under empirical laws generally, the principle of judgement is the finality of Nature as systematic unity in its multiplicity. Cf. Sections V–VIII.

29. In a like manner, when describing the relations between finality and pleasure in Section VI, Kant alludes to the need for a new principle not simply 'fused with cognition' (28/187). Having done all it can in cognition, it seems, understanding needs a further principle on which to base a systematic ordering of our knowledge of nature. Thus, Kant accepts that the 'causality of an alteration in general, presupposing as it does, empirical principles, lies altogether outside the limits of transcendental philosophy. For upon the question as to whether a cause ... is capable ... of determining [its effect] to the opposite of a given state ... the a priori understanding casts no light.' (B213).

30. G. Buchdahl, 'The Relation Between "Understanding" and "Reason" in the Architectonic of Kant's Philosophy', *PAS* (1967), *passim.* and G. Bird, *Kant's Theory of Knowledge* (1962), *passim.*

31. A419/B446, note b. 'Nature' here refers to 'the sum total of appearances so far as they stand, in virtue of a principle of causality, in thoroughgoing interconnection'. Kant is referring to the 'dynamic whole' constituted by the order and coherence issuing from systematization and totality.

32. A322/B379. Kant notes that the 'transcendental concept of reason is, therefore, none other than the concept of the *totality* of the *conditions* for any given conditioned'.

33. The principles which 'prescribe a priori to the understanding thoroughgoing unity in its employment, also hold, although only *indirectly*, of the objects of experience ... in order to indicate the procedure whereby the empirical and determinate employment of the understanding' can be given 'thoroughgoing unity' (A665/B693; italics added).

34. B702/A674. And ideas differ from objective concepts in that 'the application of the concepts of the understanding to the schema of reason does not yield knowledge of the object itself (as in the case of the application of categories in their sensible schemata) but only a rule or principle for the systematic unity of all employment of the understanding'. (B693).

35. A651/B679: the 'law of reason, which requires us to seek this unity, is a necessary law, since without it we would have no reason at all, and without reason, no coherent employment of the understanding, and in the absence of this, no criteria of empirical truth. In order, therefore, to receive an

empirical criterion, we have no option save to presuppose the systematic unity of nature as objectively valid and necessary'.

36. A664/B692.
37. Section 18, 81/236.
38. Section 40, 154/296.
39. At Section 18, 81/236, Kant writes that aesthetic pleasure does not have 'a theoretical necessity—such as would let us cognize a priori that everyone *will feel* this delight in the object that is called beautiful by me.'
40. A 'person who describes something as beautiful insists that everyone ought to give the object in question his approval'. Section 19, 82/237.
41. Section 19, 82/237.
42. Section 59, 224/353. Guyer, op. cit., 380 ff., is unable to give proper attention to this quotation because of his emphasis on epistemological problems, and H. W. Cassirer, in *A Commentary on Kant's Critique of Judgement* (1970), does not analyse this section at all. F. X. Coleman in *The Harmony of Reason: A Study of Kant's Aesthetics* (1974), because he seems to identify the common ground for the possibility of taste with the *sensus communis*, also bars himself from understanding the *sensus communis* as a practical ideal (cf. 144 ff.), and cannot give an account of the inter-relation.
43. This reference to the subject must be qualified in a number of ways. See Chapters III and VI.
44. Section 30, 134/280. Italics added.
45. Section 36, 145/288.
46. Section 6, 50/211 ff., and Section 32, 136/281.
47. Section 42, 158/299.
48. Section 45, 167/306.
49. See 'The Significance of Natural Beauty', by Salim Kemal, for a more detailed consideration of this issue.
50. See Chapter II for a more detailed account of this issue.
51. Section 16, 72/229 ff.
52. Ibid.
53. Ibid., 72/229.
54. Ibid.
55. At Section 47, 171/310, he writes 'there is still no fine art in which something *mechanical*, capable of being at once comprehended and followed in obedience to rules, and consequently something *academic* does not constitute the essential condition of the art'.
56. At Section 43, 164/304, Kant says that in 'all free arts . . . a *mechanism* [is required], without which the *soul*, which in art must be *free*, and which alone gives life to a work, would be bodiless'. It is difficult not to be reminded of the dove of speculative philosophy.

57. Where representation and expression are unequally valued, the problem will not arise.
58. Section 30, 134/280. In this context he is concerned to argue that the 'deduction of aesthetic judgements upon objects of nature must not be directed at . . . the sublime in nature, but only to the beautiful' (Section 30, 133/279).
59. Ibid.
60. Section 40, 159/300. Italics added.
61. Such precedence seems to be proposed by Maill, op. cit., 135, and is implicit in Crawford, op. cit., *passim*.
62. Section 42, 158/299: We are 'not alone pleased with nature's product in respect of its form, but [are] also pleased at its existence'.
63. H. J. Paton, *The Categorical Imperative*, 256. For a fuller treatment of this topic see Salim Kemal, 'The Significance of Natural Beauty', *British Journal of Aesthetics* (Spring, 1979). See also R. W. Hepburn, *Wonder* (1985), *passim*, for an account of natural beauty in aesthetic theory generally.
64. Section 42, 158/299: 'Our reflection and intuition must have as their concomitant the thought that the beauty in question is *nature's* handiwork; and this is the *sole* basis of the immediate interest that is taken in it' (italics added).
65. In Sections 42, 52, and 59 Kant talks of the support beauty gives our moral efforts, but in Section 59 he gives an extensive presentation of the symbolic relation which is used to exemplify the necessity of beauty.
66. At Section 52, 191/326, Kant writes that where 'fine arts are not, either proximately or remotely, brought into combination with moral ideas, which alone are attended with self-sufficing delight . . . [the fate that awaits them is] that they render the soul dull [and] the object in the course of time distasteful . . . owing to a consciousness that in the judgement of reason its disposition is perverse'. In disposing the soul to ideas, 'the beauties of nature are in general more beneficial'.
67. Section 59, 223–4/353.
68. Section 42, 160/301.
69. Ibid., Italics added: Kant writes that the analogy between pure, disinterested judgements of taste and moral judgements, '*conduces to a like immediate interest* being taken in the objects of the former as in those of the latter . . . . *In addition to this* there is our admiration for nature which in her beautiful prospect displays herself as art . . . designedly . . . as finality apart from any end' (Section 42, 160/301).
70. See Salim Kemal, 'The Importance of Artistic Beauty', *KS* (1980), 488.
71. Ibid., 505–6.
72. Section 52, 191/326.
73. Especially in talk about 'genius': cf. sections 46–50 of *Anthropology*; and 'The Production of Fine Art' below.

74. Section 60, 226–7/355–6.
75. Ibid.
76. Ibid., 227/356.
77. Ibid.
78. See below, 'The Production of Fine Art'.
79. Purposiveness or finality is but 'a concept of the reflective judgement . . . since the end is posited not in the object but always in the subject, and, in fact, in the latter's capacity for reflection'. The actual order of nature is constituted by causal determinations. (*First Introduction*, Section V.)
80. *Lectures on Ethics*, *KrdpV*, *passim*.
81. *Foundations*, 393; *KrdpV*, 114/110.
82. Section 42, 158/299, Italics added.
83. On the need to conceive of nature by analogy with art, see T. E. Wartenberg, 'Order through Reason: Kant's Transcendental Justification of Science', *KS* 70 (1974). The issue is discussed further in Gerhard Lehmann, 'Kant's Nachlasswerk und die Kritik der Urteilskraft', 293–373, in *Beiträge zur Geschichte und Interpretation der Philosophie Kants* (Berlin, 1968). We examine nature in terms of purposes and activity, and are led to ascribe design, because of our self-consciousness of our nature as purposive and rational beings.
84. *KrdpV*, 116.
85. *Anthropology*, Section 88, 143/271.
86. Further, fine art is based on the supposition of a free and active will having the production of a work in the phenomenal world as its end. But we may have reason to find such a supposition implausible and may deny that any empirical object can be seen as a product of some intention. However, in a sense, the very existence of natural beauty provides a defence of the supposition that some objects are produced by some intention. It evinces that the ascription of the creation of an object to a free and active will is not inconceivable: the occurrence of natural beauty depends on nature co-operating with reason, showing nature capable of purposiveness in its satisfaction of taste and in being directed to satisfying human rational ends in the empirical world. That is, in its finality and its existence natural beauty is conditioned by the demands of fine art, and the relative significance of particular characteristics of natural beauty is determined by our conception of fine art.

    Fine art's status as a paradigm is really a point about the methodological principles which we use to regulate our experience. Beauty leads us to assess objects in terms of their intentionality. So far as this intentionality is used to account for its aesthetic qualities, then something that promises a wider range and greater depth of quality by showing that it can properly claim to introduce them into an object will be more suitable to our exploration of what constitutes a pleasurable aesthetic judgement and aesthetic preference.

87. The latter provides another sort of support for our moral aspirations, and the former symbolizes nature: but neither of these points contradicts the claims being made here.
88. cf. Crawford op. cit., 143–6, and Elliott, op. cit., 244.
89. Section GR, II, 159/482.
90. Section 59, *passim.*
91. Crawford, op. cit., 143–9.
92. Section 59, 225/354.
93. Elliot, op. cit., 246.
94. T. Cohen, 'Why Beauty is a Symbol of Morality', in Cohen and Guyer (eds.), *Essays on Kant's Aesthetics* (1982). As Cohen fails to distinguish fine art from natural beauty, he cannot give a satisfactory account of taste being 'both the limiting case of, and an emblem of, our ability to make sense of *objects*' (231, italics added).
95. 223–4/352–4.
96. Section 59, 224/353.
97. See below, Chapter V.
98. Section 70, II, 36/387.
99. See 'Fine Art and Natural Necessity' below.
100. Preface, 7/170.
101. Section VIII, 36/194.
102. Section VIII, 35/193.
103. Preface, 7/170.
104. Ibid., 7/170.
105. Fisher and Maitland, op. cit., 726-51.
106. Elliot op. cit., 244–59 and Crawford, op. cit., 146 ff.

II. The Production of Fine Art

1. R. Burch, 'Kant's Ideal Theory of Beauty' in G. Dickie and R. Sclafani (eds.), *Aesthetics*, (1977), 688–703.
2. It is 'only in respect of judgement [of taste] that the name of fine art is deserved' (Section 50, 182/314).
3. It 'depends on production through freedom, i.e., through an act of will that places reason at the basis of its actions' (Section 43, 163/303).
4. Art is always based on a 'definite intention of producing something' (Section 45, 167/306).
5. The suggestion is that what pleases us in a judgement of taste is called beautiful. (Section 5, 50/211).
6. Section 46, 168/307.
7. Section 45, 166/306.
8. Section 43, 162/303: Art is distinguished from nature as 'making (*facere*) is from acting or operating in general'.

9. Cf. Section 47, 171/310; see also Sections 43–6, 162–9/303–8. Kant talks of 'definite concepts' at Section 16, 72/239.
10. Section 45, 167/307.
11. Section 48, 172/311.
12. Op. cit., 162–3/303–4.
13. See below, 'Kant on genius'.
14. Initially, Kant identifies genius as 'a talent which gives the rule to art' (Section 46, 168/307); and we may better understand this talent by examining the nature of its object. Kant explains this further when he defines genius also as a talent for *making* or '*inventing* things' (*Anthropology*, Section 57, 92/224)—by reference to the process rather than the product —and this serves to clarify our conception of the product as, by Kant's definition, art includes 'everything *formed* in such a way that its actuality must have been preceded by a representation of the thing in its cause'. (Section 46, 168/307; italics added). That is, whether or not an object is art depends on the presence or absence of a process of production, where the 'producing cause' had 'an end in view to which the object owes *its form*' (Section 43, 163/303). Accordingly, if to possess a form is to have a rule, then genius is the talent for giving form to a constructed object; or, as a talent for making, genius is the talent for constructing art by forming objects.

Although objects of art are determined by a process of production in which genius provides guiding rules, not every object that is produced by following rules is a work of art. And Kant explains the role of genius further by contrasting art with nature, handicraft, and skill. Unlike natural objects, art works are made: there is an intention or rational will underlying the determination of an object's form. Indeed, Kant extends the concept of art to include '*everything* formed in such a way that its actuality must have been preceded by a representation of the thing in its cause' (op. cit. 163/303). While the paradigm for such formation is that where 'some work of man is always understood' (Section 43, 163/303), which 'is called absolutely a work of art', art covers even 'the case of bees[,] although the effect could not have been thought by the cause' (Section 46, 168/307). Further, art is not creation *ex nihilio*, and we do not produce art when we create by knowing—in the way God might. Similarly, art is not merely theoretical knowledge. Whatever 'one *can* do the moment one only *knows* what is to be done, hence without anything more than sufficient knowledge of the desired result, is not called art' (Section 43, 163/303). In art, as with skill, we apply ourselves to solve practical problems by manipulating given materials to achieve some end. 'To art that belongs for which the possession of the most complete knowledge does not involve one's having then and there the skill to do it' (ibid.). It involves distinctions, first, between means and ends, where we may manipulate the former to gain the latter, and, second, between planning—where we assess the end in relation to a strategy and to calculation of how the means may be used—and implementation—in which we realize a preferred plan.

However, while skill and art are alike in their differences from theoretical knowledge, they may be distinguished from each other by reference to their respective processes of production. For example, it is possible to learn a skill in that we follow an already given rule for producing an object; but we may deny that this is the case of art by showing that the pupil would be unable to proceed, were the particular materials changed, because he could not invent a new rule. Nevertheless, although art and skill differ, in the former 'something of a compulsory character is still required, or, as it is called, a *mechanism*, without which the *soul*, which in art must be *free*, and which alone gives life to a work, would be bodyless and evanescent' (Section 43, 163/303). This serves to remind us of a planned use of materials, without which art would be closer to fantasy than to practical activity.

The contrast between skill and art is also extended, by reference to interests in the process of production, to distinguish art from handicraft. Art must be seen as play, as a development and implementation of strategy to a particular goal that is considered for itself rather than some further purpose that goal may serve. Our concern is with 'an occupation that is agreeable on its own account' (ibid.). While skill involves an interest in the further ends which might be served by our goal, and though handicraft leads to an interest in using the same process of production as a routine means of attaining its object, our interest in art is in the strategy itself, not in any further goal that might be served.

15. In *Anthropology*, Kant mentions da Vinci, Newton, and Leibniz as men of '*vast* genius' or of 'intensity of spirit . . .'. Cf. *Anthropology*, Sections 57 and 58, 92–95/224–7. Kant moves from applying the 'term [genius] only to *artists*, and so *to people who know how to make things*', to talking of fine art at Section 71, 113–14/246–8.

16. *Anthropology*, Section 57, 93/225.

17. Ibid.

18. At Section 44, 165/305, Kant identifies mechanical art as that 'where art, merely seeking to actualize a possible object to the cognition of which it is adequate, does whatever acts are required for that purpose'.

19. Ibid. Kant goes on to distinguish between different sorts of works of art, usually by reference to the goals aimed at by the process. Thus, 'mechanical art seeks adequacy to cognition', whereas 'should the feeling of pleasure be what is immediately in view then it is termed *aesthetic* art' (ibid. 165/305). The latter is divided between agreeable and fine art, so that in aesthetic agreeable art 'the end of art is that the pleasure should accompany the representations considered as mere *sensations*' (ibid.). That

is, aesthetic agreeable arts 'are those which have mere enjoyment for their object'.

20. Section 44, 165/305. The end may involve pleasure, but the latter accompanies representations 'considered as *modes of cognition*' (ibid.).

21. See above. Fine art 'does not permit of the judgement of the beauty of its product being derived from any rule that has a *concept* for its determining ground, or a concept of the way in which the product is possible' (Section 46, 168/307).

22. Indeed, although Kant presents this possibility only when examining the work of genius in producing fine art, his description of the process is applicable to art in general.

23. Section 46, 168–9/307–8. Italics added. Kant proposes an etymology for *Genie* derived from the capacity for producing original ideas. See also *Anthropology*, Section 57, 93–4/224–5.

24. Ibid: 'A product can never be called art unless there is a preceding rule'.

25. The ability to originate rules need not be restricted to producing objects which satisfy judgements of taste. We may expect it of art generally in that whereas skill involves following given rules, art involves us in solving problems in attaining goals for which no rules need have been established.

26. Section 46, 168/307 ff; cf. also *Anthropology*, Section 57, 92/224 ff.

27. Ibid. Cf. *Doctrine*, 46, where Kant has more to say on the nature and role of examples.

28. Section 46, 168/307.

29. In *Anthropology*, Section 57, 92/224, Kant says we call a *person* a genius for his possession of the ability to create or make objects.

30. Section 32, 138–9/283.

31. Section 33, 141/286.

32. Section 49, 180/317.

33. Naturally, such a comparison must recognize a continuity in the history of fine art and between that and cultural history. 'There is still no fine art in which something mechanical, capable of being at once comprehended and followed in obedience to rules, and consequently something *academic* does not constitute the essential condition of the art . . .'. Its form requires 'a talent academically trained'. Indeed, as 'the artist practises and corrects his taste by a variety of examples from nature *and art*' (Sections 47 and 48, 171–2/310 and 174/312, italics added), there is little reason in theory to exclude information about fine art, its institutions, the general social structure, or its history, from our understanding (though it is not yet clear how or when they enter into our consideration of particular works). Indeed, we may even be able to justify a comparison with, say, prevalent ideologies to show the originality of a painting and to identify its role in changing the self-conception of individuals and societies.

Further, a comparative analysis avoids the problem of, so to speak, dissolving creativity by explaining it. One problem with ascribing creativity is that to explain the originality of a work may be to show how it arises from what was present before. The more thorough our explanation, the less original a work seems: we make explicit the sufficient and necessary conditions for its occurrence. Consequently we are less able to separate what is new from what determined the object or event. There are a number of issues involved in this claim, but its principal error, which a comparative analysis avoids, is that it conflates the process by which objects are produced with the originality of the object produced. Thus, a psychological theory may be able to extend its explanatory power to include an account of creativity, allowing us to show that any given creative or original work is the unsurprising consequence of the operation of certain psychological factors. But this does not show what makes a work original. Rather, the originality of a work goes to determine whether or not we would be prepared to ascribe creativity to a product or person. And we could discover originality through a comparative analysis of works.

34. Or because of the producer.
35. The development of original and exemplary works is more than a craft. Certainly, a facility with materials and techniques is important, but these are used to produce objects whose success is judged in aesthetic terms. Thus, differences in style between, say, Fra Angelico and Renaissance painters can be explained in terms of the invention of a new technique of perspective, but their techniques are used to provide the sort of pleasure from unity, balance, style, expression, interplay of shape, line, colour, and so on, that constitute aesthetic judgements. It is by analysing the techniques by which aesthetically satisfying works are produced that we give sense to talk of resolving problems in fine art. Further, to develop a technique may be to change what we expect of fine art: what we expect from the *Mona Lisa* differs from what we expect from Duchamp's *Fountain*.
36. Section 46, 169/308.
37. Section 49, 181/318. In his paper on 'The audience of originality', Gould argues that the product of genius is wrongly construed as 'metaphor' if its contrast is with 'original nonsense'. The latter is 'a failure of sense' and so, 'more ordinarily dangerous' (186). It seems to me that Gould's claim rests on attributing to beauty an importance and value that Kant does not. The production of beautiful objects is only one among a number of ways in which we may be creative. Only for writers like Schiller and Schelling is genius so important as the sole authentic instrument for access to a true and transcendent reality, and only for them will a failure of genius have the momentousness that makes it 'more than ordinarily dangerous'. Whether Kant will find such failure more than ordinarily dangerous will depend on what place and importance he gives to fine art. I shall argue later that fine art, the product of genius, is but one facet of a general cultural develop-

ment whose more urgent business leaves fine art in a less prominent position than that given to it by, say, Schiller and Schelling. Cf. Timothy Gould, 'The Audience of Originality: Kant and Wordsworth on the Reception of Genius', in Cohen and Guyer (eds.), *Essays in Kant's Aesthetics*, 184–7.

38. Section 47, 171/309–10.

39. It seems at first that Kant's claim must be mistaken since, clearly, *some* rules must be present. An artist must decide whether to work in oils or water colours, whether to use a knife or brushes, and so on. However, these are general rules that determine, or identify, what we are doing: for example, that someone is painting a picture rather than constructing an explanatory theory. Other sources of rules are found in the conventions accepted by artists through academic training or school discipline, and the mechanisms of nature that limit representational art. Although they tell us something generally of the work, classifying it with all other paintings or sculptures, these rules fail to say much about what is specific to a particular work. And it is to the latter that Kant's claim is addressed and which we must understand. For by understanding its operation in the specific instance we may be able to explain something of the formation of the rules enumerated above.

In another instance Kant writes that 'the author of a product for which he is indebted to genius does not himself know how he came by his ideas' (section 49, 181/318). This may seem to deny the presence of prescriptive rules on the basis of a claim about the psychology of the artists, suggesting that the absence of rules or order is explained by our ignorance of psychological factors. But Kant could reject this conclusion by arguing that the discovery of, say, a causal account of the brain's activity, or a psychological explanation of the transformation of artists' experiences into images and metaphors, does not contribute to an explanation of the aesthetic product. Psychological and causal explanations see the use of language only as a symptom of something else, and are not concerned with the aesthetic nature of their object. The psychological process involved may be a mystery to us and the artist; in this sense, genius can be 'just this talent, for which no rule can be prescribed', whereby the 'rapid and transient play of the imagination' is unified or ordered (ibid.). But our ignorance of psychology need not lead us to deny that rules are present. For questions of the order and rules present neither concern the process of its production nor attempt to explain the psychological process in which meanings are apprehended.

40. Further, in relation to fine art, Kant holds that expression is intransitive. (Cf. L. Wittgenstein, *Blue and Brown Books*, Section 15, 158.) What the artist expresses in a work need not be capable of being paraphrased and, so, more completely expressed in some other medium. This suggests that we

may not always be able to conceptualize our appreciation and understanding of a work in a manner necessary for formulating instructions.
Moreover, the need for interpretation in understanding metaphors and
images in fine art also suggests the presence of some equivocity in our
response. That, in turn, amounts to a further obstruction to attempts to
articulate some determinate set of instructions for creating fine art.

41. Section 49, 181/318. In effect, Kant is arguing that we produce types only
by producing tokens.

42. Kant recognized the possibility and, perhaps, necessity of continuity
between works *in* the history of fine art and *with* cultural history. Thus, his
claims about the intransitivity of works do not depend on any exhaustive
distinction of what is 'internal' to a work from what is 'external'. There is
no reason why facts about social structure or history must be excluded by
Kant from our interpretation and understanding of fine art.

43. *Religion*, 179.

44. Section 50, 180/317–19.

45. *Anthropology*, Section 57, 95/225.

46. Op. cit., 169/308.

47. Section 47, 169–70/308–9. See G. Lukacs, *Soul and Form* (Cambridge,
Mass., 1978), 73, for a development of Kant's claim that the limits of fine
art have already been reached, whereas we have a long way to go before we
reach the boundaries of science. Another consideration of this issue is to be
found in Stadler's paper on 'The Idea of Art and its Criticism: A Rational
Reconstruction of Kantian Doctrine' in Cohen and Guyer (eds.), *Essays on
Kant's Aesthetics*, 195–218. Lukacs' account seems truer to Kant, though I
would contend that Kant's meaning is rather more prosaic than either
Lukacs or Stadler is prepared to grant. It is best understood, I think, as
saying that fine art and science make distinctive claims to comprehensiveness. The former is comprehensive over all subjects while the latter aims to
cover all objects. In the history of fine art, we have long since gained the
state of universality or comprehensiveness of which fine art is capable
because we have seen or constructed numerous universally valued works.
But we have not as yet understood all of nature, and so have no right to
claim comprehensiveness for our scientific work.

Of course, this distinction between fine art and science tallies with the
claim that these are different sorts of object and that such differences do
not show us capable of being creative in only one but not both activities of
creating objects.

48. The passage contains a number of difficulties, one set of which we
considered in the text. In this note we add that by using our ignorance of
the thought processes of poets as part of his argument, Kant seems to be
confusing matters of psychology with what is an epistemological matter. If
it were taken seriously as a psychological claim, it would amount to this:

that science is concerned to explain objects, and that our knowledge of them is determined solely by their nature and behaviour. To explain how ideas about nature assemble themselves in our minds, we have to refer to the order they have in reality. We cannot hope to discover a similar correspondence in the case of fine art because there is no object— rather, the artist *constructs* his object. His psychology is unknown, though the order he gives his imaginative product is not. And as there seem to be different connections between the mind and its objects in the two cases, it seems that our thought of them must be of different sorts: only a poor scientist is unable to separate personal psychological associations from his experience of nature and, so, is likely to confuse truth and prejudice. Psychological associations are not only welcome in poetry, they may even be what distinguishes our subjective lives from the objective reality which is the object of science. If psychological factors are important, then, even if we are ignorant of their operation, because they depend on the particular subject and his experiences we are led to have certain expectations of them. By contrast, the reference our thoughts bear to reality in science will lead us to see that scientific conclusions are objective only in so far as they correspond with objects and their behaviour; and subjective factors only disrupt our search for scientific knowledge.

49. 'Special laws, as concerning those appearances which are empirically determined, cannot in their specific character be derived from the categories, although they are one and all subject to them. To obtain any knowledge whatsoever of these special laws, we must resort to experience.' (B165).

50. B860/A832: 'Systematic unity is what first raises ordinary knowledge to the rank of science: that is, makes a system out of a mere aggregate of knowledge.' See Chapter I above, and Bird, op. cit., *passim*, Buchdahl, op. cit., *passim*, and Rotenstrich, op. cit., *passim*.

51. Introduction, Section V, 25–6/186–7, and *KrdrV*, Dialectic, *passim*.

52. A crucial contrast between them, for example, may lie at the basis of being able to interpret works of fine art—and interpret them in different ways in the history of fine art—because the nature of the subject is involved in a specific way in understanding them, but this fails to show that subjects can be creative in art and not in science.

53. Further, scientists do often issue instructions in testing and exploring the limits of a theory, and research workers may carry out those instructions. But these are not instructions for creatively developing a theory, and the work required in testing a theory may itself be done imaginatively, creatively, or slavishly. If it is accepted that observation and experiment do not confirm or disconfirm a theory, then it becomes clear also that such research work is not part of the development of the theory itself—though it

may lead to that, just as an artist's perusal of his own or others' work may lead him to change his own new work.

54. GR, 86/240. This is the case with natural beauty too, where 'in the apprehension of a given object of sense the imagination is tied down to a definite form of this object and, to that extent, does not enjoy free play (as it does in poetry)' (GR 86/240). But whereas in the case of natural beauty 'it is easy to conceive that the object may supply ready made to the imagination' just that 'form of arrangement of the manifold' which 'gives the imagination free play' (ibid.), to describe an object as a work of fine art is to raise questions about the possibility of identifying phenomenal objects as the result of action by a free and rational will.

55. Kant described genius as a 'talent in the line of art, that presupposes a definite concept of its product—of its end. Hence it presupposes understanding, but, in addition, a representation, however indefinite it may be, of the material, that is, of an intuition, required for the presentation of the concept'. Consequently, we suppose that it involves 'a relation of the imagination to the understanding'. But, next, Kant qualifies the role of the concept by saying that genius will 'display itself . . . not so much in the working out of the projected end in the presentation of a definite *concept* as rather in the portrayal or expression of aesthetic ideas containing a wealth of material' (section 49, 180/317). And writing of the expression of aesthetic ideas, Kant later adds the proviso that 'with the beauty of art this idea must be excited *through the medium of the concept* of the object' (section 51, 183–4/320; italics added). For example, poetry, the highest form of art, offers 'from among the boundless multiplicity of possible forms concordant with a given concept, *to whose bounds it is restricted*, that one which couples with the presentation of the concept a wealth of thought to which no verbal expression is completely adequate' (section 53, 191/326). Elsewhere, Kant says that 'the *beautiful*. . . requires the representation of a certain *Quality* of the object, that permits of being understood and reduced to concepts. . . ' (GR, 117/266). Clearly, concepts have a useful role in our response to fine art, though the details remain unclear.

56. Section 49, 176/314.

57. Section 50, *passim*.

58. Kant later explains this response—expression—by reference to a process where, to 'the presentation of a concept', there is '*coupled*' a 'wealth of thought to which no verbal expression is completely adequate' (Section 53, 191/326). Our consciousness, this wealth of thought, will not allow language to 'get on level terms' with itself. The vocabulary Kant uses is of imagination 'leading the understanding'. Instead of being the recipient faculty which in cognition brings representations under concepts, 'imagination displays a creative faculty towards an extension of thought that, while germane . . . to the concept of the object, exceeds what can be

laid hold of in that representation or clearly expressed' (Section 49, 176/
314). That is, if conceptualization is a measure of clarity and of the
objectivity of experience, its contrast with expression is developed here in
terms of the latter '*exceeding*' concepts, of an '*extension* of thought', and of a
'*creative* faculty'. Elsewhere Kant writes that the 'representation of the
imagination' is '*annexed* to a given concept' (Section 49, 177/315–16), or that
the imagination furnishes 'a wealth of under-developed' material '*over and
above* . . . agreement with a concept'. It seems that not only is expression not
determinately conceptual, but that it becomes so by *adding to* concepts such
thoughts and associations as they do not possess in experience. This
addition is exemplified in the way our thought or consciousness does not,
for example, 'represent what lies in our concepts of the majesty and
sublimity of creation but something else, which gives occasion for it to
spread itself over a number of kindred representations which arouse more
thought than can be expressed in a concept' (ibid.). As it develops its
themes, imagination is not restricted to repeating the representation of a
single concept under which it is subsumed but, instead, develops
metaphors, images, analogies, and idioms, which form different parts of the
whole. They 'induce . . . a wealth of thought as would never admit of
comprehension in a *definite* concept'. As a 'consequence [imagination gives]
aesthetically unbounded *expansion* to the concept itself' (section 47, 177/
315–16). What is expressed by associating 'kindred representations' is
'indefinable in words' if these are tied to cognition. And it is by contrast with
standards of causality and conceptualization, and because of the addition of
kindred representations, that Kant can say that beauty is '*like* a presentation
of an indeterminate concept of understanding' (section 46, 176/214).

59. Section 49, 179/316.
60. In the course of his account of ideas, Kant give two examples which suggest
   that he wants to distinguish aesthetic ideas which are somehow native to
   beauty from those allegedly belonging to the sublime.
   The first example shows how a rational idea is 'enlivened by imaginative
   representations', while his second example illustrates that 'an intellectual
   concept' can 'serve as an attribute for a representation of sense, and so
   quicken the latter by means of the idea of the supersensible, but only by the
   aesthetic element, that subjectively attaches to the latter being employed
   here'. In the second, Kant says of the 'consciousness of virtue' that 'if we
   substitute it in our thoughts for a virtuous man' it 'diffuses in the mind a
   multitude of sublime . . . feelings, and a boundless prospect of a joyful future,
   to which no expression that is measured by a definite concept completely
   attains' (Section 49, 178–9/316). It appears Kant wants to hold that
   expressiveness in beauty is best understood as a case where a rational idea
   acts as a schema by which the imagination develops, whereas in our
   experience of the sublime an intellectual idea has a *symbolic* function.

However, Kant's conception of expression does not fit well with such a distinction. He describes aesthetic ideas as a development of the imagination—a process of continuously producing thoughts commensurate with our inability to articulate completely what is meant—with a subsequent appeal to reason as a guiding force. That is, the process is construed as one of thoughts coming into the mind rather than as one of paying attention to an object: we are bound to a flow of thought and lack access to external criteria. So, for 'schema' or 'symbol' to be applicable, they must permit a distinction *within* our thoughts that is in some way based *on* our thoughts, as if it were inherent in them. That is, it must be shown that the distinction makes itself obvious in our thoughts. But this has not been done. Further, as we are dealing with a 'flow of imagination', and given that there is an absence of clearly stated rules—which must, in any case, be gained from our thoughts because expression is intransitive—it becomes difficult to sustain claims for a distinction based on those rules. The nature of the process makes it cognitively meaningless to try to distinguish a schematic part, producing beauty, from a symbolic one, which produces sublime feelings, for we are bound to the flow of imagination and thought; and, to make the proposed distinction is at best to make a formal pronouncement.

61. It becomes so by 'adding to' concepts such thoughts as suit our response to the concept.

62. Section 49, 179/316.

63. This addition serves for 'quickening the cognitive faculties, and hence also indirectly for cognitions,' and is to rely on the deduction for its validity.

64. Further, Kant affirms that fine art 'does not permit the judgement on the beauty of its products being derived from any rule that has a *concept* for its determining ground, and that depends, consequently, on a concept of the way in which the product is possible' (op. cit.). But *this* independence from determination by a concept only points to a distinction we must make between judging the work and understanding the process of its production.

65. However, if there are all these additions, the concept is so different in its new character that we should be reluctant to continue to talk of *concepts* when we consider their aesthetic use.

66. That is, the epistemology of the former does not differ from that of the latter. An artist may give the complex its order, but it also needs an audience to understand and organize it in a similar or related way for the practice of appreciating particular works of fine art to be instituted. This is an essential trait of fine art.

67. Section 49, 173/315.

68. It does this by introducing 'a clearness and order into the plentitude of thought' (section 50, 183/319).

69. However, the importance of the work in which expression is embodied must not be underplayed. Although it is essential that we can communicate

what is presented in a particular work of fine art, it is not clear that there must be a relation of subject to subject before we can make an aesthetic judgement. For in a sense we do not so much recognize another subject in making a judgement as understand what is said in the work. In this sense, the work may be said to be ruptured, first, from the artist, so far as it may reveal more about itself than he can tell us, and second, from the audience, so far as our response is directed to understanding the work rather than to making it suit our purposes. The claims made by artist or audience would have to fit the work, and meanings must be gathered 'from the performance'.

Further, in judging a work and its adequacy to a state of mind, the audience judges itself. If the work presents us with a 'second nature', a 'remodelled experience' that 'surpasses nature', then in understanding and appreciating it the subject seeks to enter into its world, giving to his own imagination a direction and resonance gained from the work. Similarly, because their judgements are autonomous, subjects must understand their own relations to a work, and must act to enter its world, because judging is an act individuals must perform for themselves. But not every feature of the subject's nature is significant, and it does not carry more weight than the work.

We may further explain the salientness of the work in the following way. The complex of thoughts we instantiate in fine art is not determined by objective causal determinations between objects, and is not conceptual, in one sense in which Kant uses the term, and is not assessed in terms of truth or falsity. It depends rather on appropriateness to a particular pleasurable state of mind. Nevertheless, we cannot suppose that aesthetic judgements depend on 'types of pleasure' which are 'beyond concepts' and 'comparable independently of their objects' (Fisher and Maitland, op. cit., 745). Kant does not claim that a pleasure is distinctively aesthetic, as if it exhibited some inherent, perhaps phenomenological, and qualitative difference in moral or cognitive cases (ibid.), so that we need only attend to the pleasure we experience in order to discover whether it is a case of beauty.

Rather, to gain an experience of beauty we may (1) consider explanations and justifications that attempt to persuade individuals to judge the object good or bad; (2) seek to show that our response to the work is universally communicable, and (3) consider a work and criticize it. In each of these cases, the work must be the object of our attention (cf. Sections 32, 34, 38, and 50).

Further, it is clear that the complex of thoughts in judgement has properties, of being interesting or boring, clear or confused, vital or dull, and so on, which are not determined merely by skill or by rules for its construction. A brilliant draughtsman remains a poor artist to the extent that the ideas he expresses in his works remain uninspired or fail to be creative. Rather than being a matter of skill, for Kant genius 'properly consists in the happy relation, which science cannot teach nor industry learn, enabling one to find out ideas for a given concept, and, besides, to hit upon the *expression* for them—the expression by means of which the subjective mental condition induced by the ideas as the concomitant of a concept may be communicated to others'. It requires 'a faculty for laying hold of the rapid and transient play of the imagination, and for unifying it in a concept . . . that admits of communication without any constraint of rules' (Section 49, 179–80/317), where such communication is embodied in a work.

Similarly, a psychological explanation of an individual's construal of meanings would fail to grasp their aesthetic character because by this account the use of language is seen only as a symptom of individual psychology. Nor can aesthetic expression be merely a matter of skill if that consists of following a set of rules determined by a predefined goal. For, of skill, it makes sense for us to talk of an agent succeeding or failing to follow rules to gain a determinate end. By contrast, in an important sense, works of art cannot be successful or unsuccessful because there are no criteria external to our experience of a work with which it can be compared and its 'success, in following a rule', judged. In this vein, Kant can be taken to emphasize the centrality of the work when, in arguing that fine art precludes mannerism, he states that 'the distinction between them is this: the former possesses no standard other than the *feeling* of unity in the presentation, whereas the latter here follows definite principles' (Section 47, 182/319). That is, a work of fine art is judged in its own terms by reference to a harmonious relation of faculties. Only on the basis of the experience of unity can we articulate the order we discover in a work of fine art. And rules are gained *from* such a work, instead of being applied in its construction. This is at least a part of what Kant means by writing that fine art 'reveals a new rule which could not have been inferred from any preceding principles or examples' (Section 49, 180/317).

Further, the exemplariness and originality of expression in a work must be understood in commensurate ways. Just as the explanation given above showed that creativity in fine art must satisfy demands dissimilar from those in science, similarly, exemplariness and originality must be assessed in 'aesthetic' terms. Accordingly, when Kant says that a work is exemplary if it serves as a model 'inspiring' other artists in their development, there need be nothing mysterious in such inspirational or generative powers. For they may be simply a matter of one school or artist influencing another, as when Signac, Cézanne and Neo-Impressionism influenced, and so inspired, Matisse. Indeed, we may develop the example to show how these influences led Matisse to an interest in the effect of one pure colour on another and in the correct placing of brush strokes. A consequence of this, in turn, was his use of red and green to exclude the natural spectrum from his paintings. And because he developed and used this technique under the influence of the movement and artists mentioned above, we place his work in a tradition that, say, is opposed to Classicism. The point of developing the example is to show that whereas a new scientific theory may result in a set of prescriptions setting out tasks for shallow-pates to carry out, works of fine art will serve only to inspire others to produce their own works when they serve as models—not by providing separately formulated prescriptive rules but by being exemplary works. Further, that the absence of prescriptive rules in construction does not deprive a work of intelligibility shows that the same is true of appreciation. We may say that ultimately a work is understandable *and* its construction free of prescriptive rules because the *artist* organizes the 'play of his imagination' *in order to* attain a unity *in* his work. Consequently, our appreciation of his product is a matter of grasping the order present: a grasp that must follow the work rather than attempt to fit it to a prescribed set of appreciative rules—for no previously given set of rules will encompass the varied ways in which an action manifests an intention.

As we said earlier, psychological knowledge is not important here. Just as the artist may misunderstand his own work, so the audience may fail to understand. The point is to look at the work itself. The artist does not have any more privileged a position than the audience in construing the meaning of a work. Further, as imaginative freedom is based on the freedom of the subject, the audience is not made up of people who are merely spectators. They are spectators who must be able to judge *and* act (cf. the sense of genius as actor and taste as spectator which H. Arendt, in *Lectures on Kant's Political Philosophy* (Chicago, 1982), 42 ff., sees as central to Kant's political philosophy in the third *Critique*).

70. See Schiller, *AEM, passim*, and for example, F. W. Schelling, *System des Transcendentalen Idealismus, Sämtliche Werke*, vol. iii (1957), 612 ff., and *The Philosophy of Fine Art; An Oration on the Relation between the Plastic Arts and Nature*. Tr. A. Johnson (London, 1845), *passim*.

71. In a later chapter we will show that Kant can locate the activity of genius in our present reality.

72. Herder, *Yet Another Philosophy of History for the Enlightenment of Man*, quoted in Engell, *The Creative Imagination*, 233. See also D. Jähnig, *Schelling, die Kunst in der Philosophie*, 2 vols. (Pfulligen, 1968–9).

73. Hamann, *Socratic Memorabilia*, Section 70, 74–5; cf. also *Doctrine*, 46/467 ff., and Herder, op. cit.

74. Cf. H. Honour, *Romanticism, passim*, cf. also J. C. Goethe's 'Künstlergedichte', written in 1773–4, and included in *Von Deutscher Baukunst*, in *Goethe, Gedenhausgabe der Werke, Briefe und Gespräche* (Zurich, 1948–54), vol. x.

75. Heine, in *Religion and Philosophy in Germany*, writes that 'the history of great men [geniuses] is always a martyrology: when they are not sufferers for the great human race, they suffer for their own greatness, for the manner of their being, for their hatred of philistinism, for the discomfort they feel among the pretentious and commonplace, for the mean trivialities of their surrounding—a discomfort that readily leads to extravagances . . .'. See also Goethe on 'Schöpterkraft' or 'creative power', in *An Kenner und Liebhaber* (1774), included in *Aus Goethe Brieftasche*, in *Goethe*, op. cit.

76. Benjamin Constant develops this picture of genius further in connection with the notion of '*l'art pour l'art*', which he derives from Kant's aesthetic theory. Cf. J. Wilcox, 'The Beginnings of l'Art pour l'Art', *JAAC* 11 (1953), 360–77, and R. Wellek and A. Warren, *Theory of Literature* (New York, 1942).

77. *Anthropology*, Section 58, 94/226.

78. Section 5, 49/201:That is, for beings who are 'at once animal *and* rational'.

79. Further, Kant's explanation of genius militates against some ways of using the distinction between form and content to talk about aesthetic objects. Kant seems to accept some version of this dichotomy when he compares 'aesthetic form with the form of objective judgements' and insists that 'we abstract at the outset from all content of the judgements' in order to carry out this comparison (Section 31, 136/281) or when he writes of the 'mutual subjective finality' of faculties, 'the *form* of which in a given representation has been shown . . . to constitute the beauty of their object' (Section 34, 141/286).

'Form' suggests a contrast with either a conceptualized content or a material that cannot be made sense of without the introduction of form. Neither contrast is straightforwardly true of Kant's use. The first can be used to argue that the more formal a work is, the more it is also non-conceptual. A corollary of this would be to argue that Kant thinks aesthetic judgements do not use concepts at all but merely provide an immediate and pleasurable experience. This conception is hinted at, it seems, by the first quotation with its reference to an abstraction from all content. But Kant is concerned to abstract from the content of judgements only in the sense that he wants to deny that pleasure in aesthetic judgements results from the particular concepts used in the judgement. His requirement is that Cézanne's *Still life with Apples and Oranges* (1895–1900), for example, must not be thought beautiful merely because it contains representations of apples where we are pleased with it for the reason that we like apples.

The second contrast too may be denied. The judgement of taste is applied to something which, in one sense, already has the form of experienceable matter and consequently is awaiting neither form nor experience. At the same time, for the aesthetic material of a work to gain the coherence necessary for us to appreciate its beauty is for it to possess form. Kant writes that taste gives form to a work, where form is 'the *means* by which the product of genius is universally communicated' (Section 49, 174/312). But he does not propose a contrast of this form with any content and, in this vein, uses the phrase '*Gestalt öder spiel*' to explain the nature of the coherence or unity of form. Clearly, this precludes any interpretation similar to the formalist position propounded by aestheticians such as Clive Bell in *Art* (London, 1931). Instead, form is something dynamic and developing, suggesting movement and a constant grappling with objects, meanings, and intentions in appreciating fine art by considering the order and interrelations occasioned in the expression of aesthetic ideas. And in this sense, form is the expression of aesthetic ideas, so that to express anything in a work is to give form to that expression. Its complex of images, metaphors, and other imaginative products becomes a unified complex just where it occasions a 'mutual subjective finality' of faculties. It is a finality that is intransitive and cannot support the contention that the 'content must be capable of independent conceptualization'.

Thus, attempts to force Kant's explanations into a dichotomy of form and content are merely artificial. Nor are there, for Kant, some 'formal' principles or 'sensuous' impulses that, as for Schiller, externally determine a work. To give form is to construct a work, and our actions need not be referred to these strange capacities of genius in order for us to understand the work itself—unless we want to conflate the process of production with the object produced *and* seek some supranatural source for *each* concept such as 'form' or 'content' that we apply to works of fine art.

80. *Anthropology*, Section 57, 93/224.
81. See Chapter IV, Section 'Reason and Freedom: Intentions and Causes'.
82. 'That is, through an act of will that places reason at the basis of its action' (op. cit., 163/303).
83. Op. cit., 168/307.
84. Section II, 12/174, italics added.
85. Op. cit., 167/306.
86. Although finality is ascribed by judgement, Kant claims it is 'to their creator that we ascribe natural objects as art' Section 43, 163/303.
87. Cf. The Deduction in *KrdrV*, and also Section 70, II, 38/387.
88. Section 70, II, 38/387.
89. Ibid.
90. Ibid.
91. Section 59, 224/353.
92. Section 46, 168/307. In Section 57, Remark I (212/344), Kant explains this claim further, pointing out that genius may also be defined as the 'faculty of aesthetic ideas'. Consequently, the beautiful may be estimated 'by the final mode in which the imagination is attuned so as to accord with

the faculty of concepts generally, and so rule and precept are incapable of serving as the requisite subjective standard for that aesthetic and unconditioned finality in fine art which has to make a warranted claim to being bound to please everyone. Rather must such a standard be sought in the element of mere *nature in the Subject,* which cannot be comprehended under rules or concepts, that is to say, the supersensible substrate of all the Subject's faculties ... ' (italics added). I take this too to refer us to the capacity for reason *and* natural inclination which we possess by our nature, and to the unity between reason and nature which Kant thinks is possible in the 'suprasensible'. This, in turn, raises the issue of what fine art reveals of human nature in the sense of what answers it provides to the question: 'What is man?'.

93. *First Introduction,* Section V, 35/231.
94. cf. *KrdU,* Sections 85, 86, 87 ff., and 'Conjectural Beginnings', *passim.*
95. See *On History,* 'Enlightenment' and 'Universal History'; and *KrdU,* Section 83 ff.
96. Section 59, 224/353.
97. Section 84 ff.
98. Sections 85 and 86 ff.
99. Section 60, 277/356.
100. Section 83 ff.
101. 'Conjectural Beginnings', *passim.*
102. Section 26 ff.
103. Section 40, 150/293.
104. *Anthropology,* 112/244.
105. 'Universal History', 21/26.

III. Fine Art and Culture

1. Comparing the sublime with beauty, for example, Kant writes that while the sublime 'in no way conduces to our culture', beauty 'cultivates, as it instructs us to attend to finality in the feeling of pleasure' (GR, 117–18/266). Both the creation of and response to fine art, then, refer us to culture.
2. The beautiful, for instance, 'is final in reference to the moral feeling' and 'prepares us to love something' (GR, 119/267).
3. See books by Guyer, op. cit., and Podro, op. cit.; and papers by Aquila, op. cit., Fisher and Maitland, op. cit., Gotshalk, op. cit., Maill, op. cit., Maitland, op. cit., and Osborne, op. cit..
4. Cf. Paul Schilpp, *Kant's Pre-Critical Ethics* and James Engell, *The Creative Imagination: Enlightenment to Romanticism.* Kant writes of these influences also in *Anthropology.*
5. Although the following examples are limited to English aestheticians, a corresponding association of taste with moral perfection is found amongst rationalist philosophers.

6. Hutcheson, *Inquiry*, 34: the capacity to receive the pleasant ideas that make up beauty generally is called '*a fine genius* or *taste*'.

7. Ibid., VII, Article II.

8. Hume, *Essays*, 6.

9. At Section 50, 153/319, Kant writes that taste 'qualifies [fine art] for culture'.

10. Section 44, 166/308: fine art 'has the effect of advancing the culture of mental powers'.

11. Section 83, II, 92/430.

12. In *Doctrine*, 51/91, Kant says this is a matter of being 'independent of nature'.

13. *Doctrine*, 45/386.

14. Earlier, in 'Universal History', 21/26, Kant has affirmed that 'the ideal of morality belongs to culture'.

15. In Section 83, II, 94/431, skill is defined as the 'principal subjective condition of the aptitude for further ends of all kinds'.

16. Skill is 'incompetent for giving assistance to the *will* in its determination and choice of ends' (ibid.).

17. Section 83, II, 94/431.

18. Bemerkungen, G.S., xx, 31.15, quoted in Kelly, *Idealism, Politics and History*, 92.

19. *Doctrine*, 51/91 . The 'power to set an end—any end whatsoever—is the characteristic of humanity (as distinguished from animality)'.

20. Section 83 ff.

21. 'Universal History', 21/20 and 'Human Race' 81/104.

22. A number of Kant's writings may be cited here: 'Universal History', 'Old Saw', *Perpetual Peace*, and 'Orientation'.

23. Kant's thought is not speculative here. He is considering the extent to which nature is compatible with reason, not arguing to a necessary and predetermined end for human development.

24. Section 91, II, 147/472.

25. 'Conjectural Beginnings', 62/117, note 2.

26. In *Religion*, Kant draws this contrast in terms of ethico-civil and juridical-civil states or conditions. The latter replaces a 'juridical state of nature' in which 'each individual prescribes the law for himself' (*Religion*, 87 ff).

27. *Religion*, 87 ff.

28. And even though there may not be any hostility actually present, the community organization is based on the supposition that hostility and violence are endemic. That is, although there is no actual war in progress between 'men who stand under external and public laws, nevertheless the state (*status irridicus*) is that same; that is, the relationship in and through which men are fitted for the acquisition and maintenance of rights—a state in which each wants to be judge of what shall be his right against others, but

for which rights he has no security against others, and gives others no security; each has only his private strength. This is a state of war in which each must be perpetually armed against everyone else'. (*Religion*, 89).

29. *Perpetual Peace*, 'First Supplement', 112/366.
30. *Religion*, 89.
31. *Religion*, 86.
32. Section 83, II, 95/432.
33. 'End', 82/140.
34. *Religion*, 62.
35. 'Conjectural Beginnings', note 62/118.
36. 'Universal History', *passim*.
37. 'Conjectural Beginnings', 67/121.
38. Section 65, II, n 25/375.
39. This is implicit in the essays on history and explicit in the *Critique of Practical Reason*.
40. *Religion*, 87.
41. The reasons are set out in *Justice*. Further, according to Kant, in political life, 'given a multitude of rational beings requiring universal laws for their preservation, each of whom is secretly inclined to exempt himself from them,' the problem is 'to establish a constitution in such a way that, although their private intentions conflict, they check each other, with the result that their public conduct is the same as if they had no such intentions' (*Perpetual Peace*, 112/366).
42. A316/B373.
43. *Strife*, 178.
44. *Perpetual Peace*, 112/366.
45. Ibid. Kant later qualifies the claim that in politics our concern is only with a formal balance between self-interested individuals. In the two appendices to *Perpetual Peace* and in other essays, he argues to the effect that political maxims 'must not be deduced from volition as the supreme yet empirical principle of political wisdom, but rather from the pure concept of the duty of right, from the *ought* whose principle is given a priori by pure reason, regardless of what the . . . consequences may be', (*Perpetual Peace*, 127/379). Nevertheless, politics remains 'the art of using coercive mechanisms for ruling men. At best, in the case of political coercion, morality serves as the limiting condition' (op. cit.).

Kant later contends that 'all maxims that *stand in need* of publicity in order not to fail their end, agree with politics and morality combined' (ibid., 134/386). To accept this assertion it is necessary to explain how the proposed harmony between politics and morality can be maintained or why it should be. Assuming that they are co-terminous, however, we may ask how culture is to be distinguished from politics in the search for man's self-government and for a unity between coexisting individuals. An important factor here is the distinctive claim to legitimacy made by each practice. One contrast is that in our cultural activity we try to dissolve those 'hindrances', 'arising out of human nature', that politics bypasses in seeking to liberate men from subjugation to laws based on impure ideas (*KvdrV*, op. cit.).

46. *Perpetual Peace*, 94/351, where Kant identifies the limitations of a democratic government and contrasts it unfavourably with a republic.

47. *Doctrine*, 163, cf. *Perpetual Peace*, 134/386.

48. In *Perpetual Peace*, 134/386, Kant writes that the validity of the law as a rule for citizens is all that is defended in arguments which begin with 'the pure concept of duty' and proceed, 'by means of publicity, i.e., by removing all distrust in the maxims of politics' to 'conform to the rights of the public, for only in this [public sphere] is the union of the goals of all possible'.

49. It may seem that all this fails to provide guidelines for problem cases, as where a political restriction is so closely tied to cultural practice that we cannot easily separate out political from cultural features. Although discovering how the distinction applies is an empirical matter, the possi-bility of making a distinction must be defended by arguments. However, part of the defence can only consist in describing how particular cultural practices—such as aesthetic and artistic activity—operate to achieve unity between subjects without using the compulsions and processes prevalent in political practices. These descriptions are not based on vague distinc-tions, arbitrarily accepted, but point to real features whose importance must be grasped for the complex relations of nature to be understood.

Some differences have already been suggested above. Other contrasts between culture and politics may be drawn from Kant's writings in *Perpetual Peace*, 'Orientation', 'Strife', and 'Old Saw'. One conclusion we can draw from this comparison is that cultural development has political consequences. For example, cultural development may oppose con-tingently formed political organization because we can use fine art to sustain a particular relation between subjects who are also citizens, or because in fine art we can express ideas that are political in presenting relations between citizens and institutions in a particular light. Not every aspect of the tension between subject and citizen is a priori or in principle already worked out, and fine art and culture participate in developing their interrelation.

50. *Religion*, 51.

51. 'Old Saw', n 61/278.

52. *KrdpV*, 63/62.

53. *Doctrine*, 41/483.

54. Kelly, *Idealism, Politics and History*, 142, see also *Doctrine* 41/483 ff.

55. See *Religion*, Pt. III, *passim*.

56. 'Conjectural Beginnings', 62/117.

57. Ibid., 61/116.

58. Ibid.
59. I. Berlin, *Vico and Herder*, 195–9.
60. C. Antoni, *From History to Sociology*, *passim*.
61. Z. Bauman, *Culture and Praxis*, Ch. 1.
62. 'Universal History', 15–16/20–22.
63. *Doctrine*, 45/386, italics added.
64. *Religion*, Preface.
65. *Religion*, 95–6.
66. A 407/B434; See Chapter I, above.
67. A 327/B383.
68. Section 91, II, 147/472.
69. *KrdpV*, 108.
70. *Religion*, 89.
71. A number of quotations from Kant can be given to illustrate the social nature of humanity's co-operative effort to promote the highest good. Not all of them need to be taken from his later writings, although it is in these, especially in *Religion Within the Limits of Reason Alone*, that he expounds the notion of an ethical community as something that will provide a continuity *in this world* for the intentions of active moral personalities and for the consequences of their acts.
72. *Anthropology*, 160/374.
73. 'Universal History', 15/21.
74. *Doctrine*, 132/467.
75. 'Universal History', 15/21; cf. *KrdrV*, *Perpetual Peace*, and 'Strife'.
76. Section 41, 155/297.
77. Ibid., see below note 80.
78. Section 87, II n 116/449.
79. 'Human Race', 137/79.
80. *Anthropology*, 188/328: It may be that 'nature within man tries to lead him from culture to morality and not (as reason prescribes), from morality and its laws as a starting point, to a culture designed to conform with morality . . . . This course inevitably perverts his tendency and turns it against its end.'
81. Cf. Yovel, *Kant's Philosophy of History*, Chapter 1.
82. Hegel, *The Phenomenology of Spirit*, Preface, 29 ff.
83. Section 83 ff.
84. But see Chapter IV, below.
85. Section 49, 174/312.
86. Section 49, 174/312–13.
87. Section 50, 183/319.
88. At *Doctrine*, 145/472, an interest in social communication is justified by moral reason. It can determine aesthetic judgements only at the price of disinterestedness.

89. At Section 50, 182/318, Kant proposes that as judgement is an 'indispen-
sible condition' it is 'at least what one must look to in forming an estimate of
art as fine art'. That is, we may compare the different sorts of judgement we
make in order to understand the nature of the objects considered.
90. Section 32, 137/282.
91. Section 33, 139/284.
92. Ibid., 141/285.
93. All of which, in turn, point to its position in the history of fine art and
culture.
94. Section 34, 141–2/285. Cf. also Section 29, GR, 117–18/261.
95. See S. Cavell, *Must we mean what we say?* Unlike Hume, who compares a
critic to someone who can tell there *is* a leather thong at the bottom of the
barrel, Kant supposes that aesthetic argument enables a subject to divine
the taste of metal and leather.
96. At Section 40, 151/293, common sense is the 'least we may expect from
anyone claiming the name of man'. It carries a connotation of vulgarity.
97. Section 20, 83/238.
98. Section 40, 153/285.
99. Section 40, 152/294.
100. Ibid., 152/295.
101. It fancies 'nature not to be subject to rules which the understanding by
virtue of its essential law lays at its bases' (ibid.).
102. Section 40, 151/293.
103. Section 75, II, 56/401 and *Anthropology*, 88/219.
104. Ibid., 56/402.
105. 'Conjectural Beginnings', loc. cit.
106. Section 40, title.
107. Section 22, 84/239.
108. Section 57, Remark 1, 212/344.
109. Section 51, 184/320: 'i.e. not merely in respect of their concepts but in
respect of their sensations also'. This involves 'thought' rather than merely
the application of concepts, but 'thought' covers a wide range of mental
activities for Kant. In *Logic*, for example, he seems loath to describe even
logical or tautological statements as anything but 'mere thought' because
they cannot be demonstrated (cf. *Logic*, Section 9, 92–3), but is happy to
describe expression in beauty as involving thought (Section 49, *passim*).
110. Ibid.; cf. also Section 51, 189/323. The division does not follow a theory of
fine arts so much as assess them from the point of view of culture generally.
It merely associates the fine arts 'under a principle' without any 'positive
and deliberate derivation of the connection'. Thus, the nature of the work
of fine art is not intended to provide a basis for the hierarchy proposed.
This is not to say that no justification is possible, and we may propose one
based on the nature of fine art.

111. Section 51, 184/320–1.
112. Ibid., italics added. Poetry for example, 'must have the appearance of being undesigned and a spontaneous occurrence—otherwise it is not *fine* art'. The poet plays with ideas (Section 51, 184/320–1), guiding this play without 'ulterior regard to any end, and yet with a feeling of satisfaction and stimulation . . .'. Indeed, poetry 'expands the mind by giving freedom to the imagination by offering from among *the boundless multiplicity of possible forms* accordant with a given concept to whose bounds it is restricted, *the one* that couples with the *presentation of a concept a wealth of thought* to which no verbal expression is completely adequate, and by this rising aesthetically to ideas'.

 Similarly, while painting is intended only to 'entertain the imagination in free play with ideas, and to engage actively the aesthetic judgement', its importance here is that 'the artist furnishes a bodily *expression* for the substance and character of his thought, and makes the thing itself speak, as it were, in mimic language—a very common play of our fancy, that attributes to lifeless things *a soul suitable to their form*, and that uses them as a mouthpiece'.

113. In music, and the art of colour, too, form is primary. Communication through the expression of aesthetic ideas being difficult to specify in relation to particular forms, these associations are not rationalized in great depth in our appreciation. Although associations and sensations are obviously present and could result in our pleasure, Kant suggests that we consider 'the mathematical character both of the proportion of variation in music, and our judgement upon it, and, as is reasonable, form an estimate of colour contrasts on the analogy with the latter'. Intelligible distinctions can still be made between sensations, and bearing these in mind, 'we may feel compelled to look upon the sensations afforded by both, not as mere sense-impressions, but as the effect of an estimate of form in the play of a number of sensations' (ibid.).

114. Section 52, 195/329.
115. Kant's argument for comparative worth may be extended to the distinctions between fine art and natural beauty. If fine art is better able to possess expressive imaginative freedom, it must have an aesthetic priority over natural beauty. This is suggested in 'The Importance of Artistic Beauty' by Salim Kemal. This is not to say that fine art is always more beautiful, only that it is more capable of beauty because it gives rise to intersubjective pleasure through expression in many more different forms.
116. Section 53, 192/326–7.
117. Loc. cit.
118. Art is 'capable of being at times directed to ends intrinsically legitimate and praiseworthy' (loc. cit.).
119. Rhetoric becomes 'reprehensible on account of the subjective injury done

in this way to maxims and sentiments, even where objectively the action may be lawful. For it is not enough to do what is right, but we should practise it solely on the ground of its being right' (loc. cit.). Consequently, it can be recommended 'neither for the pulpit nor for the bar' nor for any place where 'correct knowledge' and 'conscientious observance of duty is at stake'.

120. Section 53, 196/330.

121. Kant goes on to argue that the formative arts are preferable to music, which, first, is more agreeable than productive of an expansion of the faculties, second, forces itself on our attention because 'it scatters its attention abroad to an uncalled for extent . . . , and thus, as it were, becomes obtrusive and deprives others, outside of the musical circle, of their freedom', (loc. cit.) and third, is only fleeting, for it evokes ideas only in its performance.

122. At times Kant writes as if fine art were quite unimportant to our progress, and describes science and art as the 'less necessary branches of culture' (Section 83, II, 95/432). But the context makes clear that this reference is to art, not fine art (See Chapter II), and to science merely as technology. We saw that the former merely seeks 'to actualize a possible object to the cognition of which it is adequate' and 'does whatever acts are required for that purpose'. It is part of the development of skill only, and Kant adds now that it is commensurable with an 'inequality among men'. It 'keeps the masses in a state of oppression, with hard work and little enjoyment'. The 'culmination point' of this sort of culture, 'where devotion to what is superfluous begins to be prejudicial to what is indispensable, is called luxury' (ibid.). If this were all that culture meant, then fine art's unimportance to culture should not worry us, for the only art submerged in such a culture would not be fine art.

123. Cf. Schiller, *The Aesthetic Education of Man, passim.*

124. Ibid.

125. *Religion*, 97.

126. Schiller, Letter 15, *AEM*.

127. We do not know what sort of duplication in experience we could achieve of a *summum bonum* which is, in any case, itself to be realized in this world, and we cannot easily discover examples of non-persuasive culture to be contrasted with beauty.

128. Schiller argues something like this in *Kalliasbriefe*. Cf. Ellis, cited below.

129. Which is why the necessity of taste cannot be justified by the analogy between beauty and morality.

130. Section 38, *passim.*

131. The need for this explanation was suggested by Prof. R. W. Hepburn and by the academic adviser at Oxford University Press who read my typescript.

132. e.g. J. M. Ellis, *Schiller's* Kalliasbriefe *and the Study of his Aesthetic Theory* (*Anglica Germanica*), (The Hague, 1969), 47–83.
133. Section 43 ff.
134. *AEM*, L. 9.
135. Schaper, *Studies in Kant's Aesthetics*.
136. Schiller, *On Tragedy*, italics added; quoted in Ellis, op. cit.
137. In Kant's understanding of 'expression'.
138. *AEM*, L. 12; see also *Briefweschsel zwischen Schiller und Kroner von 1784 bis zum Tode Schillers*, with an Introduction by L. Geiger (Stuttgart, 1892–4), for example the letter dated Jan. 25th, 1793; but see also letter to Goethe, 7th July, 1797 in *Correspondence with Goethe*, op. cit.
139. See Chapter I, above.
140. R. D. Miller, *Schiller and the Ideal of Freedom*, Ch. V, and Ellis, op. cit.
141. Section 66, *Anthropology*.
142. *AEM*, LL. 4 and 13. A correspondence between them began after the publication of the *Vocation of a Scholar*.
143. *SR*, 79 ff.
144. *SR*, 159 ff.
145. *AEM*, LL. 2, 3, and 4.
146. *VS*, 23.
147. Section 59, 225/354.
148. M. C. Ives, *The Analogue of Harmony*, and Ellis, op. cit., 78–9; cf. also H. Reiner, *Duty and Inclination*, Chs. I and II.
149. See Schaper; Hegel, in *Aesthetics*, Tr. C. Karelis (Oxford, 1979), 61, writes 'It is Schiller who must be given the credit for venturing on an attempt to get beyond this [distinction between subject and object] by intellectually grasping unity and reconciliation as the truth'.
150. Fichte develops this in *The Science of Knowledge* (Part III, Second Discourse – Eighth Discourse, 218).
151. *AEM*, L. 13.
152. *AEM*, LL. 14, 15 and 16.
153. *AEM* L. 20–27.
154. *AEM* L. 27.
155. Op. cit.
156. Cf. *Anthropology, passim*.
157. Section 17, 76/233.
158. Section 17, 80/235.
159. Ibid.
160. Ibid.
161. Forrest Williams, 'Philosophical Anthropology and the Critique of Aesthetic Judgement', 172–88, and Van de Pitte, *Kant as Philosophical Anthropologist* (1971).
162. Forrest Williams, op. cit., 174.

163. Forrest Williams, op. cit., 185.
164. Van de Pitte, op. cit., *passim*.
165. See Weiler, who gives cogent reasons for the impossibility of a Kantian anthropology of the sort needed here.

IV. Fine Art and Natural Necessity

1. J. Maitland, op. cit., 350; Ameriks, op. cit., 3, claims something similar.
2. Section 87 ff.
3. We strive to live '*under* moral laws *in this* world' (Section 86, 110–11/444).
4. *Religion*, n. 45.
5. Section 43, 163/303.
6. *KrdpV*, 119/118. See also B. Harrison, 'Kant and the Sincere Fanatic', *passim*.
7. And so best expresses or exhibits our 'free rationality'. Cf. Harrison, op. cit.
8. *KrdpV*, 98/101.
9. *Foundations*, 446/114.
10. *Religion*, 191.
11. The exercise of virtue, as we shall see, no longer refers to a separate and transcendental world in which it gains some ahistorical realization. Further, in the development of skill we see examples of the unintentional or accidental reorganization of nature. See also J. R. Silber, 'Kant's Conception of the Highest Good as Immanent and Transcendent', *Philosophical Review* 48 (1959); Y. Yovel, 'The Highest Good and History in Kant's Thought', *Archiv für Geschichte der Philosophie* 54 (1972), and M. B. Zeldin, 'The *summum bonum*, the Moral Law, and the Existence of God', *KS* 42 (1971).
12. He regards the world as 'a *consistent whole* of interconnected ends' and the *summum bonum* becomes 'the existence of rational beings under moral laws ...' (Section 86, II, 110–11/444). The *summum bonum* co-ordinates natural and moral orders generally, and 'has to be realized *in the world* through freedom' (Section 91, II, 142/469 italics added). It is 'the highest good *in the world* possible through freedom' (Section 87, II, 118/450), being concerned with 'mankind ... in its moral perspective' (*Religion*, 80) and with making actual 'the kingdom of God *on earth*' (*Religion*, 136; italics added). And to make sense of these claims we must understand the moral connotations of the 'complex of objects of all possible experience', taken 'as no more than phenomena'. The last quotation is from the programmatic statement made early in the *Critique of Judgement*. Whether our concern is with theoretical *or* practical reason, 'the territory upon which its realm is established, and over which it *exercises* its legislative authority, is still *always* confined to *the complex of objects of all possible experience, taken as no more than phenomena*'. Or, as Kant concludes, the 'concept of freedom is *meant to actualize in the sensible world the end proposed by its laws*' (Section II, 12/174);

for 'reason cannot command us to pursue an end that is recognized to be nothing but a fiction of the brain' (Section 91, II, 147/472).

13. *KrdpV*, 108–12/110–14.
14. *Religion*, 4.
15. *Religion*, 5.
16. Section 87, II, 118/450.
17. Ibid. Kant's argument is that God is the *moral* author of nature.
18. In *Religion*, 5n, Kant says we must do this at least 'in representation and intention'.
19. Ibid. It is an idea arising 'out of morality' only, and 'is not its basis'.
20. *KrdpV*, 118.
21. Yovel, *Kant's Philosophy of History*, 64.
22. Ibid.
23. Section 87, II, 116/448.
24. Section 87, II, 115/448.
25. Section 87, II, n. 117/448.
26. Section II, 14/175–6: Although 'between the realm of the natural concept . . . and the concept of freedom . . . there is a great gulf fixed', Kant writes, 'still the latter is meant to influence the former—that is to say, the concept of freedom is meant to actualize in the sensible world the end proposed by its laws'.
27. Section 87, II, 118/450. For if it were impossible to actualize moral ends, then moral claims would become vacuous—a 'mere fiction of the brain' that lacked rational motivation—and we could not extract a final end from the moral law because 'a final end cannot be commanded by any law of reason unless reason . . . also promises its attainability' (Section 50, 146/472).
28. A643/B671 ff, *KrdU* Introduction, and A832/B860 ff.
29. 'For instance, understanding says: all change has its cause; [here] transcendental judgement has nothing further to do than to furnish a priori the condition of subsumption under the concept of understanding placed before it'. But besides this a priori necessity, 'the objects of empirical cognition are determined, or, so far as we can judge a priori, are determinable, in diverse ways, so that specifically differentiated natures, over and above what they have in common as things of nature in general, are further capable of being causes in an infinite variety of ways' (Section V, 22/183).
30. Ibid.
31. 'As otherwise we should not have a thoroughgoing connection of empirical cognitions in a whole of experience' (ibid.).
32. See S. Kemal, 'Aesthetic Necessity, Culture, and Epistemology', *KS* (1983).
33. Section IV, 18/179–80.
34. Section IV, 18/179.
35. Ibid.

36. Section IV, 18–19/180.
37. Section IV, 19/180.
38. Cf. J. D. McFarland, *Kant's Concept of Teleology* (1970); *KrdU*, Sections IV and V; B727, where Kant argues that the meaning of the regulative idea of God is to be understood as divine wisdom and 'nature as the source of purposiveness in the world'; and S. Kemal, 'Systematic Ideas in Aesthetics', *BJA* (1975).
39. Section V, 23/184.
40. Section VIII, 34/193 where aesthetic judgement is 'the faculty of estimating formal finality (otherwise called subjective) by the feeling of pleasure or displeasure' and teleology is that of 'estimating the real finality (objective) of nature by means of the understanding and reason'.
41. There 'our own imagination is the agent employed' (ibid.).
42. Ibid.
43. Here 'the concept of an object, so far as it contains at the same time the ground of the actuality of this object, is called its end, and the agreement of a thing with that constitution of things which is only possible according to ends, is called the *finality* of its form' (Section IV, 19/180). Kant later expresses this in terms of causality: 'an end is the object of a concept so far as this concept is regarded as the cause of the object (the real ground of its possibility); and the causality of a *concept* in respect of its object is finality (*forma finalis*)' (Section 10, 61/220).
44. E. Cassirer, *Kant's Life and Thought*, tr. J. Haden (New Haven, 1981), 343.
45. Section IV, 19–20/181.
46. Section 10, 61/220.
47. Section 70, II, 38/387.
48. Cf. Buchdahl, op. cit.
49. A648/B676. We would then 'assert a *transcendental* principle of reason and would make the synthetic unity necessary, not only subjectively and logically, as method, but objectively also'.
50. Section 70, II, 38/387.
51. Ibid.
52. Ibid.
53. Section 77, II, 60/405: The antinomy arises if we mistake a 'peculiarity of *our* [human] understanding' and think it yields 'objective predicates transferred to things themselves' (ibid.).
54. McFarland, op. cit., Chapter 3, *passim.*
55. Section 77, II, 66/409. The use of either principle does not preclude use of its rival. But teleology and causality 'are not capable of being applied in conjunction to one and the same thing in nature as co-ordinate truths available for the explanation or deduction of one thing from another'. That is, once a satisfactory causal explanation for the occurrence of a particular event or object is given in terms of sufficient and necessary conditions and

mechanical laws, 'I cannot then turn around and derive the same product from the same substance as a causality that acts from ends' (Section 78, II, 69/411–12).

56. Section 78, II, 79/415.

57. Kant holds that this is true also in the case of organisms. He writes that it 'is quite certain that we can never get a sufficient knowledge of organized beings and their possibility, much less get an explanation of them, by looking merely to mechanical principles of nature. Indeed, so certain is it, that we may confidently assert that it is absurd for men even to entertain any thought of so doing or to hope that maybe another Newton may some day arise, to make intelligible to us even the genesis of but a blade of grass from natural laws that no design has ordered. Such insight we must absolutely deny to mankind'. (Section 75, 54/400). That is, no one can divine the purpose of the creation of an object through mechanical causes—its inner possibility—and so mechanistic science can never hope to explain it.

58. It may be necessary to point out that Kant clearly does not seek to explain fine art as a matter of creation *ex nihilo* but as an ordering of existent material.

59. E. Cassirer, op. cit. 346–7.

60. We need not be detained by issues concerning organisms. What we are interested in is that reflective teleological judgements allow us to conceive of some objects in nature as possessed of an organization that we can and must ascribe to 'an intelligent cause, distinct from the matter and parts of a thing' (Section 65, II, 20/373). Art and organisms both are ends, but Kant distinguishes between them on other grounds: both possess design, but while works are objects and ends 'whose causality, in bringing together and combining parts, is determined by its idea of the whole made possible through the idea, and consequently, not by external nature', organisms must satisfy another criterion. To conceive of an object as an organism—as something 'possible independently of the causality of the conceptions of external rational agents'—a 'second requisite is involved' *in addition to our thinking of it as an end*: 'namely that the parts of a thing combine themselves into a unity of a whole by being reciprocally cause and effect of their form' (ibid.). An object that satisfies both these criteria is an 'organized and self-organizing being'. Basically, this seems to mean that they are able to reproduce themselves whereas works of art must be brought about by 'the causality of conceptions of external agents' (Section 64/5).

61. Cf. S. Kemal (1975), for the distinction of 'finality *in* nature' from 'Finality of Nature'.

62. Section 78, II, 74/415.

63. Ibid.

64. Section 64, II, 17/370, italics added.

65. Section 64, II, 17–18/320, italics added.

66. Op. cit.
67. Op. cit. I am indebted to publications by K.–O. Apel, which clarify how these arguments may be drawn from what Kant says.
68. This understanding of their relation makes possible the claim that counter-examples refute generalizations—that is, that hypotheses are at risk.
69. Section 58, 216/347.
70. Ibid.
71. Section 58, 217/347–8.
72. Section 58, 219/349.
73. Other examples are given in chemistry, where particles seem to 'shoot together' to form beautiful patterns. As Kant thought that chemistry was only a 'systematic art', concerned with qualities and not at all scientific, mathematical, or quantitative, examples from that discipline suggest to him that 'we have only what may be ascribed to nature in its capacity for originating in *free* activity aesthetically final forms independently of any particular guiding ends, according to chemical laws by means of the chemical integration of the substance requisite for the organization' (Section 58, 219/349). Thus, Kant thinks that these examples do not support claims that nature has an interest in producing beauty—that is, its possession of 'an end acting in the interest of the imagination' (ibid.). The reference to '*free* formations' and '*free* activity' in Section 58 is meant to indicate the unscientific nature of chemistry. Those laws are supposedly only contingent, and 'carry no consciousness of their *necessity* with them (they are not apodeictically certain)' (*Metaphysical Foundations of Natural Science*). As a body of knowledge becomes a science only when it is organized into a system and based on 'ultimately certain principles', Kant held that chemistry was not the latter. We presumably know better. And, so, for us, chemical formations best illustrate that nature does seem to have an end in our aesthetic judgements. Chemical formations are lawful, based on 'ultimately certain principles' and, apparently, directed toward the creation of beautiful formations.
74. Kant's main argument for his conclusion depends on Occam's Razor: 'not alone does reason, with its maxims enjoining upon us in all cases to avoid, as far as possible, any unnecessary multiplication of principles, set itself against this assumption [of nature having an end in our experience of beauty], but we have nature in its free formations displaying on all sides extensive mechanical proclivity to producing forms seemingly made, as it were, for the aesthetic employment of our judgement, without affording the least support to the supposition of a need for anything over and above its mechanism, as mere nature, to enable them to be final for our judgement apart from their being grounded upon an idea' (ibid.).
75. Section 58, 221/351.
76. Cf. C. G. Hempel, 'Rational Action', *passim*.

77. Ibid.
78. Section 70, 36/387.
79. Section 2, n. 44/206.
80. Section 41, 154/296.
81. See above, Chapter 2.
82. I contend that history and culture are identical in this respect.
83. Section 82, II, 88/426.
84. Section 83, II, 93/430.
85. Section 83, II, 94/431.
86. Ibid.
87. Ibid.
88. Section 87, II, 114–122/449–453.
89. Section 86, II, 110/444.
90. Section 87, II, 118/450. Cf. Despland, op. cit.
91. Section 87, II, 120–1/452–3. Cf. McFarland, 'The Bogus Unity Between Physical and Moral Teleology', *passim*.
92. Cf. Despland, op. cit., 65 ff, and McFarland, op. cit.
93. Section 86, II, 111/445.
94. GR on Teleology, II, 159/482.
95. *KrdpV* 139/134.
96. Section 86, Remark, II, 113/446.
97. Ibid.
98. GR on Teleology,II, n. 159/482.
99. Ibid.
100. Section 86, Remark, II, 114/447.
101. Michael Despland, *Kant on History and Religion*, 65.
102. Ibid.
103. GR on Teleology, 154–5/478. Cf. also McFarland on 'The Bogus Unity'.
104. Section 88, 126/459; cf. McFarland, op. cit.
105. Section 88, II, 126/459.
106. GR on Teleology, 158–9/482.
107. Cf. Y. Yovel, 'The God of Kant'.
108. E. L. Fackenheim, 'Kant's Concept of History', 381–98. See also Y. Yovel, 'The Highest Good and History in Kant's Thought'; Crawford's (op. cit.) argument also depends on the unity of this supersensible substratum.
109. Section 87, II, 121/452.
110. Nor can the problem of the relation of nature to reason be solved by relegating each to a different realm. Even if the rational will at the basis of setting and pursuing ends is not determined by the casual mechanisms of nature, nevertheless, if it is to be part of the development of humanity it must intervene in nature in some way. The 'concept of freedom is meant to actualize in the sensible world the end proposed by its law' (Section II, 14/ 176). Were this impossible, then 'the moral law ... must be fantastic,

directed to empty, imaginary ends, and consequently, inherently false' (*KrdpV* 114/110).

As we saw, the inadequacy of such a resolution is suggested also by the analogy between beauty and moral good. In keeping with their relegation to separate realms, the analogy would take a particular form. For example, given that the experience of beauty belongs to nature, it might be thought enough to focus on similarities between nature and reason—such as the lawful casual determination and empirical necessitation characteristic of nature and its analogy with the lawful casuality of freedom and moral necessitation. Nature and morality may be alike in that both have to do with casuality and necessity; but the casuality and necessity characteristic of morality are diametrically opposed to those of nature. Their analogy is based on the most acute opposition between them. However, the necessity of beauty has a more positive connection with moral good. It occurs in the phenomenal world, has an exemplary necessity and imputes agreement to others. Its necessity is like moral obligation and unlike empirical necessity. And Kant's interest is in showing how a transition between them is possible, not in leaving them distinct.

111. From the nature of fine art, similarly, we may be led to see that cognition is complementary to aesthetic practice in culture. Works are sometimes unclear or ambiguous, so that the relation between subjects cannot be sustained simply by virtue of understanding and interpretation, and we need to look at features of the object.

The work is the focus of our attention and understanding. It is the basis of our interpretation, and its link to the artist can be broken in the sense that we may understand the artist through his work rather than seek to clarify his intention in order to interpret the work. Both artist and audience would have to satisfy the same criteria if their claims about a work are to be justified, and both would have to point to features of the object itself.

Where there is ambiguity or ambivalence we may refer to the object's 'non-aesthetic' features to defend or reject aesthetic ascriptions. Kant may have these features in mind when he writes first that in art we initially seek 'to actualize a possible object' (Section 44, 165/305); second, that we must interpret the work; and, third, that fine art presupposes culture. In this context, the complementarity between cognitive and aesthetic judgements may be expressed by saying that the former facilitate our deeper, fuller understanding of a work of fine art. This may be explained in the following way.

Cognition may count among the 'external witnesses' to interpretation. The object to be understood as a goal or as subject to aesthetic judgement must first of all conform to the general laws of understanding (Section 22, GR, 86/241), whose determinate expression is found in the transcendentally necessary categories. Hence the work must be an object whose properties we can experience in the phenomenal world. However, the general laws of the understanding alone fail to explain the possibility of interpretation. Kant's association of fine art with culture adds to the possibility of interpretation by placing the object and the artist within the wider context of social and intersubjective conditions such as schools and exemplary works. As Kant writes, to understand a work we must have 'a concept of what the thing is *intended to be*' (Section 48, 173/311, italics added) and intentions, here, are understood within the context of originating works in relation to other examples or schools. (See Sections 43, 47 and 49, *passim*.) Indeed Kant goes as far as to claim that genius 'can do no more than furnish rich *material* for products of fine art; its elaboration and its *form require a talent academically trained* . . . ' (Section 47, 171/310, italics added). Both critic and artist, who might be the same person, must be cognizant of this background to works. So much so that there may be an art to knowing how 'taste proceeds' (Section 34, 142/286; cf. also Sections 51–4).

V. The Necessities of Taste, Fine Art and the *Summum Bonum*

1. Section 31, 135/280. Aesthetic judgements, he explains, claim 'the concurrence of everyone, albeit the judgement is not a cognitive judgement, but only one of pleasure or displeasure in a given object'. This is because they involve 'an assumption of a subjective finality that has thoroughgoing validity for everyone, and which, since the judgement is one of taste, is not grounded upon any concept of the thing'. Therefore, their legitimacy may be defended by deducing their subjective universality.

2. For example, Ameriks, in his paper, sets aside one for the other. Guyer, in Chapter 4 of his book, seems to propose the same thing. Cf. *Kant and the Claims of Taste*, 144 and 163 f.

3. Guyer, op. cit., 163 ff. I shall use features of Guyer's account in what follows.

4. In the Deduction itself, the sequence of argument moves from justifying the possibility of a subjectively universal judgement to considering questions of the communication of sensations and of taste as a kind of *sensus communis*. That is, from the success of the deduction, which validates subjectively universal judgements, Kant raises claims about the communication of particular judgements, suggesting that the former grounds conclusions about our relation to other subjects. Just as the move from the Second to the Fourth Moments is one from universality to necessity, similarly the argument of the Deduction turns from considering the possibility of aesthetic judgements generally to justifying our general expectations of particular judgements. This is done in order to show that the Analysis of the Beautiful, laid out in the earlier part of the text, can be defended and justified.

5. Like our empirical cognitive judgements, aesthetic judgements may also be mistaken, but as their basis is in the subject's experience of a pleasurable state of mind, his conviction that his is an aesthetic judgement cannot rely on the sort of compulsion available in cognitive judgements. It makes sense to dismiss a cognitive judgement that contradicts our own as a false one which does not correspond with the way the world is. For to show that it is false we may adduce evidence and compel agreement because a subject cannot accept the grounds for a conclusion yet reject the conclusion without contradicting himself or being irrational. And the judgement is objective in that while it is made by a subject, its criteria depend on the state and nature of objects and involve general rules for classifying them as being of a particular type. By contrast, aesthetic judgements not only do not attempt to classify objects as belonging to a particular type, but they are also based on an experience that cannot have any cognitive content because it is only a subjective experience of pleasure. Aesthetic judgements, therefore, are autonomous, and the frequency, conviction, or expertise with which they are made by other subjects does not serve to justify our own judgements. Only our own experience of a pleasurable state of mind can serve as the basis for judgements, and its occurrence seems unable to compel agreement from others. Consequently, whereas in cognitive judgements an acceptance of the grounds for judgement leads to conviction over the truth of the judgement, no such rational or evidential force can be deployed for aesthetic judgements of taste.

6. Section 59, 224/353.

7. The points sketched out above stand in need of explanation; but here we may say that if the proposed distinctions are defensible, then although the deduction concerns only the subjective validity of our aesthetic judgements and seems to be content to treat that as a uniquely aesthetic compulsion, that cannot be the whole story. We must treat necessity as Kant does, as something requiring a separate Moment because of the peculiar 'logic' of these judgements. If that were not the case, then the Analytic would have stopped at the Third Moment, in which Kant could clarify the uncertainty inherent in the aesthetic judgements, separate questions of their rationality from those of their certainty, and add nothing new to his analysis of taste. But he adds a Fourth Moment, and develops his analysis of taste by clarifying the special nature of the necessity gained. The Moments of universality and necessity place related but distinct demands on judgements of taste, and the Moment of necessity can be seen as proposing a practical value, which is deployed through the *sensus communis*, in addition to a merely epistemological one.

8. Cf. P. Guyer, *Kant and the Claims of Taste*, and D. W. Crawford, *Kant's Aesthetic Theory*, among others. The quotation is from Guyer, 122–3.

9. Guyer, Chapter 3.

10. It becomes clear from considering Kant's deductions that as they only justify a general transcendental possibility—in this case, of making aesthetic judgements—they fail to give us an account of actual instances. Thus, we understand that aesthetic judgements generally are singular and subjective, and depend on the state of mind of the subject responding to a particular object. And so we may expect of aesthetic judgements generally that our disinterestedness and concern with finality will show that our pleasure is universalizable. However, this remains a general account of particulars: we have only a general account of the possibility of aesthetic judgements, but still lack an explanation of how we are to deal with actual instances.

11. One sense of intersubjectivity was proposed earlier when we argued that in making aesthetic judgements subjects treat each other as rational and feeling ends in themselves. This sense depends on a meaning of intersubjectivity which is epistemological but contrasts with subjective and objective judgements.

12. A218/B266.

13. *Logic*, op. cit., A222/B269.

14. *Prolegomena*, Section 18, 56.

15. Section 6, 51/211.

16. The qualifications involved here have been proposed in Chapter 3 above.

17. This seems to hold true regardless of the particular conception of truth, objectivity, or theory we use.

18. Section VII, 29/189.

19. See above, Introduction.

20. Ibid.

21. Such a claim is made by Fisher and Maitland, op. cit., 750.

22. A104–5.

23. Section 38, 146/290.

24. Section 32, 136/281.

25. Section 33, 140/285.

26. Section 34, 141/285: 'A principle of taste would mean a fundamental premise under which one might subsume the concept of an object, and then, by a syllogism, draw the inference that it is beautiful. That, however, is absolutely impossible. For I must feel the pleasure immediately in the representation of the object and cannot be talked into it by any grounds of proof'.

27. Section 8, 55/215.

28. Section 33, 284–5/239–40. Kant clarifies the autonomy of taste further, adding details to the account given at Section 8.

29. Cf. Guyer, *Kant and the Claims of Taste*, ch. 3 and 4.

30. Section 18, *passim*.

31. Ibid.

32. Guyer, 163 ff.

33. Section 8, 57/216.
34. Ibid.
35. Ibid.
36. Guyer, 'Pleasure and Society in Kant's Theory of Taste', Section II ff, claims this is the case.
37. Section 9, 57/217.
38. Kant's concern here is with actual judgements. He says, first, that at this point in the discussion what we have in view calls for something more than psychological or empirical explanations of our pleasure in communication, and then, second, at the end of the same paragraph, says that discussion of questions of *necessity* 'must be reserved until we have answered the *further* one of whether, and how, aesthetic judgements are possible a priori' (Section 9, 59/218, italics added). Thus, issues of the ability to communicate one's mental state, and of the necessity of the demands consequent on such an ability, are to be separated from, first, empirical or psychological explanations of pleasure in communication and, second, from the transcendental a priori justification of the possibility of aesthetic judgements.
39. In the next chapter some of the over-simplifications present here will be mitigated.
40. Section 9, 58–9/218, italics added.
41. Ibid.
42. Ibid.
43. Section 40, 153/295.
44. Section 6, 50/211.
45. In Section 18 Kant explains that 'what we have in mind in the case of the beautiful is a *necessary* reference on its part to delight. However, this necessity is of a special kind.'
46. At Section 18, 81/236, Kant adds that in the case of practical necessity 'thanks to concepts of pure rational will, in which free agents are supplied with a rule, this delight is a necessary consequence of an objective law, and simply means that one ought absolutely (without ulterior object) to act in a certain way'.
47. Section 18, *passim*.
48. Ibid.
49. Ibid.
50. Section 19, 82/237, italics added.
51. So far as they depend on the transcendental deduction, their constitution is not a recommendation to others, for if the categories were not accepted, there would be no experience at all. Therefore, any such judgement must presuppose the constitution of experience and cannot recommend it. However, there is a sense in which cognition is tied to a recommendation; for science, the constructed system of our knowledge of nature, follows regulative ideas. And while there is need for some systematic order if we

are to have knowledge, because it is conceivable that the particular order we gain could have been otherwise, we cannot predict whether it will be acceptable. Consequently, science itself may be said to be based on a recommendation where the constitutive role of causality in the deduction leads the subject to suppose that 'I *ought* at all times to reflect upon [the order of natural events] according to the simple mechanism of nature' (Section 70, II, 38/387). That is, given a distinction between empirical a priori necessity and the use of reflection in constructing the order of our knowledge of nature, the compulsion guiding our construction is expressed by an 'ought'. This is what subjects should agree with so far as the order of their experience of objects is to be rational.

52. When Kant writes that each judgement 'exacts agreement from everyone; and a person who describes something as beautiful insists that everyone *ought* to give the object in question his approval and follow suit in describing it as beautiful' (loc. cit.), he is denoting the subject who makes the proposal.

53. Section 19, 82/237.

54. Loc. cit.

55. Section 19, 82/237.

56. Ibid.

57. At Section 19 Kant only reminds us of these problems by pointing out that in addition to the ground common to all, which is a condition of the transcendental *possibility* of taste, we need to explain its success also. While he considers the sorts of necessity proposed above once the deduction of taste has been secured, in the present context Kant's concern is only to show what sort of transcendental possibility enters the picture and what sorts of necessity are involved. He will have more to say of the latter in Section 22, to clarify the relation between its two forms.

58. Section 19 ff.; Section 40 ff., and Section 59 ff., among others.

59. The precise role of the distinction between common sense as the ground of the possibility of judgements of taste and the role of the idea of a *sensus communis* as ground of necessity is left obscure at this point in the *Critique* because Kant is not here attempting a deduction but only clarifying our expectations of judgements of taste in preparation for such a deduction and for a justification of necessity. The latter comes to the fore in Sections 21 and 40, where Kant characterizes the *sensus communis* as 'the faculty for estimating a priori the communicability of the feelings which are connected with a given representation', and where he describes taste as 'the faculty of estimating that which makes our feeling in a given representation universally communicable'. Whereas 'possibility' is a question of the validity of making judgements, and is justified by the transcendental deduction, their communication concerns the actual subjective judgements we make and the compulsion they can generate. The latter may be

justified, but requires a claim about the validity of Ideas rather than a transcendental deduction.

60. Section 20, 83/238. Cf. also Guyer, *Kant and the Claims of Taste*, ch. 3 and 4.

61. Section R1, 209/343.

62. It is not an 'external sense' in that our representations are such as we would gain from sight, or sound, and so on, and their order is not simply that owed to our forms of intuition.

63 Section 20, 83/238.

64. It may be that at this point the *sensus communis* as an idea is what is expressed in beauty generally, so that the recommendation made in a judgement is gained through its expressive qualities, perhaps at some higher level. But this new theory is one which Kant has not prepared us for, and it may only be a misreading of ambiguities in Kant's expression.

65. And, as we have seen, on the basis of a general argument against scepticism and by showing that our assumption of a 'common sense' in either use is well founded because it does not introduce any irrational elements, Kant goes on to deny that our putative judgement is 'merely a conglomerate constituting a mere subjective play of the powers of representation, just as scepticism would have it' (Section 21, 83/238). However, the universal validity and subjective or objective necessity of taste are far from being proven at this point—nor, I suggest, is it intended that they should be validated by these claims. All we have done is to show that 'we do not have to take our stand on psychological observations, but we assume a common sense as a necessary condition of the universal communicability of our knowledge, which is presupposed in every logic and every principle of knowledge that is not scepticism' (Section 22, 84/234). That is, the present claim is only that taste is not a matter of mere psychology or physiology: if we were sceptical about judgements of taste we would have to be sceptical about our claims to knowledge. But to justify the possibility of taste we would have to deepen the concept-dependent deduction that constitutes our experience to show how a feeling not dependent on concepts may yet be said to be intersubjective. We would have to show also what justification there is for using the idea of a common sense to legislate over particular judgements.

Moreover, we have yet to argue against a second doubt—that directed against our success or our assurance of correct subsumption. For 'nothing is postulated in a [particular] judgement of taste but the idea of a *universal voice* in respect of delight that is not mediated by concepts; consequently, only the *possibility* of an aesthetic judgement capable of being at the same time deemed valid for everyone' is relied on, and *that* still '*looks for confirmation*, not from concepts, but from the concurrence of others' (op. cit.).

66. Section 8, 56/216.
67. Section 22, title.
68. Section 40, 150/293.
69. The contrast with 'public' here might be 'secret', in that an entirely idiosyncratic pleasure could easily give rise to a 'maxim which I cannot divulge publicly without defeating my own purpose. It must be kept secret if it is to succeed . . . ' (*Perpetual Peace*, 129–30, in *On History*). A 'regard to universal communicability', Kant says, 'is something which everyone expects and requires from everyone else, just as if it were part of an original compact dictated by humanity itself' (Section 41, 155/297). And this must require 'publicity'.
70. Cf. Guyer, 280–2.
71. Section 20, 82/237.
72. Section 22, 84/239. Although Kant does not specify that he is talking only of successful judgements, I hold that the title of this Section, with its reference to 'assent', limits our attention to just that.
73. Section 22, 84/239.
74. Cf. Section 17, 76/232 for Kant's account of an ideal; cf. also *Doctrine*, n. 152/479, for Kant on the use of examples.
75. Section 22, 85/239, italics added.
76. Section VII, 29/189.
77. Section 32, 136/281, italics added.
78. Here, Kant ends Section 21 with a number of questions. He feels he has shown how common sense is involved in the necessity of aesthetic judgements and has made progress in showing what sort of justifications are needed; but the business of deducing the possibility of taste and of accounting for its necessity are to be left for the Deduction of Taste. Further, although we have drawn out the different uses of 'common sense' and suggested their relation to questions of possibility and subjective or objective necessity, Kant does not himself argue for their different logical status. Consequently, at this point in the *Critique* he can claim it is still an open question whether the common sense is constitutive or regulative. As we shall see, and as what has been said above may already have suggested, Kant wants and is able to have it both ways. So that where the last paragraph of Section 21 raises the possibility of a moral justification of taste, we may take this to serve as a hint of what he wants to conclude.
79. At Section 31, 135/280–1: 'The obligation to furnish a deduction, that is, a guarantee of the legitimacy of the judgements of necessity in question must be that arising from transcendental possibility, not one that is subjective or objective'.
80. Later he adds that if we '*demonstrate* the *universal validity* of a *singular* judgement expressing the subjective finality of an empirical representation of the form of an object, we shall do all that is needed to explain how it is

possible that something can please in the mere formation of an estimate of it
... and how, *just as* the estimate of an object for the sake of a *cognition*
generally has universal rules, the delight of any one person may be
pronounced as a rule for every other' (at Section 31, 135/280–1). Such a
demonstration cannot be an empirical one because the question is whether
there are judgements of taste—whether pleasure can be given a special
status in some of its occurrences—not whether there are different sorts of
pleasure. Further, while indicating what special characteristics this deduction will consider, Kant compares his present exercise with the transcendental deduction of objective experience.

81. This peculiarity follows from the nature of the beautiful presented in the
first three Moments, which requires us to explain whether the disinterested pleasure arising from the subjective finality of an object can be
ascribed to all subjects.

82. Loc. cit.

83. This is iterated in Section 37 when Kant considers 'What exactly it is, that
is asserted a priori of an object in a judgement of taste' (Section 37, title).
He concludes that 'what is represented a priori as a universal rule for the
judgement and as valid for everyone, is not the pleasure but the *universal
validity* of this pleasure perceived as it is, to be combined in the mind with
the mere estimate of the object'. Given that pleasure is associated with 'our
mere estimate' of the object—with the finality of its form with respect to a
mutual accord of our faculties—we suppose that the case is of the mind
following rational rules or making a judgement that we may attribute to
others as we do to ourselves. As we said, it is not the pleasure that is
deduced or constituted—pleasure already exists—but the legitimacy of
seeing that some grounds for pleasure are grounds we may use to attribute
pleasure to everyone else.

Of course, our pleasure arises from our estimation of an object, and our
claim that this pleasure is intersubjectively valid does not entail that
everyone will feel that pleasure. The latter can only be confirmed by other
subjects making their own judgements and feeling that the same pleasure is
'combined in the mind with the mere estimate of the object' (op. cit.).
Thus, although an aesthetic judgement 'has merely subjective validity, still
it extends its claim to *all* subjects, as universally as it would if it were an
objective judgement, resting on grounds of cognition and capable of being
proved to demonstration' (Section 33, 141/285). But in the case of
cognition we organize our representations by using concepts of an objective world, and so can impose our judgements upon others. In the other
case, such objective validity is not available, and being unable to rely on the
categorical framework to give validity to the 'wealth of underdeveloped
material' involved, we need to establish that there is some condition,
satisfied by all subjects, which makes such a judgement possible in spite of

the subjectivity of our experience and the absence of a basis in a categorical or objective framework.

84. Section 22, 85/249, italics added.

85. Op. cit., 56/216.

86. Section 37, 146/289: If a judgement 'asserts that I think the object beautiful' then 'I may attribute the delight to everyone as necessary' and it 'is then an a priori judgement' or is based on an a priori principle.

87. See below, 'Beauty, the *Sensus Communis*, and Culture' and the rest of the present section.

88. Section 38, 146–7/290.

89. Section R1, 147/290. That we might be mistaken in any particular claim of this latter sort, of course, does not cast doubt on the validity of the principle that we can subsume correctly; but certainly whether we can subsume correctly or not depends on whether we can at all suppose that the same conditions are present in every person. We may, therefore, set aside the second claim in order to establish the first one.

90. Section 38, n. 147/290. A second condition will be left aside for the moment. The point is reiterated at Section 21, but the claim is not given justification there and so fails to constitute a deduction. That is, the 'subjective condition' referred to in Section 38 may be seen as a 'common ground' because the latter is defined by reference to an order of representations which, if the deduction is right, depends on an identical relation between similar faculties.

91. Section 21, 83/238.

92. Further consideration of this issue will be found in the paper read by M. Gregor at the Fifth Interntional Kant Congress, 1981. This paper clarifies a number of issues. See also C. MacMillan, 'Kant's Deduction of Pure Aesthetic Judgements', *KS* (1985), 43–54, where an argument similar to mine is proposed.

93. B195, italics added; cf. A154/B193 – A158/B197.

94. Ibid.

95. Cf. Strawson, *The Bounds of Sense* (1966).

96. B166.

97. Cf. also A58/B82; A157/B196; A237/B296; A820/B848.

98. That is, in keeping with the principle of significance.

99. B137.

100. B138.

101. A354–5; cf. also B423, note, and B407–10.

102. A398.

103. B131.

104. A341/B399. Cf. also B406.

105. A155–6; cf. also B166; B195.

106. A155/B194 – A157/B196.

107. Section 38, n. 147/291.
108. In Section 21, 83/238, Kant writes: the 'disposition of the cognitive powers has a relative proportion differing with the diversity of the objects that are given. However, there must be *one* in which this internal ratio . . . is *best* adapted for both mental powers in respect of cognition generally.' (Italics added.)
109. The condition expressed in Sections 38 and 39 is weaker than the proposal at Section 21.
110. And what Kant says of the latter is presented in Section 39, where his positive claims show he uses a version of the second condition which not only depends on the first, but does not insist on a single proportion.
111. Section 39, 159/292–3.
112. Op. cit. With this in mind, we must see that for a judgement to be justified generally 'in claiming universal agreement', it may be enough to know that aesthetic judgements are possible. If the second condition were treated as of one best proportion, of success, and as a part of the deduction, Kant would be overstepping the limits he has set himself in the Analytic: for there he distinguished universality from necessity, and his deduction only argued to the possibility of universally valid judgements which were subjective and singular. Moreover, we cannot deduce the necessity of aesthetic judgements because of their nature. A subject cannot feel another's pleasure for him, nor make his judgements. While 'objectively' necessary aesthetic judgements require that other subjects make these judgements, and this is what success involves, all that subjects can do in aesthetic judgements is to give the reasons for their judgement and see whether by attending to these reasons others can make aesthetic judgements for themselves. In this, a subject cannot *communicate* a representation and base his action only on the supposition that we share the same faculties—he needs more to be assured of success.
113. Section 39, 150/292.
114. Section 40, 150/293.
115. Section 40, 150/293.
116. Where we postulate a 'universal voice', this concerns only particular judgements of taste, of which the subject claims subjective necessity on the basis of his own reflection, and so feels warranted in seeking 'concurrence from others'. Of course, the particular judgement itself 'does not postulate the agreement of everyone' (Section 8, 56/216), for we may make erroneous judgements. But, in any case, the point is that when Kant says that the 'universal voice' concerns the possibility of an aesthetic judgement and characterizes it as an ideal, he is concerned to identify the idea or ideal which governs the particular judgements we make, not their transcendental possibility.
  We do not even need a separate deduction of successful judgements, for

all that is necessary for them to be possible is the possession of a common ground. We do not add anything to the character of this subjective condition by claiming that there are conditions for the success of particular actual judgements.

117. Op. cit., 82/237.

118. Op. cit., 84/239.

119. Section 40, 151/293.

120. Section 22, 84–5/239. The next previous quotation is from the same source.

121. Section 40, 151/294.

122. Cf. 'Fine Art and Culture'.

123. Section 8, 57/216. In this context Kant also says we 'postulate a universal voice', and explains what he means by the latter in *Logic*, Section 38, 112. In his book Guyer quotes this passage on 145 but seems to misunderstand just what is being postulated. As his argument is based on the claim that judgements are not immediately certain, this suggests he thinks agreement or success is being postulated when it is clear that only the possibility of taste is postulated, and must be if we attempt to make actual such judgements. Moreover, it must be postulated whether our actual judgements are correct or not.

124. Section 40, 151/293.

125. Section 22, 85–4/239, italics added.

126. Cf. Section 17, 76/232, where Kant characterizes an *ideal* as the 'representation of an individual existence as *adequate* to an idea'. As this adequacy is gained only by successful particular judgements, only then is it an ideal claiming necessity and able to *demand* agreement.

127. Op. cit.

128. Section 8, 56/216.

129. Ibid.

130. This suggests that the argument holds even if subjective necessity is not understood in terms of 'postulating the idea of a universal voice', but is considered only as a judgement warranted in the deduction of taste.

131. And the latter would have no part to play in the '*Critique* as science'. See Sections 18 and 19.

132. Section 40, 151/294.

133. Ibid.

134. Op. cit., 154/296.

135. *Anthropology*, Section 53, 88/219.

136. Cf. 'Fine Art and Culture', above.

137. Section 41, 155/247.

138. *Anthropology*, Section 44, 72/200. Cf. also Section 48, 80/209.

139. 'Universal History', 13/19, and 'Enlightenment', *passim*.

140. *KrdrV*, 'Doctrine of Method', *passim*.

141. *Religion, passim.*
142. Op. cit., 212/344.
143. See above, 'Fine Art and Culture; Kant on Culture'.
144. Section 40, 151/293: the maxim of collective reason states this clearly.
145. *Perpetual Peace*, 129/381.
146. Section 65, II, n. 23/375.
147. *Foundations*, 223.
148. It is in the Kingdom of Ends that these criteria are 'realized'.
149. *Perpetual Peace*, 129/381.
150. Ibid., 129/381.
151. Section 40, 151/294.
152. *Anthropology*, Section 42, 71/200.
153. Section 40, 153/295.
154. 'Fine Art and Culture', above.
155. Chapter I, above.
156. See Chapter I, above, n. 9.
157. See Chapter I, above, n. 10.
158. At Section 42, Kant hints at, then dismisses, a justification derived from a duty to social communication, and we propose that it be seen as a cultural necessity.
159. The position outlined above is compatible with those taken by Crawford, Guyer, and Maitland, in so far as they distinguish the possibility of judgements of taste from the necessity we try to satisfy by making them. But it differs from them so long as Guyer takes the argument to concern only a regulative epistemic ideal; or Crawford holds that aesthetic necessity can be accounted for, and the deduction completed, through the symbolic relation of beauty to moral good; or Maitland thinks Kant is unable to justify the importance of our experience of beauty. In other respects it differs also from those who treat the argument for necessity only in epistemological terms (see above, Chapter I) or who hold that the universality and necessity of judgements of taste 'are practically indistinguishable' (Karl Ameriks, op. cit.). It may also be distinguished from claims by other commentators, who use variations on the symbolic relation between beauty and morality proposed by Kant to deduce a necessity for aesthetic judgements (Richard Kuhns, 'That Kant did not complete his argument examining the relation of Art to Morality and how it might be completed', *Idealistic Studies* 5 (1975), 190–206), or argue that the deduction is merely a practical one (Rogerson, *JAAC* 40 (1982)), or that aesthetic necessity is justified through considering man as an ideal for beauty (D. A. White, 'On Bridging the Gulf Between Nature and Morality in the *Critique of Judgement*', *JAAC* 38 (1979), 179–88).
160. Section 19, 82/237; cf. Section 22, 84/239.
161. Section 70, II, 38/387.

162. One shortsighted objection may be dealt with here. This is the claim that it is fundamentally unKantian to look for an objective principle of aesthetic necessity. The objection becomes relevant because it seems that what is being sought here is precisely that: that we are ascribing objective moral necessity to beauty. First, I am not sure that it is unKantian to look for objective necessity for beauty. It is not as if Kantian themes have some precise delimitation that clearly excludes such necessity. Second, the necessity of beauty being suggested here is subjective in the sense that is true of the epistemological argument as well. It is a claim that depends on subjects making their own judgements, by reference to their own subjective character, and by reference to a subjective experience of pleasure. As Kant says, aesthetic judgement 'can demand assent *like* objective principles, provided our subsumption under them is correct (op. cit.). Which objective principles, though? My claim is that what Kant says is ambiguous between moral and epistemological principles and that the *sensus communis* can actually be both at the same time without contradiction. Further, as we suggested above, among the reasons that they are not actually objective principles but only *like* them is a reference to the nature of our experience. It is subjective and exemplary in the important sense of being a *feeling* I have from judging *this* object. It cannot be objective though it may be *like* an objective principle because it is demanded from other autonomous subjects. That is, arguing from moral necessity does not give judgements of taste an objective necessity, and we must misunderstand this to see it as the claim that the necessity of our experience of beauty *is* an objective necessity. It is not. The experience is subjective and an example, and the judgement autonomous. But this does not render it incapable of association with, or of meeting, a demand that carries a necessity derived from objective *moral* necessity.

163. And so far as our understanding of the latter underlies our conception of natural beauty, may also be discovered there.

164. In any case, if we attempt to reconcile natural necessity with the existence of freedom by separating nature and freedom into distinctive ontological realms and thereby find them compatible or incommensurable with each other, we will not have found a unity that satisfies the case of fine art. For we have seen that Kant conjoins fine art with a cultural development of reason in which nature must be effected by reason and freedom. A relegation to different realms would only make it more difficult to explain their interaction in fine art.

165. Section II, 14/176.

166. Cf. 'Fine Art and Natural Necessity', above.

167. Section 87, II, 118/450.

168. Section 87, II, 115/448.

169. Section 40, 154/296, italics added.

170. Section 22, 84/234.
171. Section 40, 154/292.

VI. Culture and Morality: Aesthetic Necessity

1. Section 40, 153/295.
2. Section 18, 81/237.
3. Section 59, 224/353. The details of this unity are obscured by Cohen's (op. cit.) failure to consider what might be called the mechanics of aesthetic and cultural *activity*.
4. This seems to be what Cohen (op. cit., 235) is suggesting.
5. See Bernard Harrison, 'Kant and the Sincere Fanatic', 237.
6. Ibid., 236.
7. J. R. Silber, 'Procedural Formalism in Kant's Ethics', *RM* (1982), *passim*.
8. As distinct from the conditions any individual must accept in order to act in public or with other agents.
9. It is necessary to consider these duties in some more detail. One's 'own happiness and the *perfection of others* cannot be made into obligatory ends for the same person' (*Doctrine*, 44/485). Duty 'is *necessitation* to an end we adopt reluctantly', but men naturally seek the state of satisfaction of desire which is happiness. Hence 'it is contradictory to say that we are *under an obligation* to promote our own happiness to the best of our ability'. Similarly, we cannot have a duty to promote another's perfection. Kant conceives of another person's perfection to consist in 'precisely *his own* power to adopt his ends in accordance with his own conception of duty'. Since we cannot do what only another person can do for himself, it cannot be our duty to promote his perfection. We only have a duty to make ourselves perfect and others happy. As we will see, the first duty qualifies the second.
10. M. J. Gregor, *The Laws of Freedom* (1963), Chapter I, *passim*.
11. See 'Moral Culture and Culture in General', below.
12. *Doctrine*, 45/486: Kant takes 'the perfection characteristic of men as such (humanity really)' to lie in 'what man can bring into being by his actions, not the mere gifts he receives from nature'.
13. *Doctrine*, 51/491: The 'power to set an end is characteristic of humanity (as distinct from animality).'
14. *Doctrine*, 45/486: That is, they are obliged to the 'cultivation of *understanding*, the power of concepts and so too of those concepts that belong to duty. At the same time, this duty includes the cultivation of one's will (moral aptitude) to fulfil every duty as such.'
15. *Doctrine*, 51/491.
16. Ibid.
17. *Doctrine*, 38/380.
18. *Doctrine*, 44/385. The context makes clear that Kant is concerned with the perfection of other agents. But he is considering 'another man *as a person*'.

And if his moral theory is to examine universalizable ends, the case of 'another man' must be equally applicable to ourselves when *we* are considered by other individuals.

19. Ibid., italics added.
20. Section 83, *passim*.
21. Sections 22, 29, 50, 83 and 84 of the *KrdU*.
22. *Doctrine*, 51/491.
23. *Doctrine*, 51/492, italics added.
24. Nor can it include the unqualified promotion of others' animal being as a duty to their happiness. If individuals are to treat each other as ends, it is because of their rational character that they must be so treated. And this would require us to treat them as ends through the duty of their happiness only so far as their natural inclinations are compatible with the capacity for reason. The one qualifies the other; and natural perfection can be required to be cognizant of the needs of moral perfection.
25. *Doctrine*, 45/486.
26. *Doctrine*, 43/485; cf. Section 43, 163/303.
27. Section II, 12/174.
28. *Foundations*, 460.
29. *KrdpV*, 31–50/30–51.
30. *Doctrine*, 11/444: the 'ground on which man should develop his powers is not regard for the *advantage* that can be gained by cultivating them.'
31. *Doctrine*, 51/391.
32. Cf. Chapter III, above.
33. *Doctrine*, 152/479.
34. Ibid.
35. Section 46, 168–9/309.
36. Section 59, 224/353.
37. *KrdrV*, Transcendental Deduction of Categories.
38. Kant thinks of this distinction in terms of a 'free' as opposed to a 'bound' imagination, but these terms are questionable.
39. See above, Chapter IV, Section 'From Consciousness to Community'.
40. L. W. Beck, *Commentary*; B. Aune, *Kant's Theory of Morals*; R. C. S. Walker, *Kant*; H. Reiner, *Duty and Inclination*.
41. *KrdU*, Preface 6/170. 'The present investigation of taste . . . is not being undertaken with a view to the formation of culture or taste . . . but merely directed to its transcendental aspects.'
42. *Anthropology*, 199/71.
43. *Old Saw*, 41/275; H. J. Paton, *The Moral Law* (London, 1966), 57, and GR, 389.
44. Section 22, 85/239.
45. It is worth mentioning that a failed work of fine art can also contribute to culture—but not for its beauty. Similarly, the imitation of a work may be an

end, but this does not increase our capacity for setting and gaining ends through making and appreciating work. For a successful imitation will not be considered fine art for the excellence of its copy even though the copy may be appreciated as a work of fine art.

46. *Doctrine* and *KrdU* Sections 42, 86, *passim*.

47. Maitland, op. cit., 351.

48. Ch. III above.

49. Section 22, 84/239.

50. Ibid.

51. The claim that it is a matter of psychology seems to be the substance of an argument against Kant put forward by Fisher and Maitland, op. cit.

52. Section 8, 55/216.

53. Section 22, 85/239.

54. P. Kivy, 'Breaking the Circle', *BJA* 7 (1967).

55. Section 22, 85–6/239.

56. *Doctrine*, 71/408.

57. Section 50, 183/319.

58. Section 60, 227/356.

59. Section 60, 226/355.

60. Cf. F. Nietzsche, *The Will to Power*, 233 et al.

61. Section 60, 227/356.

62. *Anthropology*, 143/277.

63. *Human Race*, 143–4/85; italics added.

64. Section 59, op. cit.

65. Erwin Panofsky, *Meaning in the Visual Arts*, 200 f. Michael Podro, writing in *The Critical Historians of Art* (New Haven, 1982), shows the influence of Kant's aesthetic writings on Panofsky's critical work.

66. C. A. Raschke, *Moral Action, God, and History in the Thought of Immanuel Kant*, Chs. 1 and 2, *passim*.

67. W. Benjamin, *The Origins of German Tragic Drama* 152. See also E. Panofsky, *The Life and Art of Albrecht Dürer* (Princeton, 1955), 193 f. and 242 ff.

68. *AEM*, op. cit.; see also *Correspondence with Goethe*, tr. L. Dora Schmitz (London, 1877).

69. *AEM*. It seems to me that a similar, Schillerian, conception of symbols and necessity underlies the arguments for necessity proposed by Crawford, Elliott, Cohen, and White.

70. See above, Chapter V, n. 4 ff.

71. Indeed, it seems that real agreement is anticipated in *every* judgement claiming participation in the indefinite history of the *sensus communis*.

72. On the other hand, it is also not enough to maintain that a judgement can claim to promote unity only where it does, in fact, participate in the community in the sense that everyone does in fact and not only in theory

judge a work beautiful. Such a claim would make the promotion of unity redundant: it would require everyone to assent to a judgement only when they already do so.

73. Section 40, 151/293–4 and above.
74. A316/B373.
75. B113, where Kant gives an account of this exercise.
76. See Chapter IV.
77. Section 38.
78. Mario Amya, *Pop as Art* (London, 1975).
79. See S. Kemal, 'The Importance of Artistic Beauty', *KS* (1980).
80. P. Ricoeur, *Freud and Philosophy*, 34.
81. Section VI, 28/187.

Select Bibliography

I

Kant, Immanuel, 'An Old Question Raised Again: Is the Human Race Constantly Progressing?' Tr. R. E. Anchor, in *On History*. Ed. L. W. Beck (Indianapolis, 1957, 1963).

——, *Anthropology from a Pragmatic Point of View*. Tr. M. J. Gregor (The Hague, 1974).

——, 'Conjectural Beginnings of Human History'. Tr. E. L. Fackenheim, in *On History*.

——, *Critique of Judgement*. Tr. J. C. Meredith (Oxford, 1952).

——, *Critique of Practical Reason*. Tr. L. W. Beck (Indianapolis, 1956).

——, *Critique of Pure Reason*. Tr. N. Kemp Smith (London, 1958).

——, *The Doctrine of Virtue: Part II of The Metaphysics of Morals*. Tr. M. J. Gregor (Philadelphia, 1964).

——, 'The End of All Things'. Tr. R. E. Anchor, in *On History*.

——, *First Introduction to the Critique of Judgement*. Tr. J. Haden (Indianapolis, 1965).

——, 'Idea for a Universal History from a Cosmopolitan Point of View'. Tr. L. W. Beck, in *On History*.

——, *Kant on the Foundation of Morality: A Modern Version of the Grundlegung*. Tr. with commentary by B. A. Liddell (Bloomington, 1970).

——, *Kant's Political Writings*. Tr. H. B. Nisbet and ed. Hans Reiss (Cambridge, 1970).

——, *Logic*. Tr. and ed. K. Abbott (Indianapolis, 1965).

——, *The Metaphysical Elements of Justice: Part I of the Metaphysics of Morals*. Tr. J. Ladd (Indianapolis, 1965).

——, *On the Old Saw: That May Be True in Theory But it won't Work in Practice*. Tr. E. B. Ashton (Philadelphia, 1974).

——, *Perpetual Peace*. Tr. L. W. Beck, in *On History*.

——, *Prolegomena to any Future Metaphysics that will be able to present itself as a Science*. Tr. P. G. Lucas (Manchester, 1953).

——, *Religion with the Limits of Reason Alone*. Tr. T. M. Greene and H. H. Hudson, with an Introductory Essay by J. Silber (Illinois, 1960).

——, 'Strife of Faculties' in *Kant's Political Writings*.

——, 'What is Enlightenment?' Tr. L. W. Beck, in *On History*.

——, 'What is Orientation in Thinking?' Tr. L. W. Beck, in *Critique of Practical Reason and Other Writings* (Chicago, 1949).

II

Burke, Edmund, *Philosophical Enquiry into the Origin of our Ideas of the Sublime and the Beautiful* (ed. J. T. Boulton) (London, 1958).
Fichte, G., *Vocation of a Scholar*, tr. William Smith (London, 1947).
——, *Science of Knowledge*, tr. Peter Heath and John Lachs (New York, 1970).
——, *Science of Rights*, tr. A. E. Kroeger (London, 1970).
Hamann, J. G., *Socratic Memorabilia*, tr. J. C. O'Flaherty (Baltimore, 1967).
Hegel, G. F. W., *Aesthetics*, tr. A. Miller (Oxford, 1975).
——, *The Phenomenology of Spirit*. Tr. A. Miller (Oxford, 1977).
Hume, D., *Essays, Moral Political and Literary* (Oxford, 1963).
Hutcheson, F., *An Inquiry concerning Beauty, Order, Harmony, Design*, ed. P. Kivy (The Hague, 1973).
Nietzsche, F., *The Will to Power*, tr. W. Kaufmann and R. J. Holingdale (New York, 1968).
Rousseau, J. J., *The Social Contract and Discourses* tr. G. D. H. Cole (London, 1973).
Schiller, F., *The Aesthetic Education of Man*. (1) Ed. and tr. Wilkinson and Willoughby (Oxford, 1967) and (2) ed. and tr. R. Snell (1927).
——, *On the Naïve and Sentimental in Literature*, tr. Helen O'Kelly (Carcanet, 1982).

III

Ameriks, K., 'Kant and the Objectivity of Taste', *BJA* 23 (1983), 3–17.
Antoni, C., *From History to Sociology* (London, 1959).
Apel, K.-O., *Towards a Transformation of Philosophy* (London, 1981).
——, *Understanding and Explanation* (Massachusetts, 1985).
Aquila, R., 'A New Look at Aesthetic Judgements', *KS* 70 (1979). Reprinted in *Essays on Kant's Aesthetics*, ed. Cohen and Guyer (Chicago, 1982), 87–114.
Arendt, H., *Lectures on Kant's Political Philosophy* (Chicago, 1982).
Aune, B., *Kant's Theory of Morals* (Princeton, 1979).
Bauman Z., *Culture and Praxis* (London, 1973).
Beck, L. W., *A Commentary on Kant's Critique of Practical Reason* (Chicago, 1960).
——, *Essays on Kant and Hume* (New Haven, 1978).
——, (ed.) *Kant Studies Today* (Illinois, 1969).
Beimel, W., *Die Bedeutung von Kant's Begrundung der Aesthetik für die Philosophie der Kunst*, Kant-Studien Ergänzungshefte (Cologne, 1959).
Benjamin, W., *The Origins of German Tragic Drama* (London, 1977).
Berlin, I., *Vico and Herder* (London, 1976).
Bernstein, J. A., *Shaftesbury, Rousseau and Kant* (London, 1980).
Bird, G., *Kant's Theory of Knowledge* (London, 1962).

Blocker, H., 'Kant's Theory of the Relation of Imagination and Understanding', *BJA* 5 (1965), 37–45.

Buchdahl, G., 'The Relation between "Understanding" and "Reason" in the Architectonic of Kant's Philosophy', *PAS*, 1967.

Cassirer, E., *Kant's Life and Thought*, tr. J. Haden (New Haven, 1981).

Cassirer, H. W., *A Commentary on Kant's Critique of Judgement* (London, 1970).

Cavell, S., *Must we mean what we say?* (Cambridge, 1976).

Cohen, T., 'Why Beauty is a Symbol of Morality', in Cohen and Guyer, 221–236.

Cohen, T. and Guyer, P. (eds.), *Essays on Kant's Aesthetics* (Chicago, 1982).

Coleman, F. X., *The Harmony of Reason: A Study of Kant's Aesthetics* (Pittsburgh, 1974).

Cooley, K. W., 'Universality in Kant's Aesthetic Judgement', *Kinesis* 1 (1968), 43–50.

Crawford, D. W., *Kant's Aesthetic Theory* (Wisconsin, 1974).

Despland, M., *Kant on History and Religion* (Montreal, 1973).

Ellis, J. M., *Schiller's Kalliasbriefe and the Study of his Aesthetic Theory* (The Hague, 1969).

Elliott, R. K., 'The Unity of Kant's "Critique of Aesthetic Judgement"', *BJA* 8 (1968), 244–59.

Engell, J., *The Creative Imagination: Enlightenment to Romanticism* (Massachusetts, 1981).

Fackenheim, E. L., 'Kant's Concept of History', *KS* 48 (1957), 381–398.

Fisher, J. and Maitland, J., 'The Subjectivist turn in aesthetics: A critical analysis of Kant's theory of appreciation', *RM* 27 (1974), 726–51.

Gadamer, H.-G., *Truth and Method* (London, 1975).

Genova, A., 'Kant's Transcendental Deduction of Aesthetic Judgements', *JAAC* 30 (1972), 459–75.

Gotshalk, D. W., 'Form and Expression in Kant's Aesthetics', *BJA* 7 (1967), 250–60.

Gould, T., 'The Audience of Originality: Kant and Wordsworth on the Reception of Genius', in Cohen and Guyer, 179–94.

Gregor, M. J., *The Laws of Freedom* (Oxford, 1963).

——, 'Kant's First Deduction of Taste', *Proceedings of the Fifth International Kant Congress* (1981).

Guyer, P., 'Formalism and the Theory of Expression in Kant's Aesthetics', *KS* 68 (1977), 46–70.

——, *Kant and the Claims of Taste* (Massachusetts, 1979).

——, 'Pleasure and Society in Kant's Aesthetic Theory' in Cohen and Guyer, 21–54.

Harrison, A., *Making and Thinking: A Study of Intelligent Activities* (Sussex, 1978).

Harrison, B., 'Kant and the Sincere Fanatic' in S. C. Brown (ed.), *Philosophers of the Enlightenment* (London, 1977).

Heine, H., *Religion and Philosophy in Germany* (1834). Tr. J. Snodgrass (Boston, 1959).

Hempel, C. G., 'Rational Action' in *Proceedings and Addresses of the American Philosophy Association* (35, 1962).

Hepburn, R. W., *Wonder* (Edinburgh, 1985).

Hirsch, E. D., *Aims of Interpretation* (Yale, 1968).

Hofstader, A., 'Kant's Aesthetic Revolution', *Journal of Religious Ethics* 3 (1975), 171–91.

Honour, H., *Romanticism* (London, 1979).

Ives, M. C., *The Analogue of Harmony* (Pittsburgh, 1971).

Johnson, M., 'Kant's Unified Theory of Beauty', *JAAC* 38 (1979), 167–78.

Kelly, G. A., *Idealism, Politics and History; Sources of Hegelian Thought* (Cambridge, 1969).

Kemal, S., 'Systematic Ideas in Aesthetics', *BJA* 15 (1975), 144–58, and 16 (1976), 68–79.

——, 'The Significance of Natural Beauty', *BJA* 19 (1979), 147–66.

——, 'The Importance of Artistic Beauty', *KS* 71 (1980), 488–507.

——, 'Aesthetic Necessity, Culture, and Epistemology', *KS* 74 (1983), 196–205.

Kivy, P., 'Breaking the Circle', *BJA* 7 (1967).

Knox, I., *The Aesthetic Theories of Kant, Hegel, and Schopenhauer* (New York, 1958).

Kuhns, R., 'That Kant did not complete his argument examining the relation of Art to Morality and how it might be completed', *Idealistic Studies* 5 (1975), 190–206.

Kuspit, D., 'A Phenomenological Interpretation of Kant's A Priori of Beauty', *Philosophy and Phenomenological Research* 34 (1974), 551–9.

Kuypers, K., *Kants Kunsttheorie und die Einheit der Kritik der Urteilskraft* (Amsterdam, 1972).

Lehmann, G., Kants Nachlasswerk und die Kritik der Urteilskraft, in *Beiträge zur Geschichte und Interpretation der Philosophie Kants* (Berlin, 1968).

McFarland, J. D., *Kant's Concept of Teleology* (Edinburgh, 1970).

——, 'The Bogus Unity Between Physical and Moral Teleology', in P. Laberge, F. Duchesneau, B. E. Morrissey (eds.), *Proceedings of the Ottawa Congress on Kant in the Anglo-American and Continental Traditions* (Ottawa, 1976).

MacMillan, C., 'Kant's Deduction of Pure Aesthetic Judgements', *KS* 76 (1985).

Maill, D., 'Kant's *Critique of Judgement*: a biased aesthetics', *BJA* 20 (1980), 135–45.

Maitland, J., 'Two senses of necessity in Kant's aesthetics', *BJA* 16 (1976), 347–53.

Malraux, A., *Days of Hope* (London, 1934).

Miller, R. D., *Schiller and the Ideal of Freedom* (Oxford, 1970).
Mischel, T., 'Kant and the possibility of a science of psychology' in *Kant Studies Today* (ed. L. W. Beck).
Osborne, H., 'On Mr. Elliott's Kant', *BJA* 8 (1968), 260–8.
Panofsky, E., *Meaning in the Visual Arts* (Harmondsworth, 1970).
Paton, H. J., *The Categorical Imperative* (London, 1947).
Pippin, R. B., *Kant's Theory of Form* (New Haven, 1982).
Podro, M., *The Manifold in Perception: Theories of Art from Kant to Hildebrand* (Oxford, 1972).
——, *The Critical Historians of Art* (New Haven, 1982).
Raschke, C. A., *Moral Action, God, and History in the thought of Immanuel Kant* (Montana, 1975).
Reiner, Hans, *Duty and Inclination* (The Hague, 1983).
Ricoeur, P., *Freud and Philosophy* (New Haven, 1976).
Riley, P., *Kant's Political Philosophy* (New Jersey, 1983).
Rogerson, K. F., 'The Meaning of Universal Validity in Kant's Aesthetics', *JAAC* 40 (1982).
Rotenstreich, N., *Experience and its Systematisation: Studies on Kant*, 2nd edn. (The Hague, 1972).
Schaper, E., *Studies in Kant's Aesthetics* (Edinburgh, 1979).
Schilpp, P., *Kant's Pre-Critical Ethics*. 2nd edn. (Evanston, 1960).
Silber, J. R., 'Kant's conception of the Highest Good as Immanent and Transcendent', *Philosophical Review* 48 (1959), 469–92.
——, 'Procedural Formalism in Kant's Ethics', *RM* (1982).
Strawson, P. F., *The Bounds of Sense* (London, 1966).
Tonelli, G., 'Kant's Early Theory of Genius', *Journal of the History of Philosophy* 4 (1966), 109–31, 209–24.
van de Pitte, F., *Kant as Philosophical Anthropologist* (The Hague, 1971).
Walker, R. C. S., *Kant: the Arguments of Philosophers* (London, 1978).
Wartenberg, T. E., 'Order through reason: Kant's transcendental justification of science', *KS* 70 (1974).
Weiler, G., 'Kant's "Indeterminate Concept" and the concept of Man', *Revue internationale de Philosophie* 16 (1962).
White, D. A., 'On Bridging the Gulf between Nature and Morality in the *Critique of Judgement*', *JAAC* 38 (1979), 239–48.
Wilbur, J. B., 'Kant's Critique of Art and the Good Will', *KS* 61 (1970).
Wilcox, J., 'The Beginnings of l'Art pour l'Art', *JAAC* 11 (1953).
Williams, F., 'Philosophical Anthropology and the Critique of Aesthetic Judgement', *KS* 46 (1954–55), 172–88.
Wittgenstein, L., *The Blue and Brown Books* (Oxford, 1960).
Wood, A. W., *Kant's Moral Religion* (Ithaca, 1970).
Yovel, Y., *Kant's Philosophy of History* (Princeton, 1980).
——, 'The God of Kant', *Scripto Hierosolymitana* 20 (1966).

——, 'The Highest Good and History in Kant's Thought', *Archiv für Geschichte der Philosophie* 54 (1972).

Zeldin, M. B., 'The *summum bonum*, the Moral Law and the Existence of God', *KS* 42 (1971).

——, *Freedom and the Critical Undertaking: Essays on Kant's Later Critiques* (Ann Arbor, 1980).

Index